ISBN 978-0-282-62592-4
PIBN 10859504

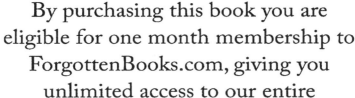

date * has assured us of the talents and virtues of these people; but it remained for the close of the eighteenth century to realize the scene, from a state of abject degeneracy:—to exhibit, a horde of negroes emancipating themselves from the vilest slavery, and at once filling the relations of society, enacting laws, and commanding armies, in the colonies of Europe.

The same period has witnessed a great and polished nation, not merely returning to the barbarism of the earliest periods, but descending to the characters of assassins and executioners; and, removing the boundaries which civilization had prescribed even to war, rendering it a wild conflict of brutes and a midnight massacre.

To attract a serious attention to circumstances, which constitute an æra in the history of human nature and of martial affairs, is the purpose of the present disquisition; which, it is hoped, will tend to furnish an awful, yet practical lesson, as well as to excite and gratify a laudable curiosity.

To this subject, the attention of the writer was peculiarly led, from a long acquaintance with the West-Indies, and opportunities of considerable observation of the colonies in that Archipelago. To the French colony of St. Domingo, his notice was early and particularly attracted; several of his military friends were afterward

* Adanson, Voyage à l'Afrique, 1749-53.

emplo-

employed on its shores, and ultimately an accident caused a personal visit; the information resulting from which, on account of its subsequent effects, could not fail to be deeply impressed on his memory.

Of *Hispaniola*, or *St. Domingo*, there is no particular history, in any language, similar to those of the British colonies, so ably executed by Sir HANS SLOANE and others. The earliest accounts are incorporated with the voyage of the great discoverer, his Spanish coadjutors, and the legends of the missionaries. Of these the description of COLUMBUS, and that of PETER MARTYR, are the most intelligent, while the account of LAS CASAS is particularly interesting, and the History of HERRERA acute and correct. That of VESPUCCI ought scarcely to be named, in retribution for his injury to Columbus. After the establishment of the French colony, when priests from the mother-country settled upon the island, they furnished accounts of the establishment, and of the manners of its inhabitants, generally interesting and correct; the most celebrated of these are by the Fathers DU PERS, CHARLEVOIX, DU TERTRE, and LABAT. Neither are the accounts of the Buccaniers (the first founders of the French colony), by themselves—nor the observations of an anonymous writer in the *Histoire Generale des Voïages*,* without merit. From these sources, with the assistance of the able compilation of the ABBE RAYNAL, and occasional reference to the most polished of modern historians, Dr. ROBERTSON, the *facts* with which the present work commences, are drawn.—

* Paris, 1759.

For

For the different light in which some incidents will appear, from their authorities, as well as the opinions or sentiments which are occasionally interspersed, the writer alone is answerable.

When the circumstances which ultimately led to the independence of the island commenced, the first English work, exclusively on St. Domingo made its appearance;* and, though in the form of a pamphlet, contained a correct account of facts, with no other fault than an inflammatory style, easily imparted by such a subject at the period it was written. Not long after, Mr. BRYAN EDWARDS, who had been successful in a General History of the British Colonies in the West-Indies, and who had intended to write a similar one of the French colonies,† published a quarto volume on the subject, comprising all the information he could collect. This work, however, although it contained documents of the most authentic kind, did not increase Mr. Edwards's fame as an accurate writer; being, in point of fact, as well as topographically, incorrect; it provoked a volume of equal size in answer, from a gentleman, who, for many reasons, was well acquainted with his subject; M. de CHARMILLY,‡ the commissioner empowered by a number of the colonists to offer a capitulation of St. Domingo to Great Britain. Though replete with errors arising from personal interest, and local prejudices, some facts are furnished

* An Inquiry into the Causes of the Insurrection in St. Domingo, 1792.

† Hist. Survey. Preface.

‡ To Mr. Edwards he says, (in his "*Lettre en Refutation de son Ouvrage sur St. Domingue*" "You should have acknowledged, that all your information was derived from others, during a stay

furnished by both these writers which could not be obtained by any other means. About the same time, there appeared at Paris, a work in two small volumes, in the form of Letters, under the name of the " Baron de WIMPFFEN ;" which, from external evidence, appear to be a collection of facts, arranged in an agreeable manner, on a subject occupying the attention of the French public, at the time. Whether it were or not a real voyage, among a variety of observations calculated to suit a temporary purpose, there are some that deserve a much better character. To these were added in France, a short time after, a work containing some authentic facts in a memoir of Toussaint, and a life of that great man, distorted for the purposes of party, by a popular writer, DU BROCAS. The Remarks of Colonel CHALMERS, in England, succeeded; from whose experience and local opportunities much was to be expected.* Of these, with a variety of private documents obtained from an extensive and intelligent correspondence, the writer has

few weeks only, in a time of general disorder, shut up in the town of the Cape; while the inhabitants of the colony, and even the city, were divided into different parties; and that you could not speak the French language, or very badly."

" Il fallait dire—'Pendant un séjour de quelques semaines seulement que j'ai demeuré enfermé dans la ville du Cap, aussitôt après la révolte des negres en 1791, j'ai rassemblé dans un tems de désordre et de troubles, les importans matériaux qui m'ont servi :—' que vous aviez rien vu par vous-même,' " &c.

M. de Charmilly, at the same time, views the conquest of St. Domingo by the English as very easy—ridicules the idea of the blacks ever attaining any force, and hangs the fate of the whole of the Antilles on the prosecution of his favorite project.

* It is amusing to see the confidence with which the subjugation of St. Domingo constantly inspired its advocates. Col. Chalmers, in other respects, a well-informed soldier and gentleman, incautious enough to have the following assertion in his preface :—" The late events in St. Domingo

has availed himself, in his third and fifth chapters, in a way, he trusts, neither injurious to their authors, nor unacceptable to the public.

Two other works have arisen out of the subject more recent than the foregoing, which deserve to be mentioned: that of M. d'ARCHENHOLTZ on the *Buccaniers*, published in Germany; and Mr. DALLAS's English History of the *Maroons*, furnished from the materials of their superintendant, Mr. Quarrell, of Jamaica. On the former, while it furnishes illustrations of human nature, little dependence is to be placed in point of historical fact; for it follows the Spanish accounts of the people of whom it treats, and conveys an obvious calumny on their most respectable members.* From the latter, some inferences are to be drawn, applicable to the subject of this volume, though the source, enveloped in interest, and the prejudice inseparable from a fa-

mingo have been much misunderstood, or highly exaggerated: he trusts that he has clearly proved that the *temporary* misfortunes sustained by France were occasioned by her impolicy, cruelty, or other causes, totally independent of the power of her black enemies, whose strength, as stated, is utterly inadequate to render them independent of that empire, or of any other *much less formidable power*. If so, it is humiliating to hear senators gravely pronounce that France has lost St. Domingo." The colonel adds, from Homer,---

"To few, and wonderous few, has Heaven assign'd
"A *wise, extensive, all-considering* mind!!!"

* Of the intrepid, generous, and intelligent Morgan (among others), M. d'Archenholtz asserts, "The horrors he committed are more dreadful than those of any of his colleagues. This *monster* filled the highest posts in the (*British*) state, and enjoyed with perfect security that enormous wealth which had cost the tears and blood of so many victims to his avarice, without suffering the smallest remorse to approach his hardened heart!"

vourite

vourite project, is not so pure as could be wished on such an important occasion.

To the abstracts of these works may be added a variety of temporary productions (including the foreign and English public journals), to which proper reference has been had, with the caution necessary for consulting such an heterogeneous mass of materials. Thus, no correct or comprehensive account, has been given in our language, of this interesting country; even those who have enlightened the public mind on other great occasions, falling in with the general apathy, have forborne on this wonderful revolution.*

To supply this omission, in a small degree, the writer, on a former occasion,† submitted to the public his ideas in a crude and imperfect state; and the attention they received from some intelligent minds, afforded sufficient proof, that the public only required to be roused to entertain the considerations they suggested; while the adoption of his humble narrative in the journals of those countries‡ that might

* From this censure, however, must be excepted Mr. Cobbett, (the author of the Political Register) who has in more than this instance deserved the character he has obtained of an enlightened politician.

† In the winter of 1801-2.

‡ See "The Merchant," a respectable paper published in Rotterdam in the beginning of 1802, &c. &c.

might be supposed to possess the priority of information, evinces the necessity of such a communication as the present.*

In it, will be found a succinct, and he trusts candid, view of the early history of the Spanish colony, in which the *impolicy* of cruelty, and the *errors* of injustice, are exposed, in preference to any national prejudice, or habit. The same ideas are continued, regarding the French establishment; and a reference to human nature is preferred, when considering the character of those, whose actions of terrific splendour could be tried by no other test. In regard to the height of the French colonial prosperity, he has not dilated the account by so minute a view of their domestic life as by some might be wished; but, in what is necessary to give a correct idea of manners and conduct, it is hoped no deficiency will appear. In any case where the question of slavery interferes, considering the subject on a broad basis, without regard to party, he has shewn its general *inexpediency*, rather than scrutinized its measures. And in tracing the revolutionary spirit to its source, he has endeavoured to point out moral delinquency without any other expression of rigidity than that which arose from the subject itself. In cotemporary history, that hazardous, and perhaps invidious enterprize, he has rather adopted those facts, wherever such could be found, which have already received the common consent, than obtruded his own, in their place; and where the latter are of necessity introduced, they have been scrupulously

* See also "The Monthly," and other Reviews of this period.

examined and confirmed. His own sojourn at Cape François and Fort Dauphin is the unaffected tale of a way-worn soldier,* experienced in the cross-roads of life, equally happy in the hospitality of an Indian cottage, or that of a magnificent empire—yet not regardless of each exclusive excellence, nor appropriating that of the one, to the other, or denying either. With regard to the transactions of the Black Republic (the appellation first given to the black government by the author), great care has been used to obtain the medium of truth between a variety of conflicting accounts; and, for the better comprehending their direct intent and views, much attention has been paid to give in the translation of their public papers, their original spirit.

Of one prominent subject of the present volume, it is painful to speak—yet an application to the general reader is necessary, as well as an apology to the sensibility of that sex, which the author would be much afflicted to forego—for the representations of cruelty, which will, he trusts, prevent such another violation of the human character. He is also desirous to avoid the appearance of enlarging on a subject which regards a country against whom his own is in hostilities. It must, therefore, be recollected, that it was during the peace which afforded an opportunity for the commission of crimes against human nature, of which he complains, that he first attacked the expedition against St. Domingo, and the immediate recourse to the assistance of the ferocious animals, which were surpassed by the cruelty of those,

* The writer, at the time of his first publication, had been *twenty-four* years an officer in his Majesty's service.

by whom they were employed. Mere description conveys not with so much force as when accompanied by graphic illustration, those horrors which are wished to be impressed upon the public mind. The existence of blood-hounds in the Spanish settlements in America, though disgraceful to the nation by which it is permitted, may yet continue, without any effect more extensive than with regard to the colonists, or their visitants; but the practice of, and terrible reference to, the savage custom of a barbarous age (only employed exclusively against the worst criminals) in a European army, is a subject of the most alarming kind. That every public exhibition of even the forms of cruelty is productive of dangerous effects on the human mind, cannot be denied; and should be avoided; what then must be the callous insensibility produced on a soldier by circumstances such as are here delineated? It is reducing the heroism of war, to a base contrivance of death. This cautionary memorial records the first step; it is for the public only, by marking it with a general sentiment of detestation, to preclude another and more dreadful, because more extensive, employment of the means. Such measures increase upon those who adopt them by insensible gradations, and once admitted, may extend even beyond their own intentions. The modern art of war is already removed to a sufficient distance from the magnanimity of ancient combat. Let not the breach be rendered wider by adoptions such as these.

CONTENTS

CONTENTS.

CHAP.

APPENDIX.

VIII. *Extract*

ERRATA.

Page 28, line 19, erase "their;" after "clergyman," insert *who*.

p. 40, l. 16, erase "of whom I am about to speak."

p. 42, l. 20, for "it," read *Tortuga*.

p. 45, l. 18, erase "truly gallant."

p. 88, l. 8, for "confined," read *conferred*.

p. 101, l. 11, for "I am considering this subject," read *this subject is now considered*.

p. 107, l. 21, begin *Thus concludes*.

p. 112, insert *March* 8, as a side-note opposite the resolution of the assembly.

p. 121, l. 20, after "armed," insert *indirectly*.

p. 139, l. 7, after *society* substitute the following sentence: "Mr. Edwards's account is here quoted as the most authentic."

p. 168, l. 7, for "disinclined," read *inclined*.

——— l. 23, for "the government afforded," read, *the Spanish government refused to afford*.

p. 202, l. 16, for "became," read *becoming*.

——— l. 21, for "its possessors," read *the conquerors*.

p. 203, l. 13, before "government," insert *the British*.

p. 245, l. 24, erase "perhaps."

p. 265, l. 2, for "the same month," read *of January, when*.

p. 276, l. last, after "sons," insert *dressed in the uniform of his enemies*.

p. 311, l. 22, before "weakness," insert *mental*.

p. 323, l. 17, erase "period of."

p. 324, l. 6, for "its," read *his*.

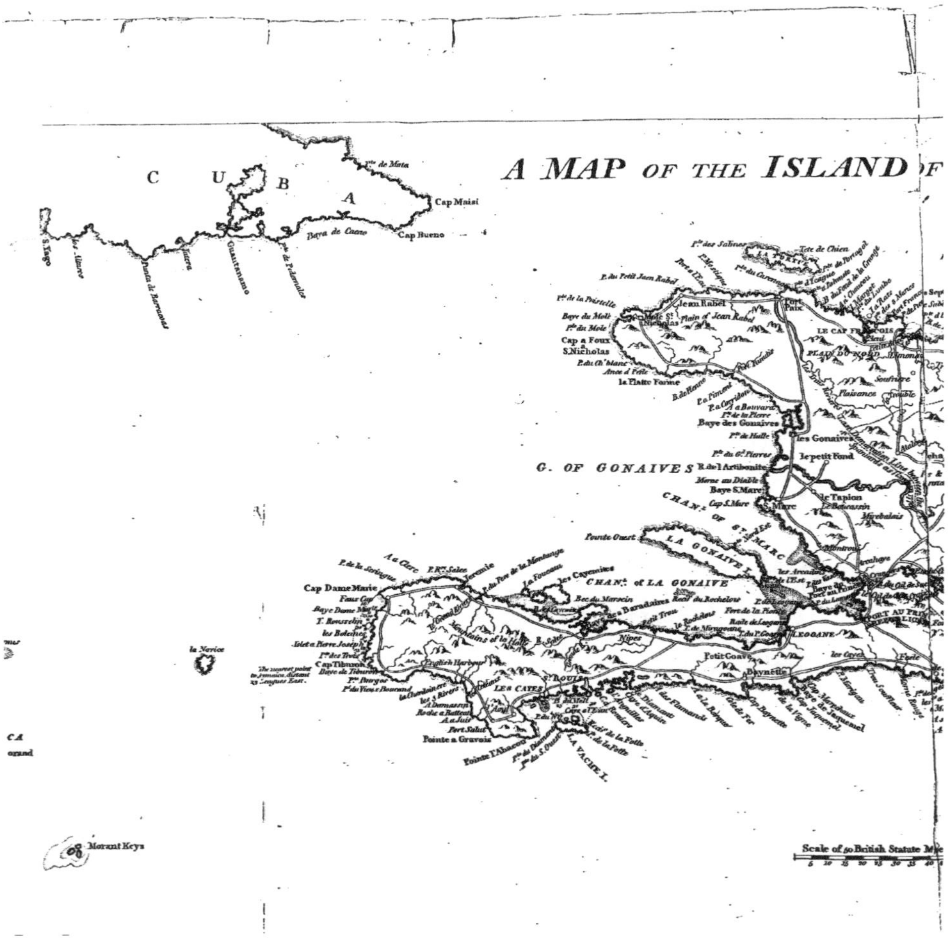
A MAP OF THE ISLAND OF
CUBA
Cap Maisi
Cap Bueno
G. OF GONAIVES
CHAN. of LA GONAIVE
LA GONAIVE I.
LA VACHE I.
LE CAP FRANCOIS
LES CAYES
LEOGANE
Cap Dame Marie
Cap Tiburon
Morant Keys
la Navice
Scale of 50 British Statute Miles

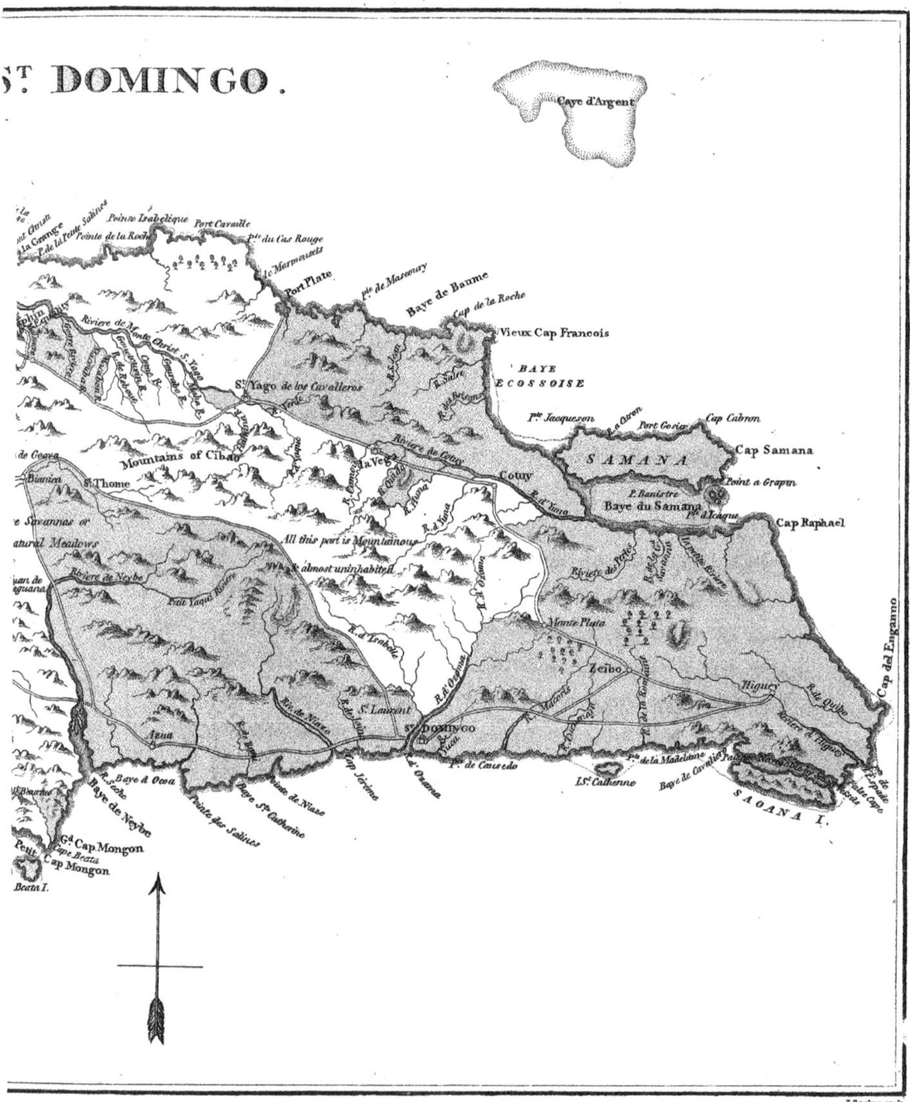
ST. DOMINGO.
Caye d'Argent
Port Plate
Baye de Baume
Vieux Cap Francois
BAYE ECOSSOISE
St. Yago de los Cavalleros
Mountains of Cibao
St. Thome
Couy
SAMANA
Cap Samana
Cap Cabron
Baye du Samana
Cap Raphael
All this part is Mountainous & almost uninhabited
Monte Plata
Zeibo
Higuey
Cap del Enganno
St. Laurent
St. DOMINGO
Azua
Baye d'Ocoa
Baye de Neybe
Gd. Cap Mongon
Petit Cap Mongon
Beata I.
SAOANA I.
Isle St. Catherine
J. Barlow sculp.

SUCCINCT HISTORICAL

VIEW OF ST. DOMINGO.

CHAP. I.

From the Period of its Discovery, by Columbus, to its highest State of Prosperity in 1789.

CHAP. I.
1492.

Situation of St. Domingo.

HAYTI, Hispaniola, or St. Domingo, the largest and most valuable of the West India Islands, is situated in the Atlantic ocean, between the island of Porto Rico on the east, and Jamaica and Cuba on the west; a small part of the rocks and shelves which form the Bahama islands lie at no great distance to the north; and it is bounded on the south by the Caribbean sea, and ultimately by the continent of South America. It lies in the latitude of 18 deg. 20 min. north, and in 68 deg. 40 min. west longitude from Greenwich. It is in length, according to the best accounts, more than 450 miles from east to west, and 150 in breadth. = 67,500 sq. m.

CHAP. I.
1492.

This beautiful island was the sixth discovered by the enterprising and unfortunate Columbus in his progress towards the discovery of a new world, of the honor of which, in the appropriation of a name, he was to be deprived by the caprice of his contemporaries, in favor of an obscure adventurer, of no other merit in the discovery, than that of having trodden in his steps*. It was the first on which he formed a settlement, or made any stay in his first voyage, and appears to have afterwards received the principal marks of his consideration. To it he was directed by the natives of Cuba, where he had previously landed, as more rich in its mines of that fertile ore with which it was necessary to bribe the avarice of the Spaniards, to prolong that ardour of discovery which it had cost him so much labour to excite.

Original name, *Hayti*.

Columbus first arrived at *Hayti*, for so this country was called by its natives, on the 6th day of December, 1492. He landed at a small bay, which he called St. Nicholas, and then named the island Espagnola, in honor of the country by whose king he was employed: from thence he sailed along the northern coast till he found a more convenient harbour, which he named Conception, and where he first had access to the inhabitants, through the

Named by Columbus Espagnola, or *Hispaniola*.

* When the prosecution of discoveries in Spain had fallen into the hands of private adventurers, *Alonzo de Ojeda*, who had accompanied Columbus in his second voyage, was among the first to propose an expedition under his own command. With this active and gallant officer sailed Amerigo Vespucci, a Florentine gentleman, apparently of no ostensible character whatever; but having framed a fraudulent narrative of his voyage with some elegance, which formed the first description of any part of the new world, he obtained from its circulation the honor of giving name to America.

2 means

CHAP. I.
1492.

means of a female whom his people overtook, and prepossessed in their favor, by the usual means of trifling presents and gentle behaviour.

Original inhabitants.

It is our wish to pursue in this place a sober narrative of fact, rather than to give loose to the fascinations of romantic description, or else the early Spanish writers have handed down such accounts of the aborigines of Cuba, Hispaniola, and Jamaica, as would warrant the most extravagant eulogy on their personal appearance, manners, and ingenuity. It may, however, naturally be supposed possessing the necessaries of life without labour, on a soil the most fertile, and in a benignant climate, in a state of the utmost simplicity, and consequently free from the general enemies to beauty, they would have personal advantages not to be expected in their descendants under the combined evils of slavery in a voluptuous state. Even the rigidity of history has been softened into the most pleasing descriptions of them: "They appeared," says Robertson *, "in the simple innocence of nature, entirely naked, their black hair, long and uncurled, floated upon their shoulders, or was bound in tresses around their heads.—They had no beards, and every part of their bodies was perfectly smooth. Their complexion was of a dusky copper colour; their features singular, rather than disagreeable; their aspect gentle and timid; though not tall, they were well shaped and active." "The industry and ingenuity of this race," says another elegant writer,

* Hist. of America, vol. i. l. 2.

"must

CHAP. I. 1492. "must have exceeded the measure of their wants. Placed in a medium between savage life, properly so called, and the refinement of polished society, they were perhaps equally exempt from the bodily distresses and sanguinary passions of the former conditions, and from the artificial necessities and solicitudes of the latter." They were unquestionably the most unoffending, gentle, and benevolent of the human race*.

That there were some grounds for a belief in the ingenuity ascribed to them by Peter Martyr† and others, as far as it related to their simple agriculture, and some progress in the arts of ornament as well as utility, may, perhaps, be proved by a fact of another nature which tends to illustrate the character of this people, while it may afford a lesson to our own times;—would that we could not say to our own country.

When, among the numerous disasters of Columbus, he was wrecked on the eastern coast of the island, and if he had before impressed the natives with admiration of the superior nature of their visitors, was now placed in a situation the best calculated to prove their natural equality, and even to tempt by an unlucky opportunity any inclination to their injury, instead of the smallest hostility. Guacanahari, the cazique, or king of this division of their island, of which it appeared to be governed by seven, having been informed of his misfortune, expressed great grief for his loss,

* Hist. Jamaica, Dallas's Hist. vol. i. 23.

† De Rebus Oceanis, &c.

and

CHAP. I. 1492.

and immediately sent aboard all the people in the place in many large canoes; they soon unloaded the ship of every thing that was upon deck, as the king gave them great assistance: "He himself," says Columbus, who records it, "with his brothers and relations, took all possible care that every thing should be properly done both aboard and on shore; and from time to time he sent some of his relations weeping, to beg of me not to be dejected, for he would give me all that he had. I can assure your Highnesses," he adds, "that so much care would not have been taken of securing our effects in any part of Spain; as all our property was put together in one place near his palace, until the houses which he wanted to prepare for the custody of it were emptied; he immediately placed a guard of armed men, who watched during the whole night, and those on shore lamented as much as if they had been interested in our loss*. They are supposed to have migrated originally from the neighbouring continent, and are ascribed by Sir Walter Raleigh to the Arrowauk tribe of Guiana †.

Report of them to his monarch by Columbus.

Thus far we have preserved the necessary sobriety in collecting a description of the first inhabitants of St. Domingo; but when we come to speak of the territory itself, this caution ceases, for, no description that we have yet seen is adequate to the appearance, even

Description of the country.

* Letter of Columbus to Ferdinand and Isabella of Spain. See his Life in Churchill's Voyages, as written by his younger son Ferdinand, an ecclesiastic, and founder of the Columbine Library at Seville; also Herrera's General History.

† Raleigh's Voyages.

CHAP. I. 1492. even at the present day, of a country which requires all the aid of romance to imagine, much less to describe.—Of fertility, which it requires but the fostering hand of man to guide to all the purposes of life, and of a climate the most salubrious among the Antilles, and in which longevity is general.—"In these delightful countries too," observes Robertson, "Nature seemed to assume another form; every tree and plant, and animal, was different from those of the ancient hemisphere;"—Columbus boasted of having discovered the *original seat of Paradise.*—"In these delightful vales," exclaims the Abbé Raynal*, "all the sweets of spring are enjoyed, without either winter or summer. There are but two seasons in the year, and they are equally fine. The ground always laden with fruit, and covered with flowers, realizes the delights and riches of poetical descriptions. Wherever we turn our eyes, we are enchanted with a variety of objects, coloured and reflected by the clearest light. The air is temperate in the day time, and the nights are constantly cool."—"In a country of such magnitude," says Edwards†, "diversified with plains of vast extent, and mountains of prodigious height, is probably to be found every species of soil which nature has assigned to all the tropical parts of the earth. In general it is fertile in the highest degree, every where well watered, and producing almost every variety of vegetable nature and beauty for use, for food, and luxury, which the lavish hand of a bountiful providence has bestowed on the richest portion of the globe." "The possessions of *France* in this noble

* East and West Indies, vol. iv. 231.

† Historical Survey, chap. 19.

island,"

island," he continues, "were considered as the garden of the West Indies, and for beautiful scenery, richness of soil, salubrity, and variety of climate, might justly be deemed the paradise of the new world."—"What you have said," replies De Charmilly *, animadverting on the preceding passage, "is *nothing* when it is known that the extent of the French part is but one half of that of the Spanish division, and that this is yet more fertile than the French part, requiring only cultivators, &c." Of even such an account, when contemplating the various parts of St. Domingo in which we have been, with an eye well accustomed to tropical scenery, and satiated with the luxury natural to its soil, we could be almost inclined to say too, *this is nothing.*

It is not to be wondered at, that the inhabitants should consider the Spaniards, on their first interview, as preternatural beings, a circumstance, however, very favorable to their intercourse, and which might have been turned to more advantage in a better purpose than that to which it was applied. They possessed gold, which they found in the beds of the rivers, or washed by the heavy rains from the mountains, and which they gladly exchanged for bells, beads, or pins. A prince, or cazique of the country, who visited Columbus, was carried in a sort of seat upon mens' shoulders, and derived great respect from his attendants. He was extremely courteous, and presented the

* Lettre à M. Edwards, p. 70.

admiral

CHAP. I. 1492.

admiral with many articles of curious workmanship, and received with complacency some trifles in return.

They had no idea of the imaginary value attributed by their visitors to gold, and readily pointed out the mountains, which yet retain their original name of Cibao, as the great repository of the ore they so much desired.

Distresses of the great discoverer.

It was at this period that Columbus lost one of his ships through the carelessness of a pilot, and experienced the tenderness which has been already mentioned. Of another of his vessels out of three, he had procured no intelligence since his arrival, and suspected some treachery in the captain who commanded it. The third was of course insufficient to receive the whole of his crew, and he was desirous to return to Spain. The simplicity of the natives, and their terror from the incursions of the people who inhabited several islands to the south east, whom they called Caribbeans*, and who were of a very opposite character to themselves, being fierce and warlike, and devouring the flesh of their prisoners, gave confidence to Columbus, in the proposition of leaving a part of his crew behind, which would embrace the two advantages of forming a settlement on the island, and enable him to return to Spain immediately. They agreed without a murmur.

* M. de Charmilly constantly confounds the character of the inoffensive aborigines of St. Domingo, with that of the Charaibs, or Cannibals, and of the African negroes in their present state of slavery, and thence draws deductions, which must consequently fall to the ground.

murmur, and even assisted in the erection of a fort which was to be afterwards used as a means of their own subjection. CHAP. I. 1493.

Thirty-eight Spaniards were appointed to remain on the island, under the command of Diego de Arado, a gentleman of Cordova, to whom Columbus communicated his own powers, and every thing requisite for their establishment; having first endeavoured very successfully to impress the natives in their behalf, by acts of beneficence and exhibitions of power. He promised to revisit them soon, and in the interim to make respectable mention of them to their country. Columbus left the little colony on the 4th of January 1493, and arrived in Spain in the month of March following.

1493.

Departure of Columbus after establishing a colony.

The departure of Columbus had not long taken place, when, as too often happens, the garrison he had left behind grew impatient of restraint, and threw off the command of their newly appointed governor. Regardless of the prudent instructions which had been given them, the men who composed it became insolently independant, and gratified their avaricious and licentious desires at the expence of the natives, making a wasteful prey of their gold, their women, and their provisions; thus, instead of supporting the estimation in which they were held, exhibiting themselves as the most depraved of human beings. At length the cazique of Cibao, whose country the Spaniards chiefly infested, cut off a part of the colonists, surrounded the remainder, and destroyed their fort.

The colony destroyed.

CHAP. I. 1493.

Columbus having employed himself for six months at the court of Spain in receiving the rewards of his distresses, and in interesting it in behalf of the splendid enterprize of which he was the author, no sooner accomplished his aim, and procured a sufficient fleet, under the papal sanction, on the part of the king of Spain, than he became impatient to revisit his colony. He accordingly departed on his second voyage, and after touching at several other islands towards the north west of his route, arrived at Hispaniola on the 22d of November following.

Return of Columbus.

His surprize may easily be conceived to find that his colony no longer existed; and while the Spaniards in dismay were weeping over the fate of their countrymen, a brother of the friendly cazique Guacanahari arrived, and related to him the account of their fate.

Instead of wasting his time by a retaliation of injuries, Columbus set about the erection of a town, of which he traced the scite in a large plain, near a spacious bay. He obliged every person in his suite, of whatever quality, to assist in a work so necessary to the common safety. This City, the first which obtained that appellation in the new world, was named Isabella, in honor of his patroness the queen of Castile.

City of Isabella built.

Columbus experienced all the difficulties attendant on an infant colony, and a timely excursion in great pomp to the mountains of Cibao, which they found to answer the description of the Indians, in the possession of gold in considerable quantities, perhaps

haps only saved the establishment from final ruin. As soon as concord was restored by the prospect of the mines, Columbus again purposed to leave his colony for the prosecution of new discoveries. He appointed his brother Diego, with a council of officers, to govern in his absence; and a body of soldiers, under the command of Don Pedro Margarita, were sent to visit the different parts of the island, and to establish the authority of the Spaniards. He then set sail on the 24th of April, but after an absence of five months, during which time he had not been distant many leagues, and had experienced the most disastrous circumstances, he returned almost dead to the colony, where he found a brother Bartholomew, whom he had not seen for thirteen years, who had arrived in his absence, and whose unexpected appearance, after sustaining distresses scarcely inferior to his own, so much revived his spirits as to produce a speedy convalescence*. CHAP. I. 1494.

During the absence of Columbus, the soldiery under Margarita had repeated the conduct of the first colony, while the necessities even of abstemious Spaniards rendered them unwelcome neighbours to a race who, requiring very little food to support a life of indolence and innocence, made but proportional provisions when any care was necessary. Maize, with a few vegetables,

* Bartholomew Columbus had been dispatched by the great navigator to England, to negociate with Henry VII. his project of discoveries, in case he should be disappointed in Spain, as he had been in Portugal. On his voyage, the negociator fell into the hands of pirates, who stripped him, and retained him several years a prisoner. At length, having escaped, he arrived in London, but in such poverty, that he was incapable of appearing at court on his mission, till, by drawing maps for sale, in the execution of which he was very ingenious, he procured decent clothing, and a moderate subsistence.

CHAP. I. 1494. and very little, if any animal food, formed their only necessary stock, and on this a body of men fortifying themselves in towns, must have made a formidable inroad. Famine, and the success of their former revolt, with long repeated grievance, at length provoked other attempts to rid themselves of the burthen, and Columbus was compelled to have recourse to arms, which he had hitherto with much solicitude avoided. The Indians were defeated by their precipitance: instead of the mode natural to them, of drawing the enemy into their fortresses, they rushed into an open plain, the Vega Real, and numbers being thrown into consternation by the first appearance of European warfare, the impetuosity of cavalry, (which they conceived, like the Thessalonians, to be Centaurs,) and the fierce onset of the *dogs* *, they yielded to Columbus an easy victory; and those who were not taken prisoners, and reduced to servitude, resigned themselves entirely to despair. Such was the disparity of power, that though near an hundred thousand Indians took the field with missile weapons of their rude fashion, the victory was obtained by two hundred foot, twenty horse, and twenty large dogs, which formed the whole disposable force of the Spaniards.

Conflict with the Indians, March 24, 1495.

Columbus employed several months in passing through the island to complete its subjection, and impose a tribute on all the natives above the age of fourteen, which was one of the first effects of a policy adopted against his own inclination to gratify the avarice of the Spanish court, at which he was attempted to be

* Of the mode of introducing these combatants into Spanish tactics, some account will be found in a future chapter.

undermined,

CHAP. I.

undermined, and which proved afterwards, however moderately used by himself, a means of tyranny and cruelty in the hands of 1494.
others. This taxation was an insurmountable infringment on the habits of the Indians, to whom restraint on labour was an intolerable evil. It induced an attempt at another kind of hostility, that of starving the appetites of the Spaniards, on the gratification of whose voracity they conceived so much to depend. They pulled up the roots, and suspended all their simple agricul- 1495.
tural operations, and retiring to inaccessible mountains, they produced in themselves the effects they vainly hoped to produce in their usurpers. Few as were their wants, they were soon totally unsupplied, and more than a third part became victims to their self-created famine.

Origin of the slavery of the natives.

It was at this time that divisions began to be created in the island through the intrigues of the enemies of Columbus in Spain; they procured one Aguado, a groom of the bed-chamber, to be sent commissioner to Hispaniola, who displayed all the insolence of mean minds disordered by sudden elevation. To relieve himself, and obtain an explanation with his enemies before his monarch, Columbus returned to Spain, leaving his brother 1496.
Bartholomew as adelantado, or lieutenant-governor, and through a misplaced trust, appointing Francis Roldan, a gentleman of rank and character, chief justice.

Columbus undermined, and *Aguado* sent commissioner to Hispaniola.

Though as usual experiencing difficulties in his passage, he so far gained over Ferdinand and Isabella, as to obtain further provisions

Columbus visits Spain, and returns with a fleet of colonists,

CHAP. I. 1498. after discovering the American continent. 1498.

visions for his colony, in a digested plan, and on a more permanent and extensive scale. Women, artificers, and husbandmen, were joined to the new expedition, but, as all his acquisitions received some alloy, to these were unadvisedly added, the criminals from the jails, that fatal resource for population which has so often miscarried. It was almost two years, however, before Columbus set out on his third voyage, and several months after before he returned to Hispaniola, having in the interim discovered the continent of America, the crown of all his enterprises, and of all his sorrows. He returned weary and sick, but he found the colony in a state that admitted of no repose.

Capital of St. Domingo built.

Don Diego Columbus had, at the desire of his brother, during his absence, removed the colony to a more eligible station on the opposite side of the island, where he had founded a city, which he dedicated to St. Domingo, or Dominica, in honor of the name of his father, and which remained so long the seat of Spanish dominion in the new world.

1499.

Restless spirits will sometimes be found, however inconsistently, in the highest stations, and political troubles arise from very unexpected sources; such was the case with Roldan, whose appointment was to have preserved peace and order; and, when Diego had reduced to subjection what remained of the island unsubdued by his brother, this man excited rebellion among his countrymen, and even the Indians, with such artifices, as caused the most alarming effects, and was only quelled by the temperate, conciliatory,

conciliatory, and expedient policy of Columbus. Of the bad consequences of this restoration of tranquillity, however, was the re-establishment of Roldan, and a concession to the avarice of the Spaniards, which was the first step in reducing the Indians to actual slavery. Lands being allotted to the mutineers in different parts of the island, the Indians of the district were appointed, in lieu of their tribute, to cultivate a certain portion of ground for the use of their new masters, from the characters of many of whom may be easily derived the origin of numberless calamities to that unhappy people. CHAP. I. 1499.

Of the mutiny, the effects were by no means terminated in appearances, the progress of discovery was stopped, and such false representations were made by his opponents, that a knight of Calatravia, called Francis de Bovadillo, was sent to supersede Columbus, and by means known only to courts, to send him immediately a criminal in chains to Spain. Thus closed the fifteenth century in St. Domingo, a period which, while it saw the founder of an empire disgraced and wretched, afforded a better prospect to the colony than had hitherto appeared. Such provisions had been made for working the mines, and cultivating the country, as assured *not* only its existence, but a considerable revenue to the monarch, who suffered Columbus to be circumvented and abused. 1500. *Bovadillo* appointed governor.

Bovadillo proceeded, as might be expected, to render himself popular, by gratifying the entire inclinations of his countrymen. He numbered all the remaining Indians, and dividing them into classes,

CHAP. I. 1500. classes, distributed them as property among the Spaniards, who, disregarding the only true means of obtaining wealth by agriculture, sent them to the mines, and imposed on them such a disproportioned labour as threatened their utter and speedy extinction.

To prevent this dreadful event, and preserve the shew of decency to the world, on the arrival of Columbus in Spain, and his appeal to the justice of Ferdinand, another knight of the military order of Alcantara, Nicholas de *Ovando*, was sent to replace

1501. *Bovadillo*. Regulations were adopted to prevent the licentious

Ovando governor. spirit which had arisen in the colony under his government; and, to check the inordinate progress of wealth, the gold was ordered to be all brought to a smelting-house, where one half should become the property of the crown. Columbus remained in Spain many months soliciting attention in vain, till his proposition of an attempt at discoveries to the east was accepted; and he sat out on his fourth voyage in May, 1502.

Ovando brought to St. Domingo the most respectable armament hitherto seen in the new world, consisting of thirty-two ships, with two thousand five hundred settlers. On his arrival, Bovadillo, with Roldan and his accomplices, were ordered to return to Spain.

Columbus having experienced some inconvenience from one of his vessels, altered the course in which he steered, and bore away for St. Domingo, with a hope of exchanging it for some ship of Ovando's fleet; eighteen of which, however, he found

3 laden,

laden, and preparing to depart for Spain. He requested permission to enter the harbour, (first acquainting Ovando with his destination,) that he might negotiate an exchange, and avoid a violent hurricane that he saw approaching, and which he advised the departing fleet also to avoid. To neither of these objects did he obtain an acquiescence. He, however, took precautions against the tempest, and saved himself, while nearly the whole of the eighteen ships of his enemies were lost. In them perished Bovadillo, Roldan, and the greater part of those who had persecuted Columbus and the Indians, with the whole of their ill-gotten wealth, amounting in worth to upwards of fifty thousand pounds sterling; a sum at that time equal to many multiplications of its value at present. 1502.

Columbus refused admission to the island of his own discovery.

Columbus did not long remain on the inhospitable shore of a country to which he was refused access, by those who owed to him entirely its possession, but prosecuted his voyage in the fruitless hope of discovering the Indian ocean.

In the mean time Ovando, who had received a commission more favorable to humanity than his predecessors, relieved the Indians from compulsory toil, and the colony, though retarded by deficiency of labourers, began to advance in its approaches to a regular society; but, alas! in no instance is the constant variance between justice and expedience in what is called the social state to be more regretted than in the present. The Spaniards became incapable, without the assistance of the inha- 1503.

CHAP. I. bitants, (which no inducement could procure) to cultivate the
1503. soil, or to work the mines, and many of the new settlers died of disorders incident to the climate, not yet understood, while others quitted the island when deprived of their slaves. These
1504. circumstances demanded some attention, and the consequence once more returned to the unoffending Indians.

Columbus again visits St. Domingo.

Columbus, persevering through misfortune, this year again paid a visit to his favorite isle, after having been not only unsuccessful in his attempt at farther discoveries, but a sufferer by complete shipwreck, and detained near twelve months in the island of Jamaica, which he had discovered nine years before, but of which no farther notice had been taken. Ovando appears to have been cautious of admitting into the country, under his government, a man of such vast powers, and to whom belonged, by the most determinate of all rules, the dominion of a world he had found: he at length, however, furnished the means for his escape, and received him with every public honor on his arrival at St. Domingo.

He remained only a month upon the island; with his usual ill-fortune, encountering violent storms, sailed seven hundred leagues with jury-masts on his way to Spain, where, exhausted by his sufferings, and disgusted with the dissimulation and injustice of a monarch whose reign he had immortalized, he died fifteen months after *, aged fifty-nine years. It is useless to

* On the 20th of May, 1506.

lament

lament in this place the melancholy end of a man whose me- CHAP. I.
mory is eternized. The recollection of it rather communicates 1504.
a balm to the sorrows of inferior multitudes; and the details of history will apply the event with advantage to the instruction of future ages.

A few months before Columbus, died his patroness Isabella; so that a powerful influence was withdrawn from the interests of humanity, as they regarded the new world; and as Ovando 1505.
began to experience the ill effects of a liberal conduct, he began also to relax in the execution of the royal edicts. He made a new distribution of the Indians among the Spaniards, with the difference only, that they were to be paid for their labour, reduced the royal share of the gold to one third, and afterwards to a fifth part; for which he obtained, (with better success than Columbus,) the sanction of the court.

Notwithstanding the apparent mildness of the present governor, it was at this period that the rage for cruelties commenced which have stained the page of history with more horrors than can be conceived by those possessing even an ordinary love for the species. No treachery was too gross, no violation of sex or dignity too painful for this unhappy people in the hands of the Spaniards; all regulations tending to mitigate the rigour of their servitude were forgotten, while their labour was increased. Ferdinand conferred grants of them as rewards to his courtiers,

Cruelty of the Spaniards to the Indians.

CHAP. I. 1505. who farmed them out, being no longer treated or considered but as animals of an inferior species, of no other use than as instruments of wealth, and I could almost say, subjects of oppression. At their expence, however, the colony increased in riches and in consequence; for with such rapidity and success were the mines explored, that for several years the gold brought into the royal smelting-house, amounted in value to more than half a million sterling, (according to the present standard of money). Sudden fortunes arose among private persons, which tempted others to embrace the opportunity of enriching themselves both at the expence of health and reason; and the effect was for a time highly advantageous to the colonists, and to the government of the mother country. Like the progress of a conflagration, however, the blaze was short in proportion to its extent. The same exertions which exhausted the unhappy Indians enriched the Spaniards, both as related to the nature of the operations, and to the government of Ovando, who is described to have introduced much wisdom and justice into his jurisdiction over his countrymen, but a proportionate rigour towards the original inhabitants of the country.

Flourishing state of the colony.

1506.

Ovando first gave a permanence to the laws he had established by executing them impartially, the only means of procuring regard for any establishment. He seems also to have attended to every object of advantage to the colony, and, among others, endeavoured to turn the attention of some of the Spaniards to the

the more laudable pursuits of agriculture. Having obtained from the Canary Islands some slips of the sugar-cane, which throve exceedingly, he tempted them to form plantations, and to erect sugar-works, which fortunately became an important support when the bowels of the earth were exhausted. The conduct and success of Ovando soon apprized Ferdinand of the value of those discoveries, he had hitherto appeared to depreciate, and on the author of which he had conferred only disgrace and misery; he accordingly set about forming commercial and ecclesiastical regulations, and at length established a system of policy the most profound, and every way calculated to secure to Spain the entire advantages of her colonies.

CHAP. I. 1506. Culture of sugar introduced.

While these provisions were taking place for its government, some circumstances began to make their appearance, for which, however to be dreaded, no remedy could be found; and therefore, notwithstanding all other advantages, immediately threatened the dissolution of the colony. The consumption of the natives, which was the natural consequence of the inconsiderate oppression of the Spaniards, (and in whom rested the source of all their prosperity,) became so evident, as to afford serious cause for alarm. Fatigue, to which they were unequal; diseases, the result of an inattention to their change of habit; famine, the effect of preferring so long the search of wealth in the mines to agriculture; and self-violence, the consequence of despair, conspired so forcibly, as to reduce their number upwards of 40,000 in the space of fifteen years, there remaining but about

1507.

Rapid decrease of the native population.

60,000

CHAP. I. 1507. 60,000 out of more than a million, to which the original population amounted*.

This diminution continued with such rapidity, as to occasion a stagnation not only of the colonial improvements, but of the common operations of life, which demanded immediate relief, and Ovando in consequence adopted an expedient which was again the source of enormities that seemed to increase in proportion to the progress of their society. The description will afford a mild example of the temper and conduct experienced by the simple, [illegible] benevolent beings of whom, Columbus, with an ingenuousness natural to great minds, had spoken in such exalted
1508. terms to the Spanish court. He proposed to seduce the inhabitants of the Lucay Islands†, which had been previously discovered, to Hispaniola, "under the pretence that they might be civilized with more facility, and instructed to greater advantage in the Christian religion, if they were united to the Spanish

* M. Charmilly, (Lettre à M. Edwards,) has a long, and, in some respects, sufficiently accurate calculation, to prove the original diminutive population of St. Domingo, in opposition to Mr. Edwards's general description of the massacre of a million of inhabitants. He falls, however, as is usual with those influenced by a spirit of party, into self-contradictions and inconsistency: for he alludes to a perfect knowledge of the topographical antiquities of the country, the existence of which he has proved to be impossible; and he supposes his author to have believed in the instantaneous sacrifice of a million of persons in the four chief mines of the country. General assertions are certainly distracting, and Mr. Edwards is too frequently superficial; but in this instance he is perfectly right. It is from Herrera, the most correct and intelligent of the Spanish historians, whom Dr. Robertson has also adopted, that the fact in the present text is derived, and not Oviedo, to whose amplifications M. de Charmilly ascribes the supposed error. Benzoni states the original population at two millions.

† The same with the Bahamas.

colony,

CHAP. I.
1508.

colony, and placed under the immediate inspection of the missionaries settled there." Ferdinand, deceived by this artifice, or willing to connive at an act of violence which policy represented as necessary, gave his assent to the proposal. Several vessels were fitted out for the Lucayos, the commanders of which informed the natives, with whose language they were now well acquainted, that they came from a delicious country, in which the departed ancestors of the Indians resided, by whom they were sent to invite their descendants to resort thither to partake of the bliss enjoyed there by happy spirits. That simple people listened with wonder and credulity; and fond of visiting their relations and friends in that happy region, followed the Spaniards with eagerness. By this artifice above forty thousand were decoyed into Hispaniola to share in the sufferings which were the lot of the inhabitants of that island, and to mingle their groans and tears with those of that wretched race of men *.

Natives of the Lucayos seduced to supply the deficiency of labourers.

The ardour for discovery, which had languished during the anxiety for the wealth of the mines, began to be renewed by an expedition under Juan Ponce de Leon, (who commanded under Ovando in the eastern district,) to the island of Puerto Rico, which in a few years was subjected to the fate of Hispaniola. Ovando also commissioned an officer, named Sebastian de Ocampo, to ascertain the insular situation of Cuba, which

Cuba and Porto Rico explored by expeditions from St. Domingo.

* Hist. of Amer. vol. i. p. 263. I have quoted this from Dr. Robertson, as the best and most moderate description. His authorities are, Herrera, Dec. 1. lib. 7. c. 3.; Oviedo, lib. 3. c. 6.; Gomara Hist. c. 41.

VOL. I.   Columbus

CHAP. I. 1508. Columbus had supposed to be a part of the neighbouring continent.

But though late and unexpected, by a perseverance the most constant, a degree of justice was at length to be accorded to Columbus in the person of his son Diego. Almost wearied out in the courtly delay which had exhausted his father, he determined upon the bold alternative of an appeal against his monarch to a council for Indian affairs, which he had himself established. Unequal as the parties were, and recent as was its own existence, the court honourably sustained its integrity, and determined on the side of justice, even against the king: with this decision, and the support of powerful connections, subsequently acquired by marriage, he soon obtained (though but a partial concession of his rights) the government of St. Domingo, and such privileges as enabled him to arrive in the island with more splendour and magnificence than had hitherto been witnessed: Ovando was of course recalled. That splendour, and the numerous retinue with which it was supported, while it added lustre to the settlement, effected no other change to the unhappy aborigines, than the seal of a more determinate slavery, by a numerical division of them among the Spaniards, according to the rank of the latter.

Honor and integrity of a court of justice.

Diego, the son of Columbus, restored to the government.

1509.

The destruction of the labourers proportionally decreasing the produce of wealth to their masters, naturally excited an impatience in those who had been glutted with wealth, and satiated with dissipation. They had already began to contemplate other

4 countries,

countries, whose inhabitants were yet unexhausted; they had established a pearl-fishery at the small island of Cubagua, and lodged a small colony on the continent, at the gulf of Darien, under the brave and enterprising, though as usual, unfortunate, Vasco Nugnez de Balboa, when Diego Columbus made a proposition to which they readily acceded. This was the establishment of a colony in the neighbouring island of Cuba, to which an armament immediately embarked under the command of Diego Velasquez, one of the companions of the great discoverer on his second voyage. The only circumstance concerning this expedition, as it regards the island which is more immediately under our consideration, besides its relief from a number of discontented members, was the opposition of Hatuey, a cazique, or prince, who having fled thither from St. Domingo, indignant at the destruction of his innocent subjects, might naturally be expected to oppose the intrusion of their destroyers into the place of his refuge. His feeble party (for they were of the same inhostile nature with his former subjects) were soon dispersed, himself taken prisoner, and condemned to the flames under the *barbarous maxim*, which considered him only as a slave, who had taken arms against his master. "When Hatuey," says Dr. Robertson*, "was fastened to the stake, a Franciscan Friar, labouring to convert him, promised him immediate admittance into the joys of Heaven, if he would embrace the Christian faith."—"Are there any Spaniards," says he, (after some pause), "in that region of bliss which you describe?" "Yes," replied the monk, "but only such as are worthy and good." "The best of them," re-

CHAP. I.

1509.

1511.

Bravery and repartee of Hatuey, a cazique of St. Domingo.

* Hist. of America, vol. i. p. 277. edit. 1800.

CHAP. I. 1511. joined the indignant cazique, "have neither worth nor goodness; I will not go to a place, where I may meet with one of that accursed race!"

Another expedition soon took place from St. Domingo, to assist in the discovery of the South Sea, by the justly celebrated Balboa,
1512. from whose incursions in the continent on which he was established, he had sent home such quantities of gold, as tempted a number by no means contemptible to join him. It comes not into my promise to shed fruitless tears on the perverted fortunes of this truly great man; his name, consigned to unfading memorials, has, I trust, its use with those who possess a fertile mind without the power to sustain its operations.—Though the passage to the Indian ocean was not obtained, as was expected, they reached the South Sea, and prepared the way for more important discoveries.

1514. In 1514, died more peaceably than he had lived, Bartholomus, the uncle of the present Governor; a man of very respectable powers, and an unsullied character; who had occasionally filled offices of high importance in the island, and who, it would appear, was more closely connected with its history than his contemporaries have enabled us to state.

The government of Diego Columbus was neither inefficient nor violent; neither did he want inclination or ability to render the colony both prosperous and happy: but that justice which had been unwillingly accorded him, on the part of the deceased Monarch,

CHAP. I.

1514.

A minister, named *Albuquerque*, appointed to the island.

1517.

Monarch, was, as much as possible, impeded by every political artifice that could be employed. The meaner officers of the government were encouraged to thwart the authority of the governor, in a variety of measures, and at length the power of distributing the *Repartimientos* was created into an office, and conferred upon Roderigo Albuquerque, the relation of a confidential minister called *Zapata*. On the loss of this necessary advantage, in addition to the embarrassment he had already experienced, Diego resolved on returning to Spain for the purpose of remonstrance: leaving behind him the best administration in his power, reached his destination in safety, but he soon found with very small hopes of redress in the object of his voyage.

In his new capacity Albuquerque discovered no other care than to repair his own indigent circumstances, for which purpose he first ordered a renumeration of the Indians, (now reduced to 14,000,) and then put them up to sale in different lots. This was the only stroke wanting to complete the extinction of this unhappy race, by a consequent separation from the habitations to which they had been accustomed, and the imposition of additional labour for the indemnification of their purchasers.

As is too frequently the case when political injuries become irreparable, those measures which, earlier adopted, would have preserved a sacrificed people; now served, only to excite useless controversy and public disturbance; the Monks, who, since the ecclesiastical establishment of Ferdinand, had arisen to consider-

able

CHAP. I. 1517. able power, began to oppose their eloquence publicly to the system on which the natives were reduced to absolute slavery, or rather, consigned to perish in progressive misery. They could not be insensible to the impolicy of the measure; and, no doubt, impressed with the inutility of a mission to a people who were rapidly ceasing to exist, they had early remonstrated, but appear to have been easily silenced, till the present period. Even now, but a part of the mission, the Dominicans, stood forth to represent the mild precepts of religion; the Franciscans attached themselves to the more popular cause; and while they could not unblushingly defend the *Repartimientos*, palliated the principle on the ground of expedience, so often improperly assumed in society.

Las Casas defends the Indians.

The consequence was, an application to the king by both parties, of which the only circumstance of importance, was the interference of Las Casas, a man of romantic disposition, and benevolent mind; whose exertions, though unsuccessful, were neither wanting in genius or perseverance; whose character cannot be omitted even in the compression of abridgment. It may be previously observed, that the appeal was terminated on the side of the Franciscans, a few regulations of their labour only being for decency promulgated; Albuquerque pursuing his violence and rapacity with impunity.

Bartholomew de las Casas, (a Clergyman,) came hither on the second voyage of Columbus, and who had early exerted himself in the cause of the Indians, was not to be diverted from his purpose; finding the rapacious governor deaf to all expostulation

postulation that militated against his immediate interest, he embarked for Spain, to make a personal appeal to the Emperor, and to exert that eloquence, of which he was so eminently possessed, in their behalf. Aided by fortuitous circumstances, he was particularly successful, with the Emperor, then on the point of death, and with Cardinal Ximenes, who became Regent. The effect of this success was the appointment of three Superintendants of the colonies, to whom were added a lawyer of probity named Zuazo, with judicial power, and Las Casas, with the title of Protector of the Indians. These soon arrived in St. Domingo, and began their career by the auspicious act of liberating all the natives who had been granted to the Spanish courtiers, or to any person not residing in America. To avoid the influence of party spirit, neither of those orders, who had contended the subject were suffered to have a member among these Superintendants; they were composed of three Monks of the order of St. Jerome, who appear to have exercised not only ability, but a knowledge of the world, which is seldom to be obtained in a cloister. The result of this mission was, as might be expected, only negatively advantageous to the Indians, without whose labour, reduced as it was, the colony could not be hoped to exist; the best regulations that could be formed were adopted for the prevention of excessive rigour and of cruelty towards them, while, without coercion, they ceased to work, and were obstinate in proportion to their power.

Las Casas still dissatisfied with any thing less than the entire freedom of the Aborigines, and finding no countenance in the island,

CHAP. I. 1517. island, with undiminished perseverance, again returned to Spain, and found Ximenes, as he had before found Ferdinand, on the point of death. With the Emperor, (Charles V.) who immediately arrived from the Low Countries, and with his Flemish minister, he prevailed so far, as to induce the recal of the superintendant and his colleague Zuazo; and Roderigo de Figuerra was appointed Chief Justice of the Island, with directions to moderate the sufferings of the Indians, and to prevent their threatened extinction. Finding that this, was all that could be accomplished, in the hurry of imagination which always marks such characters, (not more eminently successful on some occasions, than dangerous on others,) Las Casas now proposed, in support of his favourite scheme, to substitute, in the place of those he wished to liberate from slavery in their own country, the inhabitants of a distant one, whom he appeared to consider more capable of labour, and more patient under sorrow.

The earliest advantage of the Portugueze in Africa had arisen from a trade in slaves*, but it had been abolished, and was considered ineffectual. About fourteen years before, the importation of a few slaves had been permitted by Ferdinand, but not as a public concern, and in 1511 the number was increased, without producing any effect on the population. This plan, which had been peremptorily refused by Ximenes, was adopted by Charles, who granted a patent to one of his Flemish favorites for an importation of the limited number of four

* For the origin of this traffic the reader is referred to a future chapter, to which it is more closely connected.

thousand,

thousand; this privilege being sold to some Genoese merchants, proved the first formation of a regular trade for supplying the island, which has continued to increase through the whole Archipelago. CHAP. I. 1517.

Even the farther introduction of other Slaves produced so small a change in the Colony, that the invention of Las Casas was directed to other substitutes; and with a more plausible view, it occurred to him, that if *Labourers* could be induced to emigrate from the Mother Country, their habits of life would enable them to bear the effects of the climate under agricultural operations; and that they might, by soon becoming opulent citizens, introduce habits of industry, and a promotion of virtue:—but, though countenanced by the ministry, his laudable plan was defeated by an ecclesiastic, who had long opposed him, the Bishop of Burgos. Thus deprived, of all his hopes with regard to his favourite Island, this extraordinary man turned his attention to the Continent, and his schemes to the prevention of similar abuses in that part of the new world, which was yet but little explored. After many unsuccessful applications in behalf of this colony of labourers, he at length obtained permission to form one in Cumana; but with such opposition, that the number of colonists whom he could persuade to accompany him did not exceed two hundred. It is not within our plan to follow this unfortunate party through their various distresses, occasioned by the bewildered cruelty of their countrymen:—prevented from arriving at their destined country by the detestation which was every where excited against the Spanish name, and unpopular with Spaniards as the followers 1518.

 of

CHAP. I. 1518.

of Las Casas, they became the innocent victims of both parties; while their leader, driven from every asylum, shut out from all resource, abandoned, and houseless, took refuge in the Dominican convent in the city of St. Domingo; where he soon after assumed the habit of the order, and, as it may be readily supposed, did not long survive the death of all his happiness.

The occasion of that violence which had every way met the party of Las Casas, originated more particularly in the predacious excursions of the Spaniards, who would seem in these piracies to have left no means of cruelty or depredation unattempted. When, by the extinction of the Natives, every exertion of industry began to stagnate in St. Domingo, and even Slaves, were sold at a price beyond the reach of many, they fitted out a sort of Privateers, which, cruizing along the coast of the continent, under the pretence of trading with the unsuspecting natives; whenever they found an opportunity, seized upon and sold them as slaves on their return: this conduct, however, combined all the Indians to revenge it, and in consequence, among others, two Dominican Missionaries were killed. This was the signal for more extensive hostilities, and Diego Ocampo, with five ships, and three hundred men, were dispatched to lay waste the country of Cumana, and to transport all the inhabitants that could be procured as slaves to St. Domingo.

Expedition of Diego Ocampo from St. Domingo against Cumana. 1520.

About this time, to add to the embarrassments of the colony, it suffered considerably from those extraordinary swarms of ants which sometimes used to infest the Archipelago, and injure the vegetation. After ineffectual many endeavours to destroy them, the Spaniards (according to Herrera) determined on appealing to the saints; but some time elapsed before they could fix upon one for so singular a business; at last, however, being relieved from the disastrous effects of the insects, and happening to invoke St. Saturninus at the same time, that saint acquired the merit of a miracle. CHAP. I. 1520.

The return of Diego Columbus to Spain appears to have been attended with some circumstances which are yet unknown, for he shewed no inclination to return to the new world, till we find him in 1523 called to Jamaica to suppress a revolt of the Indians, in the absence of Francis de Garay, its governor, who had embarked in an expedition against Panuco, which had, without his knowledge, already submitted to the government. Among the political arrangements of Ferdinand, was that which separated from the power of Diego the island of Jamaica, attaching it to that division of the continent, not subject to his dominion: he, however, acted with a spirit no less creditable to his character than on former occasions, and regained the island; which afterwards descended to his heirs, and, yielded the title of Marquis, among other honors, which descended to his family. Diego Columbus died in 1525. 1523. 1525. Death of Diego Columbus.

To return to the domestic situation of Hispaniola, that quick decline, which we have already described, continued to be acce- 1528.

 lerated

CHAP. I. 1528. City of St. Domingo.

lerated, by the cruelty and impolicy of those, to whom no means were exceptionable in the search of wealth. In external appearances, however, this decline was not perceptible, and the capital of St. Domingo, as is the case with all falling states, still presented an august reverse to the internal poverty of its inhabitants. In 1528, the city is described by some Spanish historians, and particularly Oviedo, who was there at that time, as "not inferior to any in Spain, the houses mostly built of stone like those of Barcelona, but the streets much better, being large and plain, crossing each other at right angles. With the sea on the right, and the river Ozamo on the left, health and beauty were united more than in any other part of the world. Ships heavy laden discharged their cargoes in a manner under the house windows. The citadel, which stood exactly in the centre, also gave security to an extensive command. The houses were fit to receive any nobleman of Spain with his suite, and the grandeur of Don Diego's palace as viceroy was beyond conception, and every way fitting to receive the king his master. The cathedral was of exquisite workmanship, and well endowed; the dignity of its bishop and canons well supported. There were three monasteries, dedicated to St. Dominic, St. Francis, and St. Mary de Mercedes, and an hospital founded by Michael Passamont, the treasurer-general."

How much were it to have been wished, that such public splendour had argued equal prosperity; that it did not, however, is certain, from every account; and Benzoni asserts, that towards

the

the middle of the sixteenth century, scarce one hundred and fifty of the native Indians remained alive *. CHAP. I. 1550.

The dealers in slaves, however, beginning to lessen their demands, as time and competition affected their trade, the colony might have once more recovered itself by an attention to agriculture; but that cruelty which appeared to be inherent in the breasts of these early colonists, (increased by disappointment and pecuniary difficulties,) excited in their new servants a spirit of insurrection that soon broke into open revolt, and which, though unsuccessful, compelled their masters to a relaxation of their severity and inordinate avarice.

The consequences produced by the smallest degree of moderation, became soon perceivable in the increased cultivation, and sugar, tobacco, cocoa, ginger, cotton, peltry, &c. were shipped for Spain in such quantities, as induced the best hopes of their increase continuing; but these flattering hopes were not to be realized, the Spaniards remaining inactive, weak, unprotected, and useless.

In 1586, Sir Francis Drake came before the island, and pillaged the capital with a degree of barbarity, surprizing in the present refinement of European warfare. The invaders held possession of St. Domingo for a month, during the latter part of 1586. Invasion of Sir Francis Drake.

* Benzoni, Nov. Orb. Hist.

 which

CHAP. I. 1586.

which they employed every means from day-break, till the heat became intense in the forenoon, to destroy the beautiful edifices that surrounded the town, but on which, from being composed of stone, fire made no great progress, and ordinary means became too laborious; after two hundred sailors, with as many soldiers to protect them, had been employed for several days only to destroy one third part of the town, and were completely wearied with the task, they condescended to accept of about 7000l. sterling as a ransom for the rest.

Among the severities which were practised, the following will afford an example, which, notwithstanding its cruelty, some will think from the circumstances of the times, not badly imagined: a negro boy having been sent on a message to the Spanish governor with a flag of truce, was run through the body by some straggling Spanish officers, and only lived to complain to the English general; he immediately ordered two friars, who were his prisoners, to be taken to the same spot, and hanged, commissioning another at the same time to acquaint the Spaniards, that until the party, who had thus murdered the general's messenger, should be delivered into his hands, there should no day pass without the execution of two prisoners; on the following day the offender was produced, and his countrymen compelled to be his executioners.

* See the account of this expedition in Hackluit's Voyages.—Sir Anthony Shirley pursued a similar conduct in Jamaica in 1596.

The

The decline of the mother country could not fail to weaken the situation of her colonists, who had suffered neglect, even from the importance of her acquisitions at home. Those who remained, rather from a want of power to quit the island, than any other cause, sunk into a kind of debility and sloth that resigned them to every evil. Gradually degenerating from the spirit and manners of their ancestors, they became little anxious about any thing beyond an indulgence, as degrading as fatal. Associating in common with their female slaves, they propagated a people of almost every *grade* of colour, and became entirely a mixed colony, of which, Spaniards formed in fact a very small part. Their mines were deserted, agriculture was neglected, and their cattle ran wild in the plains. They employed themselves, as may be expected from such an irregular establishment, not only in an illicit foreign trade, but in piracies against the property of their own country, of which the practice of fitting out ships clandestinely, for the purpose of procuring slaves, (as has been already observed,) afforded them the best opportunities, and a secret understanding with the ships of war, guaranteed their safety and success. Instead of an attempt to remedy this evil, of which there were many means *, the short-sighted policy of the Spanish court chose rather to complete the dejection of the islanders, by demolishing the sea-ports which had been illicitly employed, and compelling the inhabitants to

CHAP. I. 1586.

Degeneration of the Spanish colony.

1600.

* Among others, even the Flemish were refused the permission they requested to clear the lands of this fertile country, and revive its splendour by the more solid pursuits of agriculture.

retire

CHAP. I. 1600. retire to the interior of the country. History is silent, during a considerable period of the existence of this miserable people, whose actions could indeed admit but of little variety; who are described as "demi-savages, plunged in the extremes of sloth, living upon fruits and roots, in cottages without furniture, and most of them, without clothes *."—"Their slaves had little more to do," says Raynal, "than to swing them in their hammocks;" nor can a more striking proof be given of the wretched situation of that country which had supplied empires with gold, than the necessity to which it was reduced, of adopting pieces of leather as a circulating medium among its inhabitants †.

While the government of Spain, however, was so remiss in regard to the colony, which might be considered as the centre of their possessions in the new world, they were as much the reverse, with respect to the admission of any other power into a participation of its produce, or its territory:—their caution extended even to absurdity; and all ships were stopped who were met
1620. beyond the tropics. Notwithstanding this care, during a war with Spain, the English and French, had become acquainted with the Windward Islands, (whose warlike and sullen inhabitants, the Charibs, generally repelled the Spaniards,) equipped a small fleet to interrupt the Spanish vessels in those seas, whose piracies were not interrupted by peace; in conse-

* The Abbé Raynal,—History of the Trade and Settlements in the East and West Indies, vol. iv. p. 18.

† Edwards's History of the British West Indies, b. ii.

quence

quence of the jealous policy already described. A part of these under an enterprizing Englishman named Warner, and the captain of a French privateer called Desnambuc, took possession of the island of St. Christopher on the same day *, and divided it into two equal shares; the fierce inhabitants, who had been more favorable to the enemies of the Spaniards than to themselves, retiring from the parts on which they were fixed, telling them nevertheless, with usual Indian acuteness, that "land must be very bad, or very scarce with them, since they had traversed such a distance with so much difficulty, to seek for it among savages." CHAP. I. 1623.

The court of Madrid immediately alarmed, at the vicinity of these members of two active and industrious nations, ordered Frederic of Toledo, on his way against the Dutch in Brazil, to attack these newly established powers while they were yet weak in their new establishment; they were soon defeated, and those who were not either killed or taken prisoners, fled for refuge to the neighbouring islands. The greater part, however, returned to their possessions as soon as the danger was over, except a small number who remained on the little barren isle of Tortuga lying off the north-west coast of Hispaniola, and within a few leagues of Port Paix. These, inconsiderable as they were in their outset, were the founders of a race which giving rise to 1630.

* Some writers state that Mr. Warner had obtained possession two years before, and had suffered the loss of his plantations by an hurricane.

4 the

CHAP. I. 1630. the French colony that is soon to become an important part of this history, and being hitherto but imperfectly described, demands particular attention.

1655. Previously, however, it is but justice to the Spanish colony to say, that after the first surprize at seeing a large English fleet commanded by Admiral Penn, with nine thousand land forces under Colonel Venables, (the same which afterwards conquered Jamaica,) who had been dispatched by Oliver Cromwell to obtain for England a portion of the new world, they compelled the enemy to re-embark with disgrace. A want of unanimity was the apology made on the part of the English, who ill brooking such a reception, determined on no alternative between victory and death on their next and more successful attempt.

1660. By the middle of the seventeenth century these incursers, of whom I am about to speak, had received some accessions from the French colonies, which had by that time been established, and assumed an appearance as formidable as it was singular. They had gradually obtained notice under the appellation of Buccaniers from their mode of curing animal food, which was derived from the savages, being slowly dried, or rather smoked, over fires of green wood, in places from thence called by the Spanish term, *Buccans*, a custom yet retained by the Spaniards. As they were for a time destitute of wives and children, they associated pairs, (as recorded by former historians); property was common, and survivor inherited the residence; theft was unknown amongst them, though no precaution was used against it, a virtue they borrowed from the savages. They seldom disputed, but if any were obstinate, they decided with arms; and if any foul appearance occurred in the combat, as a back or side wound, the assassin was put to death. Every member of the fraternity assumed a warlike name on admission into the body, which descended to their several successors. Their dress consisted of a shirt died with the blood of the animals they killed in hunting; an apron, or trowsers, yet dirtier; a leathern girdle, containing a short sabre, and other knives; a sort of military cap, and shoes, without stockings. A Buccanier was satisfied if he could supply himself with a small gun, and a pack of dogs, to the number of twenty or thirty. Their employment consisted chiefly in hunting the bulls, with which the Spaniards had furnished the neighbouring island; which they killed chiefly for the skins, regaling, perhaps, on a small part of the flesh, preparing it sometimes with a seasoning of pimento, and the juice of orange. CHAP. I. 1660.

The remainder of the indolent colonists could not, however, bear with the idea of more active neighbours; which gave rise to several unavailing conflicts, that ended in a determination to destroy all the bulls by a general chase, a scheme which had the effect of turning the attention of the Buccaniers to the more permanent pursuits of agriculture.—Tobacco soon became a profitable culture, which, with the produce of several excur-

 sions

CHAP. I. 1660.

sions made by the most intrepid in their cruisers, amply repaid their difficulties. However, another Spanish armament was commissioned for their extirpation, which inspirited them to deeds that will live to future ages—pregnant with bravery and horror.

Possessed of an island eight leagues long and two broad, in a fine air, and with capability of improvement, unshackled by the prescriptions of ancient society, with a vast territory open to their predatory incursions, and numerous channels accessible to their maritime courage, the success of the Buccaniers may be easily supposed to have spread. To this lawless, yet far from unsalutary dominion, those who sought a refuge from the tyranny of creditors, or of want, as well as enterprizing spirits without opportunity for action, in their mother-country, (particularly from Normandy,) had a resource, which formed a considerable acquisition to its power. Envious of the establishment, the court of Spain made an attempt to dislodge them, which is worthy of notice, only from its wonted cruelty; the general of the galloons exerted his commission while the greater part were at sea, or hunting on the large island; he put all he found to death, leaving it as desolate as possible.

The effects of these cruelties, and the sentiments of revenge they inspired, produced a closer combination of the Buccaniers; for which purpose they agreed to sacrifice personal independence, to social safety, and accordingly appointed a leader,

leader, much in the same way, as the origin of all monarchies; as they were yet composed of English and French united, an Englishman, distinguished for his prudence and valour, named WILLES, was the first appointed, who appears to have excited jealousy, by an invitation of his countrymen to the settlement, and the use too frequently made of power, when its origin becomes forgotten in its advantages. A governor-general had, therefore, no sooner been appointed over the French windward islands,* than finding the opportunities probably agreeable, and being, perhaps, privately solicited, he sent a small force from St. Vincent, who, joined by the Frenchmen on the island, suddenly ordered all the English to withdraw from it; when supposing an order of such, audacity supported by a much greater force, they immediately agreed to evacuate the island, and never returned. They still pursued the bold career in which they had embarked, and afterwards obtained regular commissions from the English government to act against the common enemy, though the settlements and navigations of the Spaniards continued the prominent objects of their hostility. One of them afterwards arrived at situations of honour and emolument, having received the dignity of

CHAP. I. 1660.

* This Governor, who was named De Poincy, appears to have held his appointment on the same tenor as Willes, receiving it when the increased followers of Warner and Desnambuc had, in 1660, joined in a treaty independent of their respective governments, which had regarded them with indifference. By this treaty it is pleasing to see the native Charibs considered, Dominica and St. Vincent's being appropriated to their reception. According to their respective rights of conquest, France obtained Guadaloupe, Martinico, Grenada, and some less considerable acquisitions; and England was confirmed in the possession of Barbadoes, Nevis, Antigua, Montserrat, and several other islands of little value. St. Christopher's still belonged to both nations.—See *Raynal's History, Vol. III. p.* 284. &c.

CHAP. I. 1660. knighthood, and being advanced to the high office of lieutenant-governor of Jamaica! His character, however, will be given more regularly among those of the other Buccaniers, to whom, as original founders of the French colony in St. Domingo, this history is more particularly directed.

Alternately losing and gaining the little island of Tortuga from the Spaniards, the French, under a captain of their own choice and nation, at length retained it, and obtained a firm footing on St. Domingo, which rendered it, at the same time, of less importance. Of the consequence to which they arrived (a consequence which, to this day, furnishes the West-Indies with legendary tales of their valour and honour), an idea will be best obtained by a description of their mode of life and warfare, and of those characters to whom they were indebted, for many of the exploits which have rendered them conspicuous to the admiration, if not the approbation, of the present and of future ages.

They formed themselves into small companies, from fifty to three times that number, of whom, some appear to have preferred agricultural pursuits. As the authority they had conferred on their captain did not extend to their domestic œconomy, they were at perfect liberty as to their manners, or a preference of rest or pleasure in their intervals of peace. Their armaments were formed of boats, without any difference, but in size, in which, they were exposed to all the inclemencies of the weather; as through their careless dispositions, on shore they were subject to the seve-

rest

rest extremities of hunger and thirst. After the various cruelties exercised by the Spaniards in the attempt to extirpate them, the sight of a ship is said to have transported them to frenzy;—no superiority of power affected them, they boarded as soon as possible, and the skill they had in the management of their small vessels, screened them from the fire of their enemies, while their fusleers, who presented themselves at the fore-part of their vessels by an excellent aim at the port-holes opposed to them, confounded the most experienced gunners. They seemed to have a religious notion of humility and gratitude, for they implored the aid of heaven to their success in any onset, and returned thanks to the deity for every victory obtained; such was their uninterrupted bravery, that the Spaniards, at length, trembled at their very approach, and surrendered immediately to those whom they designated as devils, as much as if they had been in reality preternatural beings. Among those whose names have come down to us, as having particularly distinguished themselves, were Montbar, a Frenchman; a truly gallant Welshman (already mentioned) named Morgan; and a Dutchman, called Van Horn. In the conduct of these men, may be seen the general character of the Buccaniers, the proportion of this sketch not admitting of a more enlarged insertion, which might otherwise be easily selected.

Montbar was born a gentleman of Languedoc, and his connection with the freebooters appears to have arisen neither from necessity nor chance, but an early spirit of romance—such as has determined

CHAP. I. 1660. determined the most heroic characters. Indeed, to those who have seen unqualified descriptions of the Spaniards in the New World, without an acquaintance with human life sufficient to discriminate, such a Quixotic idea will not excite surprize. It is said, that while at college having seen these accounts, their enormities had so strongly impressed him, that, acting in a private play the part of a Frenchman, who quarrelled with a Spaniard, it was with difficulty the performer of the latter character escaped from him with life. His imagination continuing to be heated by day-dreams, in which he beheld the expiring victims of a rage, more cruel than that of religious fanaticism, he viewed them, as calling on him for vengeance; although but imperfectly acquainted with the history of the Buccaniers, he determined to join them, and accordingly procured a ship for the expedition. On the passage they met with a Spanish vessel, which they immediately boarded, when Montbar was the first, sabre in hand, to fall upon the enemy; he broke through them, and hurrying twice from one end of the ship to the other, levelled every thing that opposed him. When the enemy surrendered, leaving to his companions the care of the booty, he desired only to contemplate, with horrid pleasure, the dead bodies of the Spaniards, which lay in heaps upon the decks, and seemed strengthened in the cause, in which he had so romantically embarked. Arriving on the coast of St. Domingo, the Buccaniers, who applied to barter provisions for brandy, pleaded, as an apology for their quality, that the Spaniards had recently taken advantage of their absence to destroy them. "And do you not seek

seek revenge?" exclaimed Montbar. He soon found they were no more tardy in destruction than himself, and offered his services as a leader: was accepted, and astonished the boldest by his bravery. He continued with them during his life; and their sufferings (from his courage and success) procured for him, among the Spaniards, the appellation of *The Exterminator.*

Van Horn was a native of Ostend, whose intrepidity in the discipline of his crew, is the only peculiar trait handed down to us. He commanded a frigate, which was his own property. In the heat of an engagement, he was constantly seen in every part of the ship; and where he observed any one shrink at the sudden report of the cannon, he instantly killed him. He became the idol of the brave, and liberally shared with his successful companions, the riches so dreadfully acquired.

It is pleasing to turn from characters terminating with the same violence with which they set out, to one who, after having blazed in the full strength of a meridian-sun of power, is seen retiring to the mild evening of domestic life.

MORGAN,* the Welshman, only remains to be mentioned, descended from respectable parents in Glamorganshire, whom he early

* I wish to be acquitted of any local preference in the description of these men, or partiality of delineations in their characters. But notwithstanding the representation given of *Morgan* (in extension of the calumnious old history of the Buccaniers) by the Abbé Raynal

CHAP. I. 1660.

early quitted (as it was then termed) in search of his fortune. His adventurous spirit leading him accidentally to Bristol, he found an opportunity of embarking for the West-Indies, in the way of many others, by indenting himself for four years to serve a planter. When released from a service executed with fidelity, he joined the Buccaniers, and adding ability to courage, soon shared their success and their riches. One of the exploits which first rendered him famous was the capture of Porto Bello (which Admiral Vernon afterwards destroyed with difficulty); for which, the plan of operations was so well contrived, that he took it without opposition. In attacking the fort, to spare the effusion of blood, he compelled the women and the priests, whom he had made prisoners, to set the scaling-ladders to the walls, from an idea, that the Spaniards would not fire at the objects of their love and reverence. *Their* omnipotent power, however, was wealth, in preference to religion or beauty; and the humane expedient miscarried, to the great injury of the besieged. The conquest of Panama seems to have been attended with prodigious difficulty, both by sea and land; but even here, he did not forget a merciful expedient—buying the fortified island of St. Catharine, which was necessary to his progress. At Panama they found immense treasures: among the dreadful sacrifices that were made, some cir-

Raynal, he is constrained to confess, that in the midst of hostility he *fell in love* with a beautiful Spaniard; and that he did not sacrifice her to his wishes, though she attempted his life. A breast capable of admitting a passion of this nature, under such circumstances, could not surely be considered as the most barbarous; and of the respectability of his subsequent character, we have certainly the best account.

cumstances

cumstances less severe are recorded: vanity received a singular punishment; and it was here that Morgan became captivated by a captive. The first of these circumstances occurred in a beggar, who, entering a castle deserted by its owners, found some rich apparel, which, in preference to every thing else, he adopted; the besiegers entered, and pressed the grotesque noble for his wealth, when, pointing to the rags he had just quitted, he received the effects of his folly and pride in a death scarcely unmerited. CHAP. I. 1660.

Morgan, appears to have addressed the lady by whom he was smitten, with respect and forbearance, sentiments not always to be found, in more refined invaders, and they met with a contrary return. "My fortune and my liberty, which depended on others," said the indignant fair, "you have already, but my honour is my own care;" upon which, she drew a poignard from beneath her dress, and attempted to plunge it into his breast; fortunately he avoided the blow.—Agonized with passion, yet incapable of violation, with more philosophy than is often called forth under such circumstances, it is probable that he wisely and nobly tore himself from the scene of his attraction, as he suddenly quitted the spot; even before his companions could accompany him. On the peace, which a few years after took place, between England and Spain, he retired to Jamaica, and having purchased a plantation, betook himself with much industry to its cultivation. He succeeded in these tranquil pursuits, and, in time, grew into equal repute in a pacific life to that which he had experienced

CHAP. I. 1660. in war; he was called to bear a part in the government of the island in which he had become a proprietor; and, finally, to the command of Lieutenant-Governor of Jamaica, and to the dignity of knighthood. He executed the duties of every situation in which he was placed with probity and honour; and a writer of the present day,* who saw some of his letters in the possession of a friend on the island, describes them as manifesting a spirit of humanity, justice, liberality, and piety.

It is painful to relate, that Sir Henry Morgan, three years before the close of his chequered and useful life, was committed to the Tower by King James II. at the instance of the Spanish Emperor, where he remained till his death without trial, and of course without conviction of any crime. Though a sacrifice to the same monarch, with his great predecessor Raleigh, his life was not, however, included, and he died in peace.

To return to the community of Buccaniers, although separated from each other, the English and French still continued to act in concert; the latter retiring, after the conflict, to St. Domingo, to share the spoil, and the former to Jamaica. When any were maimed, the first steps, were those taken for their provision in the most honourable way; no one secreted any share of the booty under pain of expulsion; nor had favour any influence in its division, which was with much judgment. Dissipation of

* Bryan Edwards, Esq. M.P. F.R.S. &c.

every

every kind succeeded their advantages, and he who was rich one day, resigned himself to poverty the next. They continued to increase in force, and to proportionably depress the Spaniards, who, at length, retired into a sullen inactivity, which passively continued, till all other communication with their mother-country ceased, than that which could be maintained by a single ship of no great burthen. CHAP. I. 1660.

Nor did the Buccaniers themselves continue to prevail as they had been accustomed. After the settlements of the French and English in the New World became established, many were killed and lost, and some adopted agriculture; till, at length, France, who had not been altogether ignorant of its progress, became attracted by the infant colony then formed in St. Domingo, if it could yet be so called. 1666.

The number of planters to whom only could be really accorded the character of colonists did not exceed four hundred; the first care of the government then was to multiply this number, and to form them into a more regular society; for this purpose it commissioned a gentleman named Bertrand D'Ogeron, who had emigrated from Anjou about nine years before, but who had evinced too much virtue and sensibility to hope for commercial success, without a better fortune. With the best contrived plans he had failed; but the ability and fortitude, he had shewn in adversity, had won him the general esteem and attachment so much, that

CHAP. I. 1665. D'Ogeron governor.

he was considered as the most proper person to direct, or rather to settle the colony.

Of the difficulty of such an enterprize, none could doubt but himself, depending much on his own powers, who knew no other wish, than the good of human kind; he began by reconciling the idle to labour, and those who had traded with all the world, to the monopoly of a privileged company, which had the year before, been established for all the French settlements. He held out allurements for new inhabitants in a country which had suffered every species of calumny: when the maritime determined to go in search of greater advantages, he seduced them to stay, even by relinquishing the revenues of his post, and procuring them commissions from Portugal to attack the Spaniards, when they had made peace with France; to the huntsmen he advanced money without interest to erect habitations: and to the planters he united every encouragement. Nor did he long suffer them to remain in a cheerless celibacy, which denied an increase of population by the best and most natural of all means, and left them without the most powerful attraction to a fixed residence—that of mild, unassuming beings, who create comforts unknown by any other means; conferring interest and felicity, while they are as ministering angels to alleviate the sorrows, and soften the asperities of man. D'Ogeron sent for women, and obtained an hundred from France—such as should be the female inhabitants of an infant colony, young, healthy, amiable, and enterprising. To prevent the effect of the most

Women first introduced to the colony.

most impetuous of passions, he contrived, that while choice was not entirely suppressed, those should first become husbands whose industry had rendered them equal to the payment of an adequate sum; and the others (who respected social justice) waited anxiously to be so blessed in their turn: but they were disappointed, and the colony injured, as is too often the case, by expedients of which their insufficiency is the most favorable objection. The females, who afterwards made their appearance from the mother country, as if all regard for the constitutions of society, had been lost, were those for whom delicacy would wish to find a better name than the refuse of cities; selected without discrimination, they were bound as to masters for three years; of such a connexion, we need not attempt the description. The only circumstance worthy of record respecting it, is the declaration of the Buccaniers, who chiefly adopted them, on their simple marriage. "I ask you no questions," said he, "respecting your former life, but you are now mine; and if you prove false, this," putting his hand to the muzzle of his gun, "will revenge me." The effects of the profligacy introduced at this time were long, very long felt. In the course of four years, however, D'Ogeron found means to increase the number of planters in proportion to the population, so that, in 1699, they amounted to more than 1,500. 1669

CHAP. I. 1665. Foundation of the colony.

In the following year the benign exertions of this good man, received a check from the elation of the India Company, which is the too frequent consequence of successful monopolies. Conceiving 1670.

CHAP. I. 1670. ceiving themselves secure in a new and extensive trade, and not satisfied with a moderate profit, they ventured to raise the prices of their goods in a proportion of two thirds; the colonists, who had not yet changed their natural inclinations to violence, had immediate recourse to arms, and the price of tranquillity was a free trade to France, except an allowance of five per cent. to the company, to be paid by all ships on their arrival and departure. Even this disaster afforded D'Ogeron an opportunity for exertions of beneficence, of which only himself was capable. He procured two ships seemingly intended for his own produce, but, in fact, for the use of the colony. Every one shipped his commodities on board these vessels at a moderate freight, and, on their return, the cargo brought from the mother-country was exposed to public sale at prime cost. A general credit was given without interest, and even without security, this generous governor hoping to inspire them with probity and noble sentiments by such a confidence: thus, under a jurisdiction so exquisite, every public disaster served but to consolidate the colony; and could not fail also to excite a regret the most poignant, on an occasion which happened much too early; for the patriotic and benevolent D'Ogeron was cut off in the
1673. midst of his parental offices in 1673, an example of every humane and social virtue.

It was three years before the much lamented death of D'Ogeron, that the town of Cape François had been founded. It is to be regretted as a consequence of religious intolerance to drive from

from their country its most useful members. Gobin, a calvinist, flew from persecution to the mild state of St. Domingo, and built the first habitation on the cape, to which he invited others, who immediately flocked thither as the ground became cleared. CHAP. I. 1673.

The place held by D'Ogeron was supplied with tolerable success by his nephew, M. Ponancey, who, although described as of a less amiable disposition than his uncle, seems to have followed him in his laudable plan of government. He had the honor of completing what his great predecessor had so ably begun, the establishment of a colony upon a regular and firm basis, without the promulgation of laws, or the coercion of military force. More virtue than could be expected, from a variety of governors, was, however, required to sustain such a government; as licentiousness, naturally increased with population, aided by the unfortunate introduction of females, of the character already mentioned, it became of course necessary to submit to ordinary forms. Two administrators were therefore commissioned from Martinico, who established courts of judicature for the several districts, accountable to a superior council at Petit Goäve. These innovations were gained by a little finesse without much disagreement, and, but for the interference of private interest, which will ever obtrude upon infant establishments, the colony might have immediately opened a mine of wealth upon its shores.

Du Casse governor. 1684. 1685.

It

CHAP. I. 1694. It may not be improper to remark here, as a glaring instance of the want of power, or capacity in the Spanish colony, that in 1685 it suffered the Duke of Albemarle, then governor of Jamaica, and Sir William Phipps, to obtain considerable wealth, by raising the wreck of a Spanish plate ship which had been stranded off the north-east coast of their own territory twenty-four years before, on a shoal between the north and south riff, almost in sight of Old Cape François.

Skins and tobacco, were hitherto, the principal articles of commerce from the French colony; for the latter, in consequence of the restrictions, they substituted indigo and cocoa; for similar reasons the profitable culture of cotton, which had been added, was soon abandoned. Hitherto the labours of the colony had been prosecuted chiefly by the poorest of the inhabitants, and a few negroes, which had been obtained by successful expeditions against the Spaniards; but in the war of 1688, several slaves being taken from the English, they began to contemplate the culture of the sugar-cane, as an additional source of wealth, and one of the greatest importance. With this view they continued to increase their stock of negroes, by every means in their power, though but slowly, till the year 1694, when, taking advantage of a combination of misfortunes which had reduced Jamaica, the governor (a spirited man, who had before desired permission to chase the Spaniards from his own colony,) landed in that island with a force, which shewed the anterior progress of St. Domingo to power, and increased it

1688.

Negroes adopted in the colony.

it more than any other event, that had hitherto occurred. Whatever were the other motives that induced this expedition, Du Casse seems to have had an eye to the principal necessities of his colony, by including in his booty a considerable number of negroes, perhaps not less than two thousand. The other captured property, added to the private wealth of some of the remaining Buccaniers, (if those embarked in privateering, could be still so called,) enabled them to employ these slaves, and furnish buildings and articles for the production of sugar. The year following, however, the English returned the compliment of M. Du Casse, by attacking the now flourishing settlement of Cape François, in conjunction with the forces of Spain, which they took, plundered, and reduced to ashes. It was soon, however, rebuilt on the same scite; and from this period no difficulty or misfortune to the colony, was sufficient to impede its gradual progress to that eminence, which obtained for it, in another century the appellation of the Garden of the West Indies.

The peace of Ryswick afforded the first regular cession of the western part of the island to the French; for the preceding treaties of Aix la Chapelle and Nimeguen in 1668 and 1678 did not, by any means, conciliate the national antipathies in St. Domingo; and even by it there were no other boundaries established to the possessions thus ceded, than a custom, constantly submitted to change from a variety of circumstances. By this cession the French appear to have obtained all the territory excluded, with-

CHAP. I. 1698. out an oblique line reaching from the then Cape François, on the north-east coast, to Cape Rosa on the west, intercepting the towns of Isabella and Jago at the one point, and those of Petit Goäve and Port Louis at the other.* Still, therefore, the scene of constant feuds between the more antient colonists and their neighbour, a large part of the colony towards the south, continued unoccupied, except by a few straggling inhabitants in miserable huts, and it remained a desirable object with the government to procure its settlement, in some way, at once both permanent and effectual. To accomplish this end, another company was privileged in France, which adopted the title of St. Louis, to whom this fine and extensive country was granted as a property for thirty years; on condition—that it should open a contraband trade with the Spanish continent, and clear the ground. The company immediately granted lands to all who chose, with certain allowances, providing them also with slaves and other necessaries, and every thing began to wear a promising aspect. The colony continued to increase with so much vigour, that, at the beginning of the next century a superior jurisdiction became necessary in Cape François, and it was accordingly esta-
1702. blished in 1702. The town of the Cape was, in every other respect, the capital of the colony, though, except in time of war, when it was removed hither, Port au Prince was the seat of the government.

* From the demarcation on the map of Herman Moll executed in less than twenty years after.

In

CHAP. I. 1702.

In proportion as the French colony rose in splendor, the Spanish inhabitants decreased in comfort, apparently shrinking from the effects of an industry they could not reach; yet, the former was not without difficulties to counterbalance its advantages: for in the year 1715, the death of nearly all the cocoa trees on the colony, deprived it of a very lucrative revenue; and shortly after, it experienced, in common with more important states, a shock that threatened its total subversion. This flourishing colony had arrived at a pitch of prosperity and refinement, sufficient to enable many of its proprietors to return with ample fortunes to France, or retire under easy circumstances when age required it; but when LAW's fatal scheme of finance exploded, those whose property had been paid for in the notes, or securities of the Mississippi company, or others, allied to them, were left destitute, without any hopes of retribution; many returned poor to the island, from which they had departed rich, and were compelled to serve those, who had formerly been their servants, for bread. The presence of these unfortunate victims, seemed to prolong a sensation with respect to that delusive stroke of policy, which nothing else could have occasioned; it, however, recovered the shock; and, in its worst moments, surrounded by the pleasing effects of successful industry, might look with pity upon the opposite situation of its neighbours; if such sentiments could be expected to prevail under a disparity of circumstances.

1715. Effect of LAW's financial scheme on St. Domingo.

CHAP. I. 1717. In 1717, the Spanish colony, (which had in the time of Herrera, according to his history, included 14,000 pure Castilians among its inhabitants, with a proportional population in every class,) had only 18,410 souls of every description; and, but for the ecclesiastical and juridical importance of its dilapidating capital, perhaps scarcely even a vestige would have remained. Without affecting, in allusion to these times, either the bigotry, which must be occasionally allowed in Edwards, or the inveteracy of Raynal, in favor of peculiar opinions, we may clearly view, in this decline, the fatal consequences of intolerance and cruelty, while we can happily contemplate with redoubled pleasure the agreeable contrast, which a mild regimen affords through every class of created beings.

1720. In 1720, the produce of the French colony amounted, according to Raynal*, to 1,200,000 pounds weight of indigo, 1,400,000 pounds of white sugar, and 21,000,000 pounds of raw sugar, and its increase was as rapid, as it was successful: never satisfied, however, with ordinary advantages, it is the very nature of monopoly to grasp at every opportunity of increasing its exclusive rights, without any regard to those which are the objects of its privileges. In consequence of a degree of insolence, with which, the introduction of a measure intended to confine the trade of slaves to themselves was conducted, a violent commotion
1722. took place in 1722, which was not quelled entirely for two years,

* Settlements and Trades in the East and West Indies, vol. iv. p. 235.

CHAP. I.

during which period the buildings and ships of the company were destroyed, and their commissioners disgraced. It will naturally 1722. be supposed that a commotion which extended with the most inconceivable firmness through every part of the island, affected the progress of cultivation and commerce for some time after the re-establishment of peace; yet, in 1734, we find a considerable 1734. increase of plantations, in which the growth of cotton, and coffee, had been added to a great extent. This increase of opulence, occasioned, naturally, an augmentation of the respectability of the government, for in 1750 we find a new establishment at Port 1750. au Prince, the capital, which now became the residence of a commander in chief, a superior council, and an intendant.

In the year 1754, the amount of the various commodities of 1754. the colony was equal to 1,261,469l., but such was its increasing prosperity, that the inhabitants received from the mother country, imports to the amount of 1,777,509l. The population of pure whites amounted to upwards of 14,000; free mulattoes nearly 4,000; and upwards of 172,000 negroes of different descriptions, There were 599 sugar plantations, and 3,379 of indigo. The cocoa trees amounted to 98,946; the cotton plants to 6,300,367; and there were near 22,000,000 of cassia trees. The provisions consisted of near 6,000,000 of banana trees; upwards of 1,000,000 plots of potatoes; 226,000 plots of yams; and near 3,000,000 trenches of manioc. The cattle, did not exceed 63,000 horses and mules, and 93,000 head of horned cattle *.

* Raynal, vol. iv. p. 236.

In

CHAP. I. 1757. In short, the remaining events of St. Domingo, up to the period of the French revolution, consists of a series of successes the most brilliant, and a display of industry and opulence the most creditable to the French character. Even the government of Madrid seems to have been excited, to some degree of emulation about the year 1757, as a company was formed at Barcelona, with exclusive privileges, to attempt a re-establishment in the eastern part of the island. The most, however, that appears to have been accomplished, was the equipment of two small vessels annually, by which they received in return, a few thousand hides, and some other trifling articles; but in 1765, when Charles III. opened a free trade to all the Windward Islands, they suddenly assumed quite an altered appearance; and Hispaniola, so long depressed by the false policy of the mother country, seem determined to attempt a renewal of her former activity. During the five years preceding 1774, the custom-house duties were more than doubled. It extended, however, comparatively to little more than a dying struggle. The
1764. French still continued to increase rapidly; in 1764, they had a force of 8,786 white men, capable of bearing arms, with whom 1414 mulattoes were enrolled, and their slaves had in-
1767. creased to 206,000. In 1767, they laded 347 ships for France, besides a considerable overplus, not less than one fifth of that number, distributed in various ways.

As if it were to temper the success of this splendid colony, a
1770. dreadful earthquake, happened on the third day of June, 1770, which

which levelled the capital, Port au Prince, with the ground. It has been, however, rebuilt with additional convenience, and enlarged with much labour, several streets having been raised upon the shore by means of causeways, though it does not possess, by any means, the elegance of Cape François; many of the buildings being composed of wood. 1770.

In 1776, a determinate cessation took place of the dreadful feuds which had constantly occurred between the Spanish and French inhabitants of the colony, by the formation of a new line of demarcation, to separate the different partitions of the island. This settlement, though from a strange avarice in the Spaniards of territory, which they knew not how to occupy, appears to encroach considerably on the former possessions of France, was a most desirable concession to the latter. Nor were the consequences of this agreement less favorable to the Spaniards in other respects: for they afterwards opened a more liberal commerce with their neighbouring colonists; whom they supplied with every description of cattle, receiving in return through their means all the productions of Europe, and expending with them the monies received from Spain for the purposes of the government. 1776.

After the conflict between Great Britain and her American colonies, the Spanish government began to pay more regard to its territories in that quarter, and it accordingly became furnished with a more respectable garrison. Since that time, the number of 1785.

CHAP. I. 1785.

of Europeans added to it, tended also to improve its respectability as a colony.

From this period, to the commencement of revolutionary activity in 1789, when those principles which had long been concealed in a smouldering flame, were about to have vent through the world, the French establishment in St. Domingo reached a height superior, not only to all other colonial possessions, but to the conception of the philosopher and politician; its private luxury, and its public grandeur, astonished the traveller; its accumulation of wealth surprized the mother country; and it was beheld with rapture by the neighbouring inhabitants of the islands of the Antilles. Like a rich beauty, surrounded with every delight, the politicians of Europe, sighed for her possession; but they sighed in vain; she was reserved for the foundation of a republic as extraordinary as it is terrible, whether it ultimately tend only, to the ascertainment of abstract opinions, or unfold a new and august empire to the world, where it has heretofore been deemed impossible to exist.

It remains only to the present division of the work, to add a brief account of the general appearance of the island, as it existed at this date of its history; which, will then subdivide itself into the different heads, under which it is proposed to consider the causes, progress, and consequences of its revolution, and present establishment.

Notwithstanding

CHAP. I. 1789.

Topography of the island.

Notwithstanding, the reduced state of that part of the island which still continued in the possession of Spain, what has been collected of its topography, or, natural history, shall, in justice to the ancient proprietors, commence the brief detail which concludes the present chapter.

Spanish division.

The Spanish division of St. Domingo is understood to have comprehended, at that period, the whole territory within the diversified line of demarcation, fixed upon a few years before, which confined the French to apparently an insignificant part of the island. Commencing with the river Du Massacre on the north, it stretched in an irregular curve towards the west, crossing all the great roads from Fort Dauphin and the Cape, passing the hills at about thirty miles distant from the coast, and intersecting the conflux of the streams of La Trouble and Plaisance; when, turning shortly round the hills at Atalaye, it assumes its southern direction, and crossing the stream of La Petite Riviere at its mouth, stretches through a delightful plain watered by the great river Artibonite: crossing this, and the river Du Fer, and winding round a single hill, it then proceeds through the little lake of Cul de Sac; returning to its eastward direction, it falls in with the river á Pitres at a point nearly opposite to that of its departure, having formed an elipsis of not less than 170 miles, the nearest point approaching within a very short distance of the town of Gonäves, situate in the bay of that name, upon the western coast*.

Last line of demarcation.

* This line is believed to be accurately delineated in the corrected map of the island prefixed to the present work.

It

CHAP. I. 1789. Topography, &c. Spanish division.

It will be perceived, what a large proportion of this delightful territory, remained in the possession of Spain; which, whatever the degraded character we have been obliged to attribute to its possessors, must have produced a very ample return for the cultivation they bestowed upon it. With an extent of coast of between five and six hundred miles, in which are not less than seven capacious bays, (with innumerable inlets,) into which twenty large rivers, besides many nameless streams, discharge themselves; while the interior, consisting of large fertile plains, well watered, and protected, rather than interrupted, by the different chains of mountains with which they are variegated; producing the most delightful and salubrious vallies: nothing was wanting but the moderate labour of the cultivator, and a liberal policy, to render it the most desirable country in the world. In wanting these, however, it sunk into a beautiful wilderness, and its sullen shores repelled the eye which had been attracted by distant fertility. On scites that would have received and encouraged the population of cities, were placed the solitary huts of fishermen; whose miserable toils, perhaps, a melancholy monk was embittering by a thousand painful restrictions of his poverty-stricken career on earth, and dreadful views of eternity; the result of morbid intellects, nursed by the wild scene around him.

City of St. Domingo.

The principal towns, after the ancient city of St. Domingo, were, Monte Christi, La Vega, St. Jago, formerly that of the Conception, Zeibo, St. Thomé, Azua, and Isabella, if the latter could deserve the appellation. The other places were merely villages

CHAP. I. 1789. Topography, &c. Spanish division. Villages.

villages of the most wretched appearance, which, instead of alluring society from the distant provinces, seemed rather to mark with desolation those natural meadows with which they abounded. The most important of these were St. Laurent, a few miles north of the capital, in which were a few villas, very inviting, from the beauty of the plain in which it was situated; Higuey, whose advantageous situation on the river of that name, might have procured for it much more importance; Baya, Bayaguana, and Monte Plata, surrounded by the finest land in the known world, and in the vicinity of forests, whose riches and utility were unappreciated; Cotuy, near the union of the rivers Yuna and Cotuy, about eight leagues from the centre of the bay of Samana; St. Juan de Maguana, delightfully placed on the banks of the Neybe, and separated by a small mountainous district from the lake of Riquille; St. Jean de Goava and Banica, served often as points of the commerce between the two colonies, as well as Atalaye, which stretched towards the extremity of the angle reaching into the French division opposite the bay of Gonäve; St. Miguel, Dejabon, Venta de Cana, Sala, Jarbon, Espani, and Amina, distributed in the course of a few leagues from the northern coasts, though inhabited by a kind of wealthy graziers, form a powerful contrast to the wild beauty of the surrounding country.

Spanish capital.

St. Domingo, the capital, and seat of the ecclesiastical government of the colonies, and at one time of the whole of the Spanish dominion in the new world, still continued an archiepiscopal see,

 to

CHAP. I. 1789. Topography, &c. Spanish division.

to which the bishops of the other islands were suffragans. It is situated, as hath been before described, near the mouth of the river Ozama, on the southern coast of the island, and on the border of a fertile and delightful level of near ninety miles in length, and thirty in breadth, significantly called Los Llanos. The cathedral, and other public buildings, yet retained no mean degree of importance; and, notwithstanding their dilapidating antiquity, wore an elegance of appearance that was not to have been expected. The remains of many other superb buildings of antiquity were yet to be seen, and those of a modern date of brick, stone, and wood, were not unworthy the capital of such a territory. It yet contained several religious establishments, and what is of more importance, the extent and safety of its harbour, containing an ample depth of water, and, protected by a bar, over which the largest vessels rode with safety, could not fail to render it of great commercial interest. The streets were principally broad, and towards the middle of the town retained their original rectangular neatness; they were also clean, and enlightened by three handsome squares. It yet contained an appearance of great strength towards the sea, and even on the side of the land it was guarded by a sufficient wall. Some remains yet exist of the ancient citadel, and also of the palace of the First Viceroy.

Monte Christi.

The town of Monte Christi still retained a busy appearance, and some degree of importance, from its continued traffic with the neighbouring continent of North America, and the vicinity of of some of the most flourishing plantations of the French colony. During the wars between England and France, while Spain was disengaged from the troubles, the Spaniards traded much to this part, as did also the English smugglers. CHAP. I. 1789. Topography, &c. Spanish division.

La Vega, neither pleasing nor convenient, situated in the extensive plain of the Viga Real, which is, in length, nearly that of half the island, though seldom exceeding thirty miles in breadth, derived its chief consequence from the surrounding pasturage, and some excellent sugar-walks in its vicinity. La Vega.

St. Jago retained a considerable air of antiquity, but no other recommendation; for all the former grandeur which it would appear to have possessed is now in ruins, and it affords but an additional monument of desolation; yet it contained a miserable monastery of Franciscans, to whom were attached some of the finest lands in the neighbourhood; but whose chief power seemed to be employed in the rule of the slaves in the adjacent plantations, in the care of whose religious duties they frequently forgot their temporal avocations. St. Jago.

Zeibo was a place of some business, from being the only town towards the eastern coast, as St. Thomas is, again, from being situated in the very centre of the island, among the mountains of Cibao. Agua was also of little other importance than from being placed in the middle of a very fine bay on the southern coast. The first and the last of these towns, besides their desolatory Zeibo.

 state,

CHAP. I. 1789. Topography, &c. Spanish division. St. Thomas. Isabella.

state, bordering on extensive swamps, were therefore unhealthy; while St. Thomé, receiving the invigorating winds, as they sweep from the mountains on one side, and the salubrious breeze from the plains on the other, was a situation desirable for the farmer, or the valetudinarian, and capable of much improvement. On the site of the first city erected in the new world, in honour of Isabella, remain a few houses and ruins, while here and there a solitary cross peeping from amidst the luxuriant grass, served just to tell us—" such things were." One little stream watered its vicinity, and a rugged road marked its few occasions to direct an inquisitive traveller to its haunts.

Ecclesiastical government.

Of the ecclesiastical government of the island, little shall here suffice. Notwithstanding that conduct on the part of the clergy which had compelled certain regulations of their conduct, and the liberality of sentiment which began to gain ground in Spain, the American church still retained an inordinate power over every class of the community, and an undue interference with every object of the colony. Independent of the papal jurisdiction,* and originally endowed with immense revenues from the wealth, and afterwards the devotion of the people, they still continued in extraordinary numbers, fattening on the very desolation of the country, to whose benefit their order had not, in

* The Emperor Ferdinand having obtained from the Popes Alexander VI. and Julius II. such an exemption on the first discovery of the New World, to favour its extension.

the

CHAP. I. 1789. Topography, &c. Spanish division.

the least, contributed.* Many of the benefices were, however, now filled by the secular clergy, according to the effort of Ferdinand VI. to remedy the vicious and abominable abuses of the regulars. It has been already stated to have been honoured with the seat of the archiepiscopal see; it had also all the minor dignities, while the *Curas*, or parish-priests, were to be found in all the sacerdotal dignity throughout the country. The inquisition was also established in this as well as all the other American islands.

Constitution.

The constitution of Hispaniola is not easily defined. The different towns were under the immediate direction of a sort of local municipality; but their power was very weak, and much infringed by the privileges of different bodies of the clergy. They confined themselves chiefly, therefore, to the minor commercial regulations of their own district, and even these were under the control of a governor of the colony. The more important ends of general justice were administered by six more respectable judges, severally appointed, for civil and criminal jurisdiction, who formed one of the eleven Courts of Audience distributed among the colonies, and which are a model of the Spanish Chancery. The decisions of these courts were subject to appeal

* "Though, by the ample provision which has been made for the American church, many of its members enjoy the ease and independance which are favourable to the cultivation of science, the body of secular clergy has hardly, during two centuries and a half, produced one author whose works contain such useful information, or possess such a degree of merit as to be ranked among those which attract the attention of enlightened nations."—*Robertson's Hist. Vol. IV. p.* 50.

to

CHAP. I. 1789. Topography, &c. Spanish division.

to the Council of the Indies in Spain, except in civil cases, where the object of litigation did not amount, in value, to a sum near fifteen hundred pounds. The vice-roy of New Spain represents the head of the government. The council over-ruled every department, civil and ecclesiastical, military and commercial, and has always preserved its dignity; with it originates every ordinance relative to the government of the colonies, which must be passed by the majority of a third of its members. At the head of this council the king is always understood to preside. There is also a commercial assembly for the purposes of an immediate attention to all its objects which could not be affected by any other means. The local officers immediately below the whole of these, consist of the different commandants, and a variety of inferior officers of almost every description; many of whose situations were sinecures, as valuable as the proprietors of the island were depreciated.

Military force.

Of the military force of the colony little can be said; for, except the garrison of St. Domingo, and a few posts established towards the line of demarcation, the regular soldiery distributed throughout the island were inconsiderable; nor could the militia, in which all capable of bearing arms were included, be said to produce an addition very effective. The principal ports along the line were those of Verettes, St. Michael, and St. Raphael.

Inhabitants.

The different inhabitants of the Spanish colony were designated as follows:—The pure Spaniards, who visited America for the purpose

purpose of employment, and who always enjoyed every situation of power, were called *Chapetones*. They looked down with disdain upon every other order of men.

CHAP. I. 1789. Topography, &c. Spanish division.

The second class of subjects were the Creoles, or descendants of Europeans settled in America. Though frequently deriving their pedigree from the noblest families in Spain, and possessing ample fortunes, yet the abjectness of political debasement—the enervation of indulgence in a warm climate, had subdued their minds, and subjected them to the vilest sloth. While the Chapetone amassed immense wealth, the Creole remained satisfied with his unimpaired patrimony; a determined hatred reigning between them.

The third was the offspring of an European with an Indian, or a negro: the former, called Mulattoes, the latter Mestizos. Of these, there was a considerable number in this, as in all the other Spanish settlements. In proportion as the number exceeded the colonies of other nations, from the early policy of encouraging an intermixture of the Spaniards with the natives, and from a greater indulgence of licentious intercourse. Among these there were a variety of different shades of colour, from the jet black of Africa, and the copper, or brown hue of America, to that of the European complexion. Those of the first and second generations, were considered not sufficiently removed, for distinction, from their parent race; in the third, the colour sensibly declined; and, in the fifth

CHAP. I. 1789. Topography, &c. Spanish division.

they embraced the characteristics and privileges of Europeans. The mechanic arts and active offices of society were left, by the proud and indolent Spaniards, to this robust and hardy race; who were lively, well-tempered, and frequently accomplished.

The Negroes compose the fourth rank; of this singular, and important part of the human species, more will be found in another department of this work. In Hispaniola, as well as several other of the Spanish colonies, the Negroes were much used in domestic service, and for purposes of luxury. They were splendidly dressed, and, in many respects, rendered so subservient to vanity, that they became themselves, more silly, vain, and imperious, than their masters*.

However, the distinctions between Europeans and the people of colour were, by no means, kept up in the Spanish colonies as in those of other nations, except with regard to ecclesiastical establishments, to which they were not generally admitted.

Country.

The Spanish coast is, in many parts, of a bold and rocky appearance, presenting high cliffs and extended promontories, and, in others, for many leagues, beautiful in the extreme, delighting the eye with an agreeable variety of hills, vallies, woods, and rivers.

* The Indians in those of the Spanish colonies where they yet remain, form a fifth, and the most depressed class of inhabitants.

The

CHAP. I. 1789. Topography, &c. Spanish division.

The generally luxurious face of the country continues the same throughout, with very little appearance of sterility even on the deserted north-east coast. The richest glades, with a most delightful foliage appear in the very bosoms of the mountains; and nothing can exceed the fertility of the cultivated lands, in every direction. The vast plain of Los Llanos, stretching along the south-east part of the island, is adapted to the growth of every tropical production, and, (abounding with rivers,) always capable of irrigation, as well as the Vega Real, which lies more towards the north, and through which flows the Yuna and the Cotuy, over a space of from fifty to an hundred miles; till meeting at a short distance from the coast, they discharge their united streams into the Bay of Samana. On the northern coast, (by which Columbus first approached the island,) is also a large tract of land which, though consigned to vast herds of wild cattle of various descriptions, exhibited its fertility, in the support of this object of commerce, as well as in several grass-farms, which lay to the northward line of demarcation. The present produce is sugar, ginger, cocoa, tobacco, cotton, indigo, maize, and the Cassava-root, of which, what they could spare (with wood for dying,) was received by the mother-country. But their principal article of exportation was the hides of the horned-cattle, which ran wild in the plains, with no other guards than the names, or the marks of their owners: at length, they regarded the carcases also, which being gladly received by their neighbours, they were found to be a valuable resource. Not confining themselves to horned-

CHAP. I. 1789. Topography, &c. Spanish division.

cattle, they furnished also great numbers of horses and mules, which required less trouble in their rearing, and were very acceptable to the French colony.

The population, though an exact account may be deemed impossible, may, probably, approach to the statement of M. de Charmilly, at 60,000; the number of whites was certainly greater than 2000, and that of the negroes *less* than half the total number; the free race of mixed blood of different grades, composing the remainder.

The Spanish division of Hispaniola, affords every species of tropical herb, and beast; as, in this respect, it is similar to the western part of the island, they will be considered together.

French division. Divided into provinces.

The French colony of St. Domingo, comprehended the whole of the territory westward of the line of demarcation, before described: with fewer natural advantages, it presented such a contrast to the inactivity of the neighbouring country, as procured for it a character almost equal to that which has been so generally given to the whole of the island at its discovery. This colony, of which we are able to give a more regular account, was divided, as indeed nature appears to have directed, into the northern, western, and southern provinces.

Northern province.

The first of these extended about forty leagues along the northern coast, from the river Massacre to Cape St. Nicholas, and contained (including the

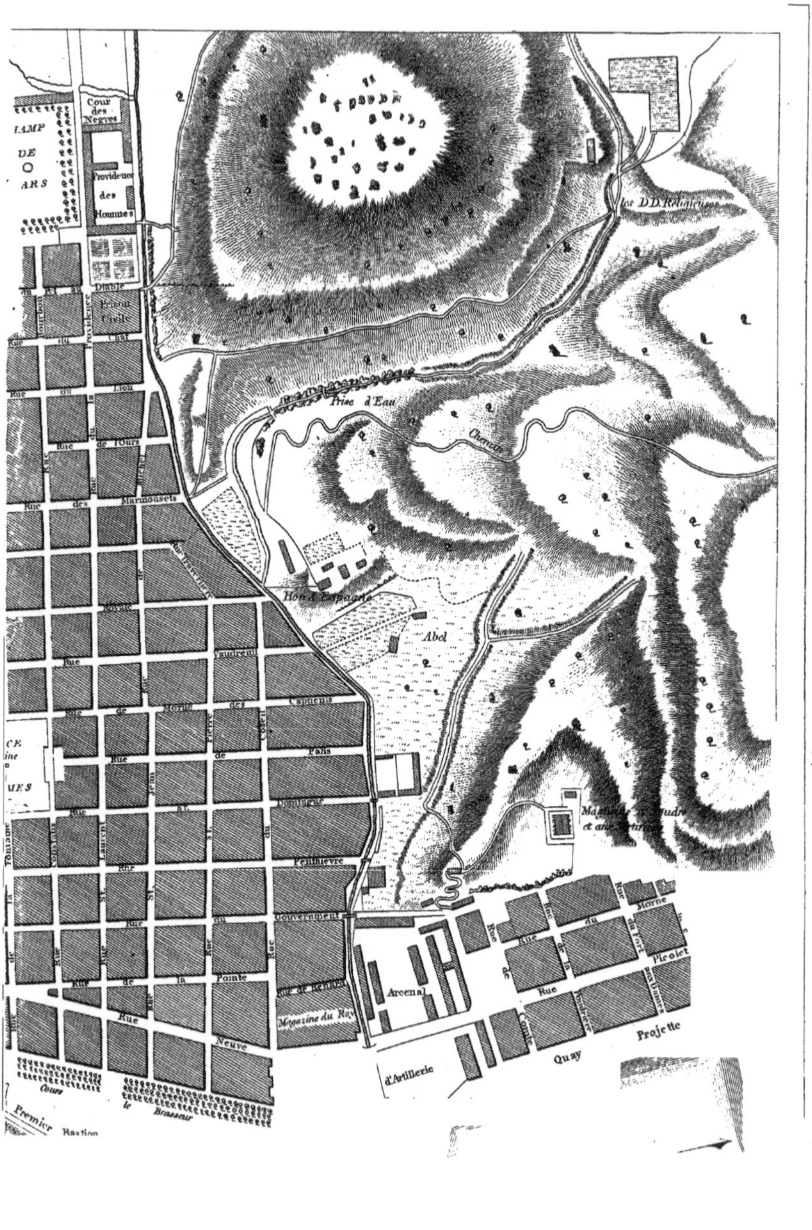

Cour des Negres
Providence des Hommes
Prison Civile
Rue du Lion
Rue de l'Ours
Rue des Marmousets
Royale
Vaudreuil
Rue de Paris
Penthievre
Gouvernement
Rue de la Pointe
Rue Neuve
Prise d'Eau
Chemin
les DD. Religieuses
Abel
Arsenal
Magazine du Roy
d'Artillerie
Quay
Projette
Picolet
Premier Bastion
Cours
le Brasseur

Topography, &c.

French division.

the island of Tortuga) twenty-six parishes. The principal towns and harbours were, Cape François, Fort Dauphin, Port Paix, and Cape St. Nicholas.

Western province.

The western province commenced at Cape St. Nicholas, and occupying the whole line of roadsted forming the Bite, or vast and general bay of Leogane, terminated at Cape Tiburon. It contained fourteen parishes, in which the chief towns were, Port-au-Prince, St. Mark, Leogane, Petit Goäve, and Jeremie; with the considerable villages of Gonaives, and Arcahaye. The best harbours are those of Port-au-Prince and Gonaives, the others are open and dangerous.

Southern province.

The southern province occupied the remaining coast from Cape Tiburon to L'Ance à Pitre, (or rather the river of that name): of the ten parishes, there were but two chief towns, those of the Cayes and Jacmel. Its roads and harbours are dangerous; and the shipping off Aux Cayes are frequently obliged to take refuge in the bay des Flamands.

Town of Cape François.

The town of Cape François, in effect the capital of the colony, stands on a small plain, as it were, hollowed out of the *Morne du Cap*, a mountain which rises on both sides from the bay. The Morne, which allows only a narrow passage to the plain, is joined by the northern mountains, extending to Fort Picolet, which is placed on the edge of the rock, and defends the entrance to the roads; though built, in some respects, disadvan-

CHAP. I. 1897. Topography, &c. French division.

tageously (except as regarded its commodious bay, and sometimes experiencing an inconvenient closeness from the situation,) it had risen to a degree of elegance concordant to the importance of the island, and which might cope with many European cities of the first order and opulence. It was composed of upwards of thirty well-formed streets, which crossed each other at right angles, and were many of them elegant. The houses built of stone and brick, were frequently handsome and commodious. It contained also two magnificent squares, those of Notre Dame and Clugny, ornamented with fountains; besides public shops, and long ranges of warehouses, suited to the commercial purposes to which this scene is dedicated. The principal public buildings after the church, which had not been erected many years, were the government-house, formerly a convent of Jesuits,* the barracks, arsenal, playhouse, and prison. There were also, I believe, two hospitals of a similar nature to our own, and two of the establishments which Raynal calls houses of Providence. Whether the *Hôpital de la Charité* (an alms or work-house), in the road to L'Haut du Cap, at a small distance from the town, was of this kind, I am not certain, though I believe it; they were, however, as Raynal observed, " truly pious and divine institutions;" being for the benefit of such Europeans as might remain in the colony destitute of resources, or who, before they had acquired by industry, an opportunity to procure subsistence,

* His Royal Highness, the Duke of Clarence, was entertained in this building at the conclusion of peace in 1783.

became

became subject to disorders often fatal. Males and females were separately taken care of, and nourished till they were disposed of in some employment in which they could help themselves. The theatre was supplied by a respectable company of comedians, who performed, with short intervals, all the year round, besides other exhibitions and entertainments.

CHAP. I. 1789. Topography, &c. French division.

Fort Dauphin, about thirty miles from the cape, from whence there is an excellent road at a small distance from the shore, supplies the place of an ancient town called Bayaha, which was situated at a greater distance from the coast: it was the last town on the eastern frontier of the French, and stands in the farthest recess of a spacious harbour, which has only one narrow outlet. It has a small river flowing by the village of Trou to the west, and the shore of Manchenillo bay to the east. The fort stands on a little peninsula to the north, and it is bounded on the south by the same luxurious and extensive plain which enhanced the riches of the town that has been just described. It was well fortified, and could have held out against a considerable force for some time. It had also a theatre well supplied, assemblies, and concerts. Though the greater part of the produce of the plain was carried to Cape François, Fort Dauphin had more than its share of contraband trade, with several advantages, derived from proximity to the forlorn part of the Spanish dominion.

Fort Dauphin.

Port Paix stands on a worse situation than either of the preceding towns, from the former of which it is distant about forty miles.

Port Paix.

CHAP. I. 1789. Topography, &c. French division.

miles. It was the first establishment of the Buccaniers on the island, when, quitting the habits of freebooters, they began to form themselves into a more peaceable society. Port Paix is healthy, though a considerable swamp is not far distant, to the north-east; and every exertion of Agrarian industry has been exercised to its advantage, even to the erection of several well-planned aqueducts. Its retirement well adapting it to the purposes of contraband trade, to the great emolument of the Americans, who frequented this port as well as the next, which forms the boundary of the northern province.

Cape St. Nicholas.

The town of Cape St. Nicholas, is situate on the sterile spot from which it derives its name, and which is considered the key to the windward passage, being directly opposite to the port of Maisi in Cuba. Its chief excellence is its harbour, which is capacious, and rendered perfectly secure by the mole, or peninsula, on the north-west, which, with the mountains on the north-east, form a bay nearly six miles long, sheltered from every wind. Behind, rise the mountains of the cape, which, altogether, renders it a place of a formidable appearance. It was rendered a free port by the French in consequence of its unproductive quality, (as before mentioned,) and to allure residents, to whom the French ministry allied a colony of Acadians and Germans.

Port-au-Prince.

Port-au-Prince was the ostensible metropolis of the French colony, and the seat of its government; except in time of war, when it was removed to Cape François. It must have been one of of the unaccountable caprices that sometimes direct the settlements of towns, that could have obtained for this place, indefensible at all points, the distinction it received. It was neither healthy nor inviting, though opulent, and well built, with every attention to convenience, but chiefly of wood. The water is of a brackish and otherwise disagreeable taste. It enjoyed, in common with the principal towns of the other provinces, the vicinity of a rich plain, the Cul de Sac, which contained no less than 150 sugar plantations, with every convenience for their advantage; while the mountains behind it, clothed with plantations of coffee, reached quite to the Spanish settlements at Riquille. The dreadful earthquake which happened in 1770, occasioned the town to be much enlarged and improved. There were many long and populous streets, but not handsome. A few public edifices ornamented situations, not the best calculated to receive them; among these, the residence of the intendant, and the theatre, were most conspicuous. There are two harbours formed by some islets, open to any attack. The town extending along the sea-shore, in the centre of the western coast, is damp, and cheerless, except from the hurry of business. It is accessible at every point, from the land. A road, about 40 miles in length, reaches from hence to the village of Sale Trou, situate between two small rivers, near L'Ance a Pitre, on the southern coast.

CHAP. I. 1789. Topography, &c. French division

The town of St. Mark, stretching along the sea-shore at the bottom of the bay of that name, was rather handsomely built, of

St. Mark.

CHAP. I. 1789. Topography, &c. French division.

freestone from the hills, which form a crescent behind it; the only instance of that kind of building in the colony. It was not large, but possessed a good trade, and received all the crops from the intervening country, to Cape St. Nicholas. It is within ten miles of the mouth of the great river Artibonite, which winds its serpentine course through the plain to which it gives name, flowing behind it at the village of Tapion, about four leagues in the interior. Being the only river on the plain, an artificial use of water, by irrigation to a great extent, was necessary for its cultivation, which was an impediment to its opulence in contrast to those plains, which, (as was generally the case,) were watered by numerous streams or rivulets.

Leogane.

Leogane stands about a mile and a half from the shore opposite the island, or peninsula, of Gonave, between the channel of Gonave and the bay of St. Mark; it is a spacious, handsome town, surrounded with fertility, and in the neighbourhood of many streams of excellent water. It is a situation capable of defence, and in many respects preferable to Port-au-Prince. It was here the seat of government was transferred from Goäve, previous to its settlement at the late capital.

Petit Goäve.

Petit Goäve, the original seat of government of the whole French colony, was long in a very decayed state, notwithstanding its importance in the first settlement of the Buccaniers, and the excellence of its harbour, still extremely good, and to which may be attributed any advantage it yet retains.

L'Anse

L'Anse de Jeremie, or, La Grand Anse, is a thriving town, well situated, healthy, and neat. Its trade was forming in a manner that left no doubt of increasing opulence, and to it, the privateers generally brought the prizes they made, in its neighbourhood. CHAP. I. 1789. Topography, &c. French division. Jeremie.

The village of Gonaves is situate on the south side of the bay of that name, immediately opposite the projecting point of the line of demarcation, so that the French colony in this part, (nearly the centre of their territory,) contained in breadth little more than twenty miles. The soil is the most productive, and the most grateful to man, of any spot in the whole of the Antilles. Its harbour was excellent in point of safety, being formed by a little island, which crossing the bay, left a narrow channel, but with sufficient depth of water. Gonaves.

Aux Cayes is completely sunk in marshy ground, without a harbour, or salubrity to recommend it; yet such is the fertility which every where surrounds this town, as to have tempted the choice of every new settler to its swampy shores, and stagnant ponds. Its population was, therefore, much greater than could have been supposed. It has also in its vicinity a variety of bays and villages, which all tend to its prosperity.—Many ships have been lost here, from the insecure and dangerous anchorage; yet, as the Abbé Raynal has observed, "even the caprices of industry are to be indulged by the government;" and "trade like a plant that only flourishes in a soil of its own Aux Cayes.

CHAP. I. 1789. Topography, &c. French division. La Vache.

choosing, disdains every kind of restraint." Vache Island, which lies off this coast, was a celebrated resort of the freebooters in their molestation of the Spaniards, and is yet the successful haunt of the privateers of an enemy.

Jaquemel.

To this island, as to that of Tortuga on the opposite coast, the colony was indebted for the foundation of a town, which, though small, is of some importance. Jaquemel, at the best of times, did not contain one hundred houses, and derives no support from its soil, which is not fruitful, and comparatively hid among the neighbouring hills. As Port-au-Prince is to L'Ance á Pitres, so is Jaquemel to Le Petit Goäve, being situated on the opposite side of the south projection of the Bight, sometimes called the Bight of Leogane. It is therefore a kind of store-house, or magazine, to the colony, receiving safely during war, (which can be done at no other place,) assistance of every kind, which is easily communicated to the western side, by a road of only twenty miles, leading to Leogane, and from thence to Port-au-Prince.

Villages.

Besides the towns, and the villages of Gonaves and Arcahaye already mentioned, there are numerous others to which either commerce, agriculture, beauty, or strength of situation, attached important advantages; among these may be ranked St. Louis, which, though poor, and containing a small number of houses, without even water to drink, till some Jews, in return for their safety, proposed to erect, at their own expence, an aqueduct; by

CHAP. I. 1789. Topography, &c. French division.

being occupied in some of the purposes of government, receiving the men of war which appeared there, and thus protecting the trade and wealth of Aux Cayes, it assumed the characterestic of a defence of the island. Baynette, about fifteen miles from Jacquemel, and Acul, at a less distance from Aux Cayes, derive a similar adventitious importance, as well as Nipes and Miragoane, on the opposite coast; while Cul de Sac, Petit Fond, and Plaisance, in the interior, are of a different character. To these many more might be added upon the northern coast, but enough hath been said to shew the different appearance of the French colony from that of Spain: suffice it to add, that every part teemed with population, and smiled with industry.

The cultivated land in the colony amounted to 2,289,480 English acres,* which was divided into 793 plantations of sugar, 3117 of coffee, 789 of cotton, 3160 of indigo, 54 of cocoa or chocolate, and 623 smaller settlements for raising grain, yams, and other vegetable food.†

Ecclesiastical government.

Of the differences which agitated the two colonies, happily religion did not form an object; for, though exempt from the interference of Rome, on one part, by express concession, and, on the other, by a light administration of ecclesiastical government, they both acknowledged the forms of her church, and

* Or 763,923 carreaux of French measurement.

† This last statement, which has every mark of authenticity, is taken from Mr. Edwards, Hist. Surv. p. 136.

entertained

CHAP. I. 1789. Topography, &c. French division.

entertained all the appendages of her hierarchy. The order of Jesuits was obtained here; that able, though insidious body, which, separated from secular projects and political intrigues, might have become benefactors to the human race. More need not be said of the local establishments of religion in a colony, whose inhabitants counted really but little upon it, and whose writers have told us still less.* The edifices of public worship did not, in elegance of building, detract any other, and that there were many excellent benefices, might be collected from the manner in which many of the ecclesiastics have been known to live.

Constitution.

The government of the French colony was composed of two principal officers, a governor-general, and an intendant, or general administrator, whose office lasted three years. They were appointed through the marine minister, and their power was unbounded; for they, in effect, enacted laws, filled all vacant offices, and presided ultimately over all councils, or courts of justice. The governor had the whole naval and military force under his command, and had the power of personal liberty throughout the colony. He had also the power, by certain impediments, to prevent arrest by any other authority, and in part to stop the course of justice. The intendant regulated and superintended every department relative to the public revenue: to this he had the occasional assistance of a court ridiculously enough

* Except the tales of some fanatics among the French missionaries, with whom many of the slaves are described as "*spiritual*," though it is sufficiently known that these people, in a state of slavery, neither comprehend, nor retain, even the forms of Christian worship.

called

called the Colonial Assembly, in which every superior public officer bore a part. A subordinate court of justice was placed at Port-au-Prince, for the provinces. The principal officers presided in it, with a president, twelve counsellors, and four assistant judges. In this court, which was formerly divided between that town and Cape François, were registered all the royal edicts, and those of the colonial government. Much, very much of the happiness of the colony, depended on the governor, who was generally a person of distinction, and most frequently selected from the army or navy. An appeal from every decision lay to the King, in which justice was insured; whatever impediments to its course might have been found in St. Domingo.

CHAP. I. 1789. Topography, &c. French division.

Military force.

The chief force of the island, though certainly inadequate to its defence, consisted of the militia, of which each parish raised from one to three companies of whites, one of mulattoes, and one of free blacks, none of which received pay; and the king's troops upon the colonial establishment generally comprised from two to three thousand men.

Inhabitants.

The inhabitants were composed, as usual, of pure whites; people of colour, and blacks of free condition; and negroes in a state of slavery. The whole of the intermediate grades were called generally mulattoes.

The character of the European planter in St. Domingo was imperious, and voluptuous to a higher degree than in the other

 islands:

CHAP. I. 1789. Topography, &c. French division.

islands: this character also shewed itself on every occasion; he was impatient of even the constraint of the laws, avaricious of wealth and honor, and a devotee to all the arts of indulgence. Hospitality, was unbounded among them, and charity, at the same time, very extensively bestowed. "'Tis the inheritance," says Father le Pers,* "which they have preserved the most entire from their ancestors; and it would seem that this excellent virtue was confined with the very air of St. Domingo.

Many circumstances combined to render the situation of the mulattoes much more eligible than in any other island, though in some respects worse. They were also more numerous. The free man of colour had the command of his own property, without any restriction, both in life and death; he could bear testimony even against the whites; he could marry as he pleased, and transmit freedom to his children; and he might embrace a liberal profession; but prejudice frequently damped his efforts, and precipitated him below what an hostile law could have done. The meanness of birth was never forgotten in his own land. They were also compelled to serve in one of the brigades of horse, furnished in all the parishes, under the appellation of the Marshalsea. The numbers of this class were to be accounted for, by several circumstances, amongst which were the superior comforts of the lower order of whites, employed in the superintendance of the

* "L'heritage qu'ils ont conservé le plus entier de leurs peres, est l'hospitalité, &c. il semble qu'on respire cette belle vertu avec l'air de S. Domingue." *Charlevoix Hist. de S. Domingue.*

plantations,

CHAP. I. 1789. Topography, &c. French division.

plantations, and the engaging manners of the women of colour, who are often elegant, if not sometimes really beautiful. The mulattoes were frequently opulent and respected.

The next class, the enslaved negro, appears to have been comparatively happy, rather than otherwise; not condemned to an unreasonable duration of labor, they were sufficiently provided, without any anxiety for their future existence. They had gardens which produced the necessaries of life; pigs, poultry, and even horses; and were sufficiently clothed, agreeably to the climate; but they were considered and treated, as much beneath, the ordinary class of human beings: yet, M. de Charmilly, whose judgment in this particular need not to be doubted, says, "that this race of men is naturally good; that if nature has denied them attention, reflexion, observation, perseverance, and all the advantages which render the whites superior to them, she has done every thing for them necessary to the climate in which they exist, not only in physical advantages, but also in those of the heart; for she has given that sensibility for the sex which makes them forget so many sorrows, and the most lively affection for their children, which renders every thing supportable to them."*

* —" Que cette race d'hommes est naturellement bonne; que si la nature lui refusé l'attention, la réflexion, l'observation, la persévérance, & tous les avantages qui rendent les blancs supérieurs à eux, elle a tout fait pour eux du côté du climat, des avantages physiques & même du cœur; car elle leur a donné cette sensibilité pour les femmes qui fait ublier tant de malheurs! et le plus vif amour pour leurs enfans, qui leur rend tout supportable!" —*Venault de Charmilly, Lettre à M. Bryan Edwards, &c. p.* 41.

The

CHAP. I. 1789. Topography, &c. French division.

The appearance which we have already ascribed to the Spanish coast, may be naturally supposed to extend itself to that of the French division, with the difference which must be created by a continual range of cultivation, either glistening in a tropical sun, or winding in an umbrageous alley towards dwellings which might be easily conceived a second paradise. The Mole of Cape St. Nicholas, which is justly considered as a key to the windward passage, presents an appearance such as it should to the ocean, sterile and commanding. The south peninsula resounded with the language of trade, and the northern coast with arms and with agriculture.—Unlike their neighbours, the French colonists caused their land to be cultivated up to the very mountain tops, from which the cane-grounds appeared as so many thickets; while every invention that could be adopted to their purpose was readily encouraged. Their roads were in general excellent, being made and kept in repair, by the contributions of every planter, who sent a proportionate number of his slaves to work upon them, (a burthen entitled the *Corvées.*) Sometimes they overflowed in the morning, and were dusty again in the evening; although generally shaded on both sides by lime trees; and the different grounds were separated by hedges of citron trees. The approach to the residence of a planter, was through an avenue of both these, and the pimento and palm graced its extended prospect.

Their principal rivers are the Artibonite, which flows from its source in the centre of the island, through the plain of that name, till

till it empties itself in the gulf of Gonaves; that called the Three Rivers, whose mouth is at Port Paix; and the Great River, or La Grande Riviere, which reaches the sea near Jeremie.

CHAP. I. 1789. Topography, &c. French division.

To describe the productions of the French colony of St. Domingo, would be enumerating those of the whole of the Antilles. Their principal were, however, as have been before described, sugar, coffee, cotton, indigo, and cocoa, or chocolate. To these may be added a little tobacco.

In return for the useful droves of cattle for slaughter and labour, smoked beef, bacon, skins, and the greatest part of the money received from Spain, they supplied their neighbours with wearing apparel, hardware, and guns.

The population was considered at about 40,000 whites, 500,000 negro slaves, and 24,000 free people of colour; and the average exports, as stated by M. Marbois, the intendant of the colony, amounted to 4,765,129*l.* sterling.

It is not intended in this place, to satisfy the scientific views of the naturalist in regard to St. Domingo, notwithstanding that, with an inclination to that study, the writer had some opportunities for its indulgence, which were not entirely lost, but reserved for some future opportunity. The amateur of this elegant research will, no doubt, have recourse to the valuable histories which have been long furnished of a neighbouring island, in

these

CHAP. I. 1789. Topography, &c. French division.

these respects so similar, as to admit of very little variation in the subject to which I allude.

The food of the early inhabitants of St. Domingo, appears to have comprised a similar description of vegetables to that of the negroes at this day:—plantains, Indian wheat, millet, the cassavi root, potatoes, and Caribbee cabbage. Their quadrupeds included the smaller species of a lizard, yet, the delicacy of a West India table; the Agouti Rat, of which a description are yet found in some of the islands; and the Alco, a small short-tailed dog, which did not bark, with others whose names have not come down to us. Their fishery was more abundant, every bay and creek furnishing an ample supply, as many of them do to the present time. The European quadrupeds now supply the necessary food of European colonists, with only such local additions as are objects of delicacy, or introduced by custom; among these, may be named the land crab, the ortolan, and a variety of wild fowl of delicious taste and flavor. The indigenous vegetables yet remain, including plantains, yams, a species of spinage, potatoes, cassava, Indian wheat, and cabbage; to these are added the European roots, herbs, and pulse; and no want is found of cabbage, turnips, carrots, parsnips, peas beans, artichokes, &c. A variety of fruits ornament the luxury of the table, among which, the melon and pine-apple, peaches and strawberries, oranges and lemons, the cashew, apples, pears, plums, and nuts, are plenteously combined with a variety of productions introduced from different countries.

CHAP. I. 1789. Topography, &c. French division.

To describe the nature, properties, and mode of cultivation of those productions, which form the different objects of commerce, would uselessly extend the present chapter, and the accounts are to be found in different works peculiarly appropriated to these subjects *. Sufficient is now already mentioned to acquaint the

* Sugar, coffee, and cotton, are rendered familiar to almost every reader. I shall, however, briefly add here a slight description of the two other staple commodities of St. Domingo—cocoa and indigo.

The cocoa-tree presents less beauty than utility to its cultivator, for its branches form so many trunks separating from each other to a distance immediately above the parent one, and these bend with their separate branches immediately down to the earth. It seldom, therefore, rises high. Its leaves are long, terminating in a point, and emitting an agreeable smell. In the pistil of a flower blooming from every part, is contained an husk, in the form of a melon, which grows ordinarily to the length of six inches, and the breadth of four or five, composed of several small inclosures, in which the fruit, comprising a number of small nuts, of the shape of almonds, is found. It is propagated from the seed; is green in the early part of its growth, and becomes yellow at maturity. When it assumes a deep hue, it must be immediately gathered and dried; two crops of equal value are annually formed. It requires shade and moisture, and loves the protection of large trees at a sufficient distance, which must be also regarded with respect to its own plants. It requires rather due care, and a few necessary precautions, than a culture either laborious or expensive, and its returns are of the most profitable kind. Its nutritious, and other advantageous qualities, are too sufficiently known to require a recital, and its commercial value will be better known from other parts of the present account.

Indigo, an article of such general domestic service, as to be used as a beautifier of the finest part of our dress, and an important object of commerce, flourishes no where so well as at St. Domingo. It is a shrub with a thick, spreading root, about two feet high, of a faint, but not disagreeable smell. The stem is of a dry appearance, and different shades of colour. The leaves are of an oval form, and connected by a short pedicle. The pistil of its small and scentless flowers changes into a pod, and discloses its seeds, of the appearance of gunpowder. The blue is found adhering to the leaves, which, when gathered on the branches, are thrown into a tub filled with water, and fermented; it is then made to run into another, when it is discovered among the water, in the form of a subtile earth. The water is then agitated by various means, and with the utmost circumspection, to combine the coloured particles, which, when effected, are left to precipitate to the bottom. The liquid, become

CHAP. I. 1789. Topography, &c. French division.

the reader with the country, from whose rich prospects, and cloudless sky, he is to turn to scenes of conflagration, and the horrors of massacre.

---

become of a thicker consistence, is drawn off into another vessel to settle, and thence drained through sacks, from which it is removed into chests, where it becomes dry, and fit for sale. It is divided into two sorts, whimsically designated the true and the bastard. The first is finer, but the latter heavier and more profitable, and therefore more generally cultivated. They are both liable to frequent accidents, among which the most destructive is the effect of the caterpillar, which devours the leaves, and their produce, in a few mornings. It is quickly ripe, and generally cut at intervals of six weeks. At the end of two years it becomes degenerated, and fresh plants are necessary. Moisture and shade are required considerably for this plant, and the principal care is to deprive it of the weeds, which would otherwise immediately choke it. It exhausts the soil considerably, and potatoes, and other similar plants, are cultivated in its place occasionally, for the purpose of burning the leaves as manure.

Those who would enjoy an acute and curious dissertation on sugar, may consult the interesting account of Dr. Moseley, in his volume of Medical Miscellanies, &c.

CHAP. II.

Origin of the Revolutionary Spirit of this Period in St. Domingo.

CHAP. II. 1789. Origin of the revolutionary spirit.

THE origin of principles is not always to be traced to the approximating causes of an event; for, as in nature, so in morality, the seeds of many productions lie dormant through varying seasons, till the moment when an unseen influence calls them into obvious existence: hence, to be capable of discerning the signs of the times, is a power that hath always been duly appreciated, and an attention to which hath frequently changed the fate of a country, if not of mankind. Yet, it is not often that man can be hoped to distinguish with precision, the approaching evil from the good, particularly in circumstances that affect, perhaps, not only his interest, but his immediate happiness; it is thus, therefore, that surprize is so frequently excited, at the apparent blindness to the future with which principles and practices are so frequently urged in society, diametrically opposite to the dictates of nature and philosophy, and repugnant to the common experience of ages. Collateral circumstances form the general argument

CHAP. II. 1789. ment in their favor; and it may endure with them a little while; but truth is eternal.

Origin of the revolutionary spirit.

If accuracy of discrimination is not always to be found in philosophers, it is not to be expected in any large mixed body; and still less so, in those who form the population of colonies, particularly of the extent of that which is the subject of the present observations. Though the greatest empires have arisen from the overflow of cities into colonies, it cannot be contended that no feculence mixed with the flood.

To attribute to the general number of colonists any specific character, (where, collected fortuitously, they must necessarily admit of the strongest marks of variety), would be ridiculous; it is, however, certain, that among those, devoted to pursue fortune in distant dependencies upon their native country, may be ranked many who have no peculiar capacity, nor opportunity for employment at home; many of the higher classes without prospects, and of the lower without character; who cannot fail to consider their destination, as intended to supply every want; and to consider those means the best, which have the most facility. To those may, no doubt, be added many of the germs of genius, to whom, it is to be feared, the warmth of a tropical sun does not always prove more genial, than the wintry rays of their own; and, probably, some with qualities fitted for any sphere of life, to whom a spirit of enterprize alone might dictate the migration. To the self-interested, the term of his own probation will always bound

bound his considerations, and it is not the bulk of mankind who can be, nor who incline to be, legislators, much less moralists. The officers of government may be able and good, but their dominion is too short to conciliate any local affection, and an expedient temporization will and must always supersede even ordinary virtue.

CHAP. II.
1789.
Origin of the revolutionary spirit.

Of the West India colonists from France, the modern writers of that nation have afforded us no reason to think with increased tenderness, since Raynal has imputed to them a viciousness of conduct, beyond the apparent bounds of human actions; and De Charmilly (one of themselves) has described those, of whom the best conduct was to be expected, receiving appointments under the government of the colony, as the rewards of an intriguing court to its meanest dependants, and vilest accessaries! Their character, as displayed on prominent occasions, during that period which is the intent of these sheets to describe, unhappily was not often such as to controvert the assertions made from such good authority.

The man who first contemplated the *purchase* of laborers by thousands,* to be conveyed in close vessels, without the power of

* The *commencement* of the African slave-trade, like many other objects of importance, seems to have taken place from a very trifling accident. In 1440, Anthony Gonsales, one of the Portuguese navigators, in the prosecution of his discoveries, seized, and carried off some Moors near Cape Bojador, whom prince Henry afterwards ordered him to restore. When again exploring the coast of Africa about two years after, he executed this order, landing them at Rio del Oro, and received from the Moors, in exchange, *ten blacks*, and a quantity of gold dust. His success in this transaction tempted his countrymen to a repetition, till at length they fitted out ships for the purpose, and afterwards formed settlements for the trade in black slaves. Ultimately patents were granted, and the dealers in human flesh were sanctified by a bull from the holy see.

CHAP. II. 1789. Origin of the revolutionary spirit.

rest or exercise, or nourishment proper for any situation, much less for a dreary voyage to a foreign land; and, who knew these men, although little removed from a state of nature, to be susceptible of those impressions which mock the utmost refinements of civilization, to the attainment of some of which, morality often strives in vain; must have been bold to conceive that they would continue always patient of their wrongs, and resigned to compulsory labour, even though it should be in a state of comparative advantage, particularly in the constant converse of annual acquisitions of their countrymen, whose remembrances were not obliterated; yet no objection would appear to have occurred to him, and his plan proceeded till the employers of it, with a physical proportion of twelve to one against them, imagined themselves capable of coercing five hundred thousand of these men, exclusive of the descendants of others, without any determined exertion of virtue, or consideration on their own part.

Let it not be conceived that it is here intended to arraign the conduct of the planters in general, or to view with complacency the revolt of servants of any description, much less to plead their apology; I am but to state facts which are necessary to the argument intended to be produced.

The African negro is described as "frivolous, inconstant, vain, timid, jealous, and superstitious; yet good and generous, without foresight, always guided by the impression of the moment; and adding to these characteristics, the *vices of slaves*, indolence, gluttony,

CHAP. II. 1789. Origin of the revolutionary spirit.

tony, dishonesty, and falshood; vindictive also, like all weak beings, injustice driving them to despair."* I take the whole of this character for granted, from the experience of the writer, and the different opportunities which have been confided to him of judging with truth. That the dependance of colonies, then, could have been originally placed upon such beings, was a strange perversion of human judgment; but that it could be expected to continue through ages, without a superior portion of human wisdom and virtue, (instead of a very small exercise of either,) is only attributable to the blindness I have just described. The result has proved the position; for, from the first moment at which African slaves were imported, the effects of all the bad qualities ascribed to them have been frequent, in revolt, treachery, murder, and suicide; nor, at the same time, have the instances been few, of actions arising from the superior impulses, or unconquerable affection, gratitude, inviolable fidelity, or bravery, have been experienced from them by their masters and connections; and circumstances are still recited that might cope with the history of the ancient republics. No more is described than is necessary to the present purpose; for it is not the wish of the writer to discuss the question of the slave-trade, already too much agitated in this country, but to trace the origin of the revolutionary spirit which has ended so fatally to the colonies of France.

* —— " légers, inconstans, vains, timides, peureux, jalouse, bons, généreux, sans prévoyance, superstitieux, toujours conduits par l'impression du moment: ils joignent à cela les vices des esclaves: paresseux, gourmands, voleurs, menteurs, vindicatif, commes tous les êtres, faibles, l'injustice les desespere." De Charmilly, Lettre, p. 41.

CHAP. II. 1789. Origin of the revolutionary spirit.

Regardless of the frequent exercise of several minor qualities also which must tend to render men impatient of slavery, the labour of the islands continued to be performed by their means; without any other foresight, than related to expedients which might procrastinate the evil for each successive proprietor. Hence they have been successively punished by domestic means, chased as wild-beasts, combated like a foreign enemy, and treated with as independant powers! Yet, so prone are men to consider that what they wish the case, that scarcely a doubt was entertained of those who had not deserted, or *marooned*, nor were any other than coercive principles contemplated for those who remained; the same routine of purchase to supply deficiencies, and of regulations to secure their value, prevailed. The planter, instead of exhibitions of virtue and power that should impress respect and awe, appeared a feeble voluptuary, forgetting, in idle dalliance with the female labourers of his field, the utility of moral principles, and the decencies of life. The effects of such examples are incontestible, as regards private morality, without any allusion to the offices of religion; and it requires not to be depressed into a community of the most abject description of slaves to discover, that the effects of vice in undermining public virtue is the certain basis of revolt.

Thus an ignorance, in the first instance, of human nature, a blindness to actual circumstances, and a want of individual virtue in the colonists, gave birth to the revolutionary spirit in St. Domingo; which, instead of being created, was only fanned into

flame,

flame by the occurrences which took place in the relations of the colony, with the mother-country, on the change of its government.

CHAP. II. 1789. Origin of the revolutionary spirit.

The support of colonies by means of such a disproportion of African slaves, to the other population as are necessary, continually and progressively acquired, is radically impossible, from the nature of the people themselves, and the manner of obtaining them; but if it were not, the want of powers required for their management—of a policy sufficiently subtle and yet enlightened, for their government, would render it, permanently, impracticable; even with both these probabilities in their favour, that, in such a depraved state as that of the French colony in St. Domingo, every other advantage would be annihilated.

It is, perhaps, necessary here to anticipate an observation not unlikely to be made; therefore, be it understood, that the impossibility of the continued existence of slavery is not by any means asserted. It is not forgotten that there was a period when, from the happy state under which I am considering this subject, unrestricted by the check of civil or ecclesiastical tyranny, parents sold their children as slaves to a foreign country, and inherited others themselves, who were their captives, or who had been acquired by other means; but these, notwithstanding they may have

* See an account of slavery in Europe in Robertson's Charles V. vol. I. p. 272.—Also an assemblage of the different laws on this subject, in *Huntingford's Laws of Master and Servant Considered*, chap. I. p. 36.

been

CHAP. II. 1789. Origin of the revolutionary spirit.

been treated as inferior classes of society (as the productive power is too generally to this day), bore no mark*, by which they should be considered, as distinguished by nature to be scarcely belonging to the human species, as is the case with that of complexion.

Nor, is the writer at present opposing the practice of the slave-trade. He is an enemy to it, only, as he is to every employment which offers an undue power to many, not the most unlikely to abuse it; and as a principle hostile to humanity and inefficient in its purposes. He is aware, that the situation of colonial-slaves at present is, in many respects, superior to that of the labourers or the artizans of Britain. The first have not, indeed, the command of secession, neither have the two latter the power; for if they cease from labour, they cease from its advantages. When it is considered that the artizan must wander in search of employment, and submit to the optional reward of those who may chuse to employ him, after encountering distress in consequence of repeated refusals; the slave will appear more happy, though sometimes enduring corporeal punishment too severe, whose food and residence is provided without anxiety; and who is certain of employment, or of the same provision.

* It is recorded, but where I cannot, at present, refer, that St. Gregory observing some beautiful English children in the slave-market at Rome, exclaimed in a Latin pun, if I may be allowed the expression, that they were not English, but Angels, if they had but been Christians.—"*Non Angli, sed Angeli,*" &c. This practice will, however, appear to have been continued after they had the benefit of the Christian Religion. See *Anderson's History of Commerce*, vol. I. p. 99.

Nor

Nor, would the writer be supposed to sanction the means which have been used to procure an abolition of the trade, which he disapproves; much less, the emancipation of those slaves already in the colonies. Of the latter step; the humanity would be equally problematical, with that which would dictate the liberation of the poor bird long nursed in domestic comfort, to flutter a little while in solitary freedom, a stranger to his own kind, and to the winds of heaven.

CHAP. II. 1789. Origin of the revolutionary spirit.

What has been said, has arisen from a conviction that, but for the circumstances described, a revolutionary spirit would not have so soon been spread throughout St. Domingo; and to point out the beacon to the colonies of the British nation in the same sea, with that which has produced an illustration of these positions, and a picture so full of terror, on this more will be said, and with greater propriety, at the end of this work.

Flushed with opulence and dissipation, the majority of planters in St. Domingo had arrived at a state of sentiment the most vitiated, and manners equally depraved; while, injured by an example so contagious, the slaves had become more dissolute, than those of any British island. If the master was proud, voluptuous, and crafty, the slave was equally vitious, and often riotous; the punishment of one was but the consequence of his own excesses; but that of the other, was often cruel and unnatural. The proprietor could bear no rival in his parish; and would not bend even to the ordinances of justice. The creole-

CHAP. II. 1789. Origin of the revolutionary spirit.

slaves looked upon the newly-imported Africans with scorn, and sustained, in their turn, that of the mulattoes, whose complexion was browner; while all were kept at a distance from the intercourse of the whites. Nor did the boundaries of sex, it is painful to observe, keep their wonted distinction, from the stern impulses that affect men. The European ladies too often participated in the austerity and arrogance of their male kindred; while the jet-black beauty, among slaves, though scarcely a native of the island, refused all commerce with those who could not boast the same distinction with herself.

Such was the situation of the inhabitants of St. Domingo in the beginning of the year 1789, prompt to any movement that should create an effervescence among them, or afford the one party an opportunity of opposing the other; yet, while private feuds were eager for an opportunity to burst into public clamour, the situation of the country was such as hath been described, like the verdant bosom of a volcano, unconscious of the flame about to burst; the people were cheerful, the markets plentifully stocked, the lands loaded with production, and the colony, if "*overwhelmed with debt*,"* it may be admitted to be so said, flourishing every where.

In the mean time, the great kingdom, under whose care it had expanded to its present growth, and to whose government it yet looked

* —— "la colonie qui, ayant encore *beaucoup de dettes*, n'avait pas besoin de payer celles de la France." *Lettre à Edwards*, p. 48.

CHAP. II. 1789. Origin of the revolutionary spirit.

looked for parental care, disordered by embarrassment, and agitated by conflicting interests, began to approach to that period which had been considered as inevitable, by philosophers, for more than half a century. Notwithstanding the absolute tyranny which had prevailed in other respects, France, under the feeble reign of the unhappy Louis, had been the nurse of morality and philosophy; and she drew nigh, not unwittingly, to that political mortality to which it would appear all states are subject; for it had been sung by her poets under the walls of her own capital, and repeated in auguries which did not err.

Of the different expedients that had been resorted to, the colonies did not want information; nor did it fail in the effect which might be expected upon every class of their inhabitants. In a new regimen the proprietors looked to some aggrandizement either in property or consequence; the free people of colour anticipated a favourable change in their condition; and even the slaves viewed, through the political alterations that began to occupy the attention of those above them, something to excite their curiosity, and a vigilance to gratify it. Each motion of the French court became canvassed by every class throughout the island. When a spirit of deliberation upon subjects usually considered above the capacities of the vulgar begins to spread, it seldom ends precisely as it begun; whatever may be the event, it does not fail to call into notice circumstances and opinions not easily repressed, and characters in their support who might otherwise have preserved through life "the noiseless

tenor

CHAP. II. 1789. Origin of the revolutionary spirit.

tenor of their way." It had its full effect in St. Domingo, already so ripe to receive it; and when the news arrived that the States-General of France were to be summoned (the last convulsive effort of expiring monarchy), all parties resolved on making their own interests a part of the general concern.

In opposition to the wishes of a judicious few (among whom was the intelligent De Charmilly) and even to the prohibitions of the government, the impetuous proprietors summoned provincial and parochial meetings, for the purpose of electing *themselves* to legislative functions; heated resolutions were passed; and eighteen deputies were elected, to represent the island in the meeting of the States-General, without any other authority than the noise of demagogues, and their own inclinations. Twelve were never recognized in France, and the other six were received with difficulty. The mulattoes, who could have no share in this self-created body, thought it naturally time to show an attention to themselves; and, accordingly, not only communicated with numbers of their brethren then resident in the mother-country, but augmented those powerful advocates in their behalf, with much more effect than was produced by the self-created body of colonial deputies. The negroes, however, more successful than all, without either deputies or intercessors, obtained, unsolicited, the interest of such a powerful body in their behalf, as to drown the recollection of every other object. A society, in which were enrolled the names of several great and good men, under the title of "The Friends of the Blacks" (Amis

CHAP. II.

1789.

Origin of the revolutionary spirit.

(*Amis de Noirs*), circulated its protests and appeals with such vigour, that, before the negroes themselves, although eager and alert in their enquiries, were acquainted with the importance which they had obtained in the deliberations of the mother-country, they were the prominent subjects of conversation and regret in half the towns of Europe. They were not, however, tardy in acquiring this information; and though it would be difficult to contemplate any thing in human nature so bad, as to suppose that the highest and best of motives did not actuate so respectable a body as that which composed this society, or the similar establishment which had before obtained in London; yet the unhappy eloquence with which the miseries of slavery were depicted by them, and the forcible points of view in which all the errors of their opponents were placed, as well as the enthusiasm which always accompanies the exertions of ardent minds, were certainly the cause of bringing into action, on a broad basis, that spirit of revolt which only sleeps in the enslaved African, or his descendant, and which has produced on their side, and on that of the white inhabitants of the colonies, such horrors as "make ev'n the angels weep."

I conclude this account of the *origin* of the revolution of St. Domingo, with observing how much better it would have been for themselves, and perhaps for humanity, if happily discerning the signs of the times, the planters of this delightful and flourishing colony (a character which none have attempted to deny it), by resigning an overweening fondness for dominion, and an undue

 avarice

CHAP. II. 1789. Origin of the revolutionary spirit.

avarice of gain, had rather calmed than provoked the dissentions of those whose interest should have bid them to agree; and by softening the evils of a state which is so bad in its best form, have conciliated the affections of those to whose labours, under the present regimen, every thing productive of wealth or prosperity must depend. A partial concession to those who, by complexion itself, claim half a right to political existence, would have been sufficient: with a little regard for the morals of a people who require them the most, and a revolution in their own minds, as far as human nature will admit. These would have preserved to them, now lingering in a melancholy exile, if not the sudden victims of their impolicy, an island the boast of the new world, and a powerful support of the old. If they had then contemplated some more legitimate means of prosecuting the labours of their colony, they might, however immediately unavailing, have laid a foundation for their posterity more lasting than the bequest of inordinate wealth, and have claimed the approbation of society.

CHAP.

CHAP. III.

Account of the Progress and Accomplishment of the Independence of St. Domingo.

CHAP. III. 1789. M. Duchilleau, governor.

AT the commencement of these changes in the government of the mother country, and consequently of others in that of the colonies, the governor of French St. Domingo was M. Duchilleau, a man of no moderate powers, but who, from conciliating the temper of the new council of France, was continued in his office. It soon however became, in power or consequence, but nugatory; for, upon the first meeting of the assemblies before described, his proclamations were disregarded, and his government insulted, if not despised.

The states-general, at which two deputies appeared from each of the provinces, declared themselves the National Assembly in May, 1789, and on the 20th of August they made their *Declaration of Rights.* Between these two periods, the public mind had been heated against the white colonists by such

CHAP. III. 1789. such a variety of means, as to threaten their total annihilation.

The publication of the Declaration of Rights did not tend to remedy this unfavorable impression of the people against one of their own communities; for the article that, "All men are born, and continue, free and equal as to their rights," implied an entire subversion of their establishments, and created a complete ferment among the whole of the French proprietors. They conceived, and the French government appear afterwards to have done the same, that the effect of this declaration was to rouse the negroes to an assertion of those rights it was supposed to give them. Apprehensive of disorders arising in the colony, the governor soon received orders from his new constituents, the National Assembly, to call together the inhabitants for the purpose of interior regulation. The measure had been anticipated by the ready disposition of the self-constituted legislators, and a provincial assembly for the northern district had already met at Cape François; an example which was soon followed by the western and southern provinces, the former of which met at Port-au-Prince, and the latter at Aux Cayes. For more immediate communication between the people, and to accommodate every description, parochial committees were also established. These committees were of the disposition which might be expected, and, by dividing among themselves upon every occasion, they served only to inform the negroes of their frivolity, and to excite them to take advantage of their want of unanimity and power; and the principal determination in their proceedings was that, of the necessity of a full and speedy colonial representation. The order of the king, however, which was received in January 1790, tended to supersede their deliberations, by convoking a general Colonial Assembly, which was appointed to meet in the central town of Leogane. The mode which it directed of electing the members did not satisfy the provincial assemblies, and they substituted a plan of their own, changing the town of Leogane to that of St. Mark, and fixing on the 25th of March, and afterwards on the 16th of April, for the time of meeting. CHAP. III. 1790.

The mulattoes, not willing to be left behind in exertion, when they perceived the opposition of the whites to every movement of the government, determined to proceed a step still farther, and accordingly arming themselves, they proceeded to claim by force the benefit of equal privileges with the whites. Their combination was premature, and they were soon overpowered. Different parties were secured at Jacmel and Artibonite, to whom, on their submission, notwithstanding the exasperation of the whites in general against them, an unconditional pardon was given. In the division of parties, too, inconsistent as it may appear, some of the whites, among whom were included persons of high respectability, adopted the cause of the people of colour, and even seconded their inclination to revolt. Among these, an old magistrate named Ferrand de Beaudierre, was the first to become conspicuous, for the purpose of removing the disgrace which had attached to him in consequence of having offered

CHAP. III. 1790. offered marriage to a woman of colour. He drew up a memorial in their behalf, which had not time to be presented to the parochial committee, before he was seized by an enraged mob, and put to death. The deputy procureur-general, M. Dubois, also, whose duty demanded a different course, became so infatuated, as to declaim against the slavery of the negroes in their presence; but he enjoyed a milder fate; he was only arrested by the people, and dismissed from the colony by the governor, who soon after followed.

Such was the confused state of the colony, and every one seemed to be so bent upon harassing the metropolitan government, that it was, with great reason, apprehended in France, that the island was about to declare itself independant, or to submit to some foreign power. The alarm became general throughout those places which had any concern with St. Domingo, and the National Assembly on being earnestly implored to consider of the best means of saving so valuable a dependancy resolved, after a serious discussion of the subject, " That it was not the intention of the Assembly to interfere with the interior government of the colonies, or to subject them to laws incompatible, with their local establishments; they therefore authorized the inhabitants of each colony to signify their own plan of legislation and commercial arrangement, preserving only a conformity with the principles of the mother country, and a regard for the reciprocal interests of both." It superadded, that no innovation was intended in *any system of commerce in which*

2 *the*

the colonies were already concerned. It will easily be conceived that this conciliating resolution, so necessary, as regarded the discontented white colonists, would be very differently received by the people of colour. It excited among them a general clamour, which extended to every part where their cause (diffused by the means used on those occasions) was known, or even heard of. CHAP. III. 1790.

The period having arrived to which the General Assembly of St. Domingo had been prorogued, it met to the number of two hundred and thirteen members, at the town of St. Mark. These consisted of two representatives from each parish, twenty-four from the city of Cape François, sixteen from that of Port-au-Prince, and eight from Aux Cayes. The provincial assemblies continued in their self-appointments notwithstanding, and even formed committees, to act in the intervals of meeting. The new assembly commenced its functions by reviewing the objects of abuse in the old colonial government, and in proposing means for their remedy, of which the political incapacities of the mulattoes, and a revisal of the slave laws, bore a promising part. They put the mulattoes, in point of military duty, on the same footing with the whites, restricting the king's officers commanding in the towns, from those oppressive acts towards them which they had sometimes experienced; they examined into those abuses in the courts of judicature which claimed immediate redress; and set about preparing a new colonial constitution. 16th April. Peynier, governor.

CHAP. III. 1790.

To extend the divisions, which were increasing, rather than otherwise, among the proprietors and their representatives, the new governor-general was a man privately devoted to the old system, who immediately combined those who had any interest in the ancient despotism, to oppose the colonial revolution, which would be likely to deprive them of their corrupt sources of profit. As these included all the officers under the fiscal administration, tax-gatherers, appendages to the courts of civil and criminal jurisdiction, and most of those who held military commissions under the king's authority, they formed a power, by no means contemptible, and possessed an advantage in being all sincere in their attachment to one cause, while a diversity of opinions swayed the newly established party. To this association was added one, (from many of whom their country has since suffered much,) who, with considerable talents, and an enterprising genius, was bent upon counter-projects against every act of the General Assembly; this was the Colonel and Chevalier Mauduit, who commanded, and was beloved by the regiment of Port-au-Prince. He had returned from France, by way of Italy, and had last parted with the Count D'Artois, to whose fortunes he was much devoted. Thus, impressed with more than common warmth in the cause, in which he now took such an active part, he did not fail to strike a blow to the interests of the colony; by insinuating himself between the Assembly and those in whose favor they were exerting themselves, he divided them against each other, and to this effort Peynier, who was weak and uninformed, resigned all his power, or influence, into his hands.

As if to meet the insidious policy of Mauduit, the divisions of the new legislative bodies burst into open convulsion, by the conduct of the provincial assembly of the north, who endeavoured to the utmost of their power, to counteract the provisions of the General Assembly. CHAP. III. 1790.

The decree which was the result of its deliberations being completed, the plan for a new constitution was published; which, as if every thing was to coincide with the untoward disposition of affairs, was so framed as to please scarce any party, and formed the ostensible motive for the commencement of hostilities in the party of M. Peynier. The principal articles of this consitution (of which there were ten,) consisted in May 28.

I. Vesting in the "*General Assembly of the French part of St. Domingo*," the entire management of the internal concerns of the colony.

II. Preventing any act of the legislative body relative to the internal concerns of the colony, from becoming a law, until definitively sanctioned by the Representatives of the People, and confirmed by the king.

III. IV. and V. Enabling the Assembly to enact provisional laws for their own government. Nevertheless, to keep as a separate question the execution of those laws; and in case of the governor-general (to whom such decrees shall be notified for the purpose of being enforced) sending any observations on them to the Assembly, causing them to be entered on the Journals, ordering

a con-

CHAP. III. 1790. a consequent revision, and ultimately deciding on its confirmation, or rejection, by a majority of two thirds.

VI. Establishing a communication on all common, and commercial concerns, with the National Assembly, without which, nor until they are confirmed by the Colonial Assembly, its decrees shall not be valid.

VII. Allowing the importation of necessary articles upon pressing occasions, under the cognizance of the governor-general.

VIII. Submitting every provisional act of the Assembly to be transmitted for the royal sanction, and suspended upon its refusal.

IX. Creating a new General Assembly biennially.

X. Communicating to the King, the National Assembly, the Colonial Governor, and the different districts and parishes, the present decree.

To repeat that much difference of opinion existed with respect to this descree, is what was to be expected from every circumstance; and the power retained by the Assembly, was evidently beyond what had ever been contemplated in the colonies. The leading opinions were, however, (among those the most capable of judging,) that it was intended to declare the island an independant state, or, that it was already sold by a party to the English. That both these reports were not entirely without foundation, subsequent events will appear to have proved, for it is confessed by M. de Charmilly, one of the members of this very

 assembly,

assembly, that the former proposition "was a subject of consideration among a few of the inhabitants, the opulence and prosperity of the colony having dazzled some sanguine characters,"* and, it was not three years after, before that gentleman induced the British government to accept the submission of a part of the proprietors of the island. CHAP. III. 1790.

The inhabitants of the Cape, and of some of the western parishes, did not wait for these confirmations of their opinions; for, immediately on the publication of the new plan of government, they renounced all obedience to the Assembly, and presented a memorial to the governor, requesting its dissolution. This step could not but be agreeable to Peynier, if it was not the effect of the exertions of his party; and, another circumstance which happened, gave him the opportunity he evidently desired, of coming to an open rupture. In consequence of an espousal of the conduct of the governor and his party by M. Galisonierre, the commander of a ship of the line, called the Leopard, then in the harbour of Port-au-Prince, the crew thought proper to withdraw their obedience from him, and to oblige him to quit the ship; they then gave the command to the first lieutenant, and declared themselves waiting the orders of the General Assembly. The Assembly, by no means disinclined to such an offer, transmitted them in return a vote of thanks, and directed July 27.

* "Je conviens qu'il a été question d'indépendance parmi un petit nombre d'habitans, mais la richesse de la colonie, sa prospérité, avaient trompé quelques caracteres ardens, &c." —*Lettre*, p. 52.

them,

CHAP. III. 1790. them, in the name of the law and the King, to detain the ship in the road, there to wait till further orders. To retain this acquisition, they permitted some of their partizans to take possession of the powder magazine at Leogane. It has been disputed whether the crew of M. Galisonierre's ship had been corrupted by the party supporting the Assembly, or actuated by the caprice which so often influences seamen; but as it appears that their future movements were without the knowledge of the Assembly, it is reasonable to believe, that neither the one nor the other was the cause, but that they acted entirely by themselves, among whom might be probably some characters of more importance, than is conceived by those who view them merely in their ordinary employment.

Such are the fortuitous incidents which lead to events that decide the fate of countries.

M. Peynier now conceived himself provided with the means of criminating the party, whose power so much curtailed his own. He immediately proclaimed the dissolution of the Assembly, charging it with projects of independency, and with having traitorously possessed itself of one of the king's ships by corrupting the crew; pronouncing the whole, with their adherents, traitors to the colony, the French nation, and the King; he declared his intention of bringing them to condign punishment, and to commence hostile operations against them. He had no sooner threatened, than he attempted to put his menaces into execution.

execution. He prepared for the restoration of the ancient system, and he even applied to the neighbouring island of Cuba for the aid of foreign troops; and he commissioned Mauduit to arrest the committee of the western provincial Assembly, who had become obnoxious to him from their inclination to the measures of his opponents, at their midnight meeting in Port-au-Prince. Mauduit, however, found them protected by four hundred of the national guards, (formerly the colonial militia,) and having himself but one hundred men, he was compelled, after a short skirmish, to retire, without effecting any thing more than the seizure of the national colours, which he must have obtained by some undue means, and bore off in triumph.

The General Assembly in return summoned the people from every part of the colony, to arm for the protection of their representatives, and the summons seemed to be generally obeyed with alacrity. The western and the southern provinces were unqualified in their approbation, and immediately dispatched a force of two thousand men on their way to Port-au-Prince. The Provincial Assembly of the north, however, joined the party of the governor, and detached a part of the regular troops in that quarter, with a body of two hundred mulattoes. Thus the flames of civil war were immediately about to be lighted, and a dreadful conflict was expected on every side, when a circumstance occurred which for the present prevented it, and gave a more favourable turn to the public affairs than that which they had hitherto taken.

The

CHAP. III. 1790. The crew of the Leopard having determined upon returning to France, they brought the ship into the entrance of St. Mark's bay, to apprize the Assembly of her departure, and to wait under sail for their dispatches to the King and the National Assembly. The General Assembly was reduced by this time, in consequence of sickness and secession, to less than one hundred members, and was diminishing every day: they had found themselves at first not sufficiently competent to the art of legislation, and their task was becoming every day more arduous. The majority of them were fathers of families; and could not but perceive that a storm was gathering, in which some, if not all of them, might be involved. Whatever was the motive, or whether or not it had a portion of the eccentricity which has been ascribed to it, eighty-five members of the General Assembly came to the immediate, and unexpected resolution, of availing themselves of this opportunity to proceed to Europe, for the purpose of deriving assistance in their future conduct, and justifying themselves as to what had already passed, preventing the effusion of human blood. They took their departure, therefore, on board the Leopard, and such was the good fortune which attended this step in the outset, that it excited for them, for the first time, a very general admiration; crowds followed them to the shore with tears and blessings, and prayers were every where preferred for the success which their forbearance was considered to deserve. The armaments were mutually suspended. The heads of the government party viewed the circumstance with mixed emotions of surprize and terror, and M. Peynier tremblingly resumed his seat.

August 8.

Thus

CHAP. III. 1790.

Thus, it were to be hoped that peace would have continued during the passage of the members to France, and until the result of their journey were known; particularly as the remaining part were occupied in arrangements, and in prepossessing the French government against the General Assembly on their arrival; but, no sooner was one cause of commotion removed, than another supplied its place, of a more hostile complexion, and with less occasion—the rebellion of James Ogé, a mulatto; whose mother had a coffee-plantation about thirty miles from Cape François. During his residence at Paris, for the purpose of education, he had imbibed, in addition to the natural feelings of his class, all the prejudices entertained at this period against the white planters in the mother country. Having become connected with the society of Amis des Noirs, and inflated with an idea of his own capacity, he was easily persuaded by Robespierre, and other violent members, to attach himself to a conspiracy, supposed to be already ripe in St. Domingo, and requiring only the talents of an active leader to produce the effects desired, in behalf of the people of colour. Armed by their means, and charged with all the inveteracy of the party, Ogé arrived in St. Domingo about two months after the Assembly had left it, and immediately prepared to assume an imaginary command, for which he had no foundation. He found means to convey a quantity of arms and ammunition to a place called Grand Riviere, about fifteen miles from the Cape, where his brother had been prepared to receive it, and, having collected about two hundred followers, exerted

October 12. Ogé's rebellion.

CHAP. III. 1790.

himself every where in spreading disaffection; he wrote imperiously to M. Peynier, stating the inattention which had been paid to the execution of the Code Noir,* demanding its enforcement, and also an extension of the privileges enjoyed by the whites to all persons without distinction. He took upon himself the character of Protector of the Mulattoes, and declared his intention, if necessary, of arming in their behalf. He established his camp where he had deposited his stores, and appointed his two brothers, and another mulatto, of a ferocious character, named Mark Chavane, his lieutenants. These men commenced their unruly operations by the murder of two white men, whom they met accidentally, and by punishing with extreme cruelty those of their own complexion not disposed to revolt; one who excused himself on account of a wife and six children, they murdered, with the whole of his family. Fortunately their reign was not long, for a body of regular troops, and the Cape militia, were dispatched to invest their camp, when, with a weak resistance, they were totally routed; many were killed, sixty were taken prisoners, and the chiefs escaped into the Spanish part of the island.

This rebellion, though so easily crushed, excited a considerable animosity against the people of colour, who, in their turn, as if fearing a retaliation of cruelty, took to arms, and formed camps in different parts of the island, each of them of much

* The laws for the protection of the Blacks, instituted by Louis XIV.

greater

greater importance than that of Ogé. The white inhabitants collected themselves in force to oppose them. But Colonel Mauduit, (by means not publicly communicated,) in a conference, had, singly and unattended, with the mulatto leaders, at their chief camp at Verettes, induced them to an immediate dispersion. Various doubts existed as to the nature of the means, which were supposed not to be highly honourable to M. Mauduit: certain it is, however, the mulattoes were not perfectly satisfied; for their leader at Aux Cayes, Rigaud, declared that "it was a transient and deceitful calm, and, that no peace would be permanent until one class of people had exterminated the other."* CHAP. III. 1790.

The insurrection of the mulattoes was no sooner suppressed a second time, than a fresh object of disturbance arose, more fatal than either, and least expected. This was the arrival of a decree of the National Assembly, censuring, with great asperity, the conduct of the General Assembly of St. Domingo, charging it with disaffection to France, and insubordination; annulling all its acts, incapacitating its members from ever serving again; approving the conduct of the governor's party, particularly the Northern Provincial Assembly and Colonel Mauduit; directing a new Colonial Assembly to be formed on the principle of the decree of March 8, and the instructions of March 28, and ordering under arrest, during its pleasure, the members who had November.

* Edwards's St. Domingo, p. 46.

 quitted

CHAP. II. 1789. quitted the island, and who were still at Paris. It also recommended an additional force, both naval and military, to be sent to the colony for the better support of the authority of the government.

On the arrival of the eighty-five members of the Colonial Assembly at Brest (on the 13th of September), they had been received with the utmost respect and attention by all ranks of people; and the most liberal provision made for them in every way; but, such had been the activity of M. Peynier, that deputies had arrived before them from the provincial assembly of the north, who, with their agents, had so prejudiced the mind of M. Barnave, the minister for this department, that they met at Paris with indignities of every kind; were dismissed from the bar of the National Assembly with contempt, and refused even permission to confront their enemies as they requested. On the 16th of October the report of the committee for the colonies on the subject was presented by M. Barnave, their president, and the members placed under arrest.

A very general manifestation of surprize and indignation took place on the arrival of this decree, and a very different sentiment pervaded the public mind from that intended to be produced by the National Assembly; in every particular Mauduit and his regiment became objects of the warmest resentment. Many of the parishes would send no other deputies to form the new Colonial Assembly, because they considered those in France as their legal

legal representatives, the annulling of whose decrees, they attributed to the revival of the ancient system of despotism. CHAP. III. 1791.

Whether it was from intimidation at these succeeding disorders, or from the wish of the National Assembly, does not appear; M. Peynier, however, to the great satisfaction of the majority of the planters, at this time resigned his office to the gentleman next in command, General Blanchelandè, a field-officer in the French service, who entered upon the government with peculiar vigour. Blanchelande governor.

The first exercise of his power, and one rather unexpected, was to demand of the Spaniards the fugitives from the rebellion of Ogé, who were accordingly delivered up, and placed in the jail of Cape François, till a commission should be issued to bring them to trial. It was soon commenced, but lasted for a considerable time, during which they were strictly examined, and, of course, condemned. December.

Ogé and his lieutenant, Chavane, were sentenced to be broken alive upon the wheel, and left to perish. His followers, including one of his brothers (the other not being found), to the number of twenty, were condemned to be hanged. Ogé was not a man calculated for a leader of rebellion. His mother having been enabled to support him in France as a gentleman, he had cherished a delicacy of sentiment very incompatible with the ferocity March.

CHAP. III. 1791. ferocity of revolt; but it would appear also that he wanted personal courage, and that fidelity to his colleagues which alone inspires respect in his circumstances. When he heard the judgment of the court, he wept bitterly, and implored mercy in the most abject manner; proposing to purchase life by exposing the secrets of numerous conspiracies, which he described as impending over the colony: he, however, extended it only by a reprieve for twenty-four hours, just time enough to make a brief deposition of facts of the highest importance, if they had been immediately attended to; and was then hurried to execution with a celerity rather barbarous, and an impolicy which afterwards met with its consequences. Chavane preserved the appearance of courage to the last, and resigned himself to his fate without a groan.

The persons before whom the deposition of Ogé was taken, (Ruotte and Vertierres, members of the Northern Provincial Assembly,) had been appointed to examine the revolters; and were devotees to the ancient system; from what motive, perhaps, may be seen afterwards, whether by the desire of the principal officer in the colonial administration, or of the Northern Provincial Assembly, is not minutely ascertained; but these men suppressed entirely the information communicated by Ogé, and reported that he had said nothing of importance, burying his secret, if he had any, with himself. That this was not the case will appear hereafter.

The

The decisive spirit of the new governor did not prevent the people from viewing the detention of their representatives in France with a general dissatisfaction, and those to whom they attributed the original cause of it, with additional dislike. Mauduit continued to be the object of their censure in a particular degree; they avowedly disapproved of that conduct at St. Marc's, which the National Assembly had made a subject of particular approbation; one act of which they availed themselves with reason; this was, taking from a detachment of the national guards, as before-mentioned, their colours, which had never been returned. This deprivation the whole of the national guards regarded as an insult to their body, which they would have immediately revenged, but that the veteran regiment of Port-au-Prince was remarkable for its superior discipline, and attachment to the commanding officer, whose bounty was always open to them. They had long given him a particular token of their regard, in supplanting the national cockade, by a white feather, the avowed insigne of royalty. The regiment therefore, as well as its colonel, became obnoxious to the whole of the army, who were attached to the new constitution. At this time, a reinforcement of troops from France, comprising two battalions of the regiments of Artois and Normandy, arrived in the frigates Le Fougueux and Le Borée, who, having communicated in some way with the crew of the Leopard (the vessel which carried the Colonial Assembly to France), no sooner landed at Port-au-Prince, than they discovered the same animosity against the regiment of Mauduit, as was manifested

CHAP. III. 1791.

CHAP. III. 1791. by the national guards. They treated them as traitors, which, no doubt, the peculiarity of the white feather confirmed, and refused all kind of intercourse with them. The conduct of the national guards had hitherto passed unheeded, but when two other regiments, and those arrived from the mother-country, became leagued against them, it occasioned a visible effect upon the minds of the officers and the men. They began to view each other with distrust, and to consider the regard which they had hitherto born to their idolized commander, as almost criminal. A sullen discontent appeared on every face, and their actions, amongst which was a contemptuous dismissal of the white feather, augured no good intentions towards him who, but a few weeks before, might have led them over the world. Mauduit was not insensible of the change, or of the probability of danger; and he prepared for some arrangement to induce a return of the good opinion of his troops; before he made the experiment, however, he bravely insisted on the governor removing himself and his family to Cape François, that he might not have a chance of sharing in his own ruin if it was unavoidable, to which M. Blanchelande (rather pitifully) consented.

Colonel Mauduit prepared, as the first effort of conciliation, for a restitution of the colours to the national guards, the unfortunate cause of the alienation of his own troops; and proposed, if they would support him, to carry them with his own hands, at their head to the church, in which they should be deposited. He harangued his grenadiers to that purpose, and they promised to support

support him with their lives. On the succeeding day he put his proposed plan in execution, before the whole community of Port-au-Prince. A considerable murmur took place, but means were taken by the citizens (among whom it is said were some he had most injured) to prevent any accident.* He had replaced the colours, and was turning, no doubt, to meet the gratulations of his troops, which had so often cheered him, when one of them commanded him aloud, to ask pardon of the national guards, *on his knees!* He started with indignation at the proposition, and intending to offer them his life, rather than his honour, exposed to them his naked bosom. In an instant, an hundred bayonets seemed to vie with each other which should wound the deepest, and he fell, gored all over; while scarce an arm of the number he had so often made happy, was raised to save him, or a voice among those so often exerted in his praise, to bid his spirit rest.† The spectators, however unfriendly they might have been to the deceased, were petrified with astonishment and disgust. Not contented with the extinction of life, this unmanly and treacherous number, whose conduct is, it is hoped, unparalleled, not content with destroying his house, and

* The exertions on this occasion of the brave Beausobre were too striking to be passed in silence. He had been struck with a shot, when protecting the Colonial Committee, in the affair for which Mauduit was now attempting an extenuation; yet, with a generosity not often equalled, he was among the foremost to step forward on the present occasion, and was wounded by a sabre in defending the life of Mauduit.

† Two officers named Galefeau and Germain, to their honour, did not desert their colonel till the last moment, but their exertions were of no avail; and the indignation of the soldiers being at its height, there was no time for preparation.

CHAP. III. 1791. every thing belonging to him, gratified themselves with mutilating the dead body of their once-loved commander; and, by a thousand diabolical contrivances, rendering disgusting in death a form which, through life, had been always beloved and honoured, and sometimes respected and admired. This wretched regiment met the proper fate of all such dastardly perpetrators. They were despised even by the soldiery whom they meant to oblige, compelled to lay down their arms, and sent prisoners to France, where, in some shape or other, punishment failed not to await them.

During these dreadful transactions, as if eager to provide fresh fuel to light up in this unhappy island, the society of Amis des Noirs continued to devise new projects that thoroughly effected that purpose. There was great reason to suppose, at this time, that the general body of mulattoes were not averse to conciliation, while there was as much cause to desire it on the part of the whites. The president of the colonial committee in France, (M. Barnave,) had also, after the most strenuous opposition to the planters, avowed his conviction, that all interference of the mother-country with their internal regulations should cease. But the principal members of this society, among whom were Gregoire, La Fayette, and Brissot, determined otherwise, and the foundation of their plan was in making the National Assembly the medium, in obedience to the chapter of instructions for its proceedings, which had followed the decree of March 8. These instructions, which consisted of eighteen articles,

cles, directed "that every person of the age of twenty-five and upwards, possessing property, or, having resided two years in the colony, and paid taxes, should be enabled to vote in the formation of the Colonial Assembly." This direction, repugnant to the very decree it was to accompany, was asserted by those who procured it, to regard only the privilege of voting in the Parochial Assemblies; as under the old government it was known that they were constituted solely of white persons, the mulattoes had expressed no inclination to intrude themselves. To induce them to do so, they were apprised that not being excepted, they were virtually included, and after much entreaty, were persuaded to send deputies to France, to procure an explanation from the National Assembly. This was the chief point required, for it produced a public debate on the subject, in which was also introduced the claim of the mulattoes to all the privileges of whites. The fascinating eloquence of the Abbé Gregoire was exerted on the subject with its usual vigour, and, to give additional aid, the death of Ogé became known at the same time, which afforded a popular subject for the theatres. Every mode was exerted to render the proprietors of the colonies detestable; and with such success, that they could not, at length, appear in public with safety. "Perish the colonies," exclaimed Robespierre, "rather than sacrifice our principles!"—Gregoire, Condorcet, La Fayette, and Brissot, names which often excited admiration, all joined in the cry. The National Assembly forgetting, at once, its former acts, and the principles it had acknowledged, decreed to the people

CHAP. III. 1791.

May 15.

CHAP. III. 1791. people of colour "an equal right with the white proprietors, in the choice of representatives and to seats in the colonial government." The colonial committee at Paris, which had formerly opposed the General Assembly, immediately declared itself useless; and the deputies of the colonies declined further attendance. These decisive steps had no other effect, however, than that of hastening the departure of three commissioners, (who had been appointed some time previous) to St. Domingo, for the better regulation of its affairs. The proceedings of the colonial officers in the mother-country, afforded but a faint presentiment of those which took place in St. Domingo on the arrival of

June. the first information of this last decree in that island. There then existed a variety of opposite opinions, and parties inveterate against each other, but it immediately consolidated them all. They heard it with doubt, which was soon succeeded by the frenzy of despair. All the divisions of party united themselves against the mother-country; every violence was projected and commenced; the preparations making for the federation of the 14th of July were suspended; they determined to reject the civic oath; an embargo was laid on all vessels in the harbour; and even a motion was made in the Northern Provincial Assembly, to erect the British standard in the place of the national colours; all subordination was done away, and it is said, "the people of colour being threatened to be fired upon in the streets, fled from the city, retiring to the woods and other retreats for safety."* At length it was determined

* "Inquiry into the Causes of the Insurrection in St. Domingo," &c. 1792.

to

to elect a new general Colonial Assembly, which had its first meeting, to the number of one hundred and seventy-six members, at Leogane, from whence they adjourned to Cape François, proposing to open their session at the expiration of a fortnight. CHAP. III. 1791. August 9.

During the whole of these transactions the governor-general, M. Blanchelande, remained a political cypher, without any other power, than to give a formal assent to proceedings which he could neither impede nor amend. He wrote to the king's ministers an account of the disturbances, and expressed his fears that the decree would prove " the death-warrant of many thousands of the inhabitants;" he sent a copy of his letter to the Provincial Assembly, with a solemn assurance, that he would suspend the execution of the decree whenever it should come to him.

Alarmed at the various symptoms of hostility manifested towards them, the mulattoes collected in armed bodies in different places, and fears were entertained of fresh conflicts between them and the whites; but the latter were too much occupied in the hopes entertained from the meeting of the Colonial Assembly to notice them, and, in fact, a complete removal of grievances was fully expected.

As little cessation had been experienced, from the occurrence of one disaster to another, on the expectation of pacific measures (from the auspicious sentiments of the new assembly,) another

CHAP. III. 1791. another misfortune arose, which, however it might have been long expected, was still more unlooked-for than any other. Witnesses of the general commotion of the colony, and perceiving that, notwithstanding the attention which had been paid by the mother-country to the people of colour, (except interweaving their sufferings with the subject, for the purposes of oratory,) nothing was proposed with regard to them; the negroes began to consider of some melioration for themselves among the new arrangements then taking place. As they had unfortunately perceived that the first step in all the disputes of their masters had consisted of outrage, so they determined to follow those means which promised such certain success, and at the same time, afforded objects the most grateful to people in a state of slavery. It cannot be denied, that they may have felt no great pleasure in contemplating an acquisition of power by the mulattoes, who, from being, according to their own account, more conversant with their habits, and better acquainted with their dispositions, had always been considered by the negroes as their severest masters; it is very probable, that they exercised the same, or greater rigor, over the negroes, than they received themselves from the whites. Be this as it may, August 23. while a perfect calm seemed to pervade every contending interest, one morning before day-break a sudden and confused alarm spread throughout the town of the Cape, that the negro slaves in the neighbouring parishes had revolted, were murdering the whites, and setting fire to the plantations. The governor immediately assembled all the military officers, but nothing certain could be collected till dawn, when the reports were too sadly confirmed by the arrival of numbers, just escaped with life, who, begging for protection in the town, communicated the particulars. CHAP. III. 1791.

From them they found, that the negroes in a plantation called Noé, in the parish of Acul, were the ringleaders, fourteen of whom, after having murdered the principal managers of the plantation, followed by the remainder, hastened to the adjoining one, and repeated the same enormities. The slaves of this estate immediately joined them. Their determination seemed, that it was necessary none should escape, for they shewed not the same discrimination they afterwards used. M. Clements, the owner of the latter plantation received his death from one he had regarded with much tenderness, and promoted (for so it was considered) to be his postilion. The same occurred at the largest plantation on the plain of the Cape, that of M. Galifet, whose negroes, the whole of whom joined the insurrection, were proverbial for receiving good treatment. Similar circumstances took place at the very time, on the estate of M. Flaville, a few miles distant, from whence they carried off the wife, and three daughters, of the Procureur, after murdering him before their faces. Day-light convinced the astonished inhabitants that the revolt was concerted, for some parties of observation sent from the town, soon perceived that the rising was general throughout the province, and the flames quickly burst from all quarters. The terror of the

whole

CHAP. III. 1791. whole community now became excessive, and the shrieks of women and children as the appearances of horror spread, wildly running from door to door, inquiring their fate of each other, produced a most distressing effect. The men armed themselves, and the General Assembly invested the governor with the command of the National Guards. As soon as any plan could be matured, it was determined, to send the white women and children on board the ships in the harbour; and the ablest of the domestic negroes in the town were also sent, under a guard, lest they should be concerned in any treacherous connection.

The next transaction which took place was relative to a considerable body of mulattoes in the town, who, although they had not joined the previous disputes, were immediately marked as objects of vengeance by the lower classes of white people, and it became necessary for the Assembly to afford them protection. This circumstance became the medium of an agreeable conciliation; for, in return, all the able men among them, proposed themselves to march against the rebels, leaving their wives and children as hostages for their fidelity. They were, therefore, enrolled in the militia, and a mutual confidence, to a certain degree, established itself between them.

As many seamen as could be spared from the ships were joined to the inhabitants, and the whole formed into a military order, when M. de Touzard, an officer who had distinguished himself in North America, took the command of a detachment of militia and troops of the line, and marched to attack the most powerful body of the revolters in the neighbourhood. They were posted at the plantation of M. Latour, to the number of 4,000 negroes, a large portion of whom were destroyed, but their places were supplied by such increased numbers, that M. de Touzard was compelled to retreat. The weakness of the town obliged the governor to stand on the defensive, till he could contrive means to strengthen the only position he could command; if the negroes had proceeded to Cape François at that time, they might have easily taken the town, and effected every enormity they chose. CHAP. III. 1791.

On the river which intersected the main road from the plain at the east end of the town, over which there was a ferry, a battery of cannon was raised on boats, protected by two small camps at a short distance; at the other principal road lying over the Haut du Cap, a considerable body of troops, with artillery, was stationed, while a strong palisade and chevaux-de-frize, surrounded the town on the land side; an embargo was laid on the shipping, for the purpose of retreat, and retaining the assistance of the sailors. The whole of the inhabitants, without distinction, laboured at the fortifications.

Every method was used to communicate the information of the insurrection, when it could be conveyed with safety, and several camps were formed, which seemed to arrest the progress

 of

CHAP. III. 1791. of the rebellion; nevertheless, those at Grande Riviere and Dondon were attacked by the negroes, joined by mulattoes, and after a sharp contest, forced with great slaughter. The surviving whites from Dondon took refuge in the Spanish territory.

The whole of the plain, of the Cape, and the district of Grande Riviere, now in the possession of the insurgents, and abandoned to their ravages, as were the miserable inhabitants, to whom no assistance could be given, who, therefore, suffered every injury, that bewildered licentiousness could devise, before a death, in this instance merciful, but of more than common torments, closed for them the scene.

It serves few of the purposes of history to describe the various modes of torture which occurred to the savage insurgents, or to relate accounts of the grossest violations of virgins and pregnant women, in the presence of their dying husbands, or parents; much it is to be regretted, that civilized states should ever find it necessary to render torture of any kind familiar to vulgar minds, for they are exhibitions that live in the memory, and steel the heart against those affections which form the grandest boundary of our nature. There is reason to fear that the perpetrators of those horrid deeds, had been witnesses to the ridicule of misery in others who should have evinced themselves superior to such conduct, by the godlike attributes of mercy and benevolence; the licentiousness of their intercourse with the female slaves, could leave no impression to prevent a retaliation on the occa-

sion

sion, with objects, too, of such superior attraction, alas! unhappily for themselves. CHAP. III. 1791.

It is pleasing, however, to alleviate these horrors by the recital of an instance of fidelity, and affectionate solicitude, in one of the revolted negroes, which has been already narrated, but which cannot be too much impressed upon the minds of the people in every relation of society. I quote Mr. Edwards's words, as I know of no more authentic source to which I can refer.

"Monsieur and Madam Baillen, their daughter and son-in-law, and two white servants, residing on a mountain plantation about thirty miles from Cape François, were apprized of the revolt by one of their own slaves, who was himself in the conspiracy, but promised, if possible, to save the lives of his master and his family. Having no immediate means of providing for their escape, he conducted them into an adjacent wood; after which he went and joined the revolters. The following night he found an opportunity of bringing them provisions from the rebel camp. The second night he returned again with a further supply of provisions, but declared it would be out of his power to give them any further assistance. After this they saw nothing of the negro for three days; but at the end of that time he came again, and directed the family how to make their way to a river which led to Port Margot, assuring them they would find a canoe on a part of the river which he described. They followed

his

CHAP. III. 1791. his directions; found the canoe, and got safely into it, but were overset by the rapidity of the current, and after a narrow escape, thought it best to return to their retreat in the mountains. The negro, anxious for their safety, again found them out, and directed them to a broader part of the river, where he assured them he had provided a boat; but said it was the last effort he could make to save them. They went accordingly, but not finding the boat, gave themselves up for lost, when the faithful negro again appeared, like their guardian angel. He brought with him pigeons, poultry, and bread; and conducted the family, by slow marches in the night, along the banks of the river, until they were within sight of the wharf at Port Margot; when, telling them they were entirely out of danger, he took his leave for ever, and went to join the rebels. The family were in the woods nineteen nights." *.

The town of the Cape being somewhat strengthened, the governor, with the advice of the Colonial Assembly, came to the resolution of re-commencing offensive operations against the rebels; accordingly, a small force, under the command of M. Rouvray, encamped at a place called Roucooa, in the eastern part of the plain. A division of the negroes at the same time took possession of the principal buildings on the estate of the amiable M. Galifet, and mounted on the walls several pieces of heavy artillery, which they had procured from the different har-

* Edwards's Hist. chap. vi. p. 75.

bours

bours on the coast. In this intrenchment, they began to shew somewhat of regular manœuvres; though they seldom stood more than a single volley in their skirmishes, yet they were repeated with alacrity, and with such success, that they harassed the whites by perpetual alarms, and desolated the country. After their first stock of ammunition was exhausted, it was discovered they had been supplied from the king's arsenal, by some negroes in Cape François; in a short time the small American vessels opened a brisk trade with them in this article, for the sugar and rum of their masters.

In two months of the rebellion, upwards of two thousand white persons had fallen, of all conditions and ages; it appeared, one thousand two hundred families were "reduced from opulence to such a state of misery, as to depend altogether for their clothing and sustenance on public and private charity;" one hundred and eighty plantations of sugar, about nine hundred of coffee, cotton, and indigo, had been destroyed, and the buildings consumed by fire. On the side of the rebels it was computed, that upwards of ten thousand had perished in the different accidents attendant on their horrid warfare, besides several hundreds by the execution of the law. It is to be lamented, that a retaliation of cruelty took place upon all rebel prisoners who were taken, which could produce no advantage to those who had already suffered, and might cause additional miseries to the unfortunate objects who afterwards fell in the way of the enemy. One description of punishment at the Cape, has been often

quoted

CHAP. III. 1791. quoted from the gentleman who witnessed it. I cannot perfectly coincide with him in the oblique censure conveyed against the unfortunate persons who expressed a degree of satisfaction at the death of their enemies, for it is a difficult sentiment to repress on such an occasion; nor, while I lament, can I deny the necessity of such executions, ON SUCH OCCASIONS; they are not intended as a feast for the philosopher, but they are a gratification to those whose services, whatever their feelings and their sentiments, demand and obtain *from all enlightened politicians* on *all* occasions respect.

"Two of these unhappy men," says Mr. Edwards, "suffered in this manner under the window of the author's lodgings, and in his presence, at Cape François, on Thursday the 28th of September, 1791. They were broken on two pieces of timber placed crosswise. One of them expired on receiving the third stroke on his stomach, each of his legs and arms having been first broken in two places; the three first blows he bore without a groan. The other had a harder fate. When the executioner, after breaking his legs and arms, lifted up the instrument to give the finishing stroke upon the breast, and which, (by putting the criminal out of his pain,) is called *le coup de grace*, the mob, with the ferociousness of cannibals, called out *arretez*, (stop,) and compelled him to leave his work unfinished. In that condition, the miserable wretch, with his broken limbs doubled up, was put on a cart-wheel, which was placed horizontally, one end of the axle-tree being driven into the earth. He seemed perfectly sensible,

sible, but uttered not a groan. At the end of forty minutes, some English seamen, who were spectators of the tragedy, strangled him in mercy. As to all the French spectators, (many of them persons of fashion, who beheld the scene from the windows of their upper apartments,) it grieves me to say, that they looked on with the most perfect composure and *sang-froid*. Some of the ladies, as I was told, even ridiculed, with a great deal of unseemly mirth, the sympathy manifested by the English * at the sufferings of the wretched criminals." †

Having mentioned the residence of Mr. Edwards at the Cape, it may not be amiss to repeat in this place the account he gives of the appearance of the island, to a stranger, at that time. He had returned from Jamaica with the commissioners, who had been sent thither, and to the different neighbouring powers, to request the assistance of troops, arms, ammunition, and provisions; when Admiral Affleck ordered the Blonde and the Daphne frigates to repair to that place to overawe the insurgents.

* Will the present writer merit censure if he ventures to observe in this place, for the honor of a sex, of whom he feels a difficulty in recording a slander, that there was not, perhaps, one of these unhappy fair spectators who had not lost, through the means of the victims before them, a *father*, a *mother*, *brother*, or *sister*, or some of the tenderest connexions in human existence; and that despair, mingled with revenge, assumed the place of a sensibility too exquisite for their loss. This place need not be occupied with instances in the memory of every one, of the change effected in the best dispositions under such circumstances as these; and, while he eagerly joins his tribute of praise to the sympathy of his brave countrymen in this instance, he cannot forget that the inhabitants of St. Domingo, may not always have seen them in a light equally amiable; so that the contrast, added to the accompanying circumstances, may have excited a risibility, perhaps, convulsive. It is necessary to view all sides of a question which affects the character of a nation.

† Edwards's Hist. ch. vi. p. 78.

"We

CHAP. III. 1791. "We arrived," says he, "in the harbour of Cape François, in the evening of the 26th of September, and the first object which arrested our attention, as we approached, was a dreadful scene of devastation by fire. The noble plain adjoining the Cape was covered with ashes; and the surrounding hills, as far as the eye could reach, every where presented to us ruins still smoking, and houses and plantations at that moment in flames. It was a sight more terrible than the mind of any man, unaccustomed to such a scene, can easily conceive.—The inhabitants of the town, being assembled on the beach, directed all their attention towards us, and we landed amidst a crowd of spectators, who, with uplifted hands and streaming eyes, gave welcome to their deliverers, (for such they considered us, and acclamations of *vivent les Anglois* resounded from every quarter.

"The governor of St. Domingo, at that time, was the unfortunate Blanchelande, a *marechal de camp* in the French service, who has since perished on the scaffold. He did us the honor to receive us on the quay. A committee of the Colonial Assembly, accompanied by the governor's only son, an amiable and accomplished youth, had before attended us on board the Blonde, and we were immediately conducted to the place of their meeting. The scene was striking and solemn. The hall was splendidly illuminated, and all the members appeared in mourning. Chairs were placed for us within the bar, and the governor having taken his seat on the right hand of the president, the latter addressed us in an elegant and affecting oration, of which the following is as literal a translation as the idiom of the two languages will admit: CHAP. III. 1791.

'We were not mistaken, Gentlemen, when we placed our confidence in your generosity; but we could hardly entertain a hope, that, besides sending us succours, you would come in person to give us consolation. You have quitted, without reluctance, the peaceful enjoyments of happiness at home, to come and participate in the misfortunes of strangers, and blend your tears with ours. Scenes of misery (the contemplation of which, to those who are unaccustomed to misfortune, is commonly disgusting) have not suppressed *your* feelings. You have been willing to ascertain the full extent of our distresses, and to pour into our wounds the salutary balm of your sensibility and compassion.

'The picture which has been drawn of our calamities, you will find has fallen short of the reality. That verdure with which our fields were lately arrayed, is no longer visible; discoloured by the flames, and laid waste by the devastations of war, our coasts exhibit no prospect but that of desolation. The emblems which we wear on our persons, are the tokens of our grief for the loss of our brethren, who were surprized, and cruelly assassinated by the revolters.

'It is by the glare of the conflagrations that every way surround us, that we now deliberate; we are compelled to sit armed and watchful through the night, to keep the enemy from our

 sanctuary,

CHAP. III. 1791. sanctuary. For a long time past our bosoms have been depressed by sorrow; they experience this day, for the first time, the sweet emotions of pleasure, in beholding you amongst us.

'Generous islanders! humanity has operated powerfully on your hearts;—you have yielded to the first emotion of your generosity, in the hopes of snatching us from death; for it is already too late to save us from misery. What a contrast between your conduct, and that of other nations! We will avail ourselves of your benevolence; but the days you preserve to us, will not be sufficient to manifest our gratitude; our children shall keep it in remembrance.

'Regenerated France, unapprized that such calamities might befal us, has taken no measures to protect us against their effects; with what admiration will she learn, that, without your assistance, we should no longer exist as a dependency to any nation.

'The commissioners deputed by us to the island of Jamaica, have informed us of your exertions to serve us.—Receive the assurance of our attachment and sensibility.

'The governor-general of this island, whose sentiments perfectly accord with our own, participates equally in the joy we receive at your presence, and in our gratitude for the assistance you have brought us.'

At

"At this juncture, the French colonists in St. Domingo, however they might have been divided in political sentiments on former occasions, seemed to be softened into perfect unanimity. All descriptions of persons joined in one general cry against the National Assembly, to whose proceedings were imputed all their disasters. This opinion was indeed so widely disseminated, and so deeply rooted, as to create a very strong disposition, in all classes of the whites, to renounce their allegiance to the mother country. The black cockade was universally substituted in place of the tri-colored one, and very earnest wishes were avowed in all companies, without scruple or restraint, that the British administration would send an armament to conquer the island, or rather to receive its voluntary surrender from the inhabitants. What they wished might happen, they persuaded themselves to believe was actually in contemplation. CHAP. III. 1791.

"The ravages of the rebellion during the time that I remained at Cape François, extended in all directions. The whole of the plain of the Cape, with the exception of one plantation which adjoined the town, was in ruins; as were likewise the parish of Limonade, and most of the settlements in the mountains adjacent. The parish of Limbé was every where on fire; and, before my departure, the rebels had obtained possession of the bay and forts at L'Acul, as well as the districts of Fort Dauphin, Dondon, and La Grande Rivière.

"Destruction every where marked their progress, and resist-

CHAP. III. 1791. ance seemed to be considered by the whites, not only as unavailing in the present conjuncture, but as hopeless in the future. To fill up the measure of their calamities, their Spanish neighbours in the same island, with a spirit of bigotry and hatred which is, I believe, without an example in the world, refused to lend any assistance towards suppressing a revolt, in the issue of which, common reason should have informed them, that their own preservation was implicated equally with that of the French. They were even accused, not only of supplying the rebels with arms and provisions, but also of delivering up to them to be murdered, many unhappy French planters who had fled for refuge to the Spanish territories, and receiving money from the rebels as the price of their blood.

"The merchants and importers of European manufactures, apprehending every hour the destruction of the town, as much from incendiaries within, as from the rebels without, offered their goods, for ready money, at half the usual prices; and applications were made to Captain Affleck, by persons of all descriptions, for permission to embark in the Blonde for Jamaica. The interposition of the Colonial Government obliged him to reject their solicitations; but means were contrived to send on board consignments of money to a great amount; and I know that other conveyances were found, by which effects to a considerable value were exported both to Jamaica, and the states of North America."*

* Edwards's St. Domingo, Preface, p. v.

From

CHAP. III. 1791.

From the northern province the rebellion, rapidly spread to the west; in which quarter it assumed a new appearance; for the revolters being chiefly men of colour, to whom about six hundred negroes had attached themselves, it tended to confirm the opinion and the prejudices of those who conceived the men of colour to have been the original cause of the rebellion. A detachment sent against them from Port-au-Prince was repulsed, and the enemy advanced to set fire to the city; when, happily, some of the mulatto chiefs obtained its redemption, and began to express sentiments of amity, which was attributed, with some reason, to the tardiness of the negroes, at their head-quarters, in joining them. Anxious to embrace any opportunity of quelling the disturbance, a planter of eminence, M. de Jumecourt, undertook to mediate between the two parties, and immediately obtained attention. The effect of this interference was a treaty, called the *Concordat*, which was determined upon the 12th of September, between the insurgents of the neighbourhood, and the white inhabitants of Port-au-Prince. The principal provisions were, an amnesty for the past, and an engagement by the whites to admit the full force of the decree of the 15th May. The honourable conduct of the mulattoes in Cape François, precluded any objection in the General Assembly to the ratification of this agreement; from the most rational policy, they extended their care to those who had been born of enslaved parents; military companies of mulattoes were formed, in which men of colour, under certain regulations, were permitted to hold commissions.

Treaty of the Concordat.

CHAP. III. 1791.

Thus circumstances, as far as respected the mulattoes, began to wear a promising appearance, when with that eagerness with which we supplant the remembrance of evil, by the prospect of good, the return of general quiet was contemplated. But a fresh and most tremendous blow was about to fall on this devoted colony, when least intended, by the mother country; whose regard, in this instance, similar to that of some animals, was not less fatal than its vengeance. This was the information, which at this time arrived in the colony, of the repeal of the decree of the 15th of May, which had been the original cause of the present disturbance, and which the white inhabitants had just agreed to allow.

Repeal of the decree of 15th May.

On the accounts arriving in France the beginning of September of the dreadful consequences attendant on this fatal decree, it excited general consternation throughout the trading districts; the loss of the colonial commerce by a civil war between the whites and the mulattoes, was an event to be dreaded from the probable issue; still they never apprehended any interference of the negroes; so blind are we to the approach of political danger. The idea of immense losses, and all the accompanying considerations, produced such an effect upon the merchants principally concerned, that they, with their connections, did not fail to press the National Assembly by every mode of appeal and remonstrance, for the immediate relief of the planters from the restrictions then operating so destructively upon the interests of the mother country. There is in every thing a certain satiety, resulting from attainment or enjoyment, which produces relaxation; in the present instance it appears to have had a remarkable effect; for, of all the violent members of the society, "Amis des Noirs," but few appear to have exerted themselves on the present occasion, and that few to have been as little attended to. In fact, the popular opinion seemed changed to another direction, and the Constituent Assembly being on the point of dissolution, the obnoxious decree was annulled by the sanction of a large majority, at the moment in which it was becoming the medium of peace in the colony. CHAP. III. 1791.

When it became known in the colony none would believe, (nor indeed was it reasonable they should,) that it had not been brought about at the instance of the planters, and that in consequence they were unsafe with such deceptive negotiators. They had already required repeated ratifications of the Concordat, but now every idea of amity vanished. The people of colour charged the whites with horrid duplicity, and came to the determination that one party or the other must be exterminated; accordingly, throughout the western and southern provinces, they immediately had recourse to arms, and became masters of Port St. Louis, but from Port-au-Prince having been lately reinforced, they could effect nothing more than a dreadful conflagration, which destroyed, at least, one third of the buildings. They established themselves at La Croix des Bouquets in considerable force. The contest here, assumed a more furious cha-

racter

CHAP. III. 1792.

racter; the negroes in several places joined the mulattoes, and in every action a dreadful slaughter ensued. At Cul de Sac two thousand negroes were left dead on the field, from being placed, as was frequently the case, in the front of the mulattoes. If there remained any invention in cruelty unexerted on former occasions it was now practised, with re-iterated vigor, and each party strove how they could convince the other of the fertility of their cruelty, rather than of superiority of power.

Arrival of the commissioners, Roome, Mirbeck, and St. Leger.

At length, about the middle of December, the three commissioners, who had been long before appointed at Paris, for the civil affairs of the colony, arrived, and every one began to hope from them a cessation of the accumulated horrors which every where made their appearance. They were named, Mirbeck, Roome, and St. Leger, the former two had been advocates in the parliament of Paris, and the latter (a native of Ireland) a surgeon by profession. They were neither of them in a situation of life which warranted the appointment, but had arisen through accident, in the confusion of the revolution. They were received with every degree of submission, on the part of the governor and inhabitants, by military honors, and a procession to the cathedral.

No sooner were these men in full possession of their offices, than, after announcing the new French constitution, and the decree of the 22d September, (as if every step was to be

marked

marked by some additional misfortune,) they proclaimed a general amnesty and pardon to every description of revolters who should lay down their arms, come in within a prescribed time, and take the oaths. This measure lost the desired effect with the mulattoes, from being accompanied by the repeal of the decree in their favour; in the opinion of the whites, it justified their enormities; and, tempted the negroes who yet remained faithful, to join those who experienced such an indemnification. The commissioners could not expect to obtain the confidence of the inhabitants, as Mirbeck resigned himself to every kind of low debauchery, while St. Leger employed himself in levying contributions wherever he found an opportunity. The third exerted himself with honesty to the duties prescribed to him, but wanting ability, and acting with colleagues of the character already described, could accomplish very little. The effect of these circumstances, which rendered them contemptible (and being without means to enforce authority), was their return to France, separately, after a residence of three months only. CHAP. III. 1792.

It was, however, during the stay of the commissioners, or immediately before their arrival, that, in consequence of a resolution of the General Colonial Assembly, copies of the deposition of Ogé, given during the twenty-four hours he was respited, were obtained from the Register of the Council of the Cape; but not till they had been imperiously demanded. By these it was found, that, if instead of being suppressed, as beforementioned,

 the

CHAP. III. 1792.

the evidence had been promptly and decisively acted upon, all the horrors which had blackened the colony for the last nine months might have been to a great degree, if not entirely prevented. He asserts upon oath as follows:

The neglected dying testimony of Ogé.

"That in the commencement of the month of February preceding, if the rivers had not overflowed their banks, there would have been a rising of the people of colour, who were to have fallen upon the town of the Cape in considerable numbers; that they were then re-united to the number of 11,000 men, from Mirebalais, Artibonite, Limbé, Ouanaminthe, Grand Riviére, and other parts of the colony: that, at the same time, one hundred men of colour left the Cape for the purpose of joining this band: that he was certain that the authors of this revolt were the Declains, free negroes of Grande Riviére, now under accusation; Dumas and Yvon, free negroes; Bitozin, a free Spanish mulatto; Peter Godard, and John Baptiste, his brother, free negroes; Legrand, and Toussaint Mazeau, free negroes; Peter Mauzi, Ginga Lapaire, Charles Lamadieu, the Sabourins, John Peter Goudy, Joseph Lucas, free mulattoes; and Maurice, a free negro, all under accusation.

"That the grand movers of rebellion down the coast were, Daguin, under accusation, rebel, of Mirebalais; Pinchinat and Labastille, under accusation: that the most violent partizans of the revolt, who had moved in large parties, were those who had shone in the environs of St. Mark, and who were endeavouring

to

to excite it again: that there were at that moment many people of colour in different quarters, who were very resolute to maintain their projects, notwithstanding the number of those who had lost their lives by engaging timidly in the cause: that he remembered at present the name of one only, the son of La Place, a free quadron, whose sister he had seen in the prisons, and quitting Limbé to go and raise recruits in the quarter of Ouanaminthe; that these recruits, and risings of people of colour, were continued there under the countenance of Fleury and Hirondelle Viard, deputies of the people of colour to the National Assembly, the one residing at Mirebalais, and the other in the quarter of Grand Riviére.

"That assemblies were yet held in the subterraneous passages near La Crête à Mareau, and the district of Giromen, in the parish of Grande Riviére; and that if he could be conducted to these places, he would strive hard to take the chiefs of the rebellion: that the agitation in which he found himself under his present circumstances, did not permit him to enter into more circumstantial details: that he would acquaint us with the remainder when he became a little more tranquil: that it occurred to him at the moment, that Castaing, a free mulatto of this dependency, is not concerned in any manner in the present affair, but that if his brother Ogé had followed the persuasion of Castaing, he would have been brought into much greater extremities."

The

CHAP. III
1792.

The commissioners for taking the deposition then stated, that Ogé having heard the above read on the day after it was made, and being again sworn, he confirmed it in every respect, adding, "That the two Didiers, brothers, free mulattoes, whom he had seen but that time, and that John Peter Gerard and —— Caton, free mulattoes of the Cape, were employed to gain a party of the Grande Rivière; that they kept together by the day, and dispersed at night."

They mention, that on being confronted with James Lucas, who had accused him, of threatening to hang him, he said, "it was necessary to tell them why Lucas had not insisted upon his explaining the reason of that threat, lest it should cost him his life: that the said Lucas had been always foremost in every perpetration of horror, the most active seducer of the blacks, and promoter of massacre, and had of necessity been restrained by him several times, on occasions which he repeated.

"That Fleury, Perisse, and L'Hirondelle Viard, arriving in the colony, the two former were landed at Acquin, and left at the house of Dupont, but that L'Hirondelle Viard proceeded to the Cape.

"That La Place, whose father was then in prison for raising recruits at Ouanaminthe, was of the number of those who marched from Limbé against the Cape; that to avoid suspicion, he he went to Port Margot, where he lay concealed for several days; that the senior La Place had told him that he knew his neighbour, who was a white man, would not inform against him, though he knew all his proceedings; that he was sure Girardeau, then in prison, would declare nothing, because he was too much his friend to betray him; and that, if he were denounced, he should be forced to denounce many others, both in Limbé and other quarters. CHAP. III. 1792.

"That he had omitted to mention, on the subject of Lucas seducing the slaves, that Peter Maury had brought thirty slaves to Lucas, whom Ogé and his brother sent away again, the people of colour saying that it was a future supply; that he had on the same occasion a dispute with the tallest of the Didiers, whom he wished to fight with pistols, on account of his treasons; that he had seen a short note written by Peter Maury to John Francis Tessiers, by which he signified, that he continued to collect together, and that the negro Coquin and the widow Castaing, armed with pistols mounted with silver, and a short sword which Maury had furnished, watched every thing that passed, and gave an account every night to Maury; which was all that the accused could declare at present, conjuring the commissioners to be persuaded, that if it were possible to obtain mercy, he would willingly expose himself to every danger, to arrest the chiefs of the rebellion, and that in all circumstances he should prove his zeal and respect for the whites *.

* See the original paper in the Appendix.

He

CHAP. III. 1792. He was, however, as before stated, immediately at the close of the confession, hurried to execution, and the whole suppressed, without any proceeding upon it whatever.

The matter of the deposition has been particularly given, for this reason, it exhibits the *manner* of the rebellion, and the quality of its leaders, who appear to have been well acquainted with its various manœuvres; and if the principal persons mentioned, particularly Pinchinat, Castaing, and Viard, had been arrested at that time, they would have been prevented forming their attack of the 25th August.—Thus does party, which, as before described, in dividing the colony of St. Domingo, unconsciously act against itself, and a want of political foresight ruin the best intentions.

January. To add to the effects of the disclosure of this extraordinary error, the talents of the black leaders began to appear in an instance in the conduct of one, Jean François, whose followers having destroyed all the provision grounds, and devoured all the cattle on the plain, he compelled them to plant in the mountainous districts provisions for their future subsistence; thus judiciously preparing for an indeterminate prolongation of the war.

In the mother country fresh changes continuing to take place, new horrors were prepared for this unhappy colony from that quarter. The jacobin party, and the society of Amis des Noirs, February. were, at this period, resuming a powerful ascendancy, and on the

the 29th of February, Garan de Coulon proposed an abrogation of the last decree, (of September 24,) and a general amnesty throughout the French colonies; the formation of new colonial assemblies, whose opinions were to be submitted to them, and who should particularly aid in the abolition of negro slavery. This inconsistent plan fell immediately to the ground; but it gave birth to another, about two months after, which was considered little more beneficial to the miserable inhabitants of the colony. CHAP. III. 1792. April.

The decree of the 4th of April consisted, as related to St. Domingo, of the following items; after an acknowledgment of the political equality of the free negroes and people of colour with the whites:

I. A re-election of colonial and parochial assemblies, after the mode of the decree of the 8th March 1790, and the subsequent instructions.

II. The eligibility of free negroes and people of colour to votes and seats in the legislature, upon certain qualifications mentioned in the fourth article of these instructions.

III. IV. V. VI. VII. Three civil commissioners to be named, to enforce the decree, to dissolve the present colonial assemblies; to take every measure for convoking the others, and establishing peace and order; to determine provisionally upon all questions relating thereto, conditionally reserving an appeal to the National Assembly; to procure correct information of the authors of the troubles; to send the guilty to France for accusation,

CHAP. III. 1792.

cusation, transmitting constantly minutes of their proceedings, and of the evidence they collect; to call forth the public force to their protection, or the execution of orders.

VIII. A sufficient force of National Guards to be sent to the colonies for the various purposes.

IX. X. The Colonial Assembly to transmit their sentiments on all subjects to the mother country; and to send delegates with them proportional to the population.

XI. All former decrees, not hostile to the present, to continue in force.

D'Esparbes, governor.

September. Arrival of the commissioners, Santhonax, Polverel, and Ailhaud.

To perform its functions, three commissioners, named Santhonax, Polverel, and Ailhaud, were appointed, (who were of the most violent of the jacobin party,) and with them a force of eight thousand men, under officers whose principles were well known. M. Blanchelande was superseded by M. D'Esparbes, under the title of commander in chief. The commissioners arrived at Cape François on the 13th of September. They found the governor and the Colonial Assembly involved in disputes, and therefore sent him prisoner to France, and prepared for the first article of their decree to be carried into effect..

The arrival of these men, (from the unfavourable impressions produced by their predecessors,) instead of causing peace in the colony, which appears to be the first intention of the new decree, produced an effect entirely opposite. Amidst such a contrariety of enactions as had agitated them

 from

from the mother country the result of men coolly sitting down to provide remedies for the worst of circumstances, at so great a distance from the scene of action, and unaffected by its immediate difficulties, the people were in doubt what was intended by the new commission, they sent delegates from all quarters to inquire their intentions; some had concluded that they were merely come to exact money, but all had an indifferent opinion of their projected operations. The commissioners answered generally, and certainly with dissimulation, that their views went no farther than to enforce the decree of the 4th of April, in favor of the people of colour, and to settle the future state of the colony, so as to ensure its permanence. CHAP. III. 1792.

Notwithstanding this declaration, the inhabitants were not perfectly satisfied of their probity, and, when they found that the commissioners corresponded with the mulatto chiefs in all parts of the colony, they did not conceal their mistrust. In consequence the commissioners immediately avowed their intentions, and, strengthened by the co-operation of the people of colour, declared themselves the protectors of the negroes, and mulattoes, and seized the persons and effects of those who were most eager to oppose their measures. Many were sent to France, among whom were the superior officers of the regiment of the Cape.

When the white inhabitants denied the election of the new Colonial Assembly, they instituted an intermediate commission

CHAP. III. 1792. (*commission intermediare*) as a legislative council, formed of twelve persons, six of whom had been members of the last assembly, and six mulattoes. To these they delegated a part of their power, chiefly for financial purposes. With that promptitude for which the reign of the jacobins in France was distinguished, when the governor D'Esparbes claimed a share of dominion, he was arrested, and conveyed to France as a state-prisoner: when four of the white members of the intermediate commission objected to a financial measure of M. Santhonax, he commended their frankness, invited them to supper; and, when they came, they were surrounded by a detachment of military, and conveyed on board of ship as state-prisoners. One of them was taken prisoner in the ship in which he was confined, and brought to England, where Mr. Edwards saw and rendered him service. Another of the triumvirate dissenting from the union, more timely seceded from his situation, and returned voluntarily to the mother-country.

1793. The affairs of France, now drawing towards an apparent crisis, occupied the Executive Government so fully, as to leave the two commissioners, Santhonax and Polverel, absolute masters of the colony. They eagerly embraced every advantage of such enormous power, which was increased by the attachment of the military, and a considerable portion of the revolters, whom they had found means to secure to their interest. The same scenes which occupied the whole of France at this period, were acted again in St. Domingo. The inhabitants complained

in

in the bitterest manner of their wrongs, but it produced no other amendment, than the appointment, as governor, of M. Galbaud, a respectable officer of artillery, and a proprietor in the colony, whom they dispatched (on the declaration of war against Great Britain and Holland), with directions to put the colony in a proper state of defence against a foreign enemy. CHAP. III. 1793. Galbaud, governor.

Again was the arrangements of the French government respecting this unhappy colony, the cause of commotion and bloodshed. When M. Galbaud arrived with his suite at the Cape, they were received with transport by the municipality and the inhabitants, immediately took the oaths, and entered on his government; but when the commissioners, who (at the time of his landing) were quelling an insurrection in the western province, found he was invested with powers independent of their authority, they immediately set about disrobing him; and the readiest way being, by an existing decree, which prohibited any proprietor of an estate in the colony from holding the government, they attacked and defeated his claims on that score. They ordered him to depart on board the sloop La Normande, for the purpose of returning to France, and invited M. de la Salle, whom they had previously made commandant at Port-au-Prince, to receive the command of the colony in the name of the French republic. May 7. De la Salle, governor.

The indignity thus offered to Galbaud was not tacitly re-

 ceived

CHAP. III. 1793. ceived by his brother, who collected from the inhabitants, the Cape militia, and the seamen in the harbour, a strong party to support his authority. At the expiration of seven days the two brothers landed, at the head of a powerful party, and proceeded in array towards the government house, where the commissioners were prepared, with a greater force, to receive them; being defended by the people of colour, a body of regulars, and a piece of cannon. A bloody contest ensued; but, in consequence of the seamen getting possession of a wine-cellar, the governor's party were compelled to retire and take refuge in the royal arsenal, where they remained the whole of the night. In the ensuing morning the governor issued a proclamation, inviting all good citizens to join him, and several skirmishes took place between the two parties, but without any remarkable occurrence, till Galbaud's brother being taken prisoner, by the commissioners, and the son of Polverel by the party of Galbaud, it was proposed by the governor to exchange the one for the other. "My son," replied Polverel, "knows his duty, and is prepared to die in the service of the republic!"

June 20. The fatal stroke still remained to be put to the fate of St. Domingo, as a colony of France. The white inhabitants had, from the time of the arrival of the commissioners, anticipated the measure; yet with that want of discernment which had led them into their difficulties; thereby creating a degree of stupor amongst them, inasmuch that they had not been able to attempt any method to divert

CHAP. III. 1793.

divert the blow.*" This was *the emancipation of all the slaves in the colony*. When the intentions of Galbaud became known to the commissioners, and that he was supported by so large a body of seamen, they immediately dispatched agents to call to their assistance the revolted negroes, with the offer of a free pardon for the past, the plunder of the city at present, and perfect freedom in future. The first to whom they applied among the leaders, and those of the most conspicuous eminence amidst the blacks, refused the invitation; but another, named Macaya, formerly a negro slave, accepted it, and on the 21st, about noon, entered the town with upwards of three thousand slaves, and begun an indiscriminate slaughter. M. Galbaud and his adherents had, despairing of success, on the same morning, retired to the ships, to which the whole of the whites endeavoured to follow, when their retreat being interrupted by the mulattoes, all that could not escape were immediately murdered. This confusion and slaughter continued through the whole of the two succeeding days, at the end of which they set fire to the principal buildings, and more than half of the city was consumed. The commissioners themselves, astonished at the devastation they had occasioned, and intimidated by the conduct of the allies they had chosen, sought protection under the cover of a ship of the line.

* "J'avoit écrit dans la colonie, des 1792, que c'étoit le plan confié aux commissaires. On pouvoit employer des mesures vigoreuses pour l'empêcher, elles étoient indiquées, &c. Mais l'esprit de vertige qui accompagné tout a qui s'est fait pour empêcher les maux de la revolution eut lieu dans cette circonstance, &c." *Charmilly, Let. p.* 65.

Nor

CHAP. III. 1793.

Nor, were the mulattoes less amazed and vexed, when they found that the exertions against the whites, which they supposed confined to their interest only, extended to the liberation of their own slaves, on whose labour their fortunes depended; they now perceived that they had been made the tools of the Amis des Noirs, in obtaining their darling object, the emancipation of the whole body of negroes. There is an enthusiasm and a fanaticism in politics, as well as religion, equally dangerous in both, which, with an unaccountable bigotry to their projects, must have led the society to urge such excesses; they could not have originally desired the effusion of human blood only, as hath been asserted, however strongly they might afterwards have imbibed a spirit of revenge against their opponents.—Such is the spirit of Jacobinism, endless, and undirected by any social principle.

The effect of the declaration of freedom to the slaves themselves, was such as might be naturally expected from a people of their character and condition. A considerable part remained in their former situation with their masters, in preference to a change; a greater number joined the party of the commissioners, who manumitted them; and, perhaps, the greatest number, fearful their liberty would not be permanent, RETIRED IN SAVAGE BODIES TO THE MOUNTAINS.

During the four years, in which divisions and tumult had reigned in St. Domingo, many emigrations took place to the continent of North America, and to the several neighbouring islands.

islands. These, of course, increased as security grew less, and more particularly since the first revolt of the slaves in the northern province. To them were now added Galbaud and his party, who met, as the others had done, an asylum wherever they fled. The principal planters, however, still remained behind, attached to the colony, either lingering with hopes of returning tranquillity, or planning schemes for the independence of the island. Among them were some, conversant with the economy of politics, more active and able than those who had hitherto been distinguished; who looked forward from the year 1791, to some arrangement with the crown of Great Britain, that should place the island, and its proprietors of their description, under the government, and protection of that puissant nation; and there were a few others desirous of attaching the colony to Spain. They all saw, in the last desperate proceeding of the commissioners, nothing left to hope for from the judgment of the mother country. The latter, therefore, employed a party to apply to the government of Spanish St. Domingo, who were unsuccessful. The former, with more judgment, determined upon making a formal application to Great Britain on the same subject: for this purpose they commissioned their colleague, M. de Charmilly, a man of strong mental powers, and of great activity, to communicate with the British ministry, and to bring their plans, so long in agitation, to an issue.

M. de Charmilly commissioner to the British government.

This gentleman, it will have appeared from the preceding part of this chapter, possessed a considerable interest in the island,

and

CHAP. III. 1793. and an extensive knowledge of its concerns, which had given him a share in several of its legislative bodies, where he appears to have long communicated his inclination towards the measure now confided to him.

The British ministry, hitherto deaf to any proposition of attempting the capture of St. Domingo, became rather more disinclined from the occurrence of a war, which was commenced against the new government of France. More than a negative consent it could scarcely be called, for the arrangement was left to the option of the government of Jamaica, and, in fact, whether any thing should be ventured in its attainment. An intercourse of the most honorable nature to the British character, had already taken place between the unhappy colonists of St. Domingo and those of Jamaica, who raised considerable subscriptions for their aid, and applied them in the way best calculated for their benefit, under the friendly auspices of General Williamson, the governor; and when allured by the professions of the governor of Spanish St. Domingo, they thought they could succeed better there, they were forwarded according to their wishes, Captain Rowley undertaking their safe convoy. Mr. Henry Shirley, of the House of Representatives, appears to have exerted himself in a manner which deserves the highest eulogy. When the government afforded them an asylum in their island, M. de Charmilly lost no time in setting off for Jamaica, and by his representation of the state of St. Domingo, of the disposition of the planters towards the British nation, and the facility of obtaining some ground with a very small force, he prevailed upon General Williamson to grant him the aid he required; a force certainly inadequate to the invasion of such an island under any circumstances. CHAP. III. 1793.

The French commissioners, Santhonax and Polverel, who still retained a disputable power in St. Domingo, were quickly acquainted with the intended invasion, and began to prepare for it accordingly. Their force consisted of the remnant of the troops they brought with them from France, a body of whites who continued attached to their cause, and the slaves which had joined them, of which power little could be judged, being dispersed throughout the provinces. To render themselves in a better state to repel the invaders, they had recourse to a still more determinate step, that of procuring the aid of the whole of the negro slaves. They,* therefore, declared by proclamation, "That every kind of slavery was abolished, and that the negroes were thenceforward to consider themselves, and to be considered as free citizens †.

August. Abolition of slavery.

The inhabitants of St. Domingo, at this period, might be be considered under the following classes:—

* It was signed only by Polverel, who was alone at Port-au-Prince, from whence it was issued. Santhonax was in the northern province.

† It has been asserted that they were still to exercise the same labour, but in the condition of annual servants. Those acquainted with the proclamation, recollect no such exceptions, which would, in fact, have rendered the abolition a nullity.

1. The

CHAP. III. 1793. 1. The principal, and most intelligent of the planters, who desiring tranquillity, and the renovation of their property, (which they could not expect from the distracted state of France,) looked to the protection of a powerful nation, and perhaps most to that of England.

2dly. The remainder of the white planters, who had become republicans, and chose rather to support the commissioners as the representatives of the republic, probably from principle, than to adopt any other country, and to sacrifice their immediate interest to their allegiance:—the impartiality of history demands that this class should not receive any harsher description.

3dly. A number of those persons, to be found in all countries, particularly when under embarrassed circumstances, who, having nothing to lose, and frequently without principle, are ripe for enterprize; many of whom, by stratagem, or other means, had obtained the property of absent planters, availing themselves of the state of the colony, to their own aggrandizement. The mulattoes I consider as partaking of each of these characters: and,

4thly. The emancipated slaves, the most important body of the whole, in whom were comprised almost every description of character. Some of them had already exhibited talents of a superior nature, both in civil and military government, among the revolters; others had proved themselves equal to many of the

the higher purposes of life, and they were possessed at least of eminent physical power. CHAP. III. 1793.

If we might pause for a moment, to consider the propriety, or impropriety of the accession of the British government to the proposition of M. de Charmilly, we might lavish censure on those who could, with such small hopes of success, enter into a plan of such extent, with so little information on its nature, and such small means for its execution; but we will leave it for the partizan, with every local or supposed advantage of judging, to condemn those without; and who, in the complex dominion of a country with many dependencies, and with as many jarring interests to reconcile, must be sometimes hurried into arrangements which may not prove ultimately successful, notwithstanding their discrimination. Sometimes, too, ambition may be supposed to intrude; nor will the brave and intelligent De Charmilly complain of having also attributed to him, in no slight degree,

"The glorious fault of angels and of gods!"

That those who had determined on adopting the British government, were prepared to sustain their engagements, there is no doubt, but they formed one class only of the numerous remains of a vast population; while the remainder had the strongest motives for opposition—interest, party, and relief from slavery. If, even the two former ideas could have been overcome, every

CHAP. III. 1793.

colonist, or other individuals acquainted with colonial affairs might have known, from the example of the black Charribes of St. Vincent, or the Maroons in Jamaica, that the last was not to be easily subdued.* Retaining all the advantages they had derived, in many instances, from the partiality of favorable masters, and particularly in the experience of the different controversies, and conflicts that had taken place, they had become, what is impossible, without an intercourse with them to conceive; an unique people.

It was hoped, however, that interest might assimilate the whole of the whites; that the hostility of the people of colour might be nearly exhausted; and that the negroes were not so far alienated from their duty, as never to be expected to return; still much was left, with great reason, to the bravery and ability of those who were to conduct the enterprize.

British invasion of St. Domingo, under Lieut. Colonel Whitlocke and Commodore Ford.

Under such circumstances, an armament was formed at Jamaica, composed of the 13th regiment of foot, seven companies of the 49th regiment, and a detachment of artillery, under Captain Smith, furnishing about 870 rank and file. With the first division of these, consisting of about 679 rank and file, Lieutenant-Colonel Whitlocke† arrived at Jeremie on the 19th of September,

* See Dallas's History of the Maroons, also Edwards's British West Indies.

† Now Major-General Whitlocke.

September, and took possession of the town and harbour on the following morning. Agents from M. de Charmilly had already arranged every point, the troops therefore disembarked without the smallest opposition. British colours were hoisted on the forts, with royal salutes, and the inhabitants immediately swore allegiance to the king of Great Britain. Commodore Ford having at that time the command on the Jamaica station, accompanied in the Europa man of war, the transport of the troops, and assisted in the necessary formalities of receiving the submission of the place. The Mole of Cape St. Nicholas, (the Gibraltar, or key of the Antilles,) immediately followed. To it, on the next day, according to the pre-arrangement, the commodore directed his course, and, on the 22nd, landing the marines only, took possession of the fortress and harbour. This port was soon after supplied by the grenadier company of the 13th regiment, to which was added the second division of the armament, comprising five companies, of forty men each. The town of St. Nicholas, however, did not capitulate, for its inhabitants were hostile to the British, and immediately joined the republican army.

Jeremie and Cape St. Nicholas surrendered.

The great extent of important coast thus coming into the possession of the English, excited the most sanguine prospects, and determined all parties in the prosecution of an enterprize which promised such brilliant success. We shall quit the exertions of the commissioners, who were at present employed in defensive operations about the capital, while their new allies, the slaves, were forming a separate interest in the interior,

CHAP. III. 1793. to follow the new possessors of the south-east and north-west districts of the colony in their united movements with the brave colonists, by whom they appear to have been cordially and respectably joined.

The neighbouring port to Jeremie, first attracted the attention of Colonel Whitlocke, who was instructed, that it would be of importance to the security of Le Grand Anse. He therefore sailed for Tiburon with his whole force, and arrived in the bay on the 4th day of October; a planter, named Morin Duval, was to proceed by land with five hundred colonial troops, and to form a junction at an appointed spot; but, unfortunately, a piece of cannon compelled Colonel Whitlocke to disembark three miles distant, and the wind intercepted the signal of Duval, who in consequence wandered about the whole of the day, in imminent danger, with a faithful and intelligent negro called John Vina, whose men formed a part of the five hundred. At the same time, a reinforcement of cavalry from Aux Cayes joining the enemy, Colonel Whitlocke was obliged to return, with a loss of twenty men, without effecting his purpose.

Meet a small check. A small check is sufficient to turn the tide of joy when it is full set in, consequently this defeat was magnified in the opinion of those, who had before only to step into possession of wealthy towns, and with well-filled magazines. It had the effect of disheartening the troops; to whom General Williamson sent as encouragement,

encouragement, till reinforcements, which were expected from England, should arrive, the remaining part of the 49th regiment, the 20th regiment, and the 1st battalion of the Royals. This addition not only served to chear the drooping spirits of the soldiery, but to increase the confidence in the planters, as to the intention of Great Britain following up the enterprize; accordingly, the parishes of Jean Rabell, St. Marc, Arcahaye, and Boucassin, became attached to the territory of Great Britain. From this period until the middle of January, no farther advance was made; when the colonists, who had established a port at Irois, a few miles distant from Tiburon, in order to overawe that place, having, for security, erected a fort in the centre of a marsh, which considerably affected their health; they became impatient to re-attempt that port, and the Privy Council of Le Grand Anse eagerly solicited Colonel Whitlocke for the purpose. On the 21st of January, therefore, the commodore received the troops on board at Jeremie; and on the 2d of February, in the evening, they arrived off Cape Tiburon. The commodore stood out to sea, and Capt. Rowley, a brave and sensible officer, had the management of the attack; while Lieutenant-Colonel Spencer,* no way inferior in any quality, commanded the troops, which consisted partly of colonists, and a detachment of the British army. The enemy appeared in considerable force, but the fire of the ships cleared the beach; they came forward again, and directed their musquetry at the boats; when the troops landing, and forming

CHAP. III. 1793.

1794.

Capture of Tiburon.

* Now Major-General Spencer.

instantly,

CHAP. III. 1794. instantly, with the gallant Colonel Spencer at their head, entirely dispirited the defenders. Their line was routed with conderable slaughter, and one hundred and fifty surrendered prisoners of war. In this, as in the former instance, they found the magazine well stored with ammunition. The loss, on the part of the victors, was extremely small.

By this victory the whole of the bay, or bight of Leogane, became under the command of the British squadron; and nothing was wanting but an additional armament, which was constantly expected, to secure Port-au-Prince, the capital of the colony, to which every one looked with an anxious eye.

In the interim, however, it was conceived expedient to obtain the possession of the ancient town of Port-Paix, an important post on the northern side of the island; and Colonel Whitlocke was induced to attempt procuring its surrender by the offer of a sum of money to the general who commanded in it. This was M. Laveaux, a man of broken fortune, though of a good family, who had been long in the service, and had a troop of dragoons before the revolution. Whether Colonel Whitlocke formed his calculation alone upon this circumstance, or, as hath been mentioned, his orders were improperly executed, cannot, at present, be determined; but, it is certain, that General Laveaux possessed considerable confidence from the republican army, and that he did not abuse it. The offer was made in a letter sent with a flag, and 5000*l.* the sum stipulated. He silently read the letter

CHAP. III. 1794.

letter, and asked the officer, upon his honour, if he knew its contents; upon being answered in the negative, he told him, that, if he had known them, he should have immediately been hung on a gibbet. He then read the letter aloud to those around him, and returned the following answer:—

Answer of the republican General Laveaux, to a compromise for his Post.

"You have endeavoured to dishonour me in the eyes of my troops, by supposing me so vile, flagitious, and base, as to be capable of betraying my trust for a bribe: this is an affront, for which you owe me personal satisfaction, and I demand it, in the name of honour. Wherefore, previous to any general action, I offer you single combat until one of us fall; leaving to you the choice of arms, either on foot, or horseback. Your situation as my enemy, on the part of your country, did not give you a right to offer me a personal insult; and, as a private person, I ask satisfaction for an injury done me by an individual."*

Of the character of Gen. Laveaux, a midst the conflicts of party, in which he was situated, it is difficult to judge. But he certainly possessed talents; and, if there were no other cause for this proposition than his circumstances, the misfortunes of a brave man should be respected. The situation and character of Col. Whitlocke, however, demanded an attention to every expedient object.†

* This answer is copied from Edwards, who is not contradicted by De Charmilly, though its terms differ from another copy in the possession of the author.

† Though the impartiality we wish to preserve on all occasions demands that the preceding facts should be fairly stated, we wish to offer a sincere tribute of respect to the conduct of Major-General Whitlocke, as an officer of undoubted bravery, honour, and talents of the highest order.

The

CHAP. III. 1794. The fortress of L'Acul, in the vicinity of Leogane, was next invested, and carried on the 19th of February, but with the loss of two valuable officers. At four in the morning, the flank-companies, a detachment of the royal artillery, and of the 13th regiment, with some colonial troops, two five half-inch howitzers, and two four-pounders, marched from Leogane, under the command of Colonel Whitlocke; while two hundred colonial troops, and a few British artillery, under the orders of the Baron de Montalembert, which were previously embarked, were to land and attack the fort from the sea at an hour appointed. Colonel Whitlocke moved forward on the great road, and took post just without cannon-shot; while Capt. Vincent, with the light infantry of the 49th, and about 80 colonial troops, were dispatched by a higher road to combine their effects with those of Montalembert, in favour of the main body. But, unfortunately, from the intoxication of the captain of one of the transports, notwithstanding the ability and propriety of the other, the *King*, Montalembert could not be landed, and all the service they could perform, was that of diverting the attention of 200 negroes and mulattoes, who were kept on the beach to receive them. The enemy cannonaded from seven till eleven, when Colonel Whitlocke ordered Captain Smith, with the howitzers and cannon, to advance, and fire upon the fort, supported by the light-infantry of the royal, and 13th regiments, under the command of Lieutenant-Colonel Spencer. On the discovery of a failure on the sea-side, it was determined to storm the fort, and Colonel Spencer, with the grenadiers of the 49th, and light-infantry of the 13th, proceeded to join Captain Vincent on the

2 Mountain-

Mountain-Road. Between four and five the two columns proceeded, and the main-body immediately received a heavy fire of cannon and musquetry. It was ordered to advance and gain the fort, which it executed with the utmost rapidity, and with more effect than could have been expected, by so small a party. After obtaining possession of the fort, considerable damage was sustained from the explosion of one of the buildings, which had been filled with combustibles by the commander, on finding he could no longer defend it. It was fired by a negro recently from the coast of Africa, who is supposed not to have known what he did, or, the use of powder; he set fire to an artillery-waggon on the spot, and perished, with thirteen privates of the besiegers and two officers, Capt. Morshead, of the 20th grenadiers, who had been previously wounded in the body, and Lieutenant Caulfield, of the 62d. They were buried with military honours, attended by the British garrison. Lieutenant M'Kerras, of the engineers, and Captain Hutchinson, of the royals, though both wounded in the attack, continued on duty till the fort was carried. Lieutenant Tilnin, of the 20th grenadiers, was wounded, but recovered.

Thus the first sharp action that was fought, ended successfully; but the same was not the case with the second, which occurred immediately after, though of less importance. This expedition was intended to punish the treachery of the German inhabitants of Bombarde, before described. It was composed chiefly of marines from the different ships, who were performing the gar-

English defeat at Bombarde.

 rison-

CHAP. III. 1794. rison-duty of the Mole with the regular troops, under the orders of Lieutenant-Colonel Spencer, and Lieutenant-Colonel Markham; two Frenchmen accompanied them, M. Deneux, the major of artillery, and Lieutenant-Colonel Charmilly, who was necessary every where, not only on account of the great responsibility under which he lay to all parties, but from the general want of knowledge, in the language of the country by the commanders.

The detachment set off at nine o'clock at night, and arrived at the redoubt about three in the morning, having marched fifteen miles in the woods and mountains. It was defended by 150 German soldiers, intrenched, with three pieces of cannon. They were relieving guard at the moment, when the troops were discovered, and the alarm-gun fired. Colonel Markham, with half the detachment, attacked the redoubt in flank, while the remainder approached the gate. The enemy suffered them to arrive within half-gun shot, when having challenged three times, calling—"*Qui vive?*" Colonel Spencer answered, "England!" and immediately the assailants received a fire, perfectly well directed, and kept up with so much order and briskness, that the enterprize was obliged to be immediately abandoned. Several of the officers advanced as far as the ditch, supported by some grenadiers, but not being sufficiently numerous; all retired in confusion. M. De Charmilly (who recounts the affair) was at the side of the ditch, ten feet from the entrenchments, which served as a rampart, and was wounded by several

1 musquet-

musquet-shot: one ball struck the plate of his belt, and another the barrel of a brass-pistol in his pocket, either of which must have killed him. There were sixteen men killed, and twenty-six taken prisoners; the remainder retreated without any further misfortune than the hardships experienced by a small party, which I shall describe from the authority of the officer just mentioned;* the retreat being very precipitate, there was no signal to indicate it, so that many of the people strayed from the main body. CHAP. III. 1794.

A young and brave officer, Lieutenant Garstin, of the first regiment of royal English infantry, who was with his detachment, found, at day-break, that he had strayed from the road with eight men belonging to his company. All his endeavours to find it led him farther from it; when, towards the middle of the day, he fell in with a German patrole, consisting of six men, who desired him to surrender. He answered by threatening to fire upon them if they attacked him. Seeing him so determined, they contented themselves with following, while he continued to stray still farther from his intended point. They acquainted him with it, and again pressed his surrender, which was as constantly refused. The Germans, fatigued with following him over the dry and sandy plains, on the approach of night retired; they continued to wander, fainting with hunger, thirst, and

Singular distress of Garstin and his men.

* M. De Charmilly, though extremely and often justly severe with Mr. Edwards in the errors which crept into his Historical Survey, is, occasionally, rather incorrect himself in his descriptions: an instance of which, it is apprehended, occurs in the affair of Lieut. Garstin, as it also did in a transport which he calls the *King Grey*.

fatigue;

CHAP. III. 1794. fatigue; at the end of two days and a night, during which time two of the number died of want and weariness, having found nothing but the fruit of Indian fig-trees and aloes, they arrived, by a fortunate chance, at the landing place of the Platform, a republican port, which had been destroyed three weeks before by Captain Rowley. Here they found an old abandoned fishing-boat, in which they embarked without provisions, fresh water, or a sail, with very bad oars. They arrived on the morning of the third day at the entrance of the bay of the Mole St. Nicholas, from whence the fishermen brought them into the town.

During this retreat from the enemy in one quarter, they were giving a repulse in another of considerable importance. One of the lieutenants of Rigaud, with 1500 men of different colours, had prepared to attack the important post of L'Acul de Leogane; on the day preceding the intended attack, they were intercepted by 400 men, (only 150 of whom were of the British legion, and the remainder of the militia of Leogane,) under the command of the Baron de Montalembert, who completely routed them, and took a piece of cannon. They charged with fixed bayonets, and upwards of 300 of the enemy lay dead upon the field.

The same success occurred in the attack which was made by the mulatto officer Rigaud, of Aux Cayes, on the fort of Tiburon, the possession of which had cost so dear. His force consisted of of 2000 men, chiefly revolted negroes, with two pieces of cannon, four-pounders. They surrounded the fort about three in the morning, and it was defended with much spirit till a quarter before nine, notwithstanding the great battery being entirely dismounted, and a number of men killed and wounded by the explosion of a quantity of gunpowder, when the besieged (a party of whom, under the command of Jean Kina, had before made a sortie on one side,) quitting the fort, routed the assailants with great slaughter, 170 of their number being left dead on the field. The pleasure of the victory, was damped, when it was found that out of the small number of British that were in the fort, 28 had fallen, besides 100 of the colonial troops. This affair, notwithstanding, was one which conferred equal honor on all the forces, and the Chevalier de Sevré, in his dispatch on the occasion to Colonel Whitlocke, pays a tribute to the small garrison, which so distinguished itself on the occasion.

May.

Still, during these occasional successes, the general spirit of the colony began to droop, on perceiving, that during a period of eight months, not the smallest re-inforcement had arrived from Great Britain, nor was it only in fears, that this despondency and diffidence began to shew themselves, for a parish which, a few months before, had voluntarily adopted the protection of England, (that of Jean Rabell,) compelled the officers of the garrison to deliver up their post to Laveaux; and it was much feared, that many others would follow their example. This defection was less felt, as between four and five

CHAP. III. 1794.

five thousand persons had returned to the plantations from their different asylums.

Reinforced under Brigadier-General Whyte.

At this moment, so temporarily inauspicious, when the British interests seemed devoted to contempt, on the 19th of May, the Belliqueux, the Irresistible, and the Fly sloop, cast anchor in the harbour of Cape St. Nicholas, with the 22d, 23d, and 41st regiments of infantry, under the command of Brigadier-General Whyte. All spirits were now resumed, the despondency which overwhelmed the colony disappeared, and all seemed, as from a general impulse, to expect the reduction of the capital of Port-au-Prince, and a considerable share of wealth from the capture.

These troops were detached by General Sir Charles Grey from Guadaloupe, after the reduction of the French Windward Islands, where they had experienced a severe campaign, and where their services were yet wanted. Great evils were ascribed to the circumstance of withdrawing them—the loss of the island they left, and the occasion of the largest and most expensive armament that ever sailed from England to the West Indies, with other misfortunes.*

Expedition against the capital of the island.

Commodore Ford had, for a considerable time, blockaded the harbour of Port-au-Prince, to the great discouragement of the

* Colonel Chalmers's Remarks on the late War in St. Domingo, p. 21.

commissioners;

CHAP. III. 1794.

commissioners; on the arrival of this re-inforcement, although inferior to what had been hoped, it was considered best that the expectation of the inhabitants should not be disappointed. General Whyte, therefore, having landed his sick at St. Nicholas, received in their place 160 of the garrison, and proceeded to the rendezvous, in the road of Arcahaye, on the 23d of May, to concert the enterprize with the Commodore, and receive such of the colonial troops as were to co-operate. On the 30th they sailed again, and arrived off Port-au-Prince in the evening. Notwithstanding the operations, in a warlike view, may not be of the first importance, it should be mentioned that the squadron comprised four ships of the line, the Europa, the Belliqueux, the Irresistible, and the Sceptre, three frigates, and four or five smaller vessels, the whole under the command of Commodore Ford. The British land-forces, under the orders of General Whyte, consisted of 1,465 rank and file, fit for duty, to whom were added 2,000 colonial troops. It is proper to remark, that at this period the French inhabitants composing the latter corps, likewise chiefly supplied the Mole, St. Marc, Leogane, Jeremie, the camps Des Rivaux and Du Centre, and Tiburon, (on which place an attack was projected, by the mulatto chief Rigaud, from Aux Cayes.)

Expedition against the capital of the island.

The necessary preparations being made, the next morning a flag was sent, demanding the surrender of the town, which, not being admitted, it was determined to cannonade the fortress

 of

CHAP. III. 1794. of Bizotton, which defended the great carriage road leading from Leogane to Port-au-Prince, which protected one part of the Bay, and in which were 500 men, eight pieces of heavy artillery, and two mortars. The fort was dismantled on the side next the sea in the course of the day, (May 31,) by two line of battle ships and a frigate, but on the land side remaining perfect, an assault became necessary. Colonel Spencer, with 300 British, and 500 colonial troops, were accordingly landed in the evening, within a mile of the fort, and night soon approached, accompanied by the horrors of a most tremendous thunder-storm, and deluge of rain. A council of war was held, consisting of the Commander, the Baron de Montalembert, Colonel de Charmilly, and the brave Captain M'Kerras of the engineers; when it was suggested by Colonel de Charmilly, who was best acquainted with the nature of the country, to attack with fixed bayonets, as the torrents from the elements would render the cannon and musquetry in the fort useless, and drown the sound of the approaching assailants. Captain Daniel, of the 41st regiment, led the advanced guard, of only sixty men, and executed the plan with such vigor and judgment, that entering a breach, and bearing down all before them, (except those who begged and obtained mercy,) the fort was carried directly, to the astonishment even of the brave Colonel Spencer. Captain Daniel was severely wounded, and his second in command, Captain Wallace, died on the glacis, as he had lived, full of bravery and honor.

May 31. Fort Bizotton taken.

It

It is a subject of deep regret to the writer, from the nature of this work, not to be able to adorn his pages with the account of numerous actions which, could he have transmitted to posterity, would immortalize many whose names and heroism the various chances of war frequently consign to oblivion. It is sometimes necessary that the historian should select his characters with a view to dramatic effect, yet a place on the roll of fame should not be denied to any; as that is often considered the noblest reward for a life of perseverance and sorrow; and the most honorable incentive to future services of danger and national glory.

The capture of Bizotton determined the fate of Port-au-Prince. The party remained in the fort till joined by the main body of the army from L'Arcahaye, which, one part by land, and the other by sea, made its approach on the side next the rich plain of Cul de Sac. On the 4th of June they arrived within three miles of the town, and, at ten in the morning, the detachment of Colonel Spencer marched to occupy a post on the heights behind the capital. When they had advanced about half way they were met by a mulatto woman, who acquainted them, to their surprize, with its evacuation. Colonel de Charmilly, with fifty of the colonial cavalry, were dispatched to ascertain the fact, which they found as she had stated; and they immediately took possession of the fort of the Gate of Leogane. About half an hour after, a cry was heard from a cellar in a very concealed situation, and upon the door being broke open, a negro was dis-

Capture of Port-au-Prince.

covered,

CHAP. III. 1794. covered, surrounded by barrels of gunpowder. The unhappy wretch had been placed there, according to the opinion of M. de Charmilly, the preceding night, to blow them up at a certain time, but his match being extinguished, his own life, as well as that of those who surrounded him, were thus spared by mere accident.

The fort De L'Hôpital was the next to be taken possession of, which was accomplished in the same manner, but with the appearances of imminent danger they escaped with their lives; for here the commissioners had planned their principal blow to destroy the new masters of the place, which had been defeated by the rain just mentioned. A train of powder was found reaching from the magazine, (where several of the barrels had their bottoms knocked out, and the powder strewed about the floor,) to the thickets behind the fort; the whole, fortunately, was wet, and by precaution every accident was prevented.

Fort Robin, in which were between two and three hundred men, who had refused to fly with the commissioners, readily surrendered to M. de Charmilly. The Baron de Montalembert was sent to take possession of Fort St. Joseph, which commanded the gate of the town leading to the Cul de Sac, and a detachment of troops from Leogane went to the Fort de St. Claire. Thus, in a few hours, the English were in full possession of Port-au-Prince. The commodore, who had entered the road, took possession

possession of Fort de l'Islet, and sent in a British flag, which De Charmilly hoisted at Port Robin, with sensations that are easier to be felt than described. "I considered," says he, "this happy event as a recompense accorded me by Fate for all my labours, and all my troubles in the salvation of St. Domingo." At six o'clock General Whyte arrived. CHAP. III. 1794.

Such was the capture of this important capital, whose character and wealth had tempted every person employed in the intended conquest of the island. Within the compass of its lines were one hundred and thirty one pieces of cannon regularly mounted in batteries. In the harbour were twenty-two vessels laden with sugar, indigo, and coffee, of which thirteen were from three to five hundred tons burthen, besides seven thousand tons of shipping in ballast, in value amounting to 400,000l. A booty much more considerable was conveyed away by the commissioners, who loaded two hundred mules with their riches, and carried away near two thousand persons in their train. Having previously arranged their affairs, and finding the people of colour, (of whose aid, they had only intended to avail themselves temporarily,) possessed of the whole natural strength of the island, under the mulatto Rigaud, and a negro named Toussaint L'Ouverture, they soon after quitted the colony, consigning immense wealth both to America and France, leaving General Laveaux in the character of commander in chief; and returned to France, where they received from the government presiding at that time a sanction of their proceedings. Polverel soon after died, the victim

Return of the French commissioners, Santhonax and Polverel, to France.

4 of

CHAP. III. 1794. of a life of dissipation, but Santhonax lived to pay the colony a triumphal visit.

Much controversy has existed on the idea of some private arrangement having taken place between them and the commodore, with whom several flags of truce passed during the three days in which the detachment from the army was kept inactive. How this was, has never been explained, but from the situation of the road from Port-au-Prince to Jacmel, it is clear, that their retreat might have been interrupted, and, according to some, the fate of the colony determined. Immediately after Port-au-Prince came into the possession of the British, more than three thousand armed inhabitants assembled in the town, ready to undertake any enterprize for the further reduction of the colony. Unfortunately, no use was made of the present advantages, but what they afforded in profit; thus an opportunity was lost, which, as is often the case, never occurred again.

The capture of Port-au-Prince, so much desired, seems to have formed the height of British power in St. Domingo. "From that period the affairs of its possessions," says an old English officer employed on the spot,* "began to decline in proportion, as it were, to the vast accumulation of expence; and

* Colonel Chambers, inspector-general of colonial troops in St. Domingo. "Remarks," p. 41.

CHAP. III. 1794.

all was languor, disease, or peculation!" As soon as the general satisfaction gave way to the necessary considerations for defence, the soldiery were compelled to assist in raising intrenchments on the side of the town next the mountains by day, and to perform military duty at night, thereby suffering the effects, alternately, of the sun and the dew. Many of these men had been six months on ship-board, and the season was unfavorable to them. At this unfortunate juncture, arrived the Experiment frigate, with the remainder of the troops ordered from the Windward Islands, under the command of the Honourable Lieutenant-Colonel Lennox,* consisting of eight flank companies belonging to the 22d, 23d, 25th, and 41st regiments. Now commenced in St. Domingo the ravages of that contagion, which, with a power more terrible than ordinary death itself, has bereft so many families of their hopes, and cut off the flower of a promising army, without the gratification of an honorable conflict.

Commencement of the yellow fever in St. Domingo.

It has been a melancholy object of dispute, whether or not the yellow fever had been generated, or even made its appearance in St. Domingo, previous to the arrival of the Experiment at Port-au-Prince. That sickness, and perhaps fevers incidental to all the colonies, had before been experienced by our troops, is certain, none of whom had gone directly from Europe, and might have been expected to be accustomed to the climate; yet it is to be remembered, that many of them had occasionally been

* Now General Lennox.

kept

CHAP. III. 1794.

kept long in the transports, that they had been sometimes posted on the burning sands of the Mole, and at others seated in marshes, which the colonists themselves could not long endure; and what was little better than either of these, they had opportunities of indulgence, which required more prudence to withstand, than could be expected from soldiers under their circumstances. They had been already harassed by new modes of warfare with the blacks, who, particularly those under Toussaint, a negro general of uncommon ability in the interior, had been trained with singular care. From the sickness arising from the former causes, the colonial troops were entirely free, in consequence of their different habits.

This pestilence is described as having been brought first to Grenada by the Hankey, from Bulam in Africa, where she had staid so long, crowded with passengers who could not be accommodated on shore for some time, as to contract a disease *sui generis*, similar to the jail distemper. The greater part died, and two only of the ship's company arrived at Grenada. The circumstances that follow, are scarcely to be conceived by those who do not know the numerous instances that occur, to prove the necessity of an establishment of a Board of Health in all the British colonies. The clothes and bedding of the deceased victims, were *sold by auction*, distributed among a variety of persons, and the contagion with which they were infected, consequently spread, not only throughout that island, but the other Antilles, and a considerable part of the continent.

It

CHAP. III. 1794.

It is unnecessary to enter into a description of this distressing malady in a medical view, as sufficient accounts of its nature and treatment may be found in the works of several medical writers of the present day.—Forty officers, and six hundred rank and file, fell victims to the fever within two months after the surrender of Port-au-Prince. June.

It is impossible for the best of generals to distinguish, and to avail themselves of every opportunity; but it is unfortunate, that so many troops should have been suffered to collect in the capital, thus increasing the means of disease, when they might have served with utility elsewhere. The same omission can now be perceived on the part of the navy, which suffered the southern coast to be open to communication with Curaçoa and the continent, from whence supplies of stores of all kinds were constantly received by the enemy, unregarded by a single ship. With common precaution even of this kind, the commissioners could not have escaped with the immense wealth with which they loaded themselves from the colony, nor could innumerable privateers have been equipped, which, for, a time, intercepted every vessel in our trade that passed through the Windward passage.

At this period the indefatigable De Charmilly, who was the soul of the British enterprize at St. Domingo, was again commissioned by his drooping countrymen to return to Europe, for the purpose of soliciting additional aid, to complete the business thus far advanced. August.

CHAP. III.

1794. September. Brigadier-General Horneck, commander.

General Whyte resigned the command in St. Domingo, on account of ill health, and was succeeded by Brigadier-General Horneck, a man qualified to ensure success in a situation of difficulty. Only fifty men followed General Horneck from Jamaica, and no reinforcement was received to enable them to make any movement for several months after; he had, therefore, to remain on the defensive for that time, and to preserve the territory already gained, from the defection which was beginning to appear.

The first success which encouraged the revolters, who were chiefly mulattoes, under Rigaud, to farther exertions and attainments, was the seizure of Leogane, where they put to death all the French planters who fell in their way. This was followed in the beginning of September, by a perfidious violation of the neutrality which had been entered into by the men of colour in the town of St. Marc. Lieutenant-Colonel Brisbane, a valuable young officer, who held that rank from the French legion of St. Marc, being a captain in the 49th regiment, had been pursuing, with only eighty British in addition to the colonial troops under his command, the most rapid successes in the neighbourhood, and had induced a large number of the rebels to submit unconditionally. In the pursuit of these successes, the town was left without troops, which afforded an irresistible temptation; they accordingly seized upon it, putting to death, as before, all who fell in their way. The garrison took refuge in a fort on the seashore, from whence they were relieved by the arrival of a fri-

Town of St. Marc taken by men of colour, and regained.

gate from the Mole of Cape St. Nicholas. Colonel Brisbane returned, and, at the expence of all the advantages he had obtained on the plain, regained the town, making upwards of three hundred of the insurgents prisoners. It had the effect, however, of inspiriting the whole of the people of colour, and of exciting them to greater excesses. Rigaud, who commanded in the south, made apparent arrangements for an attack upon the capital, by investing Fort Bizotton with three columns of his troops, consisting of two thousand men. They began their attack at 3 o'clock in the morning of the 5th of December, and were defeated with great slaughter. Captain Grant, who commanded, and Lieutenants Clunes* and Hamilton, though wounded severely in the commencement of the attack, continued at their posts, and earned an honorable fame, of which General Williamson bore a handsome testimony. CHAP. III. 1794.

Not discouraged by this repulse, Rigaud immediately prepared for a more formidable attack in another quarter, the recapture of Tiburon. His intentions were known, but, as in the escape of the commissioners, it again happened, that not a ship could be spared to intercept his armament, then lying off Aux Cayes. It sailed on the 23d of December, consisting of a brig of sixteen guns, and three schooners of fourteen guns each. His military force was composed of three thousand men, of different colours and descriptions, and the attack commenced on Christ-

* Now Lieutenant-Colonel Clunes.

CHAP. III. 1794. mas day. The garrison contained only four hundred and eighty men, the majority of whom were colonists, and the rest British convalescents; it held out four days, till three hundred of that number had fallen. The survivors, with Lieutenant Bradford of the 23d regiment, who commanded under the Chevalier de Sevré, commandant of the district, fought their way, with astonishing bravery, for five miles through the enemy, till they reached Irois. An unfortunate officer, Lieutenant Baskerville, who was from some circumstance left behind, perished by his own hands, as is supposed, to prevent a dishonourable death, or falling into those of the enemy. It is unpleasing to withhold approbation from an act which evinces the most determined bravery, yet it is to be lamented, that he did not find some other means more compatible with the institutes of society, and on which history could dwell with more pleasure.

Tiburon, Leogane, Jean Rabell, La Petite Rivière, and L'Artibonite, were in possession of the people of colour and the negroes; and the latter retaining the whole of the northern province, except the Mole and Fort Dauphin, were increasing in power and independance throughout the colony. The British army, on the contrary, was weakened every day, and the colonists viewed with anxiety and distrust, the delay which took place in the furnishing additional forces. They required them in a body capable of some grand operation, which might complete the conquest of the colony, and suppress the designs of the people of colour; a hope which nothing but

 the

CHAP. III. 1795.

the lingering fondness of these unhappy proprietors for their delightful possessions, could have retained to this period. The entire power having been confided to the British commander, the whole of the French colonists submitted themselves to him, as passive agents; but, from the neglect which they experienced, owing to the ample employment of the British government at home, they were still desirous of resuming some share of authority. There will always be found dissatisfied persons under all circumstances, and dissolute characters ever ready to fall in with their designs, for the sake of the treachery itself. Thus, while Colonel Brisbane, who was admired for his bravery, ability, and personal qualities, was quelling the disturbance of the mulattoes, whom he had particularly favored, and restoring tranquillity to the whites under his protection, a party of the latter were conspiring against his valuable life, which even war and disease had spared. They were, however, detected and their purpose defeated. But a more extensive conspiracy was soon after discovered at Port-au-Prince, where it was intended, by a similar party, to seize the garrison, and put the English to death. Twenty of the conspirators were seized, and tried by a council of war, composed of the principal commanders, among whom were five French field officers; they were found guilty, and adjudged to death. Fifteen of the number were accordingly shot on the 18th of February.

1795. January. Conspiracy against the English at Port-au-Prince discovered.

February.

Shortly after this narrow escape, however, the amiable Colonel Brisbane fell, while out on a reconnoitring party. By his

Death of Colonel Brisbane.

CHAP. III. 1795. his death the British affairs in St. Domingo lost one of the most able, indefatigable, and generous of their advocates. He acquired the affections of every one, and of those who were anxious to deprive him of life he was the decided friend, insomuch, that his constant intercourse with the mulattoes excited a degree of disapprobation in the whites: they, nevertheless, confided in his courage, and were never disappointed. He died universally lamented. March 2.

Death of Colonel Markham.

The commencement of this eventful year was clouded by the death of Lieutenant-Colonel Markham, who, to use the language of the orders issued by General Horneck, "lived universally respected and beloved, and died, leaving a bright example of military, social, and private virtue." He fell in the attack of an out-post, the enemy having again determined on besieging Fort Bizotton. Victory, however, crowned his fall, and his life was revenged upon six hundred of the enemy, who were slain on the spot. Their colours, and five pieces of cannon, were also taken.

April.

About the latter end of April a reinforcement arrived, consisting of the 81st and 96th, and a few of the 82d regiments, which, upon landing, met the fate of so many of their predecessors, and could not but consider their destination as so many graves open for their reception.

In the month of May, 1795, when the colony had become, in the

1795.

Major-General Sir Adam Williamson, K. B. Commander-in-Chief.

the estimation of the British government, a splendid object of enterprize, General Williamson, the governor of Jamaica, to whom it had been ostensibly confided, arrived at Port-au-Prince, having been appointed commander-in-chief of all the British possessions with the honour of the Order of the Bath.

The first exertions of the new commandant were directed to strengthen his position at Port-au-Prince, and to establish and strengthen a cordon from a village called Thomaseau, and from Grande Bois, at the extremity of the Cul de Sac, to Saint Mark, across a ridge of mountains, which divide the plain of L'Arcahaye from that of Artibonite, besides a chain of posts extending from thence to the Cape of Tiburon. For this purpose it became necessary to enlarge the plan, which had already taken place, of embodying corps of negroes; and many slaves were purchased for the purpose from the French planters and others, and placed under the command of officers who had been in the service of the old government, or of planters most likely to ensure their utility by proper attention. Of these, the corps of De Source, De Pyster, De Grass, La Serre, D'Alsun, and Cocherel were the most respectable; but they were, with many other of the arrangements that now took place, extremely expensive, and not always efficient.

August.

In the month of August arrived the 82d regiment, completing the quantum of the reinforcement, (a small part of which was

received

CHAP. III. 1795. received in April). It was nine hundred and eighty men strong on landing, of which number three hundred and fifty only remained alive in six weeks.

With troops thus arriving in divisions, and distressed with disease, where a combined body was required to form a decisive power, little could be done; and General Williamson, already embarrassed by the most difficult circumstances, was but ill prepared for those circumstances so dispiriting as the present; neither did his beneficence and complacency, qualities so amiable in private life, contribute to his assistance on the occasion. He was open to imposition from designing persons, and was led to countenance a system of expence fatal to the British interest; he was shortly succeeded in command by Major-General Forbes.

Major-General Forbes

This spirited and active officer commenced his career by an attentive review of the different posts, and an augmentation of the forces by every means that presented; he strengthened the cordons already established, and secured the frontiers of Mirabalais and Banica, to preserve a communication with Spanish Saint Domingo, for procuring cattle, and other purposes. The garrison of Banica, consisting, as usual, of a few British troops, colonials, and some Spaniards in British pay, he placed under the command of an officer of considerable merit, Sir William Cockburn, who was directed to keep in view the free access to the plain of Cape François, which it commanded.

Towards

Towards the close of this year, in consequence of the intrigues of a negro-general, whose character will form a prominent feature in this history, the Spanish government ceded its interest in a colony, it could no longer hold, to the representatives of the French republic.

CHAP. III. 1795. Spanish St. Domingo ceded to France.

In May, 1796, after a disastrous passage, about 7000 troops, under the command of Brigadier-General Howe, who had sailed from Cork near seven months before, arrived at the Mole of Saint Nicholas, where, as if to complete the destruction the elements had left unfinished, they were obliged to remain some weeks on board the transports. The same number of men, at any former period, would have changed the whole affairs of the colony; but they were too far gone; they, with the troops already at the disposal of General Forbes, (to use the language of an old experienced officer,) "were not such as those commanded by General Wolfe."* Among the effects of this insufficiency may be remembered the following disastrous circumstances.

1796.

The town of Leogane having been left in an unprotected state by the British troops, the republicans immediately enclosed it with a palisaded ditch, and began to strengthen the harbour, which General Forbes conceiving necessary to prevent, determined on attacking the enemy with a considerable force. Ad-

Leogane lost by the English.

* Col. Chalmers's Remarks, p. 44.

CHAP. III. 1796. miral Parker, after disembarking the troops, attacked the fort at the entrance of the creek, but was obliged to abandon it with loss. General Forbes carried no artillery with him, intending, by the advice of his engineer, Major M'Kerras, to take it without regular approaches. A few light pieces of cannon were placed to cover those who filled up the ditch, by which means the besiegers were to cross to the assault. The impolicy, however, of despising an enemy, was soon, as it is always, evinced. The besieged perceiving the contemptible consideration in which they were held, from the church-tower directed a twenty-four pounder against the assailants, with such effect, as enabled them to cross the ditch, and take their cannon, while they were glad in the opportunity afforded, by the weakness of their opponents, to re-embark without further injury.

Bombarde taken and evacuated by the English.

Bombarde, which had been so unsuccessfully attempted to be surprized before, became particularly necessary to the garrison and fleet, at the Mole, for the supply of vegetables, &c. A strong body of troops were sent to attack it, but many of them died on the road from the difficulties of the march, undertaken in the middle of the day. The fort was, however, immediately surrendered by capitulation; and soon after evacuated by its possessors.

Encouraged by these circumstances, Rigaud became confident of his prowess, and attacked Major-General Bowyer at Irois. He

2 was

was repelled, at the expence of near an hundred men killed and wounded; among the latter of whom was the general himself. CHAP. III. 1796.

In short, so languid became the progress of the British arms, that the republicans commenced operations in every quarter round the capital; besides, compelling General Forbes to fortify the mountain called Grenier, and to occupy all the surrounding heights, they employed some months in the erection of batteries, and on the fortification of two posts at St. Laurent and Le Boutilliere, within four miles of Port-au-Prince, without the smallest molestation from the English.

Affairs becoming desperate, with misfortune and expence incurring daily, government determined on sending General Simcoe, to endeavour to recover the British character; and, if experience and skill were all that were wanting, little doubt could have been entertained of success. He arrived at St. Nicholas Mole in the beginning of March 1797, and immediately proceeded through the British possessions to discover the evil, before the application of remedies with which he was well acquainted. But, alas! no ordinary remedies were applicable to the desperate circumstances with which he had to encounter; for, instructed in the science of government, and the relations of empires, by the inconsistency of one power, and improved in the art of war by the impolicy of others, the Blacks had arrived at a degree of per-

1797. March. General Simcoe commander in chief.

 fection,

CHAP. III. 1797.

fection in both, that, notwithstanding the inveteracy of prejudice, compelled itself to be accredited by its effects. An acknowledgment of this fact, incontestibly took place the same month, in which the command of the English army was confided to the wisdom and activity of General Simcoe, by the appointment of Toussaint L'Ouverture, the celebrated negro officer, by the French government, to be general in chief of the armies in St. Domingo.

Toussaint L'Ouverture appointed general in chief by the French.

General Simcoe felt the effect of the powerful situation of his opponent, to whom this nomination was but an honorary sanction of the command he had long possessed. He commenced several economical arrangements, which, even if his cause was hopeless, could not fail to render it a desirable service. He compelled a surrender of all private leases obtained of the vacated property of French absentees, to the public use; and he reformed the colonial corps, from the number 42 to 14, placing on a temporary half-pay, the officers necessarily withdrawn; and rendering more eligible the situation of those, who were the fittest for service: yet, with any other person than General Simcoe, these arrangements must have been of short duration, for Toussaint adopted every mode to harass him, and turn the war in his own favor, by every stratagem that could be devised. He menaced the important frontier post of Mireballais, which had been erected with stone at considerable expence: the commandant immediately evacuated it, and retired to Port-au-Prince, leaving

 the

the rich plain of the Cul de Sac open to the enemy, thereby impeding the communication of the English with Banica and Spanish St. Domingo.

CHAP. III. 1797.

With somewhat of spirit, and better success, the batteries, which had insulted the capital were carried; they required, however, a body of two thousand blacks, besides a reserve of British troops, and some artillery, and cost the life of a brave officer of colour, as he was leading the charge at St. Laurent, Major Pouchet. An attempt to cut off the retreat of Toussaint to Gonave, failed, from a variety of incidents.

While these operations employed the vicinity of the capital, Rigaud was as active in his quarter. With one thousand two hundred men he attacked the post at Irois, and gave the first notice of his approach, by his fire on the fort. The post was composed of a battalion of black troops under Colonel de Grasse, a company of British under Lieutenant Talbot, and twenty black artillery under M. de Brueil. Fortunately, the artillery of Rigaud was interrupted by Captain Rickets of the Magicienne frigate, which caused him to retire precipitately. To increase the eclat of this repulse, another immediately followed, of Toussaint, from the town of St. Marc: it was a repulse, nevertheless, dearly bought.

Rigaud's attempt at Irois defeated.

Wearied with the kind of warfare in which he was thus unavailingly engaged, General Simcoe returned to England in August,

August.

CHAP. III. 1797. gust, to procure a force, sufficient to pursue a career of glory; or to abandon a scene, furnishing at best but negative honors. The same causes which had before operated with respect to this ill-fated colony, yet continued.—The ministry of Great Britain were employed in the complicated affairs of Europe too much, to give more attention to St. Domingo, and General Whyte supplied the place of General Simcoe*, with no additional means of success. Before the end of the same year, this gentleman was superseded by Major General Nesbit, who did not live to arrive at a command of which he would have had no occasion to boast †. His place was supplied by his second in command, the Honourable Brigadier-General Maitland, to whom little remained, but to perform the humiliations of his country, with the grace which that country demanded, and which no one could have better executed, in all that appertained to the gentleman. He arrived in April, 1798, at Port-au-Prince, and commenced strenuously an attention to circumstances, with which he was well acquainted, from his service under General Simcoe, by whom he had been appointed to several difficult commands.

Major-General Whyte commander in chief.

General Maitland commander in chief.

1798. April.

* The writer cannot omit in this place paying his tribute of respect to this excellent and gallant officer. If all the abilities of the general, the suavity of the gentleman, and the vigorous powers of a manly understanding may be expected to unite in one person, it is in Lieutenant-General Simcoe. When commanding the Queen's Rangers, in the American war, he distinguished himself on every occasion, and in a variety of important battles crowned himself and his corps with the highest military glory.

† By the death of General Nesbit, (whose memory deserves his grateful recollection) the writer lost a very sincere friend in many respects, though he cannot regret the appointment of his Brigade-Major, with which he was to have been honoured by him on this expedition.

By

By the orders of General Nesbit, the British property in St. Domingo ceased to be valued at more than the annual sum of 300,000 l., which General Maitland soon found inadequate to the purpose of their maintenance, as the colonial revenues had decreased to 100,000 l. The evacuation of the capital and its dependencies, was therefore the first step that occupied his attention, and his arrangements were as honorable to his sensibility, as the proudest victory could have been to his courage. —After every consideration for their peculiar circumstances, he effected a truce for a month, and stipulated for the protection in person and property of all the adherents of Great Britain. He then withdrew with the remainder of his force to Jeremie, which he had formerly commanded. CHAP. III. 1798. May.

With his concentrated force at this point, he acquiesced in the wishes of Admiral Parker, to reduce Tiburon, for the purpose of its retention, with the Mole, the object so much desired for the security of the Windward passage: but the tide was now turned, the troops could not disembark for tempestuous weather, and other causes; and even the brave De Source, who marched across the peninsula to meet him, lingered on his way. August.

The Mole at length only remained, to which General Maitland retired, for the purpose of his last negotiation with the triumphant black General, Toussaint. The possessions of the English were here given up, as well as their colonial black troops, and some commercial stipulations being entered into, which recognized The English possessions surrendered.

CHAP. III. 1798. cognized the island as a neutral power, England resigned all her pretensions to St. Domingo for ever!

Such was the end of this disastrous enterprize, which had for five years fed the hopes and vanity of the British empire, to which had been latterly sacrificed many valuable lives, and an extravagant portion of the public money. That it was undertaken with too little consideration, must be always acknowledged: for, if the British ministry only meant, by finding employment for the French commissioners in St. Domingo, to prevent the seat of war from being carried to Jamaica, they might have effected this purpose, without entering upon so large a field, or sacrificing the lives and interests of a number of brave and unfortunate colonists; and if the conquest of the island was sincerely intended, the means furnished were contemptible, in comparison even with the exertions of the inhabitants. It is, however, probable, that no force which could have been furnished, would have been sufficient to cope with the power of the revolted negroes, and if the British colonies in the Antilles have been saved by these means, it is only to be lamented that their salvation cost so dear, in proportion to their advantages to the country.

Having recounted the progress and termination of the British affairs, it is necessary to recur to the circumstances of those who were left in sole and uninterrupted power in St. Domingo. It will be recollected, that the first consequence of the appearance of the English,

English, was the entire abolition of negro slavery by the French commissioners, who therefore recognized all who enlisted under their standard, as free citizens, and perfected them in the knowledge of arms: likewise, that immediately after the first onset of the insurrection in the plain of the Cape, the negro, Jean François, who was then principal in command, had evinced a foresight which exhibited the determined intentions of his followers, in employing the time of those who were unoccupied, with the women and children, in the cares of agriculture, for their future preservation. To this general was soon added several others, not inferior in ability, of whom the most conspicuous were Biassou, Boukmant, and Toussaint; but, although the last of those who declared himself, the latter soon eclipsed all the others by his conduct in a regular warfare. While Spain yet ranked among the coalesced powers who avowed the restoration of royalty in France, the first and last of the black chiefs had arrived at such consideration from their acknowledged merit, as to be presented (perhaps as an inducement to declare on the side of royalty, to which they appeared to lean, as the enemies of the commissioners, whose invitation they had not accepted) with the rank of general in the Spanish army, and the ancient military order of that country.

The departure of the French commissioners in 1794, and the conclusion of peace between France and Spain, which ceded its territory to the republic, a year after, had placed Toussaint in almost absolute power: (for his colleague preferred retiring on

his

CHAP. III. 1798. his rank to Cadiz); the brave, but cruel Rigaud, afterwards fled from the island; and every occurrence had contributed to his aggrandizement; till the whole was sanctioned, in 1797, by the executive power of the French government in their commission as the general in chief of the armies, and of the whole island of St. Domingo. This consequence was now enlarged in his acknowledgment as a neutral power by the most important of all his enemies.

Such was briefly the progress of Toussaint, which was marked by many circumstances that reflected the highest credit on his character, and gave dignity to his dominion. He had throughout been the moderator of all the different factions in the island, and was every way fitted for its legislator, as well as its chief. He was, indeed, one of those characters who invite the principle of an elective monarchy, but which are too rarely found to advise its universal adoption. His character will be more fully given in the ensuing part of this work; it is at present sufficient to say, that, although he detested the conduct of the French commissioners, he protected their office from indignity, and shielded them from vengeance; he relieved the planters from the intolerable tyranny of the commissioners; he saved the French army from punishment too often not greater than their guilt; and would not permit the increased cruelty of retaliation on the British forces, for the conduct of allies, which even the colonists regretted to adopt. He saved the life of General Laveaux, who acknowledged the fact with gratitude;

and his intercourse with general Maitland was of the noblest kind. Notwithstanding these exertions, in which he had to combat with the natural prejudices of many of his followers, he preserved their confidence in his integrity, and their obedience to his wishes, and was hailed, with great justice, by common consent, as the perfector of *the independence of St. Domingo.* CHAP. III. 1798.

CHAP. IV.

State of Manners on the Establishment of Independence, &c. in St. Domingo, with a Memoir of the Circumstances of the Author's Visit to the Island.

CHAP. IV.

THE white population of St. Domingo, now still farther decreased by the emigrations which followed the evacuation of the English, presented but a dismal semblance of the flourishing French colony: added to which, many of the whites who were encouraged to remain, now spread through the eastern districts with a spirit of wild speculation, and became more solitary, when they might have been expected to associate with stronger ties than ever. Of the Spaniards, widely scattered in their most tranquil state, many had emigrated, but more had been sent from the island, on the surrender of the Spanish territory to Toussaint. Although the defection of the whites was striking in the towns where they had been most numerous, that of the blacks was increased in a proportion so large, as to astonish those who had witnessed their losses, and the decrease

CHAP. IV.

State of Manners on the Establishment of Independence, &c. in St. Domingo, with a Memoir of the Circumstances of the Author's Visit to the Island.

CHAP. IV. 1799. State of population. Manners, &c.

THE white population of St. Domingo, now still farther decreased by the emigrations which followed the evacuation of the English, presented but a dismal semblance of the flourishing French colony; added to which, many of the whites who were encouraged to remain, now spread through the eastern districts with a spirit of wild speculation, and became more solitary, when they might have been expected to associate with stronger ties than ever. Of the Spaniards, widely scattered, in their most tranquil state, many had emigrated, but more had been sent from the island, on the surrender of the Spanish territory to Toussaint. Although the defection of the whites was striking in the towns where they had been most numerous, that of the blacks was increased in a proportion so large, as to astonish those who had witnessed their losses, and the decrease

CHAP. III. 1799. Black republic. Manners, &c.

which was remarked after the first insurrections of the negroes. This is accounted for in a satisfactory manner, by the greater degree of comforts experienced by the females, and the decrease of general labor.* Although, for some time, the change of government appeared to tinge with a melancholy hue, the parts of the island formerly in the possession of the English, yet the rude happiness of those who had now become its possessors, soon suppressed every other effect; and, notwithstanding the despotic rule of martial law, circumstances in general began to wear a promising appearance.

At this period the narrator of their history became possessed of an opportunity of judging of the state and power of the people, who form the subject of his present disquisition; and his personal observations during his detention among them, will supply the information submitted in the present chapter.

A violent hurricane having dismasted the little bark,† in which he was proceeding from Jamaica to join his regiment at Martinique, (having been before accommodated in the cabin of his friend, Admiral Smith,‡ as far as the Mole St. Nicholas,) it was driven under the walls of Cape François, and in that state compelled to wait the relief of the brigands, an appellation which

* Malouet, Memoires sur les Colonies.

† The Maria, Danish schooner, commanded by James Frazer.

‡ The liberal reception which the military always met with on board the Hanibal, is too well known to require any compliment on the present occasion.

the

Black republic. Manners, &c.

the superior policy that already appeared in this extraordinary republic, had not yet obliterated from its members. To avoid the suspicion in which, notwithstanding the recent treaty, the English yet continued to be viewed, and to prevent the probability of injury to his companions, the writer was induced to assume the character of an American, which was easy to be effected, as the vessel was ultimately bound to that continent. The crew were erm tted to land after certain ceremonies, and the first object which excited their attention, was no less than the hero of this novel empire. Toussaint was conversing with two privates of his forces on the batteries, and when he saw the Europeans approaching, immediately walked towards them, and, addressing them in French, inquired the news, from whence they came, and their destination. One served as respondent for the whole, who spoke in such terms as his character demanded, and the General civilly took his leave.

The number of Americans at this port could not fail to attract particular notice, and every attention seemed to be paid to the accommodation of their commerce, and a striking degree of interest in every occurrence that concerned them. Even the women seemed to renew a fondness long repressed for the whites, in favor of the meanest of the American sailors. The present writer, however, requiring some rest after his recent voyage, hastened, on receiving his directions to the purpose, to the Hotel de la Republique, the principal house, usually resorted to by Americans, an edifice of rather elegant appearance; and on his way,

except

CHAP. IV. 1799. Black republic. Manners, &c.

except the preponderancy of the black complexion, perceived but little difference from an European city. On entering the house, however, he immediately perceived that the usual subordinations of society were entirely disregarded, and that he was to witness, for the first time, a real system of equality.

Here were officers and privates, the colonel and the drummer, at the same table indiscriminately; and the writer had been scarcely seated at a repast in the first room to which he was conducted, when a fat negro, to initiate him in the general system, helped himself frequently from his dish, and took occasion to season his character by large draughts of the wine, accompanied with the address of "Mon Americain." The appearance of the house, and its accommodations, were not much inferior to a London coffee-house, and on particular occasions exhibited a superior degree of elegance. Toussaint not unfrequently dined here himself, but he did not sit at the head of the table, from the idea, (as was asserted,) that the hours of refection and relaxation should not be damped by the affected forms of the old regimen, and that no man should assume a real superiority in any other place than the field. He was in the evenings at the billiard-table, where the writer conversed and played with him several times; and he could not help, on some occasions, when a want of etiquette disturbed him for a moment, congratulating himself, that if he experienced not the refinement of European intercourse, he saw no room for insincerity: and that if delicate

CHAP. IV. 1799. Black republic. Manners, &c.

delicate converse did not always present itself, he was free from the affectation of sentiment.

In traversing the once superb city of the Cape, though presenting a tolerable appearance from the shore, desolation every where presented itself. On the site where elegant luxury had exhausted its powers to delight the voluptuary, all was magnificent ruin! and to mark the contrast stronger, of the wrecks were composed temporary houses for the American merchants, and petty shops inhabited by the natives. Several spacious streets towards the centre, displayed the walls of superb edifices of five and six stories, with gilded balconies, of which the beautiful structure exhibited the devastation that had occurred, with additional horror. Nor was this all, for in different parts of these ruins the sad remains of the former possessors were visibly mingled with the crumbling walls:

> "There—heedless of the dead,
> The shelter-seeking peasant rears his shed,
> And wonders man could want the larger pile."

Having been informed of a review which was to take place on the plain of the Cape, the writer availed himself of the opportunity, accompanied by some Americans, and a few of his own countrymen who resided there under that denomination. Of the grandeur of the scene he had not the smallest conception. Two thousand officers were in the field, carrying arms, from the general to the ensign, yet with the utmost attention to rank;

 without

CHAP. IV. 1799. Black republic. Manners, &c.

without the smallest symptom of the insubordination that existed in the leisure of the hotel. Each general officer had a demi-brigade, which went through the manual exercise with a degree of expertness seldom witnessed, and performed equally well several manœuvres applicable to their method of fighting. At a whistle a whole brigade ran three or four hundred yards, then separating, threw themselves flat on the ground, changing to their backs or sides, keeping up a strong fire the whole of the time, till they were recalled; they then formed again, in an instant, into their wonted regularity. This single manœuvre was executed with such facility and precision, as totally to prevent cavalry from charging them in bushy and hilly countries. Such complete subordination, such promptitude and dexterity, prevailed the whole time, as would have astonished any European soldier who had the smallest idea of their previous situation.

The pleasing sensations inspired by the ability manifested in this review, were checked by the additional monuments of human ferocity which presented themselves on his return to the city; the conflagration of which, and of the surrounding plantations, was still in the memory of several Americans, who described the effect, as awfully grand beyond conception.

In one of the squares in the north-west quarter was placed an edifice that made some amends for the desolation appearing in its vicinity, from the elegance of its execution. It was an ascent to a canopy, or dome, of which the architecture was not perfectly

View of a [illegible]

CHAP. IV. The Black republic. Message. Sun.

M Rainsford del.

View o ... ile erected t ... the Blacks to commemorate their Emanc

CHAP. IX.
1799.
Black republic.
Slanders, &c.

perfectly regular, beneath which are two seats, and above them an inscription that eminently exhibited the tolerance of Toussaint. There were two centinels to guard it, who, being asked if any one might ascend the steps, answered in the affirmative, but with a strict prohibition against touching the cap of liberty which crowned it. It was a tribute of respect to the memory of Santhonax and Polverel, the French commissioners, and had been erected by some of their advocates at a time when their largesses obtained for them what they would not otherwise have enjoyed, a transitory popularity. An extract from a speech of one of them formed part of the inscription, in French, and which countenanced the opinion, that the abolition of slavery was a primary object of their mission. It was to the following effect:

My Friends,

We came to make you free.

Frenchmen give Liberty to

You are free.

Guard your Freedom.

Vive la Liberté. Vive la République.

Vive Robespierre.

remainder of the inscription consisted of a selection from clamation for abolishing slavery. The prevailing opinion of these men, notwithstanding they had been executed for their conduct, was favorable to their talents, and to their spirit.

Though impressed with the necessity of caution, it would have required much more sangfroid than was possessed by the

perfectly regular, beneath which were two seats, and above them an inscription, that eminently exhibited the tolerance of Toussaint. There were two centinels to guard it, who, being asked if any one might ascend the steps, answered in the affirmative, but with a strict prohibition against touching the cap of liberty, which crowned it. It was a tribute of respect to the memory of Santhonax and Polverel, the French commissioners, and had been erected by some of their advocates at a time when their largesses obtained for them what they would not otherwise have enjoyed, a transitory popularity. An extract from a speech of one of them formed part of the inscription, in French, and which countenanced the opinion, that the abolition of slavery was a primary object of their mission. It was to the following effect:

CHAP. IV. 1799. Black republic. Manners, &c.

"My Friends,
We came to make you free.
Frenchmen give Liberty to the World.
You are free.
Guard your Freedom.
Vive la Liberté. Vive la Republique.
Vive Robespierre.

The remainder of the inscription consisted of a selection from the proclamation for abolishing slavery. The prevailing opinion of these men, notwithstanding they had been execrated for their conduct, was favorable to their talents, and to their spirit.

Though impressed with the necessity of caution, it would have required much more *sang-froid* than was possessed by the observer,

CHAP. IV. 1799. Black republic. Manners, &c.

server, to resist the numerous impulses of mingling with a people whose conduct presented the most generous hospitality, and objects of the most interesting contemplation. He obtained access to the houses of most whose intercourse could furnish either information or pleasure; nor did he reject the negro hut at other times, though certainly of less attraction.

As in all states of human society, particularly in the vortex of a revolution, which effected so complete a change, the able and the cunning had elevated themselves above those who were of the same rank of life. Negroes, recollected in the lowest state of slavery, including Africans, filled situations of trust and responsibility; they were, likewise, in many instances, occupied by those who had been in superior circumstances under the old regimen, free negroes, and mulattoes.

X

The superior order had attained a sumptuousness of life, with all the enjoyments which dignity could obtain, or rank confer.—The interior of their houses was, in many instances, furnished with a luxe beyond that of the most voluptuous European, while no want of trans-atlantic elegance appeared; nor, amidst a general fondness for shew, was the chasteness of true taste always neglected. Their etiquette extended to a degree of refinement scarcely to be conceived; and the service of their domestics, among whom were, from what cause was not ascertained, some mulattoes, was performed with more celerity than in many instances in Europe. A conscious ease, and certain *gaieté du*

 cœur,

Black republic. Manners, &c.

cœur," presided over every repast. Conversation had free scope, except as related to their own former circumstances, but when the defence of their country was the subject, every eye filled with fire, and every tongue shouted—Victory! The names of some, who had seceded from the black army were, the only objects that seemed to excite detestation. In many instances the writer has heard reasoning, and witnessed manners of acuteness and elegance, the relation of which would appear incredible, from those who were remembered in a state of servitude, or whose parents were in situations of abject penury; while sallies of wit, not frequently surpassed, have enlivened many an hour. It would ill become him, notwithstanding the tide of prejudice, which has always pervaded his assertions, to suppose his readers capable of gratification from the chit-chat of a St. Domingo table; and it would be equally unjust to employ the opportunities afforded him by unguarded kindness, in the accumulation of fleeting anecdotes, arising from domestic privacy; he therefore contents himself with stating, that the enjoyments of life were to be found in a high degree in the capital of St. Domingo, and that their alloy did not exceed, nor perhaps always equal, that of ancient European cities.

The men were in general sensible and polite, often dignified and impressive; the women frequently elegant and engaging. The intercourse of the sexes was on the most rational footing, and the different degrees of colour which remained, had lost most

CHAP. IV.
1799.
Black republic.
Manners, &c.

most of that natural hostility which formerly existed. Several Americans had intermarried with ladies of colour very advantageously, and to appearance happily. They were, generally, very agreeable women, and felt no inequality in their difference of complexion or nation. Like Sappho, they could plead, (in many instances, in point of wit, sprightliness, and pathos, little inferior to the Lesbian muse, though without her powers of song)

> "Brown though I am, an Ethiopian dame
> Inspir'd young Perseus with a generous flame;
> Turtles and doves of different hues unite,
> And glossy black is pair'd with shining white."

The drama, that source of rational delight, always so prevalent in St. Domingo, existed, in more strength and propriety than it had done before; and that licentiousness which appears inseparable to it in a higher state, was actually restrained. The representations were chiefly comedies *en vaudeville*, and a sort of pantomime;—sometimes serious representations, allusive to local circumstances, and sometimes merely humourous burlesques.—The conduct of the whole was highly creditable to the talents of the performers, some of whom yet remained from the French school, who, although driven to seek a livelihood under such doubtful auspices, might have shone with equal lustre to their more fortunate contemporaries on an European stage. The black performers, who preponderated in number, were not behind in talents; the writer saw a play of Moliere's performed

CHAP. IV. 1799. Black republic. Manners, &c.

with an accuracy that would not have disgraced the first theatre in Europe.—Even painting, from some recent specimens, appeared to be encouraged, and cultivated as an accomplishment, in a slight degree. A young lady of colour, of the name of La Roche, presented a large company, of which the writer was one, in the course of a few minutes, with their likenesses, very accurately cut in profile.—Music, also, though it must be confessed, not such as to vie with the harmony of the spheres, was every where prevalent to an excess, and the practice of most kinds in use, though stringed instruments were preferred.—Yet, with an ardent sensibility that appeared in many instances, and which could not fail to be cultivated under present circumstances, the rich blacks suffered the greater part of the capital to lie in ruins; they appeared to shrink from re-instating it, as if in rebuilding their former residences, they should create new masters.

The situation of those who still remained in humble privacy, and who formed the great bulk of the people, was indeed very greatly changed. Their condition, agreeably to their capacities of enjoyment, approached nearer happiness than many others which are considered its ultimatum. Crimes were by no means frequent, and those rather attributable to accident than vice. They were perfectly at liberty as regarded themselves, and were more ready to perform their social duties, than the state was urgent in requiring them. Those qualities conspicuous in the negroes, under their worst circumstances, their regard for all the relations of life, and tendernesses to each other, seemed expanded with

CHAP. IV. 1799. Black republic. Manners, &c.

with their freedom, and many of the little prejudices that had existed wore away. Those amusements, which were formerly suppressed, had now free scope, but they restrained themselves from public annoyance with more regularity than could have been effected by the strictest police.

The *menage* of the labourer in the town and its vicinity, was improved in a proportion equal to his condition. A rough, yet neat couch, supplied the place of the wretched bedding of a former period, and the visitor was not unprovided for, though it is lamentable to state, that in several instances the furniture of the cottage was beholden to the public commotions, and in one instance, painfully risible, a beautiful fire-screen, the dextrous workmanship of some fair sufferer, concealed a dog then roasting from some of their fellows, who considered it opprobrious to be *mangeurs des chiens.**

In one instance, the writer was introduced by a brigand † of peculiar intelligence, (with whom he had frequent conferences on

* Let it not excite wonder that the blacks, deriving their origin from some peculiar parts of Africa, are remarkably fond of the flesh of this animal, (of which an account may be seen at large, I believe, in *Du Tertre*,) for it has been often found an excellent substitute for other food at sea, and has been used with success by convalescents. See *Cook's Voyages*. I quote the incident from memory.

† In the recollection of my stay at Cape François, I use the term *negro* and *brigand*, (both derogatory of the ruling power of St. Domingo,) not as by any means appropriate to the people they describe at present, but as the means of distinguishing them to the European, who cannot so easily assimilate himself with their present condition.

the

CHAP. IV. 1799. Black republic. Manners, &c.

the military tactics of the black army) to the cottage of a black laborer, of whom an account may not be uninteresting. He had a family of thirteen children; eight of them by one woman, and the remainder by two others; the former only lived with him in the same cottage, with his mother, who was aged and infirm; the other two, separately, at a small distance. This man was an epitome of legislature, and his family a well regulated kingdom in miniature. His cottage consisted of three irregular apartments, the first of which was his refectory, where, as often as possible, and always on *jours de fêtes*, his subjects assembled, including on those occasions his three wives. The furniture of this apartment was entirely of his own making, even to the smallest utensil, and with an ingenuity beyond what might be expected from perfect leisure; notwithstanding the artificer, during the process, had been obliged to attend his labor in the fields, and was a considerable time in arms. On a neat shelf, appropriated peculiarly to their use, lay a mass book, and a mutilated volume of Volney's Travels, some parts of which he understood more than his visitor. Every thing convenience required was to be found on a small scale, and the whole so compact, and clean, with such an air of *properté* throughout as was absolutely attractive. His own bed-room was furnished with an improved bedstead, supported by trussels, with a mattress and bedding of equal quality with the other furniture, but that of his children and mother surpassed the whole. One bedstead contained them, yet separated the male from the female,

 the

CHAP. IV. 1799. Black republic. Manners, &c.

the young from the aged, and was separated or combined in an instant.*—The third was his kitchen and store-house, and might also be called his laboratory, for conveniences were found for chemical experiments, though not of the most scientific kind; but every utensil for culinary purposes were provided in the best manner. The wife of this laborer (for he had submitted to the ceremony of marriage with the female who had borne him the most children, as is the general custom with them) was nearly as ingenious as himself, and equally intelligent. The mode he pursued in the regulation of his domestic economy was excellent; as continence is not a virtue of the blacks, the increase of his family was not confined to his own house; yet, even in his amours he was just; and as the two mothers before-mentioned were less protected than his ostensible wife, the primary object of his consideration was to have the whole of his children under his own care. This was reconciled to all parties from the first, in so mild a way, that no distinction was perceivable but in age, while the mothers held a relationship to their domiciliated offspring similar to that of an aunt or cousin, each exerting herself for the purpose of adding to the comforts of her own child.—On festive occasions, the two mothers sat alternately on the right or left of the mistress of the house, with as much étiquette as might be perceived in a more elevated station, and

* It is a matter of regret to the author, that the plan of this singular bedstead, which might have been adapted to the European cottage with many advantages, was lost.

with

with the utmost harmony. The master of the family was absolute, but with him it was in theory, not in practice, for all seemed to vie in forbearance. As soon as the children could contribute their little powers to labor, they were employed; the younger (except as regarded their strength) being subject to the inferior offices; and, singular as it may appear, on the festive occasions alluded to, they waited upon their seniors, though but by a few years, and seemed delighted in the office. Agreeable to this rule, in accordance with that reverence for age so remarkable among blacks of every condition, the grandmother received the affection and attention of all; and though often crabbed, infirm, and discontented, no one seemed to consider her failings as such, but as a duty prescribed them to bear.

CHAP. IV. 1799. Black republic. Manners, &c.

In fact, the writer considered this numerous family, as he beheld them at their frugal meal a model for domestic life, with a proof that those jarring interests, which, in the smallest connection, as well as in the largest states, creating more embarrassment than the most adverse circumstances, or the greatest crimes, may be avoided by a generous conduct, and reciprocal kindness. He need scarcely add, happy was his humble friend, or that each individual of his family, in their separate capacities, laid up a store of happiness for themselves, and those around them.

From what could be perceived (quitting the confines of the town,) the productive system of the earth seemed to be founded

 on

CHAP. IV. 1799. Black republic. Manners, &c.

on original principles.—Every individual employed a portion of his time in labor, and received an allotted part of the produce for his reward, while all took the field, from a sense of duty to themselves. A perfect combination appeared in their conduct, and every action came directly from the heart. More than sixty thousand men were frequently exercised together on the plain of the Cape, in excellent discipline, whose united determination against an invading enemy, would be victory or death. Little coercion was necessary, and punishment was chiefly inflicted by a sense of shame produced by slight confinement, or the like. Labor was so much abridged, that no want of leisure was felt; it would be a great gratification to the feeling heart, to see the peasant in other countries with a regulated toil similar to that of the laborer in St. Domingo.

Such is a general sketch of the state of society, as it appeared in the capital of St. Domingo, which spread internally as far as its effects could be expected to reach.—There was no possibility of acquiring correct accounts of the plans of government, which had been submitted to Toussaint, much less of the forms he was disposed to adopt. A regular municipal establishment existed, and martial government, dispensed every where in all its vigour, rendered civil jurisdiction of little avail.

The writer observed, with pleasure, the delay in repairing the vessel, which afforded him an opportunity of examining objects

4 which

CHAP. IV. 1799. Black republic. Manners, &c.

which might never return. For several weeks he continued to amuse himself with observations on the manners of the people, which he had no idea at that time of preserving beyond the information and amusement of his own friends, and by sketching draughts of the principal posts that were accessible. He enjoyed the habits of a metropolis, and, except the anxiety which would obtrude on account of the delay from his duty, participated in the general happiness.

When the time arrived for the departure of the vessel, at an unexpected moment; such is the human heart, he lingered on a spot which he would have before avoided at the hazard of his life. The ship had been repaired—all was ready—and bidding farewel to new connections which had just began to engage him, he returned on board with the agreeable hopes of a speedy arrival at St. Thomas's: but—

"Heaven from all creatures hides the book of fate!"

After beating about upon the coast for three days, in the most perilous circumstances, the unfortunate vessel sprung a leak, when they were compelled to put into Fort Dauphin, or, according to the revolutionary nomenclature, Fort Egalité.

In this situation the master of the vessel and the writer apprehended no danger or impropriety in going on shore. Hoisting therefore Danish colours, they came to anchor under a small fort, when in less than half an hour the latter was arrested after landing by

CHAP. III. 1799. Black republic. Manners, &c.

by four blacks, and a mulatto officer of great ferocity. They returned with him on board, and placed him under the care of two black centinels. These informed him, in answer to his anxious inquiries, that he was suspected of being a spy, that he would be tried on the morrow, and of course be condemned. Such was the complacent idea attached to the trial of a stranger, who was afterwards to defend the character of their chief.

Apprehensions of different kinds now crowded his imagination: he did not know whether suspicions might not have occurred at Cape François; and the commandant of the district have been prepared for his arrival. He was aware, that, in a few instances, he had ventured farther than he should have done. He had also been allowed access to many of the principal people, and he knew not what might have taken place after his departure. He was, however, left unmolested, and, except his freedom, without any other deprivation; a circumstance of the most fortunate kind, as it afforded him an opportunity of destroying his baggage and papers, including a variety of documents, which must have been dangerous in the highest degree.* These he disposed of, by putting them out of the cabin-window in the middle of the night, with a weight attached

* Besides his military appointments, they included correct views of Fort Piccolet and other works, and several plans, which he hoped to have had the honour of presenting to the Duke of York; his Royal Highness having condescended to regard, with attention, other attempts which he had the honour of presenting to him.

sufficient

sufficient to sink them. Having succeeded in this affair, and the proceedings of the ensuing day continuing to occupy his attention, his situation became most unpleasant. The silence of the night, interrupted by the murmurs of the ocean, the clamours of the guard, and the distant sounds from the shore, produced the strongest melancholy; while confused surmises of the determination of the morrow, and a contemplation of the shame, rather than the terror of an ignominious death, revolving in his mind, deprived him of the possibility of rest, and totally unfitted him for the slightest preparation.

CHAP. III. 1799. Black republic. Manners, &c.

Early in the morning he was taken on shore, and examined by a black general, named Muro, the commanding officer of the district. He could not help thinking that his appearance augured well, for he bore the principal mythological characteristic of Justice. He was totally blind of one eye, and appeared to see but little through the other. He, however, relieved the prisoner from the apprehension of any charge existing previous to the moment; for he began his examination by insisting, that he was not an American, but an English spy, reconnoitering the coast; and closed it by acquainting him, that a court-martial, already summoned, would assemble on the morrow, and his trial would be prompt and decisive. He was then conducted to a dark prison, (which wanted none of the usual concomitants of such a place,) and treated with the utmost indignity. There was no bed; nor had he any other provision than some coarse, dry fish, which he could not eat—a treatment he was afterwards in-

CHAP. III. 1799. Black republic. Manners, &c.

formed was used to prisoners during the space between apprehension and trial, to prevent any opportunity for the contrivance of evasion. At the hour of ten he was brought before a regular military court, composed of twelve black general officers, the etiquette of which astonished him. General Christophé, a relative of Toussaint, being in a neighbouring district, presided, and Muro sat on his right-hand. They interrogated him with the utmost discrimination and acuteness, appearing perfectly conversant with the nature of the business. But, for the commandant already named, 'not a look nor an attitude escaped him—and he darted his eye, in which both seemed to have centered an uncommon degree of fire, over every part of the prisoner, the form of whose very head-dress, he insisted, was not *en Americain!*

He was put on his defence in equal form, but all he could urge had not the smallest effect, as he had no passports nor any American papers to exhibit. Notwithstanding every appearance to the contrary, they had had some decisive testimony of imprudent liberty on the island; and, after several hours deliberation, he was condemned to suffer death as quick as possible. The master of the vessel behaved with dignity of character, and the utmost solicitude. He protested against the judgment, but without effect; and the prisoner was remanded till the sentence should be transmitted to the General-en-Chef, for his approval.

He

CHAP. III.

formed was used to prisoners during the space between apprehension and trial, to prevent any opportunity for the continuance of evasion. At the hour of ten he was brought before a regular military court, composed of twelve black general officers, the etiquette of which astonished him. General Christophe, a relative of Toussaint, being in a neighbouring district, presided, and Muro sat on his right-hand. They interrogated him with the utmost discrimination and acuteness, appearing perfectly conversant with the nature of the business. But, for the commandant already named, not a look nor an attitude escaped him—and he darted his eye, in which both seemed to have [illegible] an uncommon degree of fire, over every part of the prisoner, the form of whose very head-dress, he insisted, was not [illegible].

He was put on his defence in equal form, but all he could urge [illegible] the smallest effect, as he had no passports nor any American papers to exhibit. Notwithstanding every appearance to the contrary, they had had some decisive [illegible] of imprudent [illegible] on the island; and, after several hours deliberation, he was [illegible] to suffer death as quick as possible. The master of the [illegible] [illegible] with dignity of character, and the [illegible]. He protested against the [illegible], but [illegible]; and the prisoner was [illegible] till the [illegible] should be transmitted to the General-in-Chief for his approval.

M. Rainsford del. J. Barlow sculp.

CHAP. IV. 1799. Black republic. Manners, &c.

He was then remanded to a different kind of prison, which, though little superior in point of accommodation, had the advantage of air, and the communication of the human species, though only by stealth. It was the remains of a dilapidated building, the part of which appropriated to the prisoner, was secured with strong iron-bars, in a fashion then very prevalent: he had also the incumbrance of a chain from the right arm to the left foot. For fourteen days he lay in the agony of suspense between life and death, with every evening the cruel intimation, that he would certainly be hanged on the next morning.

Even in this situation he could not resist the opportunity which his prison, or rather cage, afforded him, of observing the surrounding scene, which was more delightful than even fancy could picture. It was situated in the midst of a rich valley, through which a stream from the neighbouring hill meandered in romantic form. A church was nearly hid in the vale, and the rising ground was fortified in every direction. Over the whole the most exquisite foliage exhibited its charming fruits, with all the richness of a tropic region. Beneath the spreading cocoa, and the taller yam, he was nightly amused with the cheerful dance, the negroes assembling when they quitted labour, without any seeming appointment, but as a natural habit; sometimes they had, on *jours de fetes*, or holidays, a particular entertainment of activity, the principal part of which was the Calenda, or "dance of love." On these occasions they were dressed with peculiar care: those who had been recently employed in arms retaining some part of

 their

CHAP. IV. 1799. Black republic. Manners, &c.

their uniform, and the females bedecked with various jewels: they had also a refection. The animation displayed by both sexes in the dance was astonishing, which consisting entirely of amatory history, was equal to many ballets which are performed on the French or Italian stage, while the dancers might have been called, without any dereliction from the Cytherean goddess, though not exactly comporting with her in complexion,

——— "fair Venus' train."

The *hauteur* with which they passed the prison of "the white man taken" was astonishing; yet some seemed willing to pity and relieve, but it arose rather from ostentation than mercy. One circumstance, however, occurred that remains deeply impressed in his bosom, and relieves his mind while recording it, which would have done honor to the most dignified of a different complexion.

After lying two nights on a couch, formed of dried sugar-canes, with a very slender supply of food, the prisoner had resigned himself to the vacuity of despair; he was stretched out in silent agony, when, as the night closed in, and the mirthful troops had progressively retired, a gentle female voice, with the tenderest accents, aroused his attention. How long the benign object had been there, he could not ascertain; but, when he looked up, and beheld her, his feelings were indescribable: she was a fine figure, rather tall, and slender, with a face most beautiful, and a form of the finest symmetry, improved by the melancholy air which the

M Raunsford del. J Barlow sculp.

the same had given her. She was dressed in a superior style, and possessed all the elegance of European manners, improved by the most impressive carriage. She held a basket, containing the most [illegible] food, with the finest fruits; she entreated him to receive them silently, and to destroy any remnants, as a discovery would be fatal to her, and prejudicial to himself. He was about to reply with the ardour of gratitude, when, in an instant, she was gone! On the following evening she returned, and endeavoured to comfort him with the most cheering expressions; and, by evincing extreme anxiety in his behalf, once more light up the illusion of hope in his breast, which he had abandoned, with all human prospects, for ever. The next evening she repeated her visit, and condescended to favor him with more extensive communication. Still not a word occurred to disclose her name, or situation: once, indeed, she made some distant allusions to the English, which led him to imagine, she had been impressed with gratitude towards the country by some obligation. Whatever her name, or whatever her circumstances, if this slight memorial should live to reach that delightful isle, in which, as an angelic representation of mercy, she may yet stay the hand of the destroyer, it will bear to her the sincere effusions of a grateful heart, which, though bruised by those of a fairer skin, can never discharge its sense of duty.*

Black repub. &c. Manners, &c.

The

* I have ever [illegible] this adventure as highly [illegible] conveyed in the [illegible] repeat,—"I have," says he, "always remarked, [illegible] countries, and [illegible]

... when under sentence of ...

CHAP. IV. 1799. Black republic. Manners, &c.

the scene had given her. She was dressed in a superior style, and possessed all the elegance of European manners, improved by the most expressive carriage. She held a basket, containing the most delicate food, with the finest fruits: she entreated him to receive them silently, and to destroy any remnants, as a discovery would be fatal to her, and prejudicial to himself. He was about to reply with the ardour of gratitude, when, in an instant, she was gone! On the following evening, she returned, and endeavoured to comfort him with the most obliging expressions; and, by evincing extreme anxiety on his behalf, once more light up the illusion of hope in his breast, which he had abandoned, with all human prospects, for ever. The next evening she repeated her visit, and condescended to favor him with more extensive communication. Still not a word occurred to disclose her name, or situation: once, indeed, she made some distant allusions to the English, which led him to imagine, she had been impressed with gratitude towards the country, by some obligation. Whatever her name, or whatever her circumstances, if this slight memorial should live to reach that delightful isle, in which, as an angelic representation of mercy, she may yet stay the hand of the destroyer, it will bear to her the sincere effusions of a grateful heart, which, though bruised by those of a fairer skin, can never discharge its sense of duty.*

The

* I have ever conceived this adventure as highly illustrative of the character of the sex conveyed in the eulogium of Lediard, which contains sentiments I have always delighted to repeat.---"I have," says he, "always remarked, that women, in all countries, are civil, obliging,

CHAP. VI. 1799. Black republic. Manners, &c.

The faithful commander of the vessel, from whose mishap this dreadful circumstance arose, never long quitted the spot, and frequently ventured to whisper consolation, though with the greatest danger to himself; for it appeared a political method to expose the victims of justice, none being knowingly permitted to approach them. Whatever he heard, however, to relieve the dreadful suspense of his friend, the taciturnity of the jailor tended to contradict, as little could be obtained of information from him, except his assuring him every night, that he would be certainly hanged on the morrow.

However, on the morn of the fifteenth day, when he had ventured to disengage himself of a part of his dress, for the purpose of a temporary relief from the weight of his chains, the answer of Toussaint arrived, bringing, instead of (as was fully expected) the confirmation of the sentence, an order from that truly great man for his release, and to be suffered to proceed on his voyage, with this prohibition, conveyed with much shrewdness, but the greatest magnanimity, "That he must never return to this island without *proper passports!*"

obliging, tender, and humane; that they are ever inclined to be gay and cheerful, timorous and modest; and, that they do not hesitate, like men, to perform a kind, or generous action. Not haughty nor arrogant, not supercilious, they are full of courtesy, and fond of society---more liable in general to err than man, but in general, also, more virtuous, and performing more good actions than he. To a woman, whether civilized or savage, I never addressed myself in the language of decency and friendship, without receiving a decent and friendly answer. With man it has often been otherwise."

With many opportunities of judging in various countries, and in various situations, I warmly subscribe to this just encomium.

To describe his feelings on such an unexpected reverse, would be difficult and useless. Restored to himself once more, he did not long remain on a part of the island where his sufferings would have tended to efface the agreeable impressions received at Cape François. Once he tried to trace the haunts of his benevolent incognita, but in vain. She was impervious. He again bade adieu to this interesting soil, and at length reached his long-desired destination, the island of Martinique.*

CHAP. IV. 1799. Black republic. Manners, &c.

* It is necessary to add, that on his arrival he met with the usual kindness and urbanity of the commander in chief, General Cuyler, who ordered him a remuneration for the loss of his baggage, and to whom he is indebted for many polite attentions since. He has been also informed, that he was honored with a congratulatory letter from his Royal Highness the Duke of York, which, from some unaccountable accident, he did not receive.

CHAP.

CHAP. V.

View of the Black Army, and the War between the French Republic and the Independent Blacks of St. Domingo.

CHAP. V. 1800. View of the Black army. Toussaint General in Chief.

THE close of the eighteenth century, a period marked by the grandest operations and the most gigantic projects, presented to the world, a new and organised empire, where it was not only supposed to be impossible to exist, but, where even its existence was denied, although it was known by those connected with that quarter of the globe to have taken place, and under the most flourishing auspices. The beneficent and able black, Toussaint L'Ouverture, devoid of the extraneous policy of the governors of ancient states, no sooner found himself at ease from the complicated warfare with which, from the first moment of his government he had been surrounded, than he evinced equal talents for the arts of peace, with those which he had invariably displayed in the field; and that mercy which had ever accompanied him in victory, now transfused itself in a mild and humane policy in the legislature. His first care was to establish,

5 on

CHAP. V. 1800.

on a firm foundation, the ordinances of religion, according to the existing constitutions of society, to watch over the morals, and excite the industry of those who had committed themselves to his charge.

The effects of these exertions were quickly evident throughout his dominion. Such was the progress of agriculture from this period, that the succeeding crop produced (notwithstanding the various impediments, in addition to the ravages of near a ten years war) full one third of the quantity of sugar and coffee, which had ever been produced at its most prosperous period. The increase of population was such, as to astonish the planters resident in the mother country, who could not conceive the possibility of preventing that falling off, in the numbers of the negroes, which formed their absolute necessity for supplying them by the slave-trade. Health, became prevalent throughout the country, with its attendant, cheerfulness, that exhilarator of labor.

Having introduced in a prominent light the surprising character, to whose talents and energies, the inhabitants of this regenerated island were indebted for their then existing advantages, it becomes necessary to present the reader with a view of the circumstances which accompanied a life so important in the history of St. Domingo.

Life and character of Toussaint L'Ouverture.

TOUSSAINT L'OUVERTURE was born a slave in the year 1745, on the estate of the Count de Noé, at a small distance from Cape François,

M Rainsford del. J. Barlow sculp.

Toussaint Louverture.

Published as the Act directs, July 1st 1805, by Jas. Cundee, Ivy Lane, Paternoster Row

[illegible] in the [illegible] province of St. Domingo, a spot since [illegible] as the very source of revolution,* and site of a [illegible] from whence its [illegible] general has issued [illegible] more powerful than those of any monarch on the [illegible]. CHAP. [illegible] MS. account.

While tending his master's flocks, the genius of Toussaint [illegible] to expand itself, by an attention towards objects beyond [illegible] of his comprehension; and without any other opportunity than was equally possessed by those around him, who [illegible] in impenetrable ignorance, he learnt to read, [illegible] and the figures. Encouraged by the progress he rapidly made in these arts, and fired with the prospect of higher attainments, he employed himself assiduously in the farther cultivation of his talents. His acquirements, as is oftentimes the case, under such circumstances, excited the admiration of his fellow slaves, and fortunately attracted the attention of the attorney, or manager of the estate, M. Bayou de Libertas. This gentleman, with a discrimination honorable to his judgment, withdrew Toussaint from the labor of the fields, to his own house, and began the amelioration of his fortune, by appointing him his postilion, an enviable situation among slaves, for its profits, and comparative respectability.

This instance of patronage by M. Bayou, impressed itself strongly on the susceptible mind of Toussaint. True genius and ele-

* See Chap. III. of this work.

François, in the northern province of St. Domingo, a spot since remarkable as the very source of revolution,* and site of a camp, (that of Breda,) from whence its native general has issued mandates more powerful than those of any monarch on the earth. CHAP. V. 1800 MS. account.

While tending his master's flocks, the genius of Toussaint began to expand itself, by an attention towards objects beyond the reach of his comprehension; and without any other opportunity than was equally possessed by those around him, who remained nearly in impenetrable ignorance, he learnt to read, write, and use figures. Encouraged by the progress he rapidly made in these arts, and fired with the prospect of higher attainments, he employed himself assiduously in the further cultivation of his talents. His acquirements, as is oftentimes the case, under such circumstances, excited the admiration of his fellow slaves, and fortunately attracted the attention of the attorney, or manager of the estate, M. Bayou de Libertas. This gentleman, with a discrimination honorable to his judgment, withdrew Toussaint from the labor of the fields, to his own house, and began the amelioration of his fortune, by appointing him his postilion, an enviable situation among slaves, for its profit, and comparative respectability.

This instance of patronage by M. Bayou, impressed itself strongly on the susceptible mind of Toussaint. True genius and ele-

* See Chap. III. of this work.

 vated

CHAP. V. 1800. vated sentiments are inseparable; the recollection of the most trivial action, kindly bestowed in obscurity, or under the pressure of adverse circumstances, warms the heart of sensibility, even in the hour of popular favor, more than the proudest honors. This truth was exemplified by the subsequent gratitude of Toussaint towards his master. He continued to deserve and receive promotion, progressively, to offices of considerable confidence.

Oral tradition. Among other traits fondly preserved in St. Domingo of the conduct of Toussaint during the early period of his life, are his remarkable benevolence towards the brute creation, and an unconquerable patience. Of the former, many instances are related which evince a mind endued with every good quality. He knew how to avail himself so well of the sagacity of the horse, as to perform wonders with that animal, without those cruel methods used to extort from them the docility exhibited in Europe; he was frequently seen musing amongst the different cattle, seeming to hold a species of dumb converse, which they evidently understood, and produced in them undoubted marks of attention. They knew and manifested their acquaintance, whenever he appeared; and he has been frequently seen attending with the anxiety of a nurse, any accident which had befallen them; the only instance in which he could be roused to irritation, was when a slave had revenged the punishment he received from his owner upon his harmless and unoffending cattle. Proverbial became his patience, insomuch that it was a favorite amusement of the young and inconsiderate upon the same estate, to

CHAP. V. 1800.

to endeavour to provoke him by wanton tricks and affected malignity. But so perfectly he had regulated his temper, that he constantly answered with a meek smile, and accounted for their conduct by such means, as would render it strictly pardonable. To the law of self-preservation, or the misfortune of not knowing the delight of philanthropy, he would attribute an act of brutal selfishness; while he imputed to a momentary misapprehension, an inclination to rude and malicious controversy. Thus was his passive disposition never in the smallest degree affected, being ready on all occasions to conciliate and to bear, in circumstances whether frivolous or of the highest importance.

At the age of twenty-five Toussaint attached himself to a female of similar character to his own, and their union cemented by marriage, which does not appear to have been violated, conferred respectability on their offspring. Still he continued a slave; nor did the goodness of M. Bayou, although it extended to render him as happy as the state of servitude would admit, ever contemplate the manumission of one who was to become a benefactor to him and his family. Such is the effect of ancient prejudice, in obscuring, the highest excellence of our nature; he who would perform godlike actions without hesitation, from any other cause, shrinks from a breach of etiquette, or a violation of custom! MS. account.

In the comforts of a situation possessing a degree of opulence, Toussaint found leisure to extend the advantages of his early

 acquisitions,

CHAP. V. 1800. Memoires du General Toussaint. acquisitions, and by the acquaintance of some priests, who possessed little more of the character than the name, acquired the knowledge of new sources of information, and a relish for books of a superior order than first attracted his attention; the author of whom he became the most speedily enamoured, was the Abbé Raynal, on whose history and speculations in philosophy and politics he was intent for weeks together, and never quitted, but with an intention to return, with renewed and additional pleasure. A French translation of Epictetus for a time confined him to its doctrines, which he often quoted; but he soon sought higher food for his capacious mind, and found in a portion of the ancient historians, the summit of his wishes. He was there seen studiously consulting the opinion of those who teach the conduct of empires, or the management of war; yet, he neglected not those who aim to harmonize the mind, and teach man himself; MS. account. the only difference in his habits imbibing these treasures created, was, an external polish, which imparted an uncommon grace to his manners.*

* The following books were conspicuous in the library of Toussaint, a list of which was handed to the author in consequence of his inquiries respecting the progress of his mind:

Scriptores de re Militari.
Cæsar's Commentaries, French translation, by De Crisse.
Des Claison's History of Alexander and Cæsar.
D'Orleans' History of Revolutions in England and Spain.
Marshal Saxe's Military Reveries.
Guischard's Military Memoirs of the Greeks and Romans.
Herodotus, History of the Wars of the Persians against the Greeks.
Le Beau's Memoirs of the Academy of Inscriptions and Belle's Lettres.
Lloyd's Military and Political Memoirs; the Works of the English Socrates, Plutarch, Cornelius Nepos, &c. &c. &c.

5 Thus

CHAP. V. 1800.

Thus proceeded this illustrious man: like the simple acorn, first promiscuously scattered by the winds, in its slow but beauteous progress to the gigantic oak, spreading its foliage with august grandeur, above the minor growth of the forest, defending the humble shrub, and braving the fury of contending elements.

Continuing on the estate on which he was born, when the deliberations preceding the actual rebellion of the slaves, were taking place upon the plantation of Noè, the opinion of him who was always regarded with esteem and admiration was solicited. His sanction was of importance, as he had a number of slaves under his command, and a general influence over his fellow negroes. Among the leaders of this terrible revolt were several of his friends, who he had deemed worthy to make his associates for mutual intelligence; yet, from whatever cause is not ascertained, he forbore in the first instance to join in the contest of liberty. It is probable that his manly heart revolted from cruelties attendant on the first burst of revenge in slaves about to retaliate their wrongs and sufferings on their owners. He saw that the innocent would suffer with the guilty; and that the effects of revolution regarded future, more than present justice. When the cloud charged with electric fluid becomes too ponderous, it selects not the brooding murderer on the barren heath, but bursts, perhaps, indiscriminately, in wasteful vengeance, o'er innocent flocks reposing in verdant fields.

There

CHAP. V.
1800.

There were ties which connected Toussaint more strongly than the consideration of temporary circumstances. These were, gratitude for the benefits received from his master, and generosity to those who were about to fall,—not merely beneath the stroke of the assassin, for that relief from their sufferings was not to be allowed to all, but likewise the change of situations of luxury and splendour, to an exile of danger, contempt, and poverty, with all the miseries such a reverse can accumulate.

Toussaint prepared for the emigration of M. Bayou de Libertas, as if he had only removed for his pleasure, to the American continent. He found means to embark produce that should form a useful provision for the future; procured his escape with his family, and contrived every plan for his convenience; nor did his care end here, for after M. Bayou's establishment in safety, at Baltimore, in Maryland, he availed himself of every opportunity to supply any conceived deficiency, and, as he rose in circumstances, to render those of his *protégée* more qualified to his situation, and equal to that warm remembrance of the services he owed him, which would never expire.

Having provided for the safety of his master in the first instance, Toussaint no longer resisted the temptations to join the army of his country, which had (at this period) assumed a regular form.* He attached himself to the corps under the command of

* It is pleasing to reflect, that Toussaint was not the only instance of a similar conduct to the present. It occurred, with many variations, in numerous cases; an eminent instance of which will be found in the third chapter of this work.

of a courageous black chief, named Biassou, and was appointed next in command to him. Though possessed of striking abilities, the disposition of this general rendered him unfit for the situation which he held; his cruelty caused him to be deprived of a power which he abused. No one was found equally calculated to supply his place, with the new officer, Toussaint; therefore, quitting for ever a subordinate situation, he was appointed to the command of a division.

CHAP. V.
1800.
Du Broca, Vie de Toussaint, &c.

If during this early period of his life, the black general had shone conspicuously, through every disadvantage, with the brightest talents and the milder virtues, he now rose superior to all around him, with the qualities and rank of an exalted chief. Every part of his conduct was marked by judgment and benevolence. By the blacks, who had raised him to the dignity he enjoyed, he was beloved with enthusiasm; and, by the public characters of other nations, with whom he had occasion to communicate, he was regarded with every mark of respect and esteem. General Laveaux called him "the negro, the Sparactacus, foretold by Raynal, whose destiny it *was* to avenge the wrongs committed on his race:" and the Spanish Marquis d'Hermona declared, in the hyperbole of admiration, that "if the Supreme had descended on earth, he could not inhabit a heart more apparently good, than that of Toussaint L'Ouverture."

His powers of invention in the art of war, and domestic government, the wonder of those who surrounded, or opposed

him,

CHAP. V. 1800.

him, had not previously an opportunity for exhibition as at the period to which we have arrived in this history. Embarrassed by a variety of contending factions among the blacks, and by enemies of different nations and characters, he was too much occupied in evading the blows constantly meditated in different quarters, to find leisure for the display of that wisdom and magnanimity which he so eminently exercised. Nevertheless, a variety of incidents are recorded in the fleeting memorials of the day to corroborate the excellence of his character, and still more are impressed on the memory of all who have visited the scene of his government. Notwithstanding the absoluteness of military jurisdiction, which existed with extra power, no punishment ever took place without the anxious endeavours of the General-in-Chief to avoid it, exerted in every way that could be devised. No object was too mean for his remonstrance, or advice; nor any crime too great to be subjected to the rules he had prescribed to himself. The punishment of the idle or immoral laborer was, being withdrawn from agriculture, and condemned to a military service dangerous or severe. In cases of treason he was peculiarly singular in his ideas, and the following incident will afford a specimen:—

Oral tradition.

Shortly after General Maitland arrived upon the island, four Frenchmen were retaken who had deserted the black chief with aggravated treachery. Every one expected a vindictive punishment, and of course a cruel death. Leaving them, however, in suspence as to their fate, he ordered them to be produced in

church

church on the following Sabbath, and, while that part of the service was pronouncing which respects mutual forgiveness, he went with them to the front of the altar, where, impressing them with the flagitiousness of their conduct, he ordered them to be discharged without farther punishment. CHAP. V. 1800.

Character. It probably may be expected that something should be mentioned of the general character of Toussaint; and, if there was any object predominant in the wishes of the writer during his sojourn at the Cape, it was—to ascertain the traits of peculiarity in that individual,—to judge of the views, and of the motives that actuated him. The result of his observations was in every respect favorable to this truly great man. Casual acts of justice and benignity may mark the reign of anarchy itself, and complacency sometimes smooth the brow of the most brutal tyrant; but when the man, possessed for a considerable period, of unlimited power, (of whose good actions no venal journalist was the herald, but, to transcribe his errors a thousand competitors were ready) has never been charged with its abuse; but, on the contrary, has preserved one line of conduct, founded by sound sense and acute discernment on the most honorable basis, leaning only to actions of magnanimity and goodness; he has passed the strongest test to which he can be submitted; who, with the frailties of human nature, and without the adventitious aids of those born to rule, held one of the highest situations in society.

 His

CHAP. V. 1800. His government does not appear to have been sullied by the influence of any ruling passion; if a thirst of power had prompted him alone, he would have soon ceased to be a leader of insurgents; had avarice swayed him, he, like many others, could have retired early in the contest, with immense riches, to the neighbouring continent; or had a sanguinary revenge occupied his mind, he would not so often have offered those pathetic appeals to the understanding, which were the sport of his colleagues, on crimes which the governors of nations long *civilized* would have sentenced to torture! His principles, when becoming an actor in the revolution of his country, were as pure and legitimate, as those which actuated the great founders of liberty in any former age or clime.

Such was the character of Toussaint L'Ouverture, as regarded his office of Commander in Chief, and Governor of the island of St. Domingo. In his relations towards other countries, he appears to have excited admiration for his justice, and the courtesy of every enlightened state: the charges of his most inveterate enemies never extended to a fact that can diminish the well-earned eulogies he has obtained. His rules of conduct were the emanations of a mind capacious and well informed; and but for the exertions of his talents, or those of some chief equally able, indefatigable, and sincere, the country, now blooming with culture, and advancing in true civilization, might have been a ruined state, sacrificed to the conflicts of disappointed ambition, revenge, and the whole train of evils which a multiplicity of factions could

 create.

create. That there should be found partizans of each of these factions in the then divided state of France, to complain of every arrangement formed by this astonishing individual, is to be expected, rather than wondered at; and to these motives alone, there is no reason to doubt, may be ascribed all the calumnies which have been vented against him.

CHAP. V. 1800.

In his private life, Toussaint lost none of the excellence of that character which is conspicuous in his public actions. With much sensibility, he supported an even temper in domestic privacy; and in contra-distinction to the general custom of other great men, might be considered equally an hero in the closet as the field. To his wife, a sensible and affectionate woman, he behaved with the most endearing tenderness and consideration, and to his children imparted all the warmth of paternal affection; yet he had no overweening fondness to conceal their faults from his notice, even the smallest want of proper attention to an inferior was censured with severity proportionate to the difference of their condition. If they obtained not knowledge from the transitory nature of human circumstances, so necessary to check the pride of birth or situation, almost always manifest in children reared in affluence, it was not the fault of a father whose life was conspicuous for humility of disposition, and a diffidence of his powers, proportionable to the elevation of his rank, or the accumulation of his honors. As his children grew to an age capable of that education which his individual acquirements instructed

him

CHAP. V. 1800. him as necessary to the sphere of life in which they were to move. Toussaint procured for them the best tutors he could obtain, and afterwards sent them to France under their care, for the advantages of higher instruction.—His leisure, which was not great, was occupied in relieving those who suffered in any way undeservedly; nor did he, as is often the case in the world, weigh guilt by incapacity or distinction. The weak of every description were his peculiar care; the strong in intellect, the mighty in war, or the amiable in domestic life, shared alike his esteem.

In person, Toussaint was of a manly form, above the middle stature, with a countenance bold and striking, yet full of the most prepossessing suavity—terrible to an enemy, but inviting to the objects of his friendship or his love. His manners and his deportment were elegant when occasion required, but easy and familiar in common;—when an inferior addressed him, he bent with the most obliging assiduity, and adapted himself precisely, without seeming condescension, to their peculiar circumstances. He received in public a general and voluntary respect, which he was anxious to return, or rather to prevent, by the most pleasing civilities. His uniform was a kind of blue jacket, with a large red cape falling over the shoulders; red cuffs, with eight rows of lace on the arms, and a pair of large gold epaulettes thrown back; scarlet waistcoat and pantaloons, with half boots; round hat, with a red feather, and a national cockade;

these,

these, with an extreme large sword, formed his equipment.—He was an astonishing horseman, and travelled with inconceivable rapidity.

Thus are given the rough outlines of the character of Toussaint; for the shades it will be necessary to consider what foibles could have existence with the virtues described. It is not intended to sully the present account by the absurdity of attempting to hold him up as a perfect character; but thus much is certain, that if he had any peculiar vices, he had the address to conceal them from the most scrutinous and industrious observer.

Toussaint, surrounded by men of letters and science, whom various circumstances had brought from the mother country found little difficulty in the formation of a temporary constitution, of which justice and equality (of right only, not of property) should be the basis. Among those from whom he received important assistance was the Citizen Pascal, a descendant of the celebrated writer of that name, who inherited the talents of his ancestor. He had been sent to Cape François by the Executive Directory, in the fourth year of the revolution, as secretary to the agents of the republic; when he married the daughter of a mulatto in office, named Raymond, and acquired by the connection a considerable property. He attached himself early to Toussaint, with the Abbé Moliere, and an Italian ecclesiastic,

CHAP. V. 1800. ecclesiastic, of considerable talents, named Marinit, who were always about his person.*

Having settled the grand object of his care, particularly as regarded the safety of the white inhabitants, he next devoted himself to the regulation and increase of his army, on a scale fitting the importance of the country under his care. At the time of his treaty with General Maitland, his force in the northern province amounted to something less than 40,000 men, but they were soon increased to nearly double that number, and at this time exceeded all conception.† As they were necessarily divided in the different provinces, he prepared for a journey round the island for the purpose of reviewing them, and appointing the districts, as well as settling the officers to command them, with greater success and accuracy than could be done at a distance. Vast quantities of ordnance and stores of different kinds were accumulated at different posts, which would be more useful when distributed. He was desirous of becoming known to a

* Filling every public office with men of talents and letters in France, (as they confessedly do,) it was scarcely possible to appoint any but persons of ability to the foreign departments; which accounts for the easy acquisition of such persons, to the liberal Toussaint.

† Colonel Chalmers, in his "Remarks on the late War in St. Domingo," supposes certain muster-rolls, which he describes to have been in the possession of Toussaint's adjutant-general at the Mole, stating the force (in that quarter) at 35,000 men, to contain the whole effective force of the island, and even then ridicules the idea of its being so strong! It causes an involuntary smile to see such opinions seriously delivered, or to observe the mutual censures of General Maitland and Toussaint, for not continuing a war of annihilation, by Colonel Chalmers on one side, and Stephen Mentor, the black seceder, on the other.

great

great number of brave men who were attached to his army, many of whom had received a military education in the mother country, and could be placed in situations of responsibility; others, too, required local appointments, for the purpose of residing in situations with which they were acquainted; and it was the wish and policy of Toussaint, to know and gratify them all. —The animation of his presence was also necessary to troops, (in some few instances, perhaps, languid,) who were ambitious of being seen by their General in Chief, whose very name acted with electric force on all. In the capital of the Spanish part of the island, another reason proved the necessity of a visit from the General in Chief. Notwithstanding the cession of the Spanish colony to France in 1795, and that it had been taken possession of by the generals Paul L'Ouverture, (the brother of Toussaint,) and D'Hebecour, who had garrisoned the different posts, a force still remained in the city of St. Domingo, under Don Joachim Garcia, insubordinate to the present government; Toussaint, therefore, with that promptitude for which he was remarkable, though not without due consideration, set out upon this important tour.

CHAP. V. 1800. Black republic. Manners, &c.

The reception the General met with in every town and village through which he passed, and at every port he visited, was such as to have gratified the vanity of the proudest potentate. All orders, civil or military, vied with each other in their modes of respect, while the women and children lined the road sides, to bless the pacificator of their country. On every face was depicted

Tour of Toussaint L'Ouverture through the island.

content

CHAP. V. 1800.

content and health, and in every place appeared universal satisfaction. Every means were used to declare the general pleasure with which he was viewed. Garlands, and fantastic wreaths, were woven by those who could do no more. Superb decorations covered the houses of proprietors, and triumphal arches graced his entry to every town. The military, in their proudest array, were anxious to obtain approbation by a soldier-like appearance, and a variety of plans were formed by the maritime people to testify their accordance with the public respect. Innumerable instances might be mentioned which would assume the air of romance, of the singular testimonies which occurred to honor him, and do justice to his character.

Condescension of the General in Chief.

In one place, a respectable negro, of the age of ninety-nine, seated on a wicker chair, presented to him ten sons, the children of one wife, employed in agriculture, but ready to devote themselves to the service of their country whenever it should be necessary. Three sisters hung over their father, as if fearing to lose the protection of their brothers. All produced certificates of propriety and industry from their employers, and their neighbours, a part of whom surrounded them. Toussaint leaped from his horse, and knelt at the feet of the old man. "Respectable age," said he, "it is to such members as you, that your country is this day indebted for peace and freedom!" As he arose, an aid-de-camp directed his attention to a solitary youth, who stood at a short distance, unnoticed. "Who is that," exclaimed the General, "apparently miserable on such a day?" He was informed

CHAP. V. 1800.

formed it was one who had disgraced the family now presented to him, in many instances, and had lately encouraged his sister in vice. At this moment an interesting female rushed from the crowd, holding an infant in her arms, with the appearance of extreme anguish, exclaiming, "It is for me, General, that the poor Antony is calumniated."—Her tears interrupted her.—"I could not part with my child, though rejected by his father, and denied even permission to labor in the same plantation with my family, because I quitted it, and nearly starving, engaged myself to another less desirable.—My affectionate brother lent me all the aid his own labors could spare, and when I was to remove, solicited an addition from my other brothers and sisters. He was refused, and he"——"He robbed them, perhaps, to supply you," interrupted the General; "thereby violating his duty to his family, his country, and himself;—this is wrong;—there was something, likewise, erroneous in withholding your child from the protection it would have received; yet," turning to the old man who had claimed his approbation, "we must not, father, reject the unfortunate; it is not sufficient to be just, we must also be merciful, recollecting how much need we all have for mercy. Sully, not, therefore, the happiness you enjoy, with the recollection of one individual less happy by your means, much more your son, (leading him towards the old man,) or your daughter, (doing the same). The impressive manner of the General (though the transaction lasted but a few minutes) drew tears from the whole; the family instantly caressed their brother and

sister,

CHAP. V. 1800. sister, and Toussaint, re-mounting his horse, was quickly out of sight.

He never stoped to court the attention of the multitude, but having returned the civilities which every where crowded upon him, galloped on, leaving his aides, or whoever accompanied him, frequently out of sight. Innumerable acts of discriminative goodness are related of him during this route, and the day, where-ever he was, was a day of peace and pleasure.

The effects of this tour were very evident, by the uniform reformation in every part of the island. The municipal governments were brought into one general system, and a chain of communication established. The different brigades were rendered more effective by the better arrangement of the troops composing them, and armed posts were established throughout the island, well supplied with the ordnance his enemies had left behind. In fact, every part was put in a situation to withstand the utmost force of an enemy, however powerful, and to dispute with them every inch of ground. Nor, during an attention to the internal safety of the country in a military view, were its maritime interests forgotten, every commercial encouragement was offered to the neighbouring islands and the continent; the safety of the whites was established, and their power of injuring the state curtailed.

Toussaint

Toussaint returned to the Cape, accompanied by a numerous suite, in which was a selection of the principal talents of the island. He was received with redoubled pleasure to what he had previously experienced on returning to the capital, from the length of his absence, and the reports of his conduct, which had preceded him from every quarter. Neither was this fame confined to the boundaries of St. Domingo; it ran through Europe, and in France his name was frequently pronounced in the Senate with the eulogy of polished eloquence. CHAP. V. 1800.

It being necessary that the constitution, which in effect now existed, should be published, for the assurance of its permanent execution, and the proper understanding of the different inhabitants and relations of the island, it was proclaimed on the 1st of July 1801. At the head of the ceremony appeared the General in Chief, and the code was promulgated in the name *"of the people."* 1801. Declaration of Independence.

The intercourse between France and St. Domingo, which had been decreasing for some time previous to the proclamation, now ceased altogether, except by private correspondence, which was considerably checked. Still the late proprietors resident in or near the French metropolis, languished for the recovery of their former importance, and every account of the flourishing state of their beloved colony, awakened each lingering wish to new, but vain hopes of a restoration. They even imagined, in every amelioration of the island, an additional chance of succeeding to their

 desires,

CHAP. V. 1801. desires, till they had schemed plans of operation, and imagined means of execution, which themselves only could have devised or understood. These were constantly obtruded on the French government, who were too much employed in the complicated politics of Europe to admit them into their views, and all that they obtained was the promises with which they were bribed; as the price of forbearance from anti-revolutionary projects at home.

But a time was approaching when accident produced in a moment what the labor of years could not effect, and obtained for these misguided persons, the interference their restless spirits desired. The government of France, having assumed a novel and original form under the influence of a victorious dictator, for whose firm establishment it required an interval of peace; and the politics of that country, which was the remaining enemy of the republic, and the only nation in Europe capable of contending with her, suggesting a similar measure, the two countries, after communicating with *political* sincerity, came to the determination of a cessation of hostilities, and the preliminaries were accordingly executed. Thus the naval power of France, which for nine years had not sailed from her ports with impunity from the terror of the British flag throughout the globe, was at liberty to perform all its crippled state would permit, and to improve that state with every possible advantage.*

This

* It is painful (and dangerous) to hear the prevalence of an opinion, even from those who should be better informed, that the creation of a French navy is impossible, and that it is not an

CHAP. V. 1801.

This was but a part of the circumstances arising from the peace of Europe favorable to the expatriated colonists of St. Domingo. The labors of Bonaparté, First Consul of the Republic, hitherto limited in exertions of military prowess, whose rapidity and effect gave no opportunity for objection or scrutiny, were now to be submitted to the test of cool examination. That personal courage which had conquered a great part of the continent of Europe, subverted foreign states, and removed a divided senate at home, would not avail in the convictions of philosophy, or the conciliation of jarring interests in a state of peace. It became, therefore, necessary to obtain a powerful influence in the cabinet as well as in the field, and to assure to himself other interests than those of humanity.

At this period the party who had constantly beset the existing ministry, did not neglect a single opportunity of redoubling their appeals to the present government, or of availing themselves of every circumstance, to attach to their cause a more powerful weight than it then possessed. They held out, in temptations of the most florid description, the advantages daily lost to commerce; and those who had till now been occupied in fitting out numbers of privateers, began to think of an advantageous employment of their capital; others, whom the war had confined to France, contemplated with pleasure trans-atlantic views, and the

an object of contemplation in the present ruler of France. That it is both the one and the other is most certain, and the writer will be less prophetic than he has been, if a very few years do not exhibit a confirmation.

enterprizing

CHAP. V. 1801. enterprizing regarded the troubles in St. Domingo, as an inviting opportunity of distinguishing themselves. In fact, every description of people became interested in the recovery of the colony, forgetting what had passed in regard to the abolition of slavery in the same metropolis; it became a popular cause, was introduced into the assemblies, and the ladies became partizans, headed by the favorite sister of the First Consul, the lady of General Le Clerc. The mania spread into England with the beauties of the Consular court, and that nation, where the ministry and people had blindly desired the abolition, at the expence of a portion of their empire of commerce, and the ruin of a large body of colonists, still more blindly joined in the popular wish of returning to slavery, those who were completely emancipated.

Bonaparte viewed the growing spirit with silence, and, it may be, not without some regard to the character the victorious Black had obtained in the mother country. A variety of circumstances contributed to convince him of the necessity of some attention (in the first instance) to the powerful requests which poured in from every quarter; the instance, also, of a power bidding him defiance in a country which had not, by any regular process, become separated from that government over which he was called to preside, was repugnant to his feelings in the rank in which he was elevated. Madame Le Clerc, partaking in the ambition ascribed to her brother, urged the measure of reducing the island, to procure for her husband and herself something more than was to be derived from basking in the beams of the First Consul; and the appointment of General Le Clerc to a splendid conquest, was confining the dignity of it to the family. When the inclination of Bonaparté was understood to be favorable to the prospects of the colonists, means were found to interest the most powerful merchants in their behalf, and urged by those, on whose aid (in the present stage of his government) he was aware much was to depend, this penetrating man, without any other information than that derived through so partial a medium, consented to an expedition that was to become an eternal blot upon a career, if not often just or humane, at least always able, and frequently magnificent.

As, to devise and execute were the same thing with the First Consul, this baneful expedition was no sooner determined on, than after forming a plan for the government of the colonies, and submitting to the British government the circumstances of its destination, to prevent the alarm which it must naturally create, its preparation was commenced, to add another shade to the darkened side of human nature.

Expedition of the French Republic against St. Domingo.

At the head of the expedition was placed General Le Clerc, and such was the confidence of its success, that he was accompanied by his lady, and her younger brother, Jerome Bonaparté. General Rochambeau, who had been a proprietor, assisted with his advice the commander in chief, and also

CHAP. V. 1801. also commanded a division. To them were added Generals Kerversan and Boudet, with a force of twenty thousand men. The two sons of Toussaint L'Ouverture who had been educated in France, were sent as hostages for the reception of the French army by their father, under the care of the tutors who had accompanied them. Admiral Villaret (who was in the service of the regal government of France) commanded the fleet, under whom were Rear-Admiral Latouche, and Captain Magon. The fleet consisted of some of the best ships of the line, and a proportionable number of frigates, transports, &c. The prevalent sentiment seemed to be, that after the first attack, a compromise would be effected with Toussaint and the different chiefs, which would enable the French force to establish itself throughout the island, and complete the subjugation of the armed blacks.*

In the month of December the expedition sailed, amidst the acclamations of all, who were either interested in its success, or

* The absurdity of this idea, when the state of St. Domingo at the time is considered, and the accumulated strength which the General in Chief had acquired from the defeat of every enemy, as well as the experience which the different contentions had afforded him, is a sufficient proof of the inconsideration with which Bonaparté was hurried into this ill-contrived and ruinous measure. The writer did not omit any means, both with those in power and otherwise, to convince them of the futility of the scheme, and to caution the British government against the temptation afforded to Admiral Villaret, to turn his course to a more accessible destination. But such was the pre-determined state of the public mind, that his opinions and his cautions were alike disregarded. Both have, however, been fully corroborated; and if the "*feeble and divided*" blacks had not given a better account of the French expedition, worse effects of such an inattention might have been experienced. As a curiosity, when compared with the French General's dispatches, the anticipation of his fate, as published at the Military Library in London in the beginning of 1802, will be found in the Appendix to this work.

6 imagined

imagined themselves so; and arrived in the bay of Samana, on the eastern coast of the island, on the 28th of the same month. When General Kerversan was dispatched with a division to the city of St. Domingo; Rear-Admiral Latouche was ordered to carry the troops under the command of General Boudet to Port-au-Prince; and Captain Magon to land a division under General Rochambeau in Mancenillo Bay, on the northern coast. These divisions were directed so as to surprize different points of the island at the same period; General Le Clerc proceeded, with the remainder of the troops, to the attack of the Black capital, the city of Cape François, where he arrived on the 5th day. Two frigates and a cutter being sent to reconnoitre the entrance of the road and adjacent posts, were fired on from Fort Picolet.

In the mean time, the secret operations of the Consular cabinet had not been neglected; a few civic officers among the blacks, and several whites in that part of the country, intended to be first attacked, were prepared, as far as they could, to assist the designs of the invading army. The vigilance, however, of Toussaint had been exerted, and to every part of the island where invasion was expected, or the smallest signs of defection appeared, he had applied every means in his power to prevent their approach towards the interior. He had many faithful adherents distributed through the posts of danger and honor, whose confidence in him nothing could alter. Although cau-

tious

CHAP. V. 1802. tious of admitting any sanguinary law in his government, he had proved to every officer under his command the impartiality by which he was guided, in the sacrifice of his own nephew, General Moyse, when a charge of injustice had been proved against him. By attending to the prosecution of the necessary measures for the internal defence of the island, General Toussaint was away from Cape François at the time the expedition arrived.

General Christophé, who was left in command, on perceiving the approach of the French fleet, sent the port captain, an experienced black officer, named Sangos, to acquaint the commander of the expedition with the absence of the General in Chief; and "that it was necessary to wait the return of a courier he had dispatched to him, previous to any steps for the disembarkation of a military force; on a refusal of which he should consider the white people in his district as hostages for the conduct of the French; and that the consequence of attack upon any place would be its immediate conflagration."

Upon this intimation, General Le Clerc conceived it expedient to dissemble awhile, till the effects of his interest, strength, and success (in which was included the mayor of the city) should be known, and accordingly began to administer the palliatives with which he had been furnished from France. He wrote a mild letter to General Christophé, stating the benign intentions of the First

Consul

CHAP. V.
1802.

Consul and himself towards the island, and inviting him to return to his duty as a French citizen, with the most specious promises. He enclosed copies of the proclamations brought with him, and a private letter from General Bonaparté to the General in Chief, Toussaint. In this letter the Black General receives ample indemnity for all that is passed, and the most encouraging promises for the future. "We have conceived for you esteem," says the ruler of France, "and we wish to recognize and proclaim the great services you have rendered to the French people: if their colours fly on St. Domingo, it is to you, and your brave blacks, that we owe it. Called by your talents and the force of circumstances to the chief command, you have closed the civil war, put a stop to the persecutions of ferocious men, and restored to honor the religion and worship of God, from whom all things come." Also, "The situation in which you were placed, surrounded by enemies, and without the mother country being able to succour or sustain you, has rendered legitimate the articles of that constitution, which otherwise would not be so."* This dispatch was borne by a naval officer, named Le Brun, who received in return a repetition in effect, but more strongly expressed of the intimation received by Sangos.

A deputation from the town, headed by the mayor, went on board the fleet, who represented, with visible terror, that,

* See Moniteur, (the official journal of France,) March 21, 1802.—Dispatch of Le Clerc.

CHAP. V. 1802. "on the first signal of a debarkation, the city and adjoining estates would be set on fire, and the white people put to the sword; and entreated General Le Clerc to take their unhappy circumstances into consideration." He received this deputation with the greatest complacency, and sent them back with a commission to read the proclamation of the First Consul in the town, and to declare his good intentions towards the inhabitants; Cæsar Telemache, the mayor, fulfilled their wishes in the most open manner. The result was the same as before; notwithstanding the daring conduct of the chief municipal officer and others, and the satisfaction of some whites, (who had been protected and encouraged by the blacks,) at the prospect of the recapture of the colony.

General Le Clerc, conceiving his friends to be sufficiently ripe and numerous for his reception, and impatient to open his splendid career, arranged his plan for landing the troops at a point of land called Du Limbé, a few miles to the westward, from whence he conceived he might be able to gain the height of the Cape before the negroes executed their threatened purpose, or at least, land with less injury than he should be able to do, in the face of a well fortified capital. Admiral Villaret was ordered to attack the town by sea at the same time, which, with the descent of Rochambeau at Fort Dauphin, would form a powerful diversion in their favor. The whole was executed with the utmost difficulty, the blacks acting up to their orders, which were, "To defend

1

fend themselves against the French to the last extremity; if possible, to sink their vessels; and, when a position could not be maintained, to set fire to every thing in their retreat."* In the evening, when Le Clerc came within sight of Cape François, the city was entirely in flames. The troops halted with dismay to behold a scene so dreadful, the effects of which they could not arrest, and the squadron beheld it in awful horror from the water. The next morning they approached the ruins, when every remaining habitation was deserted, and the fields lying in waste. The emissaries of the French rallied around their Chief, among whom was Cæsar Telemaque, who was immediately reinstated in the mayoralty. General Humbert, who had landed a body of twelve hundred men, and reduced a fort to facilitate the entry of Le Clerc, had employed his men in extinguishing the fire, and saving the city from total destruction.

Two detachments were immediately dispatched to occupy Port Paix and the Mole, who contrived, from the means which had been used before the landing of the troops, to enlist (according to their own account) upwards of a thousand black soldiers. They, and several of the municipal officers, were attracted by the proclamations plenteously dispersed, which were as follow:

* Moniteur, March 22.

"Paris,

CHAP. V. 1802.

"*Paris, Nov.* 8, 1801.

"INHABITANTS OF ST. DOMINGO,

"Whatever your origin or your color, you are all French; you are all equal, and all free, before God, and before the Republic.

"France, like St. Domingo, has been a prey to factions, torn by intestine commotions, and foreign wars. But all has changed; all nations have embraced the French, and have sworn to them peace and amity; the French people have embraced each other, and have sworn to be all friends and brothers. Come also, embrace the French, and rejoice to see again your European friends and brothers.

"The government sends you the Captain-General Le Clerc: he has brought sufficient force for protecting you against your enemies; and against the enemies of the Republic. If it be said to you their forces are destined to ravish from you your liberty; answer, the Republic will not suffer it to be taken from us.

"Rally round the Captain-General; he brings you abundance and peace. Rally all of you around him. Whoever shall dare to separate himself from the Captain-General, will be a traitor to his country, and the indignation of the country will devour him as the fire devours your dried canes.

"Done at Paris, &c.

(Signed) "The First Consul, BONAPARTE.

"The Secretary of State, H. B. MARET."

In

In the mean time, Toussaint, who had been long preparing for the event, had carefully examined the interior, and was approaching the scene of devastation. Notwithstanding the hostile form in which the French armament had approached his seat of government, he was anxious to find, from their conduct, if he had to expect an amicable proposition, or any intention to support with integrity the relation in which he stood to his countrymen. Well acquainted with the political state of Europe, he could not conceive that the man, who had confessedly (however advantageous to his country) usurped a dictatorial power in France, could contemplate the reduction of one who had been called to equal power by the most legitimate of all authority, the voice of the people. He knew, that presenting a vast extent of coast, it would be impossible to prevent a debarkation at one point or the other, therefore had pre-determined to suffer the French to land, if they insisted upon it, after a slight annoyance from the forts, or adjacent posts; but, that previous to their landing, every preparation should be made for securing the property of the inhabitants of the metropolis, or any other town, which should then be set on fire, thus preventing them from taking that rest which, after the voyage, they would naturally require, and impede their penetration into the interior. These operations had been carefully performed, and with so much attention to the whites in particular, that many of them returned to their houses, in full possession of their property after the capital was in possession of the French. Toussaint, satisfied with the state in which he found every

preparation

CHAP. V. 1802. preparation for defence in the interior, determined to wait the event of the future motions of the French commander in chief.

The letter which the First Consul had written to Toussaint remaining undelivered, the scheme, which a reliance on the feelings of Toussaint had dictated, was not yet executed. Advices had been received from the other divisions, that they had with difficulty made good their landing, but all remained, as well as Le Clerc, upon the coast, without any attempt to penetrate into the interior. It was determined, as Toussaint's approach was announced, to try the effect of the artifice which had been prepared.

Accordingly Coisnon, the tutor of the sons of Toussaint, a confidential agent in this expedition, was commissioned to conduct an interview between the General and his children, who had been prepared by the caresses of the First Consul, and the enjoyment of every indulgence, to seduce their parent to an acquiescence with the measures of the Captain-General Le Clerc. Toussaint possessed a plantation called Ennery, about ten leagues from the Cape, where he was returning, which was fixed upon as the scene of the intended interview. Thither they repaired, but Toussaint had not returned; they, however, met such a reception as might be expected from a tender and affectionate mother to her darling children, so long absent, and to him

him who appeared in the character of their restorer. Coisnon availed himself of the pressing invitation of this good and hospitable woman to wait the return of her husband, that he might ingratiate himself upon the softness of her nature sufficiently to win her over as an advocate to his cause. In the mean time, a courier was dispatched to Toussaint, who was to bear the pleasing invitation of his children, and the letter of the First Consul. This was as follows: CHAP. V. 1802.

"To Citizen Toussaint L'Ouverture, General in Chief of the Army of St. Domingo. Letter of Bonaparté to Toussaint.

"CITIZEN-GENERAL,

"Peace with England and all the powers of Europe, which places the Republic in the first degree of greatness and power, enables at the same time the government to direct its attention to St. Domingo. We send thither Citizen Le Clerc, our brother-in-law, in quality of Captain-General, as first magistrate of the colony. He is accompanied with the necessary forces, to make the sovereignty of the French people respected. It is under these circumstances that we are disposed to hope that you will prove to us, and to all France, the sincerity of the sentiments you have constantly expressed in the different letters you have written to us. We have conceived for you esteem, and we wish to recognize and proclaim the great services you have rendered to the French people. If their colours fly on St. Domingo, it is to you, and your brave blacks, that we owe it. Called by your

CHAP. V. 1802. talents, and the force of circumstances, to the chief command, you have concluded the civil war, put a stop to the persecutions of some ferocious men, and restored the honor the religion and the worship of God, from whom all things come.

"The situation in which you were placed, surrounded on all sides by enemies, and without the mother country being able to succour or sustain you, has rendered legitimate the articles of that constitution which otherwise could not be so. But, now that circumstances are so happily changed, you will be the first to render homage to the sovereignty of the nation, which reckons you among the number of its most illustrious citizens, by the services you have rendered to it, and by the talents and the force of character with which nature has endowed you. A contrary conduct would be irreconcileable with the idea we have conceived of you. It would deprive you of your numerous claims to the gratitude and the good offices of the Republic, and would dig under your feet a precipice which, while it swallowed you up, would contribute to the misery of those brave blacks, whose courage we love, and whom we should be sorry to punish for rebellion.

"We have made known to your children, and to their preceptor, the sentiments by which we are animated. We send them back to you. Assist with your counsel, your influence, and your talents, the Captain-General.—What can you desire?—the freedom of the blacks? You know that in all the countries we have

have been in; we have given it to the people who had it not. Do you desire consideration, honor, fortune? It is not after the services you have rendered, the services you can still render, and with the personal estimation we have for you, that you ought to be doubtful with respect to your consideration, your fortune, and the honors that await you.

"Make known to the people of St. Domingo, that the solicitude which France has always evinced for their happiness, has often been rendered impotent by the imperious circumstances of war; that if men came from the Continent to nourish factions, they were the produce of those factions which destroyed the country; that in future peace, and the power of government, ensure their prosperity and freedom. Tell them, that if liberty be to them the first of wants, they cannot enjoy it but with the title of French citizens, and that every act contrary to the interests of the country, the obedience they owe to the government, and the Captain-General, who is the delegate of it, would be a crime against the national sovereignty which would eclipse their services, and render St. Domingo the theatre of a cruel war, in which fathers and children would massacre each other.

"And you, General, recollect, that if you are the first of your colour that attained such great power, and distinguished himself by his bravery and his military talents, you are also before God and us the principal person responsible for their conduct.

"If

CHAP. V. 1802. "If there be disaffected persons, who say to the individuals that have borne a principal part in the troubles of St. Domingo, that we are coming to ascertain what they have done during the times of anarchy, assure them, that we shall take cognizance of their conduct only in this last circumstance, and that we shall not recur to the past, but to find out the traits that may have distinguished them in the war carried on against the Spanish and English, who have been our enemies.

"Rely without reserve on our esteem, and conduct yourself as one of the principal citizens of the greatest nation in the world ought to do.

"The First Consul, BONAPARTE."

On the receipt of these dispatches, Toussaint set out on his return home, which he reached the next night. In the intervening day, Coisnon applied his powers of elocution on the wife of Toussaint with ardour equal to the baseness of his design. Like the serpent at the ear of the general mother, he whispered every delusion that crafty knowledge could devise, to tempt the unsuspecting woman, whose caution was enveloped in the delight of enfolding her children, (who were much improved by the advantages of European habits and manners,) to use her soft influence with her husband. Inspired by the news, that his children were at their paternal home, Toussaint arrived with more than common rapidity. The mother shrieked, and became insensible when he approached; his sons ran to meet him; and

Interview of Toussaint with his children.

(with

(with eyes glistening with the emotions of the father) he clasped them without utterance to his arms. CHAP. V. 1802.

Of a scene equal to the highest effort of the drama, narration can give no semblance, without using the language of passion so dangerous to truth. Enough, however, is learned from the self-condemning account of the tutor,* to prove, that it was of the most affecting nature. This wretch, with a heart cold as the cell in which he was bred, viewed the emotions of this interesting family, only to take advantage of their situation. When the first burst of joy and affection were over, and the hero turned to caress him, to whom he immediately owed the delight he had experienced, Coisnon began his attack. "I saw them shed tears," says he, "and, wishing to take advantage of a period which I conceived to be favorable, I stopped him at the moment when he stretched out his arms to me;" then recapitulated the letters of Bonaparté and Le Clerc, and invited him to accede to them. He painted the intentions of France towards the island in the most fascinating language; described the advantages of resuming its relation with the mother country, and declared, with the utmost solemnity, that it was not the intention to interfere with the liberty of the blacks; concluding with a wound that struck to the heart of Toussaint,—his orders to return with his charge to the Cape immediately, if he did not consent. The wife of Toussaint, recovered from the convulsive joy with

* Report of Coisnón to the French ministry.

which

CHAP. V. 1802. which she was seized, commenced solicitations of a milder kind, and, notwithstanding the check; by a frown, from that face which had always beamed with tenderness upon her, continued to urge the advantages with which she was impressed. The uncon-scious children described the happiness in which they had been nurtured, and the hero seemed to hesitate in opposing solicita-tions so tender, when the well practised tutor again assailed him, but becoming less cautious, hinted at his immediate junction with the Captain-General. Toussaint, now confirmed in his suspicions, instantly retired from the view of his wife and children, and when Coisnon expected, with infernal pleasure, his fraudulent victory, gave him this dignified determination. "Take back my children, if it must be so, I will be faithful to my brethren and my God!" The characters of father and hero could not agree in this trying situation. Toussaint did not risk another sight of his children, but in less than two hours from the moment of his arrival, departed again for the camp, from whence he returned a formal answer to the letter of General Le Clerc. This cir-cumstance appears to have developed in a clearer view the in-tentions of the invaders, and is an explanation of the marked hostility in the onset, although professed to be only intended, to re-establish the colonial relation of the island to France. The answer was conveyed by Granville, the tutor of the younger sons of Toussaint, a Frenchman; and a correspondence was con-tinued with the same demands on the one part, and an evasion of satisfactory explanation on the other.

At

CHAP. V. 1802.

At length, finding the surrender of Toussaint not to be accomplished by artifice, and wearied with the situation to which he was confined, instead of the pleasures of a court, General Le Clerc became impatient; and on the arrival of Admiral Gantheaume with a supply of two thousand three hundred men, with the prospect of an additional reinforcement under Admiral Linois, in a moment of irritation, on the 17th of February, issued a proclamation which seemed designed to hold the French army to contempt, and to resign all claim to that ability or design which at least marks their compositions of this kind.

Second proclamation of the Captain-General Le Clerc.

"I come," says he, "to restore prosperity and abundance! Every one must see what an insensible monster he is!" (Toussaint.) "I promise liberty to the people of this island. I shall make them rejoice! and I shall respect their persons and property. I order as follows:

"Art. I. The General Toussaint and the General Christophé, are put out of the protection of the law. All citizens are ordered to pursue them, and to treat them as the enemies of the French Republic.

"II. From the day on which the French army shall occupy a position, all officers, whether civil or military, who shall obey other orders than those of the generals of the army which I command, shall be treated as rebels.

"III. The

CHAP. V. 1802.

"III. The cultivators, who, seduced into error, and deceived by the perfidious insinuations of the rebel general, may have taken arms, shall be regarded as children who have strayed, and shall be sent to their plantations, provided they do not seek to excite insurrection.

"IV. The soldiers of the demi-brigade who shall abandon the army of Toussaint, shall be received into the French army.

(Signed, &c.) LE CLERC.
DUGUA."

The proclamation was followed by a commencement of the war at all quarters, and the exercise of every artifice that could be practised to procure defection in the black camp. The clergy were successfully employed to communicate with those of their own order to that effect; thus, those who should have mediated in the cause of peace, by undermining the very power which protected them, promoted a civil war of accumulated horrors.

The war was prosecuted by the Captain-General with all the vigor such haughty and hyperbolical expressions would imply, but the pride which dictates high-sounding proclamations, does not always furnish the means of executing them, and in the present instance they arose more from the disappointed ambition of Le Clerc, than from the power he possessed in the island.

Toussaint,

If Toussaint had hitherto suspended his opinion respecting the intention of the French government, he now had no room for doubt. It is not, however, to be wondered at, that he should so long have forborne to view them in the glaring light in which they presented themselves. That any experienced general, or minister, should be found so weak as to depend solely on the opinion and accounts of those who were so deeply interested in the event of a successful expedition against St. Domingo, at once vague, partial, and insufficient, was scarcely to be credited; and Le Clerc's conduct, since his arrival, had been paradoxical throughout. He brought a force professedly to support the existing constitution of the island, and renew the relation between it and the mother country, which had been resigned by the incapacity of the latter;—yet, presenting a hostile force, insists on every post being surrendered to him, and desires the immediate submission of the General in Chief, whose conduct had never been questioned. He brings with him the beloved sons of the General, as an earnest of the good intentions of the French government towards him, but scarcely allows him time to embrace them, when they are torn from him and their distracted mother with the most torpid apathy. He says, he comes to restore "peace and abundance" in a country *already* peaceful and abundant, by putting its inhabitants to the sword, and destroying its territory! The force he brought with him, when divided into the different detachments around the vast extent of coast, was insufficient, and the re-inforcements too trifling to effect any

CHAP. V. 1802.

CHAP. V. 1802. enterprize of importance, and without any provision being made till they had obtained it from the invaded country, inasmuch that the admiral was compelled to dispatch a frigate to Jamaica, to solicit aid of every description by the most artful finesse.*

Toussaint soon saw that, notwithstanding every deficiency, the mask which had been loosely worn, was entirely thrown aside, and that he had to confide in the pre-dispositions of his own forces, more than the sincerity or benevolence of the French. He therefore made preparation for a conflict, more terrible in proportion to its extent, than any he had yet sustained from the numerous enemies with whom he had had to cope. Considering the distant points as sufficiently provided, and expecting the great blow to be struck in the northern province, in which the French head-quarters were situate, he repaired thither with a select camp, to oppose himself to the Captain-General. His

* In a letter to the English admiral commanding there, dated February 15. "The disposition," he says, "of the cabinet of St. James's, and the known loyalty of your nation, Sir, permit me to hope that the ports of Jamaica will furnish us (should circumstances demand it, and should you be abundantly supplied) with provision and ammunition. One of the ministers of his Britannic Majesty has said, that the peace just concluded was not an ordinary peace, but a sincere reconciliation of two of the greatest nations in the world. If it depends on me, Sir, this happy prognostic will certainly be verified, at least I am pleased to imagine, that our pacific communications will be worthy of two nations, to whom war has only multiplied the reciprocal reasons which they had to esteem each other; and to give you authentic proofs of our confidence, I lay before you a faithful statement of our forces in the ports of St. Domingo."—*Villaret's Letter to Admiral Duckworth.*

attention

attention was still directed to every quarter, and his capacious mind revolved every object connected with his command. Expert as the whole of the black troops were, those surrounding the person of Toussaint were uncommonly so, being disciplined with inconceivable correctness. CHAP. V. 1802.

Though formed into regular divisions, the soldiers of the one were trained to the duties of the other, and all understood the management of artillery with the greatest accuracy Their chief dexterity, however, was in the use of the bayonet. With that dreadful weapon, fixed on musquets of extraordinary length in their hands, neither cavalry nor artillery could subdue infantry, although of unequal proportion; but when they were attacked in their defiles, no power could overcome them. Infinitely more skilful than the Maroons of Jamaica in their cock-pits,* though not more favored by nature, they found means to place whole lines in ambush, continuing sometimes from one post to another, and sometimes stretching from their camps, in the form of a horse-shoe. With these lines artillery was not used, to prevent their being burthened, or the chance of loss; but the surrounding heights of every camp were well fortified, according to the experience and judgment of different European engineers, with ordnance of the best kind, in proper directions. The protection afforded by these out-works, encouraged the blacks to every exertion of skill or courage; while the

* See Dallas's Hist. vol. ii.

CHAP. V. 1802. alertness constantly displayed embarrassed the enemy, who, frequently irritated, or worn out with fatigue, flew in disorder to the attack, or retreated with difficulty. Sometimes a regular battle or skirmish ensued, to seduce the enemy to a confidence in their own superiority, when in a moment reinforcements arose from an ambush in the vicinity, and turned the fortune of the day. If black troops, in the pay of the enemy, were dispatched to reconnoitre when an ambush was probable, and were discovered, not a man returned, from the hatred which their perfidy had inspired; nor could an officer venture without the lines with impunity.

With a body of tried grenadiers, and such troops as have been described, Toussaint waited the approach of the French with patient calmness at the camp of Breda, from whence he occasionally made rapid excursions to those points about which he was most anxious, on the north and north-west parts of the island.

On the 17th of February, General Le Clerc commenced his campaign, by forcing a few villages, and forming some posts; and soon after removed his head-quarters to the village of Gros Morne, on the bank of the Three Rivers, about twenty miles south-west from the Cape. From the success he had experienced in the compromises already made with the minor black generals, he had given his whole army directions to negotiate, wherever it could be done with safety, for the surrender of the different commands, and his success was greater than could possibly have been expected; it is, nevertheless, to be recollected, that every one viewed the present period as the commencement of a long war; and with those of inferior discrimination, the proclamations and verbal declarations of the French army presented the most grateful prospects; among which the officers regarded the confirmation of their power, independent of their black superiors, in the first degree.

The whole of the troops landed in this province, having received orders to form a junction, the division under General Desfourneaux advanced to the Limbé; another under General Hardy marched to the Grand Boucamp and the Mornets; and that commanded by General Rochambeau proceeded against La Tannerie, and the wood of L'Ance. A small corps, composed of the garrisons of the Cape and Fort Dauphin, advanced against St. Luzanne, Le Fren, and Volliere. These divisions had, according to their own account, "to sustain several actions, rendered very painful by the situation of the ground, and by the movements of the blacks, who concealed themselves in the impenetrable forests which bordered the vallies, and who had a secure retreat in the fastnesses." They, however, obtained a transitory possession of the position which they had been ordered to occupy.

On the 18th, the divisions of Desfourneaux, Hardy, and Rochambeau, encamped near Plaisance, at Dondon, and St. Raphael,

CHAP. V. 1802. Raphael, where, after having halted some time, they advanced on the blacks with impetuosity. "It is," observed Le Clerc in his dispatches,* "absolutely necessary to see the country, in order to be enabled to form a competent idea of the difficulties which it presented at every step. I have never seen in the Alps any obstacles equal to those with which it abounds."

On the 19th, Desfourneaux's division took possession of Plaisance without resistance. That canton was commanded by a mulatto called Jean Pierre Dumesnel, with whom the career of compromise commenced. He joined the French general, Desfourneaux, with two hundred cavalry, and three hundred infantry, and of course reversed the orders of Toussaint, and preserved the place.

General Hardy's division, before it arrived at Marmelade, made itself master of the Morne at Borspen by similar means, with the party which surrounded it. General Christophé being betrayed, evacuated the place with twelve hundred regular troops in good order. General Rochambeau took up his position at St. Michael, where he found little resistance, his right column carrying an entrenched post, Mare-a-la-Roche, defended by four hundred men and artillery, with the bayonet.

The French General perceiving Toussaint's design was to

* Moniteur,—Dispatch of Le Clerc to the Minister of Marine, dated February 26.

defend

defend the canton of Ennery and the Gonaives, mustered as much force as he could towards that point. He detached General Debelle with a division to Port Paix, and he had orders to attack General Maurepas near the Gonaives, who had two thousand regular troops, and two thousand cultivators under his command, in an entrenched post, within two leagues of Port Paix, and in the defiles of Les Trois Riviéres. He was very desirous to disperse that corps which had repulsed General Humbert, and ordered General Boudet to advance towards La Petite Riviére, for the purpose of cutting off the retreat off the enemy's corps, on whose defeat near the Gonaives he placed great reliance. Toussaint, however, prevented the execution of this movement by a skilful separation of one part of the force from the other. CHAP. V. 1802.

On the 20th of February, General Debelle marched to attack General Maurepas, but a torrent of rain falling, prevented the columns arriving in time to flank the black division, and thereby turn their position. The columns which attacked them in front were so much exhausted by fatigue, that they were unable to carry it; and those destined to turn them being attacked in every point by the black forces, were compelled to retreat with difficulty and considerable loss.

General Boudet's division, in setting out from Port-au-Prince, marched against La Croix des Bouquets, which was set fire to by the blacks on his approach; and General Dessalines, who commanded in that quarter, instead of retreating, made a feint

CHAP. V. 1802.

by marching over the mountains, and there taking a rapid turn to Leogane, which he fired in the face of a frigate dispatched by the French admiral for its protection. These difficulties increased the offers and the deception of the French, and in consequence, a powerful black general, La Plume, *submitted* to General Boudet, with the whole of his district.

On the 22d, the division of Desfourneaux advanced within two miles of Plaisance, then deserted by La Plume, notwithstanding the attempt of Christophé, with the force which remained, to resist it, in which they had a severe skirmish; he, however, cut off a part of their force, and retreated to Bayannai. The brigade of General Salm, after performing a very fatiguing march on the 22d, continued during the whole of the night, and at day-break on the 23d, arrived at the position Christophé had left to join the grand black army, where they were rewarded by the remains of a considerable booty, it having been a depôt of the blacks.

On the 23d, Rochambeau's division took a position at the head of the Ravine-a-Couleuvre, having the Coupe-au-Linde on his left, and the fastnesses where Christophé was entrenched on the right. The divisions of Desfourneaux and Hardy took a position before Ennery.

On the 24th, Desfourneaux advancing, at the Coupe-a-Pintade met the enemy. It was supported by Desplanque's division, and that of General Hardy. General Desfourneaux attacked

attacked a black out-post, which he pursued to Gonaives, and from thence to the River Ester. Salm's brigade, belonging to Hardy's division, took a position at Pateau, before La Coupe-a-Pintade.

Battle of the Ravine-a-Couleuvre.

On the same day, Rochambeau's division entered the Ravine-a-Couleuvre, where General Toussaint, with his guard, forming a corps of fifteen hundred grenadiers drawn from different demi-brigades, and about twelve hundred other chosen troops, with the addition of four hundred dragoons, waited to receive them in person. The Ravine-a-Couleuvre is extremely well protected, being flanked by lofty mountains covered with wood; in advantageous places were posted more than two thousand cultivators. They formed a considerable number of abattis, which obstructed the passage, and occupied the entrenched positions which commanded the Ravines. From the advantages of the defection, and a knowledge of the country, General Rochambeau executed his movement with a rapidity similar to that of the enemy he was encountering, and attacked their entrenchments. A battle ensued, in which Le Clerc acknowledges, "man was opposed to man, and the troops of Toussaint fought well." It was an affair deserving an accurate description in the military annals of the time. The ability and bravery of the French troops were called forth, and every manœuvre of the black tactics was displayed! On a bloody field, at the close of the day, victory remained doubtful, and each party were more anxious with

regard

CHAP. V. 1802. regard to their future movements, than the honor of superiority so dearly bought. Toussaint retired to the banks of La Petit Riviére, and Le Clerc to Gonaives. General Maurepas continued in considerable power in the western province, and repelled the attacks of Generals Debelle and Boudet, until they were reinforced by two divisions; those of Desfourneaux and Rochambeau, dispatched by the French General to support and collect their scattered forces.

On the 27th, General Boudet was master of St. Marc, but Maurepas, by his positions, still retaining the command of the province, Le Clerc summoned all the force he could collect, and putting himself at their head, prepared to march against that general. He ordered General Hardy to advance to Gros Morne with five companies of grenadiers, and eight hundred men belonging to his division. To this corps he added a company of his own guards, consisting of two hundred men, and on the night of the 27th, took a position at two miles distance. The divisions of Desfourneaux and Debelle were in motion to join, when the experiment of compromise presenting a more pleasing aspect than the doubtful issue of a battle, Maurepas submitted to General Debelle, on the conditions of the promise of General Le Clerc, to continue their rank to such officers as surrendered.

These important points effected, leisure was obtained to consider

sider the best means of attacking the Black General in Chief, against whom the great body of the French army could now be directed, with the addition of the black officers who had been induced to join it with their troops. General Le Clerc, in consequence of these acquisitions, with the advantages which they gave him, and the consternation with which the inhabitants beheld the defection of their countrymen, began to view his situation with ease, and to indulge more extensive prospects. In this mood, for the first time during the campaign, he sat down to communicate with the Minister of Marine, and to beg the confirmation of the First Consul of what he had done. It was a campaign which had already cost a profusion of blood and money, and which, nothing but the treachery of La Plume, Dumesnils, and Maurepas, with the powerful forces under their command, and in the favorable positions they occupied, could have been prolonged for an hour. General Le Clerc viewing affairs in another light, more congenial to his own wishes, considered himself at this moment, (though occupying but a few leagues of country with his whole army, and constantly in sight of the coast,) "master of the colony!" "The army of St. Domingo," says he, "in the course of five days have routed the chief of their enemies, obtained possession of a considerable quantity of their baggage, and a portion of their artillery. Desertion is frequent in the rebel camp. Clervaux, La Plume, Maurepas, and many other black chiefs, and men of color, have submitted. The plantations of the south are entirely preserved, the whole of the Spanish part

 of

CHAP. V. 1802. of the island has surrendered;" when his army had not visited the French plantations of the south; his troops still remained inactive on the Spanish coast of the island, and Clervaux had only *agreed*, through the bishop of Yago, to surrender.

Such was the progress of the French arms in St. Domingo, and such the opinion entertained by their general of the successes that had been obtained. The preceding account will be found corroborated by the dispatches of the Captain-General, in which he mentions the whole of the territory he had obtained, which was on the sea-coast, viz. Mancinello Bay, Le Limbé, Port Paix, Gonaives, St. Marc, Port-au-Prince, and Leogane. Notwithstanding the debarkations at nearly the same time at St. Domingo, Port-au-Prince, Cape François, and Fort Dauphin, and that the interior had never been attempted, they had not been able to form a junction till it was accomplished by the acquisition of the defectors from the black army, or to force Toussaint from their very centre. It has already been observed, that the maxim of the Black General in Chief, was to suffer them to harass themselves by forced marches, and to obtain positions untenable, or unavailing. More than this, it appears from their own accounts, they had not effected; while Toussaint and his forces changed their situation or position as often as they chose, never being overtaken in their retreat, or surprized on a march; but frequently falling on the enemy by an unexpected road, and routing them with the utmost dismay. A variety of these

manœuvres

manouvres were continually practised, but the blacks not fighting for the panegyric of Europeans, they are unnoticed and forgotten, except by their countrymen, and those who suffered from them. CHAP. V. 1802.

The circumstance of three Generals high in esteem, with a considerable force, going over to the enemy, and joining their local knowledge and peculiar tactics against their own cause, within a few days from each other, and at a distance, is unprecedented, and must have operated with the Commander in Chief, more than the shock of an unexpected and powerful army. In fact, such was the effect of gold and promises, of extension of command in the French army, that for a time Toussaint was uncertain, when he ordered a division to march, whether it was not about to join the enemy; while he was preparing against those with whom treaties had been formed previous to the invasion; others, on whom he most depended for the attack or repelling of the enemy, and to whom their country looked with confidence, were turning their swords against him. General La Plume, among the first to set the example of abetting the French, was one of whom Toussaint entertained the highest opinion, and entrusted with an extensive district. He seemed at a loss how to render his injuries sufficiently striking, and in consequence receives the eulogium of Le Clerc. One of the first acts of this ungrateful man, was the exposure of a letter, in which himself is mentioned with favour, and which was a principal cause, with his disobedience of Toussaint's orders, of the violence of his praise.

 It

CHAP. V. 1802.

It was addressed to the commandant of the district of Jeremie, General Domage, and dated from the black head-quarters, at that time at St. Marc, for Toussaint's communication was constantly kept up with every part of the island to which the French had obtained access.

Feb. 9, 1802.

Letter and orders of Toussaint to the black general Domage.

"MY DEAR GENERAL,

"I send to you my aid-de-camp Chaney, who is the bearer of the present dispatch, and who will communicate to you my sentiments.

"The whites have resolved to destroy our liberty, and have therefore brought a force commensurate to their intentions. The Cape, after a proper resistance, has fallen into their hands, but the enemy found only a town and plain in ashes; the forts were blown up, and all was burnt.

"The town of Port Republicain (Port-au-Prince) has been given up to them by the traitor, General of Brigade, Agé, as well as Fort Bizotton, which surrendered without an effort, in consequence of the cowardice and treachery of the Chief of Battalion, Bardet, an old officer of the south; but the General of Division, Dessalines, maintains at this moment a line at La Croix des Bouquets, and all our other places are on the defensive.

"As

"As Jeremie is rendered very strong by its natural advantages, you will maintain yourself in it, and defend yourself with the courage which I know you possess. Distrust the whites,—they will betray you if they can; their desire, evidently manifested, is the restoration of slavery.

"I therefore give you a *carte-blanche* for your conduct. All which you shall do will be well done. Raise the cultivators in mass, and convince them of this truth,—that they must place no confidence in those artful agents who may have secretly received the proclamations of the white men from France, and would circulate them clandestinely, in order to seduce the friends of liberty.

"I have ordered the General of Brigade, La Plume, to burn the town of Cayes, and every other town and plain in the district, should they be unable to resist the enemy's force; thus all the troops in the different garrisons, and all the cultivators, will be enabled to reinforce you at Jeremie. You will entertain a perfect good understanding with General La Plume, in order to execute with ease what may be necessary. You will employ in the planting of provisions all the women occupied in cultivation.

"Endeavour as much as possible to acquaint us with your situation.

"I rely

CHAP. V. 1802. "I rely entirely upon you, and leave you completely at liberty, to perform every thing which may be requisite to free us from the horrid yoke with which we are threatened.

"I wish you good health,

(Signed) "TOUSSAINT L'OUVERTURE.

"A true copy,

(Signed) "The General of Brigade commanding the Department of the South,

"LA PLUME."

Toussaint, confident in his resources, expected the completion of his wishes, by seeing his enemies, notwithstanding the aid they had received, exhaust themselves. He knew also that the recreant heart which sold its honor, and every sentiment that should be cherished, for the fleeting promise of a sanguine enemy, would be easily regained when time should change the hands in which the power that tempted it was placed; and he had some reason to doubt, whether the defection of those who had abandoned him did not arise from other motives than those which were apparent.

The public feeling in France, on receiving the distorted intelligence which the dispatches of Le Clerc conveyed, grew

more

more and more against the blacks:—those who had been their most strenuous friends became their most active enemies; and, exclusive of the common prostitutions of the press, to which party gives birth on all occasions,* books were published at Paris, avowedly for the purpose of exposing the errors of *Negrophilism*, or the love of the blacks. In England it was similar, and the voice of discretion, or discrimination, was drowned by the general clamour.

Admiral Duckworth, after receiving the frigate La Cornelie, which was expressly dispatched to him by Le Clerc, with every mark of respect, and loading her captain, Villemandrin, and his lieutenant with honors, wrote home for instructions relative to supplying the French troops with stores and provisions, as without he could not comply with the request of the French commander. The Spanish governor at the Havannah exerted himself in every way for their accommodation, by furnishing both money and clothing, of which the army was in great want. The following sentiments respecting the black army, as they form a correct delineation of the public opinion, are quoted from Admiral Duckworth's letter, in answer to the French Commander in Chief:

* The meanness of traducing characters, and, indeed, all vitiations of truth, which are permitted, and considered expedient in the policy of states, is one of the most prominent errors in British legislation, and one which, for the honor of the country, and the credit of its consistency, it is wished were remedied. Its effects are of the worst kind, as relates to the government and the governed, the relations between both, and every other country with whom they hold a correspondence.

"It

CHAP. V. 1802.

"It is with a painful sentiment I have learned the hostile reception of your excellency, and that direct violation of all the duties of colonies towards their mother country.... I perfectly agree with you on the consequences of such conduct, and I really think it interests all the powers of Europe. But, with a force so considerable as you have, the revolt cannot be of long duration; and the devastation committed by the rebels can only produce a temporary evil."

Prosecution of the campaign.

Having conveyed Madame Le Clerc by sea to Port-au-Prince, and established his head-quarters there, after making every arrangement in his power of his newly acquired force, the Captain-General re-commenced the campaign with fresh energy. Port-au-Prince was the most desirable residence they had yet obtained, not having been injured in the least, from the ease with which it was taken possession of by Boudet; but the next town in the south, Leogane, was destroyed by Dessalines, and every place that was likely to aid a passage to that quarter. Desfourneaux was left at Plaisance to protect the north, while Hardy, Rochambeau, Boudet, and Debelle, proceeded to the Spanish border of the western district. La Crete a Pierrot, a post rather advantageously situated, between St. Marc and Port-au-Prince, which had been a depôt of the blacks, and lately their apparent head-quarters, was the first object of the French; whereby they committed an error frequent in military tactics, where a necessary position is lost through the desire of booty. The Black General perceived this error, for, after appearing to guard anxiously a celebrated point, and

and finding means, first to convey away every thing desirable, he then evacuated it, leaving to the self-nominated victorious army, an empty arsenal, empty coffers, and frequently unsheltered quarters.*—Such was the case with La Crete a Pierrot, and in the defence of which, and the operations that immediately followed, the blacks covered themselves with glory, and their enemies with infamy.

CHAP. V. 1802.

The siege of La Crete a Pierrot.

The main body of the French army was put in motion against this fortress; and its defence, planned by the General in Chief, was committed to General Dessalines. Whether it was from the weakness of General Le Clerc, or the enthusiasm of his troops at the expectation of booty at this siege, is unknown; but, if the vengeance of disappointed personal ambition, and an accumulation of every bad passion, had been infused in the breasts of the soldiers, it could not have been more cruelly displayed than in the affair of Crete a Pierrot. The scythed car of the ancient Briton, or the poisoned javelin of the savage Indian, are instruments of humanity, compared with the fatal bayonet as used by the French on this day; nor, could the desperation of the blacks in their first struggle for emancipation, exceed their bitter vengeance, of which the very recital stains the page of history.

* A General cannot be too much on his guard how he gratifies the best soldiers under his command in this way. To brave and exhausted troops, rest and comfort, when they can be afforded with safety, is a due consideration; but a desire of booty in a dangerous and doubtful warfare, is like sleep in the frigid zone, always tempting, yet frequently destructive.

In

CHAP. V. 1802. In the beginning of March, the divisions of Hardy, Rochambeau, Boudet, and Debelle, marched against different posts in the vicinity of their grand object, with the hope of preventing the retreat of an enemy of whose reduction they considered themselves certain. Rochambeau first attacked a village called Cahows, from whose few inoffensive inhabitants he met no opposition; but General Hardy, with a considerable force, surrounded six hundred blacks in the Coupe de L'Inde, who bravely attempted to cut their way to Trianon, they were all taken, and murdered on the spot; and a Chief of Battalion, Henin, with a part of the same force, attacked the position Trianon, and carried it with the bayonet. Enraged by such unexampled warfare, Dessalines made a sortie from the fort, and advancing as far as La Petit Riviére, met General Debelle on his march to Verettes, whom, supposing a part of the cruel perpetrators, he drove before him to La Crete a Pierrot; but, so far from attempting a retaliation, he left them to the mercy of war, and retiring into the fort, discharged a volley of grape shot among them, by which Debelle and a considerable number were wounded. The commandant of artillery, Pambour, took the command of the division, and Debelle fell back into the rear.

General Boudet now passed the Artibonité, for the purpose of blockading Crete a Pierrot, but had scarcely come within sight of the glacis, when he received a wound which compelled him to return, and his men were thrown into disorder. General Dugua advancing

advancing with a battalion of the 19th light troops, and the 74th regiment of the line, to form the blockade, was also dangerously wounded, and his party completely routed. To revenge this, Le Clerc, who had a narrow escape, a shot having hit the center of his sash, and carried part of it away, hastened a part of his artillery from Port-au-Prince, and Rochambeau spread fire and sword through every village in his way. General Salines, likewise, with a large body, contrived to surround a small camp of the blacks, and put every man to the sword.

On the 22d of March, Rochambeau attempted to erect a battery of seven pieces of heavy artillery on a rising ground, but in vain, the fire of a redoubt bearing upon him, swept away the whole of his men. He therefore marched to attack the redoubt, but found it so secured by a projection of logwood, that it was impossible to be carried. In the mean time, every thing being prepared for evacuating the fort, Dessalines, with a part of his force, sallied forth in the night, and falling in with Desplanques, who commanded General Hardy's advanced guard, a skirmish ensued, which, nevertheless, did not prevent his departure. The absence of Dessalines inspired the besiegers with new hopes, and for the three successive days they bombarded the fort with great activity, frequently setting fire to it. On the evening of the last day, the commander of the black forces remaining at La Crete, made a vigorous sally, and forced the French lines; a small part only accomplished this measure, and passed the Arti-

bonité;

CHAP. V. 1802. bonité; the remainder were surrounded, and immediately put to the sword.

Thus ended the siege and blockade, which had cost the French army much, by the loss of some of her best generals and finest troops, but in nothing so much as in the exercise of a ferocious spirit unknown among civilized people. Besides the cruelties in cold blood which have been recited, and which were exultingly acknowledged in the dispatches of General Le Clerc, were numerous acts of private barbarity, the recital of which could answer no good purpose, while the blacks, in this instance, are not charged, even by their enemies, with the commission of any of these enormities. Nor did they avail themselves on the present occasion of those advantages which remain to be found in the fastnesses of the mountains. The fortress which they occupied had been regularly built by the English during their possession of this part of the island, and the defence of it was truly English. The remembrance of this affair will long be found on the banks of the Artibonité, to the disgrace of the one party, and the praise of the other.

Buoyed by what he conceived success, the Captain-General of the French extended his views, and prepared for the dominion to which he had always looked. He published an order in direct violation of his own proclamations, directing proprietors, or their attornies, to resume their ancient authority over the negroes.* He treated with rigor and insolence, on the smallest difference of opinion, the inhabitants who surrounded him, and with indignity the Americans who constantly traded to the coast, compelling them to sell their cargoes of flour, and other provisions, for bills on France, which was but the prelude to farther enormities. To prevent the circulation of facts, he established an official gazette at Port-au-Prince, whose bulletins solely were to be regarded. CHAP. V. 1802.

Toussaint L'Ouverture was employed in a care superior to that of contemplating his self-sufficiency. He had noticed the neglected situation in which the northern province was left, by withdrawing the whole of the French force to the recent siege, and he resolved to avail himself of it. Therefore, while General Le Clerc was revelling in the reputation of the French arms in the west, and dispatching General Rochambeau to sack Les Gonaives, which at one time had been the black head-quarters, Toussaint effected a junction with Christophé in the mountains; and poured down an accumulated force on the plain of the Cape. Reaching Plaisance by a mountain-road, he routed the forces of General Desfourneaux; passed on without molestation through Dondon and Marmelade, raising the cultivators in his way, and halted within a mile and a half of the city of Cape François. An universal consternation followed. Dispatches were sent, requiring the aid of the victorious generals, and Le

* Journal de Peltier, 1802, p. 521.

Clerc

CHAP. V. 1802. Clerc himself left his infant honors, taking a hasty passage by sea to the Cape. From the concourse of people in and about the city, a dreadful contagion began to shew itself. General Boyer, endeavoured to oppose this astonishing chief, with his whole force, including the marines and sailors from the fleet, and was quickly driven back, under the very hospital; when the blacks laid the whole plain of the Cape in ruins, in defiance of the Captain-General, commanding in the town, and of Generals Hardy and Rochambeau, who arrived by forced marches, they then retired to the mountains of Hincha.*

While these untoward circumstances were interrupting the felicity which General Le Clerc promised himself in his new quarters, another difficulty occurred where it was least expected. Among other objects destined for political use in the invasion of St. Domingo, was Rigaud, the mulatto-general, the ancient opponent of Toussaint, whose presence, it was suggested, by some of his friends, might attach his former party to the French arms, but which Le Clerc considered an expedient too dangerous to risque. Rigaud, who expected an immediate restora-

* At the time these transactions were taking place, Bonaparté addressed the French people in a message to the Legislative Body, thus: "At St. Domingo great calamities have taken place, and great calamities are to be repaired; but the revolt is daily confined to narrower bounds. Toussaint, without fortresses, without money, without an army, is now no more than a robber wandering from desert to desert, with a few vagabonds like himself, whom our intrepid clearers are in pursuit of, and who will be soon overtaken and destroyed." *Moniteur, May 7.*—Such was the blindness with which this wonderful man had been influenced, and such is political consistency.—

tion of his property and command, finding himself continued in concealment, at a distance from his native province, began to contemplate means of re-instating himself. No sooner, therefore, was the Captain-General called to the Cape, than he attempted a correspondence with General La Plume, on the subject of a visit to his friends, who immediately communicated his letter to Le Clerc. Enraged at what he conceived perfidy at so critical a moment, he immediately ordered the unfortunate chief, with his family, to be sent on board a frigate, and conveyed to France, as one whose principles could not "contribute to the re-establishment of the colony of St. Domingo." This was a circumstance, however, disagreeable to many powerful persons, and Le Clerc, with a facility which has marked the political transactions of Europe in the beginning of the nineteenth century, adds, that Rigaud had "sent emissaries into the south to stop cultivation, and alarm the peaceable citizens with terrors."* The officer whose duty it

CHAP. V. 1802.

* Gazette du Port-au-Prince,---Letter of the Captain-General to General Dugua, Chief of the Staff at Port-au-Prince. The letter of Rigaud, also given in this journal, contains some pathetic appeals, which are interesting, as coming from the hand of fallen power:---

"Persecuted" says he, "these ten years; driven away from my property for the last two years; taken prisoner by the English and other allies of my enemies, I have persevered in the same principles I had before. The French government doing justice to my conduct and fidelity, gave me an employment in the French army, and my first steps were bent towards the incendiary and murdering rebels of the northern part, whose example you were wise enough not to imitate. You are not ignorant of the deep wounds made on humanity, and destruction of my unhappy countrymen; I can only mourn their lot; the evil is irremediable; but for the sake of those who are yet living, for one who would not sink under the weight

CHAP. V. 1802. it was to perform the present order, (Dugua,) had the sensibility to solicit Admiral Villaret to escort the wrecks of fallen greatness.

The only means which remained to withstand the shock the French had sustained, were, an extension of the number and powers of the emissaries, who had been constantly kept in employment, to seduce the unconscious cultivators, and had proved successful in the districts to which they had access. Le Clerc saw his error in the premature attempt to re-establish the ancient regimen by his order at Port-au-Prince, which had evidently inclined even the defective to return to the confidence of their brethren, and strengthened in their determination those who held out, being at least three-fourths of the population of the island. To remedy this ill-judged action he adopted another, which, although too often countenanced in the complicated politics of magnificent states, was an instance of the most degrading meanness. This was

weight of misfortune, would you not think it conformable to justice, and even your duty, to give orders, without having recourse to superior authority, that every thing of which we have been deprived should be given up to us. I confine myself at present, to request you to cause my sister, or M. Deronseray, my attorney, to be put again into the possession of my cattle, and that of my brothers; our lands and houses, and their produce, from the time we have been deprived of it.*

* * * * * * * * * * * * * *

"When the banditti are destroyed in the northern part, I will bend my course towards the south, where I was born, where I have lived, and commanded with glory! I hope to find there none but brothers and friends, &c.

"A. Rigaud."

* The nature of this request is explained by the order of Le Clerc (in the amplitude of his power) at Port-au-Prince,—that the ancient proprietors, or their attornies, should resume their estates.

2 a pro-

a proclamation in which the freedom of the blacks is ASSURED, but that assurance is rendered a perfect nullity, by the arrangement of the sentence in which it is conveyed. As an example of the manner in which the French expedition against the blacks was conducted, the instrument is given in its formal state:— CHAP. V. 1802.

"LIBERTY. EQUALITY.

"In the Name of the French Government,

"A PROCLAMATION.

"*The General in Chief to the Inhabitants of St. Domingo:*

"CITIZENS,

"The time is arrived when order will succeed that chaos which has been the natural consequence of the opposition made by the rebellious to the landing of the army at St. Domingo.

"The rapid operations and progress of the army, and the necessity of providing for its subsistence and establishment, have, hitherto, prevented my attending to the definitive organization of the colony. I could not have any fixed or certain ideas of a country with which I was totally unacquainted, and consequently could not, without mature deliberation, form an opinion of a people who have been, for ten years, a prey to revolutions.

 "The

CHAP. V. 1802. "The basis of the provisionary organization which I shall give to the colony, BUT WHICH SHALL NOT BE DEFINITIVE TILL APPROVED OF BY THE FRENCH GOVERNMENT, is *Liberty and Equality to all the inhabitants of St. Domingo, without regard to colour.* This organization comprises:

"1st. The administration of justice.

"2nd. The interior administration of the colony, combined with those measures which its interior and exterior defence require.

"3d. The imposition of duties, the means of raising them, and their application.

"4th. The regulations and ordinances relative to agriculture.

"5th. The regulations and ordinances relative to commerce.

"6th. The administration of the national domains, the means of making them most beneficial to the state, so as to be less burthensome to agriculture and commerce.

"As it is of infinite interest to you, Citizens, that every institution should, in an equal degree, protect agriculture and commerce, I have not determined upon this important work, without having first recourse to, and consulted with, the most distinguished and enlightened citizens of the colony.

"In consequence, I have given orders to the generals of the south and west divisions, to select for each of these departments *seven* citizens, proprietors and merchants, (*without regard to colour,*)

colour,) who, with *eight* more, which I shall myself choose for the department of the North, are to assemble at the Cape in the course of the present month, to impart their observations to me on the plans I shall then submit to their consideration. CHAP. V. 1802.

"It is not a deliberative assembly I establish. I am sufficiently acquainted with the evils which meetings of this nature have brought upon the colony to have that idea. The citizens who are thus chosen being honest and enlightened men, to them will I communicate my views; they will make their observations upon them, and will be able to impress on the minds of their fellow citizens the liberal ideas with which the government is animated.

"Let those, then, who are thus to be called together, consider this appointment as a flattering proof of my consideration for them. Let them consider that for want of their counsels and advice, I might pursue measures disastrous to the colony, which would ultimately fall upon themselves. Let them consider this, and they will find no difficulty in leaving, for some time, their private avocations.

"Done at the Head-quarters of the Cape, 5th Floreal, year 10 of the French Republic.

(Signed) "The General in Chief, Le Clerc.

A true copy,

(Signed) "The Deputy Adjutant-General, D'Aoust."

Never

CHAP. V. 1802. Never was so much art and weakness displayed at one time in any public officer as in this instance of Le Clerc, whose mind must have been capable of the most abject baseness, and reduced to the most contemptible alternatives.* The proclamation, however, had its desired effect, and vast defections from the followers of Toussaint, even those in his last expedition, was the immediate consequence.

In the beginning of April arrived the two squadrons long expected, from Havre and Flushing, and increased the puny advantages on which General Le Clerc prided himself. If his conduct assumed the air of determination before his late alarm, it had now no bounds, and with all the spirit of jacobinism which his brother-in-law had boasted to abolish, considered every measure expedient that would destroy his opponents, or confirm his power. If a body of *suspicious* negroes were discovered, an open grave awaited them, to the brink of which they were led unconscious, and either slaughtered, or precipitated alive into the dreadful chasm, as suited the convenience of those to whom the charge was intrusted. If a person connected with the expedition, whose advice had been originally courted, began to discover *un-philosophic* views in the Captain-General, and to venture opinions

* What a noble contrast is afforded to this effort of dirty chicane, by the conduct of General Walpole in Jamaica, who, scorning an act that might appear to inveigle men who had held British troops at defiance, and entered into regular treaties, refused the honorary reward of his gallantry and benevolence from the country he had served, because he did not conceive his engagements with them perfectly fulfilled. *See his Letter in the Appendix to Dallas's History.*

upon

upon the state of affairs, a vessel was ready in an adjacent port to convey away the disapproving object. The terror of the present regimen seemed to produce for the time a more powerful effect, than all the successes of the French arms, or the defections of the black chiefs.

Several bold pushes had been made by Toussaint, considering the dangers to which he was exposed, by the loss of his bravest commanders, and consequently their different plans of operation. Notwithstanding the success of his last expedition, his followers began to view forced marches with less patience than they were wont, and the situation of their opponents with proportionate envy. Toussaint continued resolute, with innumerable advantages, contemplating nothing but the prosecution of the war; though arguments more prevailing had been introduced to the ear of Christophé, his relation, and Toussaint was condemned to experience the pangs of Cæsar, and exclaim,

"Are you too turned against me?"

Compromise of the three black chiefs.

Christophé perceived the consequences of the disaffection excited among the black troops, although its effects had been confined to, comparatively, a small part of the island. He observed the weakness of Le Clerc, and was thereby led to think his present proclamation sincere; it is not in the nature of a brave man to suspect the quibbling arts of inferior authority. He had been frequently tempted, as well as the other black generals,

CHAP. V. 1802. generals, and at length corresponded on the subject of making peace, the terms of his compromise being, a general amnesty for his troops, and the preservation of his own rank, and that of all the other officers; and extending the same terms to his colleague Dessalines, and the General in Chief. Thus the situation of the blacks became no worse by the truce, should it extend no farther, while the artifices of the French would cease to have their effect. To such terms it was hard for the proud commandant to submit, and, it might have been perceived, they could not be permanent. But Le Clerc, who considered only his own aggrandizement, thought a peace on any terms enabled him to claim the praise of restoring the colony to France; and with regard to the means, as he had practised a fraud in his proclamation in St. Domingo, so he could deceive the mother country, by his statement of the surrender. Thus, wading on through the same weakness, meanness, and infamy, the preliminaries were arranged with General Christophé, which afforded a temporary peace to this unhappy country. Public hostilities ceased about the 1st of May.

The arrangement completed with Christophé, the General in Chief was induced to commence a correspondence, which ended in a pacific invitation, and acceptance thereof, to Cape François. At his former capital he behaved with a dignity, and at the same time a gentleness, that won all hearts towards him, and obtained a general respect. With Le Clerc it was otherwise;—if the difficulties with Christophé were great, they were much more so with him

 who

who had governed the island through a long and arduous period, and Toussaint returned to his camp without concluding a treaty; though he desired no more than what Christophé had obtained, with a dignified retirement—the wish of the greatest men of all countries and ages.

The brave Dessalines alone remained without joining in the treaty of peace. He saw an unnatural amity projected, and he knew there were yet armies ready for the field, when called in defence of their freedom; yet he would not thwart the wish of his brethren, and therefore coincided in the acts of the General in Chief; as such he must be acquitted of suffering any imposition by the professions of the French general, for he believed none of them, and is not responsible for any sincerity, by his accordance with the peace, when he knew the blacks would not regard the dereliction of their leaders.

Le Clerc did not long contend the matter with Toussaint, —a few skirmishes took place, of slight importance, when the Captain-General, impatient for sovereignty, granted his wishes. "You, General, and your troops," says he, "will be employed and treated like the rest of my army. With regard to yourself, *you desire repose*, and you deserve it; after a man has sustained for several years the government of St. Domingo, I apprehend he needs repose. I leave you at liberty to retire to which of your estates you please. I rely so much on the attachment

CHAP. V. 1802. you bear the colony of St. Domingo, as to believe you will employ what moments of leisure you may have, during your retreat, in communicating to me your ideas respecting the means proper to be taken, to cause agriculture and commerce again to flourish. As soon as a list and statement of the troops under General Dessalines are transmitted to me, I will communicate

May 8. my instructions as to the positions they are to take."*

Toussaint, with his family, retired to a plantation of his own name, L'Ouverture, at Gonaives, on the western coast; the brave and faithful Dessalines continued near them, at the town of St. Marc, with an intelligent and agreeable society. Never was a more interesting retreat, than that of these two great men, resigning honors, command, and the fascinations of absolute power, for the peace of their country. They were reverenced with increased affection by the people, and Europeans could not forbear viewing them with wonder. With the despicable jealousy of the Captain-General such an admiration was dangerous, and it did not escape his attention.

To avoid the dreadful effects of the fever at the Cape, which now spread its ravages with uncommon violence, the Captain-General made an excursion to the little island of Tortuga, having previously dispatched his aid-du-camp to France, with an account

* Gazette du Cape.

of

of the *surrender* of the blacks. In this dispatch he describes them as begging their lives, and surrendering at discretion, as being hunted down, and made prisoners in their different residences, notwithstanding that his letter to Toussaint, in direct contradiction, was published in Paris at the same moment.* For the convenience of issuing his numerous contradictory edicts, he at this time established a Gazette, under the title of The Official Gazette of St. Domingo, after their publication in which, they were to be equally in force, as if promulgated in the most formal manner. To this gazette, every account of military or government transactions was confined, those at Port Republicain and other places being restricted to commercial purposes.

At Tortuga Le Clerc exercised the new power he had acquired with his usual want of discrimination, and what was scarcely credible, even from so weak a governor, he again violated the very proclamation which he had issued with so barefaced a quibble, without waiting for its effect or consequences, by directing the blacks who were on several plantations to be set compulsorily to work, under the dominion of their ancient masters. To Toussaint, (whom no compromise could deprive of the power of attending to the calls of humanity, in those who continued under his care,) several bodies made their appeal, and others respectfully acquainted him with their resolutions, not to suffer a violation of the rights which had cost them so dear. On this

* See the Appendix.

subject,

CHAP. V. subject, therefore, he addressed a letter to an official agent, named
1802. Fontaine, at the Cape, on the 27th of May.

"It is said," he writes, "that General Le Clerc is in an ill state of health at Tortuga, of this you will inform me. If you see the General in Chief, be sure to tell him that the cultivators are no longer disposed to obey me, for the planters *wish to set them to work* at Hericourt, which they certainly ought not to do.

"I have to ask you whether any one near the person of the General in Chief can be gained to procure the release of D——, who would be very useful to me, from his influence at La Nouvelle, and elsewhere.

"Acquaint Gengembre that he should not quit the Borgne, where the cultivators must not be *set to work*."

Whether Fontaine courted the favor of Le Clerc, by communicating this letter immediately, or that it fell into his hands by means of that system of *espionage* in which his mean and suspicious mind delighted, is uncertain; or whether he had not predetermined the violation of his personal treaty with Toussaint as well as his guarantee of freedom to the blacks, which is most probable. Be this as it may, within a few days after the departure of this letter, and before the expiration of the first month of his retirement, in the dead of the night, the Creole frigate,

escorted

escorted by the Hero, a 74 gun ship from Cape François, stood in close to the shore of Gonaives, when suddenly landing several boats with troops, they surrounded the tranquil dwelling of Toussaint, where his innocent family lay wrapped in sleep, unconscious of their awaiting fate. To Brunet, chief of brigade, and Ferrari, an aid-du-camp of Le Clerc, was confided this treacherous task, which they performed so as to deserve the commendations of their master.* They entered the chamber of the hero with a file of grenadiers, and demanded his immediate surrender. Great as he had always been, he was now *surprised* for the first time, by a band of authorised assassins, whom armies had never been able to perplex, Toussaint declared himself indifferent as to his own fate, but remonstrated with regard to his family. "I shall not resist the power you have obtained over me," said he, "but my wife is feeble, and my children can do no harm. Suffer them, then, to remain at home." Reasoning of this kind suited neither their policy nor their minds; the guard was increased, and before the vicinage became alarmed, they were on board the vessel, and under sail. Two brave leaders, who were roused, instantly attacked the banditti; but their bravery was useless, they were soon seized, and afterwards shot.

CHAP. V.
1802.
Seizure and exile of Toussaint.

As soon as Toussaint was sent away, the emissaries of the Captain-General, under the direction of Rochambeau, who commanded at St. Marc, set about discovering the connexions,

* Gazette de St. Domingue.

2 and

CHAP. V. 1802. and even acquaintance of the unfortunate general, as if to root the very remembrance of him from the colony: but that rested on a firmer basis, the justice and gratitude of the country, and was so deeply engraven on the hearts of its inhabitants, that it could only be expelled with their lives. The brave Dessalines was for the present politically spared, but above an hundred of those who contributed to form the enlightened society of Toussaint, or who were distinguished for knowledge, or benevolence, were seized and sent on board different vessels in the harbour, and were never more heard of; in all probability, as the same mode of execution was afterwards openly had recourse to, they were immediately slaughtered, or thrown into the sea.

The astonishment which this flagrant act of the French government occasioned, was such as to paralyse the minds of the whole people. A dread calm succeeded. The Captain-General again boasted to the deluded Bonaparté of enormities which alone were sufficient to subject his government to the execration of posterity. As if designed to hold up the transactions of this island to ridicule, the dispatches continued to display the most glaring falsehoods, and contradictory accounts; in the one alluded to he declares, that joy had been produced at the Cape by the departure of Toussaint. If that sentiment did obtain public declaration, when the town was a common pest-house, and the French army were hourly dwindling away, it was more probable to arise from the death of the sanguinary General Hardy, the second in command, who died on the 2d of June, universally

universally detested for his total want of those qualities in which a true soldier delights.

The dispatch, as relates to the circumstances it describes, is a document too striking and important to be omitted. It is as follows:—

"*Head-quarters at the Cape, June* 11.

"I informed you in one of my last dispatches of the pardon I had been induced to grant General Toussaint. This ambitious man, from the moment of his pardon, did not cease to plot in secret. Though he surrendered, it was because Generals Christophé and Dessalines intimated to him, that they clearly saw he had deceived them, and that they were determined to continue the war no longer; so finding himself deserted by them, he endeavoured to form an insurrection among the working negroes, and to raise them in a mass. The accounts which I received from all quarters, and from General Dessalines himself, with respect to the line of conduct which he held since his submission, left no room for doubt upon the subject. I intercepted letters which he had written to one Fontaine, who was agent at the Cape. These afforded an unanswerable proof that he was engaged in a conspiracy, and that he was anxious to regain his former influence in the colony. He waited only for the result of disease among the troops.

"Under these circumstances it would be improper to give him

 time

CHAP. V. 1802. time to mature his criminal designs. I ordered him to be apprehended,—a difficult task; but it succeeded from the excellent dispositions made by the General of Division Brunet, who was entrusted with its execution, and the zeal and ardour of Citizen Ferrari, a chief of squadron, and my aid-du-camp.

"I have sent to France, with all his family, this so deeply perfidious man, who, with so much hypocrisy, has done us so much mischief. The government will determine how it should dispose of him.

"The apprehension of General Toussaint occasioned some disturbances. Two leaders of the insurgents are already in custody, and I have ordered them to be shot. About an hundred of his confidential partizans have been secured, some of whom are sent on board La Muiron frigate, which is under orders for the Mediterranean, and the rest are distributed among the different ships of the squadron.

"I am daily occupied in settling the affairs of the colony, with the least possible inconvenience, but the excessive heat, and the diseases which attack us, render it a task extremely painful. I am impatient for the approach of the month of September, when the season will restore us activity.

"The departure of Toussaint has produced general joy at the Cape.

"The

"The commissary of justice, Mont Peson, is dead. The colonial prefect, Benezech, is breathing his last. The adjutant-commandant, Dampier, is dead; he was a young officer of great promise. I have the honor to salute you,

(Signed) "Le Clerc."

Le Clerc, General in Chief and Captain-General.

Having rid himself of Toussaint, and assumed the title of General in Chief, in addition to that of Captain-General, with which he came to the island, Le Clerc affected to undertake the organization of a new government for the colony, a labor in which many great men had been unsuccessful. In doing this, however, he did not risque his character, as they had done, by speculative attempts in legislation, for he decreed the continuance of every establishment as he found it in the hands of the exiled General, except as related to the customs, and even in these he admitted the regulations in favor of the English, which occasioned a strong remonstrance from the commercial interest at Paris.

On the 22d of June the decree was published, "in the name of the General in Chief Captain-General." Martial law continued in force, with certain modifications. Military commandants had the power over certain districts, with the assistance of the municipality; and each commune provided for the expences of its government, while the whole held a general understanding with each other.*

* See the Appendix.

CHAP. V. 1802. The object at this time requiring the most ardent and strict attention, was the health of the troops, which had suffered to such a degree, that in many instances where, (in consequence of their necessary dispersion throughout the colony,) small numbers were left at a post, sufficient scarcely remained to attend the sick and bury the dead, instead of performing military duty, while the rigorous service was necessarily obliged to be imposed upon the others, particularly in the south, and towards the Spanish division, where large parties of blacks, never brought into action, continued in arms, and ridiculed the idea of submission. General Le Clerc preserved in his endeavours to infuse terror by the most absolute measures, and to implore the First Consul for reinforcements. Thus, if it could be considered as ended, concluded the first campaign of the army of St. Domingo.

In the mean time, the injured Black General in Chief approached rapidly to the site of exile. During the voyage he was not permitted to see his family, and a guard was placed at the door of his cabin. On the 11th of June the ship arrived at Brest, and on the deck only this great man was permitted to take the last view of his innocent and respectable family. Their agonizing separation will be long remembered by the seamen who witnessed it, notwithstanding the means taken to impress an unfavorable opinion of the blacks, and render them insensible to the emotions of humanity; nature broke through the boundaries which had been thus infernally created, and expressed their sense of the fraudulent delusion so strenuously, that it was conceived necessary to hurry off their august prisoner. He was conveyed in a close carriage, under a strong escort of cavalry, to the Castle of Joux in Normandy, far from the knowledge of his fame or fate, with a single attendant, who was also confined and prevented from any other communication; and who, afterwards, weary of captivity, procured his own release under the pretence of betraying his master, and disclosing hidden treasures in his native island. From Joux he was removed to Besançon, and treated as the worst of criminals.—He, who had been the benefactor of white people in a country where their enormities had provoked hatred, whose power was never stained by malevolence, and who was greater in his fall, than his enemies in their assumed power, was kept in a damp and cheerless prison, without the comfort of a single friend, without trial, or even examination; a proof of his exalted innocence, and a perpetual memorial of the political error of the Conqueror of Italy, which will throw a gloom over his apotheosis, and cast a slur on a period of government otherwise not destitute of virtues. CHAP. V. 1802.

The wife and family of Toussaint remained in strict charge at Brest for two months, from whence they were removed to Bayonne, in the same province with their unhappy relative, where they long continued unnoticed, and in ignorance of his fate.*

* After a considerable period, a report gained credit that this hapless family had obtained permission to return to their native country: even miserable as the return under such circumstances must have been, the account is doubtful.

This

CHAP. V. 1802.

This prison may be considered the sepulture of Toussaint. France forgot awhile the habits of a civilized nation, to entomb one she should have graced with a public triumph; and England, instead of making a common cause to annihilate a nation of heroes, and depress the human intellect when rising to its level, should have guarded from violation the rights of humanity in its person. It has been the lot of him whose feeble hand attempts a tribute of gratitude, respect, and justice to his character, to regret the ill-requited life of the discoverer of the new world, and the unpropitious efforts of the enlightened and benignant D'Ogeron, to view the untimely death of many brave and exalted characters in the fluctuation of events in the different attempts to obtain possession of an island whose fate is as conspicuous as the most celebrated ancient state; but in no one instance does the mind linger with such keen sensations as on the unhappy fortune of the great, the good, the pious and benevolent Toussaint L'Ouverture.*

* The death of Toussaint is silently noticed in the Paris journals of April 27, 1803, and briefly alluded to in the London papers of the 2d of May following. In one of the most respectable of them is a paragraph nearly in these terms, whose briefness well characterizes an event which could only have been dwelt upon with shame:

"Toussaint L'Ouverture is dead. He died, according to letters from Besançon, in prison, a few days ago. The fate of this man has been singularly unfortunate, and his treatment most cruel. He died, we believe, without a friend to close his eyes. We have never heard that his wife and children, though they were brought over from St. Domingo with him, have ever been permitted to see him during his imprisonment."—*Times, May 2*, 1803.

Suspicions have been hinted of this event being accelerated by poison. The author, however, of an eloquent little popular work, states a circumstance from good authority, which would supersede the necessity for this means: "The floor of the dungeon," (in which Toussaint was confined,) he says, "was actually covered with water."—*Bonaparté in the West Indies*, &c.

6 Notwithstanding

CHAP. V.

1802.

Notwithstanding the disastrous state of the colony, General Le Clerc seemed unwilling to depreciate his government, by admitting that at the end of several months he had not accomplished what he had declared was effected in the first five days. The healthful season so much desired by him had long arrived, and the contagion had not otherwise decreased, than by the number of its victims, which every day grew less. He was himself scarcely convalescent; the best officers of his staff had fallen, and those who arrived being unacquainted with the country, and task to which they were condemned, sunk into despondency, and followed their predecessors to eternity! In the beginning of October, he commissioned an aid-du-camp to the Consular court for instructions and advice, and for once his dispatches wore the semblance of truth; they were in consequence carefully concealed from the public knowledge, but bad news finds its way through a thousand avenues, when the good is most anxiously sought for in vain.

It was therefore soon known that Christophé had rejoined the black forces with Dessalines, who could never be considered as defected. They began, by affecting in their different characters of commandant of negroes in the northern district, and superintendant-general of negroes, to retreat from those who were hostile, taking care always to leave behind them considerable quantities of ammunition and stores. A number of new generals, likewise, had arisen in arms; from the interior of the island, who began to make excursions from the mountains. Among these was

CHAP. V. 1802. was a powerful chief of negroes, of the Congo tribe, called Sans Souci, who, after committing considerable depredations, could never be discovered. Charles Bellair, with his Amazonian wife, also made a powerful diversion for a while, till they were both taken, and died under the most inconceivable tortures. Clervaux, whose submission of the eastern part of the island had been formerly boasted without grounds, now declared openly his contumacy; and Maurepas, who had surrendered, was detected in a conspiracy, and put to death. Nor were the defections from the French army confined to the blacks, or to inferior officers among the whites; General Dugua, the chief of the French staff, disgusted with the horrors attendant on the war and more particularly, with the horrid punishment of Bellair and his wife, whom he had tried, was discovered in making arrangements to quit the French army, and took the resolution of destroying himself.

The government at this period (if in the insubordinate state in which every thing appeared, any government could be considered to exist) assumed a complexion more sanguinary and terrible than can be conceived among civilized people, and formed a new æra in martial law. In attempting to disarm the black troops which had been incorporated with the French, the necessity whereof was discovered too late, the most barbarous methods were practised, ship-loads were collected, and suffocated in the holds. In one instance, six hundred being surrounded, and attempting a resistance, were massacred on the spot; and such slaughters daily

CHAP. V. 1803.

was a powerful chief of negroes, of the Congo tribe, called Sans Souci, who, after committing considerable depredations, could never be discovered. Charles Bellair, with his Amazonian wife, also made a powerful diversion for a while, till they were both taken, and died under the most inconceivable tortures. Clervaux, whose submission of the eastern part of the island had been formerly boasted without grounds, now declared openly his contumacy; and Maurepas, who had surren[illegible] was detected in a subsequency, and put to death. Nor [illegible] the desertions from the French army confined to the blacks. [illegible] inferior officers among the whites. General Dugua, the chief of the French staff, disgusted with the horrors attendant on the war and the [illegible], with the horrid punishment [illegible] had tried, was discovered in making attempts to quit the French army, and took the [illegible]

[illegible] government could be consider[illegible] sanguinary and terrible [illegible] black troops which [illegible] with the [illegible] the necessary whereof [illegible] most barbarous methods were prac[illegible] suffocated in the holds. In [illegible] six hundred being surrounded, and attempting a [illegible] were massacred on the spot; and such slaughters daily

J. Barlow sculp.

Mode of exterminating the Black Army, as practised by the French.

Published as the Act directs, July 1st 1805, by Jas. Cundee, Ivy Lane Paternoster Row, London

daily took place in the vicinity of Cape François, that the air became tainted by the putrefaction of the bodies. At the same time the French troops being driven from the field, and obliged to fortify themselves in the chief towns, contagion spread every where, and the disease became dreadfully general. In their extremity, to aid and fill up the measure of their enormities, the use of blood-hounds was resorted to, that dreadful expedient, the temporary adoption of which in a neighbouring colony, had already excited the disgust of the powers of Europe.*

Fort Dauphin, Port Paix, and several other favourite establishments, were by the middle of October completely lost to the French; and it became known to the seamen who visited the

* In this allusion to the circumstance of the introduction of blood-hounds to an English colony, the author has no other aim than to add his testimony (who was an eye-witness) to the [illegible] of the governor of Jamaica in regard to their use. Though it successful, yet it was a dangerous experiment, and one which will, it is hoped, never be again tried by British soldiers; but with the control of such men as Lord Balcarres, and General Walpole, the rights of humanity can no more [illegible] than the highest point of military honour or discipline. The writer was witness to an anxiety with regard to any employment of the dogs in the noble governor, which [illegible] eternal honor on his feelings as a gentleman and as a soldier, while the sentiments of General Walpole on the occasion are equally honourable. Strange as it may appear to those who had an opportunity of knowing the fact, the public mind (with a jealousy of national character most laudable and dignified) has never been satisfied that the Maroons were not really hunted down, and destroyed by blood-hounds; it is therefore most solemnly declared in this place, that no farther use was made of these than being marched in the rear of the army to inspire terror in the blacks, as has been mentioned in an account furnished to his respectable historian by Mr. Quarrel, although the writer is not certain that the [illegible] taken by Lord Balcarres to prevent it, was perfectly consonant to the [illegible] of that gentleman. Some accidents, and perhaps more than those stated by Mr. Dallas, did occur; but they were never let loose indiscriminately, by a British general, for the inhuman purposes for which they are bred.

Bight

daily took place in the vicinity of Cape François, that the air became tainted by the putrefaction of the bodies. At the same time the French troops being driven from the field, and obliged to fortify themselves in the chief towns, contagion spread every where, and the distress became dreadfully general. In their extremity, to aid and fill up the measure of their enormities, the use of blood-hounds was resorted to, that dreadful expedient, the temporary adoption of which in a neighbouring colony, had already excited the disgust of the powers of Europe.*

Fort Dauphin, Port Paix, and several other favourite establishments, were by the middle of October completely lost to the French; and it became known to the seamen who visited the

* In this allusion to the circumstance of the introduction of blood-hounds to an English colony, the author has no other aim than to add his testimony (who was an eye witness) to the rectitude of the governor of Jamaica in regard to their use. Though a successful, yet it was a dangerous experiment, and one which will, it is hoped, never be again tried by British soldiers; but with the control of such men as Lord Balcarras, and General Walpole, the rights of humanity can no more be violated than the highest point of military honor or discipline. The writer was witness to an anxiety with regard to *any* employment of the dogs in the noble governor, which must confer eternal honor on his feelings as a gentleman and as a soldier, while the sentiments of General Walpole on the occasion are equally honourable. Strange as it may appear to those who had an opportunity of knowing the fact, the public mind (with a jealousy of national character most laudable and dignified) has never been satisfied that the Maroons were not really hunted down, and destroyed by blood-hounds; it is therefore most solemnly declared in this place, that no farther use was made of them than being marched in the rear of the army to inspire terror in the blacks, as has been mentioned in an account furnished to his respectable historian by Mr. Quarrel, although the writer is not certain that the care taken by Lord Balcarras to prevent it, was perfectly consonant to the inclinations of that gentleman. Some accidents, and perhaps more than those stated by Mr. Dallas, did occur, but they were never let loose, indiscriminately, by a British general, for the inhuman purposes for which they are bred.

Bight

CHAP. V. 1802. Bight of Léogane, that after a considerable number of blacks had been hunted down in the neighbourhood of Port Republicain, they were hurried on board of the ships at anchor in the bay, and crowded into their holds; that under cover of the night this dishonored navy put to sea, and first either burning brimstone in the hold, or extinguishing sense by suffocation, or neither, the miserable cargoes were discharged into the sea in such quantities, that at length the tide (as if the mighty Arbiter of all, meant to hold their shame before them) brought the corpses into the bay, and rolled them on the very beach. Human nature recoils at the description, yet the scene is not ended,—under the dark concealment of night, the tender wife, the aged parent, and even the rougher comrade in arms, stealing by the watchful suspicion of their masters, were seen wandering on the sea-shore, to identify each victim as the wave produced him.

Towards the end of October, an event occurred which, however expected, produced an extraordinary effect. The General in Chief, whose health had been long impaired, and who had tried every means for its restoration, suddenly became worse, the air of the city had avowedly become mephitic, and Tortuga no longer remained as a retreat for him, being in full possession of the blacks. On the night of the 1st of November, after he had communicated his wishes as to the future government of the colony, died Victor Emanuel Le Clerc, having been only eleven months General in Chief and Captain-General of the colony of St. Domingo.

Death of the General in Chief, Le Clerc.

On

On the morning of November 2, the following proclamation was issued by the principal municipal officer of the colony: CHAP. V. 1802.

"ARMY OF ST. DOMINGO.

"*The Colonial Prefect, to the Army, and the Inhabitants of St. Domingo:*

"CITIZENS, SOLDIERS,

"The night which has passed has been a mournful night for us.

"The General in Chief, Le Clerc, your Captain-General, is no more.—He has fallen; an irresistible malady has borne him from you.

"Having scarcely attained the meridian of life, he was already a conqueror in battle and vigorous in council,—at once a hero and a sage.

"Possessing dignity without pride, generosity without ostentation;—his heart was just;—your sorrows and his were perpetually the same.

"Soldiers, although the brother of Bonaparté is no more—he will live in your hearts. The brigands, whose terror he was, will rejoice in his death;—you will punish their detested joy.

"The General of Division, Rochambeau, is about to succeed General Le Clerc. He has already delivered the South and

CHAP. V. 1802.

West from the brigands who ravaged them. He is the choice of the government, and of the General whom you lament.

"Under his standard you will continue to conquer, and your hearts alone can inform you what loss you have sustained.

"Inhabitants of St. Domingo, rally with confidence around the new Chief who is given to you.—You have long known him,—you have often blessed the success of his arms. You will have to applaud new triumphs. Forget not, Soldiers and Inhabitants, that union constitutes force; and that the only mode of honoring a man whom you loved, and who loved you, is to conduct yourselves as if he were still in the midst of you.

"The French government watches over you: it will never abandon you.

"The Colonial Prefect, D'AURE."

This communication, had it been intended to appease the manes of Le Clerc, could not have been more conformable to his ideas, or more replete with ostentation and falsehood. The body was immediately examined on account of his disease, then embalmed, and placed on board the Swiftsure man of war; Madam Le Clerc, who had no inclination to remain on an island, where, instead of a promised paradise, she had suffered the most painful deprivations, went on board in a few days, Admiral Latouche, chief in command of the naval force in St. Domingo, undertaking to escort her home, accompanied by the Chief of Brigade, Netherwood, first aid-du-camp of the

departed

departed general. His sabre and hat were placed, with much formality, upon the bier on board; all the officers attending on the occasion.

CHAP. V. 1802.

He appears to have been anxious, that the directions which he thought necessary for the future government of the island, should be put in force, and they were, as far as convenient with some persons, obeyed. As soon as the obsequies of the departed General were performed, it became necessary for some one to prepare for the repelling the blacks, who had advanced with vociferous joy to the very town of Cape François. General Rochambeau, who was appointed Chief in command, was at Port-au-Prince, and could not be expected to arrive in sufficient time, though General Watrin had set out to succeed him in the west and south; General Clausel, commanding in the north, therefore, with the remains of a dispirited army, proceeded against them, but to little effect.

Rochambeau chief in command.

A young general, of the name of Boyer, who had commanded in the Gens d'Armerie, having been appointed Chief of the Staff in the place of Dugua, was entrusted with the execution of every order, and in consequence thought it necessary to address to the French colonial minister some account of the transactions of the French army in St. Domingo from the period of the arrest of Toussaint L'Ouverture. In this dispatch, amidst a variety of matter, such as had been the custom to transmit to France, Boyer confesses the dreadful situation in which the colony then

 stood.

CHAP. V. 1802.

stood. Speaking of the first attempts after the departure of Toussaint, he says, "The heat became excessive, it was impossible to make any movement; the lowest mornes presented obstacles to us proportionate to the inconvenience of the season. The brigands increased in numbers. Our hospitals were crowded with sick, and disease daily made new ravages." He then mentions *insurrections* at Marmalade, Dondon, and Moustique, when not only those posts, but the whole plain of the Cape, covered by the black forces, from whom, they might temporarily obtain possession of a small place which they afterwards were obliged to relinquish.

He acknowledges the prosecution of the war against the leaders which had been begun by Le Clerc, in the course of which Domage, the friend of Toussaint, who had hitherto successfully repelled every attempt upon the south, fell into the hands of General Desbureaux. Loaded with the charge of an intimate connection with his exiled chief, it was not sufficient to send him "on board the squadron,"* as the end of his co-patriots was termed; he was reserved for the extremity of torture that *civilized* barbarians could inflict.

The arrival of the new Commander in Chief at head-quarters, effected little change in the situation of affairs, though much was expected, from his superior knowledge of the Island,

* Q. d. to be simply drowned.

and

and character of the blacks; but this knowledge could not effect a change in the elements, or render a power daily weakening equal to that which acquired strength from a continuation of the war. He appeared anxious to direct it to points different from that to which it was ordinarily carried; accordingly an action of considerable violence took place on the parched plains of St. Nicholas Mole, in which the French appear to have made a feeble stand. They continued to fight during the night, and to precipitate each other into the sea. The end, however, was, as it must always be in a like situation, that any advantage the whites obtained was soon relinquished. General Clausel was more successful before Fort Dauphin, which, after withstanding for some time the united attack by sea and land, surrendered to him. Before this capture, Port Republican and Les Cayes were the only towns, besides the capital, in the possession of the French.

The first public act of Rochambeau, as Captain-General of the Island, was that of calling to account the young Chief of the Staff, who appears to have been an *élève* of Le Clerc, and raised to that dignity more from the General's fondness, than his ability. He was young and spirited, and the faults with which he was charged, appear to have arisen more from errors ascribable to that period of life, than from a decided cupidity. His suspension was announced by an arrêté, thus

ARRETE

CHAP. V.
1802.

ARRÊTÉ OF THE GENERAL IN CHIEF.

December 8.

"The General in Chief orders the deposition of the Chief of Brigade, Boyer, Ex-commander of the first legion of Gens d'Armerie. He shall be detained in prison at the Cape till his accompts are given in, when he shall be sent to France.

(Signed) "ROCHAMBEAU."*

Shortly after, the General in Chief renewed the decree of Le Clerc, so obnoxious in France, permitting foreign importation into the colony, extending it to all descriptions of wares and merchandize, but increasing the duty upon them to twenty per

* This young General, with more good fortune than was ordinarily met with under the present regimen, was afterwards embarked for France, but war having recommenced, was taken, and brought to England. With the greatest impetuosity he inveighed against his treatment. But when he found that he was to be deprived of a sum of money, the fruits, probably, of defalcation in his official career, he lost all patience. Notwithstanding every thing of personal property had been returned to him, as well as the other prisoners, he complained with great virulence to his government, "that the English had *robbed* him!" He was, notwithstanding, granted his liberty on parole at Tiverton, in Devonshire, where his conduct was frequently ludicrous in the extreme; and the letters he wrote to his government occasioned many false constructions in the French papers. Notwithstanding this disagreeable circumstance, his favorable exterior, youth, and vivacity, obtained for him particular notice. On one occasion, the prisoners, having procured musical instruments, and formed a concert on a Sunday, the English peasantry conceiving it derogatory to their religion, insisted on its suppression, and the Magistrates were obliged to interfere. With great gallantry the Frenchmen hoped that, though compelled to relinquish their music, the church of England would not deny them the pleasure of drinking a few bottles of excellent wine, then in their possession, with the Magistrates: the latter declined; but were surprized at hearing nothing of Boyer all the time.---He was busily employed in a corner drawing a caricature of the whole party!

2 cent;

cent;* with this arrêté ended the most eventful year ever experienced in St. Domingo. The French troops appeared to proceed with the season in which they landed,—to rise with the progress of the year,—and to fall, with their General, at the approach of winter. Before the month of December, not ten months after their arrival, near forty thousand French troops are supposed to have been sacrificed, and a considerable number, (though by no means proportionate,) of the blacks. Troops still continued to be sent from the ports of Havre and Cherbourg, but each reinforcement was less effective than the preceding, and the conscripts at length consisted only of raw youths, Poles, Piedmontese, and Flemings. Veteran soldiers considered the army of St. Domingo as the by-word of contempt, and the once popular cause of the subjugation of that splendid colony became no more heard of, or if mentioned, it was only with sorrow, or to be treated with derision.

1802.

The commencement of the year 1803 was marked by a sullen cessation of arms, more dreadful than active war, as it gave place to secret cruelties, more extensive because less glaring. General Rochambeau was called, by the fortune of war, to a command for which, notwithstanding the local and physical experience which has been allowed to him, he was by no means competent, and to which, no talents, perhaps, would have been adequate. In the outset of the expedition he had borne a very

1803.

* See the Appendix.

CHAP. V. 1803. subordinate rank, considering his stake as a proprietor, and it was only to the death of his superiors that he owed his present appointment. He evinced no desire to change the system (if so it could be called) on which the war proceeded, nor did he exhibit sufficient ability to produce an amendment. On the 4th of March, without any other communication of importance, the French colonial minister received from the new Captain-General an intimation, that on the arrival of four thousand more troops which were expected, *offensive operations might be commenced.*

The blacks, on the contrary, during the whole of this awful cessation, were daily strengthened from every quarter, under Dessalines, who was unanimously appointed General in Chief, who resolved vigorously to push the war to a termination. With this view they collected a considerable force upon the plain of the Cape, which being observed by Rochambeau, he found it necessary to withdraw his troops from every other point, and both armies became unawares in a state of preparation for a general battle. This was not what either party designed; Dessalines, therefore, restrained his impetuous blacks, and the French forces were combined to strengthen Cape François. Several skirmishes having taken place in the vicinity of Acul, it was at length determined by Rochambeau to venture an action, for which he had many dispositions in his favor. The troops selected on either side, for the affair were admirably posted on two neighbouring

Affair of Acul.

mornes,

CHAP. V.
1803.

subordinate rank, considering his stake as a proprietor, and was only to the death of his superiors that he owed his present appointment. He evinced no desire to change the system (if so it could be called) on which the war proceeded, nor did he exhibit sufficient ability to produce an amendment. On the 4th of March, without any other communication of importance, the French colonial minister received from the new Captain-General an intimation, that on the arrival of four thousand more troops which were expected, *offensive operations might be commenced*.

The blacks, on the contrary, during the whole of this awful cessation, were daily strengthened from every quarter, under Dessalines, who was unanimously appointed General in Chief, who resolved vigorously to push the war to a termination. With this view they collected a considerable force upon the plain of the Cape, which being observed by Rochambeau, he found it necessary to withdraw his troops from every other point, and both armies became unawares in a state of preparation for a general battle. This was not what either party designed; Dessalines, therefore, restrained his impetuous blacks, and the French forces were combined to strengthen Cape François. Several skirmishes having taken place in the vicinity of Acul, it was at length determined by Rochambeau to venture an action, for which he had many dispositions in his favor. The troops selected on either side, for the affair were admirably posted on two neighbouring mornes,

Affair of Acul.

M Rainsford del | Barlow sculp.

Revenge taken by the Black Army for the Cruelties practised

camp. Rochambeau began the attack with impetuosity, and the blacks for a short time gave way, but, as he endeavoured to push the advantage, they repulsed him again, when the day closed. In penetrating the black line the French had secured a number of prisoners, and on them they determined to wreak the vengeance of which they were disappointed in the battle. Whether this determination arose from an idea that the part of the French wing which had been cut off was already absolutely sacrificed, or from the senseless policy of extermination, cannot here be determined; but the unhappy victims were, without the smallest consideration for their own men who were prisoners in the black camp, immediately put to death. As they were not carefully exterminated, many were left in a mutilated state during the whole of the night, whose moans and shrieks were heard at a distance around the spot sufficiently loud to excite a sensation of horror throughout the country. The black commander, when

mornes,* the first movement was inauspicious to the French, by the capture of a considerable body marching to strengthen one of the wings who were surrounded and driven into the black camp. Rochambeau began the attack with impetuosity, and the blacks for a short time gave way, but on his endeavouring to push the advantage, they repulsed him with loss, when the day closed. In penetrating the black line the French had secured a number of prisoners, and on them they determined to wreak the vengeance of which they were disappointed in the battle. Whether this determination arose from an idea that the part of the French wing which had been cut off were already absolutely sacrificed, or from the mistaken policy of extermination, cannot here be determined, but the unhappy victims were, without the smallest consideration for their own men who were prisoners in the black camp, immediately put to death. As they were not carefully exterminated, many were left in a mutilated state during the whole of the night, whose moans and shrieks were heard at a distance around the spot sufficiently loud to excite a sensation of horror throughout the country. The black commander, when acquainted with the case although the maxim of the benevolent Toussaint, not to retaliate, had been hitherto followed up, could no longer forbear; he instantly caused a number of gibbets to be formed, selected the officers whom he had taken, and supplying

Retaliation of the cruelty of the French by the black army.

* This French provincial term, which has become a cant phrase in the public conversation on the war in St. Domingo, the writer conceives applies to heights divided by different mounts, separated by delightful vallies, with which the island abounds.

CHAP. V. 1803. the deficiency with privates, had them tied up in every direction by break of day, in sight of the French camp, who dared not to interfere. The blacks then sallied down with the most astonishing vigor and regularity, raised the very camp, threw the whole line in disorder, and drove the French army close to the walls of Cape François. Such was the retaliation produced by this sanguinary measure; a retaliation, the justice of which, however it is lamented, cannot be called in question.

During the latter months, the fluctuating politics of Europe, which had never failed to produce some change to this unhappy island, again took a turn, and the peace, which was not inaptly termed in the British senate a "peace of experiment," had been concluded. In the middle of the ensuing May, war was recommenced between Great Britain and France, when each power directing its attention to those objects of the enemy which were most vulnerable, the former rationally looked towards the force in St. Domingo.

By the time the news arrived with the different commanders on the station, Rochambeau had permanently fixed his head-quarters at the Cape, and Dessalines had so completely lined the country about the city, that the French boundaries were confined to two miles around the Cape. As their power became weaker, an unnatural ferocity was increased, and apparently a desire to render the white complexion detestable throughout the Antilles; for no means, however extraneous, were left unattempted

M. Rainsford del. J. Barlow sculp.

Blood Hounds attacking a Black Family in the Woods.

CHAP. V. 1803. Use of blood-hounds.

to annoy the enemy. Not content with the use of a considerable number of blood-hounds, (some of which they had procured from the Spanish part of the island, but most from that of Cuba,) which they sent in pursuit of small reconnoitring parties that occasionally ventured within their lines; when they were taken (the pen shrinks from the task of describing it) they were thrown to those animals, less brutal than their barbarous owners, to be devoured alive! All the arts, which invention worse than savage could devise in the people, who continued to inspirit these animals with a ferocity not often known, was employed, to render them more terrific to the blacks, and more effective in the war. Such is the deterioration of the human mind, under a pressure of circumstances.

Dessalines, notwithstanding frequent losses, attended with the most horrid circumstances, sufficient in the relation to freeze the blood of the reader, continued the blockade, and found opportunities to decrease in the French the means of operation, both offensive and defensive. As soon as an English squadron was perceived on the coast in July, he, in conjunction with Christophé, sent a flag of truce with a proposition to act in concert against the French, and, in case of agreement, to request some assistance of stores.—It is probable, that at the same time an account of the atrocities of the French accompanied this request, for shortly after a squadron, under the command of a Commodore, blockaded Cape François in the ensuing month, when Rochambeau began to sound the Commodore

2 X 2 upon

CHAP. V. 1803. upon terms for a surrender of the French troops. About this time, so unsafe appeared the French interest, that Jerome Bonaparté, the brother of the First Consul, who had remained hitherto, (with what utility is not known,) left the island, and arrived at Baltimore, on the American continent, a young man more fond of fashionable distinction than of war, and more fitting for the *agremens* of life than its arduous occupations.*

The French affairs continued to depreciate, varying only by the increase of difficulty; attended with the same disgraceful employment of the most cruel actions, till Rochambeau actually relinquished every other merit or aim, than that of keeping possession of the city of the Cape, and fortifying it by every means that human art could devise or effect. In a dispatch on the 29th of October, he observes, "There is still some merit in defending a ravaged colony against a civil war on one side, and a foreign enemy on the other."

Such was the situation to which were reduced the conductors of an expedition, which had flattered the French people to the highest pitch,—had interested the powers of Europe,—and fed the vanity of every general whom interest could procure to be appointed to its service.—The victorious blacks, however, conti-

* Among other traits of character in this young man was, that he anxiously, and perhaps surreptitiously, obtained the London curricle of an English merchant on the island, which he used with an extravagant peculiarity in the city to which he had removed, while the executors of its owner were instituting legal proceedings to recover its value.

nuing

nuing to pour in reinforcements upon the plain of the Cape, Dessalines resolved to attack the city, and took measures accordingly. A powerful body descended from the Morne du Cap, and having passed the outer lines, and several of the block-houses, a sharp conflict ensued, and they then prepared to take the city by storm in thirty-six hours. The blacks being irresistible; and before it would be too late, reasonably expecting that every one would be put to the sword, Rochambeau offered articles of capitulation, which, to the honor of the Black General, by foregoing the desire of revenge for the conduct of the French, he accepted, granting them ten days to evacuate the city, (and in so doing the island, leaving every thing in its existing condition,) in their own ships, with the honors of war, all their private property, and leaving their sick to the care of the blacks;* an instance of forbearance and magnanimity, of which there are not many examples in the annals of ancient or modern history.

Though the British squadron under Commodore Loring, which were still stationed off Cape François, did not enter into any definitive alliance in consequence of the application of the blacks, they continued to render their cause an incalculable service, by preventing the arrival of reinforcements or supplies of any kind. Having been informed of the mode by which provisions were obtained from the Spanish part of the island, through the Curacol passage, leading to the eastern entrance of

* See the Appendix.

the

CHAP. V. 1803.

the harbour of Cape François, a frigate was placed so as to intercept them, by which thirty small vessels, several laden with bullocks, were captured in a short time.* Thus, deprived of supply by sea, and shut from an intercourse with the land, General Rochambeau became reduced to the situation he so forcibly described on a subsequent occasion. "Pressed" said he, "almost to death by absolute famine, and after waiting for a considerable time, wretchedly appeasing the desperate calls of hunger by feeding on our horses, mules, asses, and even dogs, we had no way to escape the poignards of the enraged negroes, but by trusting our fate to the sea." †

The same day on which he had treated with General Dessalines, and after he had exchanged hostages, Rochambeau thought proper to send to the English commodore a military and a naval officer, with proposals to treat for the evacuation of the Cape, with a dissimulation disgraceful to the meanest commander. These were General Boyé and Captain Barné. They proposed that General Rochambeau and his guards, comprizing about five hundred men, should be conveyed to France in two vessels, the Surveillant and Cerf, without being considered as prisoners of war. To this proposition, which nothing but the liberality they had so recently experienced could give rise, Com-

* London Gazette, Feb. 7, 1804.

† "On which," he scurrilously adds, "we were taken by the English pirates." See *Affidavit of Augustus Stenson, taken at Ashbourne, in Derbyshire, on the 27th of February*, 1804, at which time Rochambeau was prisoner there on his parole of honor.

modore

modore Loring returned his refusal, and at the same time sent Captain Moss, of the Desirée, with absolute terms. These were, —a general surrender,—that the French officers and troops in health should go to Jamaica, and the sick to France and America, security being given for the vessels which conveyed them, prohibiting at the same time the white inhabitants of the Cape from going to Jamaica. CHAP. V. 1803.

To this communication General Rochambeau returned the following answer:—

"*The General in Chief of the Army of St. Domingo to Commodore Loring, &c. &c.*

"SIR,

"I have received the letter which you have done me the honor to address to me. As your propositions are inadmissible, I must beg of you to consider the preceding letter as not having been received.

"I have the honor to be, &c.

"D. ROCHAMBEAU."

The French general flattered himself with finding an opportunity to make his escape from the Cape, and consequently forbore any farther communication with, and still concealing from the English the capitulation into which he had entered with Dessalines, but they were too vigilant for his purpose.

On

CHAP. V. 1803. On the 2nd of December, Captain Loring summoned the General of Brigade, Noailles, who maintained unmolested a species of solitary command at the Mole, to surrender, who, while equivocating as to the mode of his capitulation, embarked with his garrison in the night on board six vessels, five of which fell into the hands of the commander of the La Pique, the sixth escaping, with General Noailles on board.

Port-au-Prince having been evacuated at different periods, was under the command of the General of Division, Petion, a black officer of experience and ability, who had been regularly educated at the Military School in France; St. Domingo thus became again in the full possession of the native army. The force which had arrived with the first body of troops, and stationed at the Spanish capital under General Kerversan, had remained without the power of interfering in the war, and contented itself with the parade of communication between the French and Spanish inhabitants, and with the island of Cuba, between whom they found sufficient employment, in those petty political intrigues that are always better avoided, as regard both the character and advantage of the countries using them.

Immediately on the cessation of hostilities, which promised to be more permanent than any former one, the General in Chief, with the two Generals between whom the jurisdiction of the island was become divided, Christophé and Clervaux, began to consider of the proclamation of independance, and those measures

measures which were necessary for the public tranquillity. In a proclamation on November 29, by the three officers, from head-quarters, in the Name of the Black People and Men of Colour, they declared the "General Freedom," and invited the return of those proprietors who fled during the conflict, without having become obnoxious by any cruelty of disposition towards their servants, or inclination to the continuance of slavery; at the same time, avowing, that to those of a contrary temper, no protection would be promised; and that as to soldiery employed in any future expedition, mercy was not to be expected. They declared their disapprobation of, and palliated the cruelties which were the unavoidable consequence of civil dissentions in all countries, and proposed that a new regimen, founded on the basis of justice, should prevail in St. Domingo.* In the execution of these propositions, and in preparations for the pacific state of the Island, to which they now looked, closed the year 1803. It will scarcely be believed, that to this gratifying occupation of restoring order, in the place of distraction, perpetual caution was rendered necessary, by some infatuated people who remained at the Cape, still devoted to the hope of replacing the old constitution, and the principle of slavery. CHAP. V. 1803.

Hearing no more from General Rochambeau, although acquainted, by Dessalines, with the capitulation, and perceiving no movement, the English commodore addressed that general

* See the Appendix.

CHAP. V. 1803. as the term had nearly expired, expressive of his hopes that no retraction would take place, and requesting pilots, to conduct a part of the squadron into the harbour, to take possession of the shipping. He received the following answer:

"LIBERTY OR DEATH!

Head-Quarters, Nov. 27.

"*The Commander in Chief of the Native Army to Commodore Loring, &c. &c.*

"SIR,

"I acknowledge the receipt of your letter, and you may be assured that my dispositions towards you, and against General Rochambeau, are invariable. I shall take possession of the Cape to-morrow morning, at the head of my army. It is a matter of great regret to me, that I cannot send you the pilots which you require. I presume that you will not have occasion for them, as I shall compel the French vessels to quit the road, and you will do with them, what you shall think proper.

"I have the honor to be, &c. &c.

"DESSALINES."

On the 30th, the Colours of the blacks were flying at the different forts, which induced Commodore Loring to send Captain Bligh to the Black General, to enquire the circumstances which occasioned the change, when, on entering the harbour, he met

 Captain

1803.

Captain Barré, who entreated him to go on board the Surveillante, and enter into some capitulation with the French, that they might be placed under the protection of the English, the blacks having threatened to sink the vessels with red-hot shot, in consequence of the terms of the capitulation not being complied with in point of time. This he agreed to, and articles being drawn, in which the English continuing the liberality they had already experienced from the Blacks, agreed to their sailing out under French colours, and firing their broadsides previous to surrender; Captain Bligh went to acquaint the Black General with the capture, and to request his desistance from firing, till a wind should be fair for their departure, which was then directly contrary; his acquiescence was obtained with much difficulty.

The force being taken possession of by Commodore Loring, comprizing eight thousand men, with the shipping, consisting of three frigates, and seventeen merchantmen, were conveyed to Jamaica, from whence Admiral Duckworth immediately dispatched General Rochambeau, and the officers particularly in his confidence, to England.*

1804.

The island resumes its ancient name of HAYTI.

With the new year, a new name and a new constitution was given to St. Domingo. Desirous of obliterating every mark

* The words of that officer are, "I send a vessel of war to England, with General Rochambeau, and those officers who are said to have participated in his cruelties at the Cape." —*London Gazette, Feb. 7; Letter of Sir J. T. Duckworth.* They arrived at Portsmouth on the 3d of February, and were afterwards sent on their parole into the interior. See the Appendix.

of

CHAP. V. 1804. of its recent state, the chiefs who had effected its freedom determined upon resuming, with its pristine simplicity of government, its ancient name. Aware of the failings of his too credulous countrymen, and knowing that nothing but the firmest consolidation of their whole force, could preserve the advantages they had gained, he appointed the first day of the year for a solemn pledge of hatred to the French government, and an abjuration of all ideas of conquest and aggrandizement. The terms of this declaration of union are dreadful, they were acceded to by the people with the enthusiasm he desired, and proclaimed throughout Hayti.

"It is not enough," says he, "to have expelled from your country the barbarians who have for two ages stained it with blood. It is not enough to have curbed the factions which, succeeding one another by turns, sported with a phantom of liberty which France exposed to their eyes. It is become necessary by a last act of national authority, to ensure for ever the empire of liberty in the country which has given us birth."*

The truth of this declaration soon became exemplified by the intrigues of some of the unhappy persons who still retained their property in the Island, and who, notwithstanding the effervescence of the public mind, which was apparent in every occurrence, could not desist from plans of aggrandizement and assumption of

* See the Appendix.

power;

power; some, were so imprudent; as to retain the dogs which had created such a fatal hatred. Even experience was not sufficient to cause them to remain quiet, and those whom the strictest caution could hardly be expected to preserve from infuriated revenge, adopted the least. The blacks in their turn, indiscriminately perhaps, viewed in every Frenchman a tyrant; thus, mutually repulsive, amity could not be expected. CHAP. V. 1804.

One of the first civil acts of the black governor reflects considerable honor upon the consideration by which it must have been actuated. It arose from the following circumstances. In the early emigrations, different wealthy proprietors had taken with them for the purposes of pomp, a number of their domestic negroes; afterwards, when they ceased to receive remittances from their estates, and were unable to support a retinue, they abandoned them under various pretexts; others had voluntarily emigrated, during the sway of different factions, and thereby fallen into distress; while both were without the means of returning to their own country. The following proclamation was published, which, as it could have birth in no political view, but was a pure emanation of humanity, is an act worthy the imitation of older states.

CHAP. V.
1804.

" LIBERTY OR DEATH!

" GOVERNMENT OF HAYTI.

" *Head-Quarters, Jan.* 14.

" *1st Year of the Independence of Hayti.*

" The Governor-General considering that a great number of Native Blacks, and Men of Colour, are suffering in the United States of America, for want of the means of returning,

" Decrees,

" That there shall be allowed to the Captains of American Vessels the sum of Forty Dollars for each Individual they may restore to this Country. He orders that this Decree shall be printed, published, and posted up, and that a copy thereof be immediately forwarded to the Congress of the United States.

" By the Governor-General,

" DESSALINES."

During the period, in which he was occupied in these pleasing cares, his attention was called to others of a troublesome nature. A number of persons yet remaining in the different towns of the island, who had been the tools of every faction, and whose inclinations, and interests had always led them to foment discontent, and sow the seeds of rebellion. To root out these emissaries was necessary to the public peace, and if the expulsion had gone no farther, without sanguinary measures, it would probably have been better for all parties.

The

The official notice which then presented itself, was the publication of an extract, drawn from the reports of the proceedings of the Government on that subject. It was as follows: CHAP. V. 1804.

"*Extract from the Secret Deliberations of the Government of the Island of Hayti.*

"LIBERTY! INDEPENDENCE! OR DEATH!

"The Governor-General considering that there still remains in the Island of Hayti, Individuals who have contributed, either by their guilty writings, or by their sanguinary accusations, to the drowning, suffocating, assassinating, hanging, and shooting, of more than sixty thousand of our brethren, under the inhuman government of Le Clerc and Rochambeau, considering that every man who has dishonored human nature, by prostituting himself with enthusiasm to the vile offices of informers and executioners, ought to be classed with assassins, and delivered up without remorse to the sword of justice, decrees as follows:—

"1. Every Commandant of a Division shall cause to be arrested within their respective commands those persons who are, or shall be known to have taken an active part in the different massacres and assassinations ordered by Le Clerc or Rochambeau, &c.

"2. Before proceeding to the arrest of an individual, (as it often happens that many are innocent, who, nevertheless, may be strongly suspected,) we order each Commander to make all necessary

CHAP. V. 1804. cessary inquiries for producing proofs, and above all, not to confound with true and faithful reports those denunciations too frequently suggested by hatred or envy.

"3. The names and surnames of persons executed, shall be inscribed and sent to the General in Chief, who will make them public. This measure is adopted in order to inform the Nations of the World, that although we grant an asylum and protection to those who act candidly and friendly towards us, nothing shall ever turn our vengeance from those murderers who have delighted to bathe themselves in the blood of the innocent children of Hayti.

"4. Any Chief, who, in contempt of the orders, and unalterable will of the government, shall sacrifice to his ambition, to his hatred, or to any other passion, any person whose guilt shall not have been previously well ascertained and proved, shall undergo the same punishment which he shall have thus inflicted; and the property of every such unjust officer shall be confiscated, one half to the government, and the other half to the relations of the innocent victim, if any there may be in the island at the time of his death.

(Signed) "DESSALINES.

"A true copy, B. AIME, Secretary.

"Done at Head-quarters, Feb. 22."

CHAP. V. 1804.

Dessalines Governor General for life.

To enable the General in Chief to prosecute with that vigor and decision, which the complection of the times required, the different functions of the legislature, it was determined by the deliberative meeting which had assembled throughout the month of April, to invest Dessalines with the Government for life, which was accordingly done in the beginning of May, with the power of making peace and war, and nominating his successor. It is thus, that the advantageous principle of a monarchy, in an extensive population arises, self-evident, without the contending interests which afterwards surround it, and the factitious principles by which it is obscured.

A small French force remains in the city of St. Domingo, favored by distance and the treachery of the Spaniards.

During this period, the French Government commissioned the Governor of Guadaloupe, to treat as pirates all neutral vessels going to Hayti, which had been executed with a rigor as ridiculous as unjust. The division stationed in the city of St. Domingo, to whom reinforcements were reported would be sent, having never been called into action, except a few skirmishes on their debarkation, had suffered less than any other division on the island: the Spaniards, also, apparently glad of an opportunity for treachery, had supported and rendered them familiar to the country, nevertheless they were still confined to the Capital, without the power of advancing, or annoying the new Government, any other way than by their continuance in any shape upon the island. Kerversan, who commanded the division on the arrival of the expedition, had long since fallen, and the

 present

CHAP. V. 1804. present commander was Freron, a man of some talents, but little principle.

Dissatisfied with the Spaniards for their treachery, desirous of removing the French, and impressed with the necessity of preparing for the worst, although nothing hostile was then apparent, Dessalines determined on proceeding round the island, to examine every post or station, and observe the effect of the regulations he had established, many of which required to be enforced. Ever vigilant, Dessalines was never known to make a false movement, or to be surprised * on his post, except by treachery, and of this he had now too much experience to suffer any flagrant imposition.

Previous to his departure, however, it became necessary to address the people, to explain his intended journey, conciliate all parties, and render them firm in the support of his government, in proportion to his exertions in their behalf. The proclamation issued on this occasion (April 28) is a specimen of this kind of composition, and is a positive refutation of those who, in opposition to reason and notoriety, describe the inhabitants of

* The writer cannot resist this opportunity of observing, that it were well if this principle of conduct were always equally acted on in regular armies. It is regretted, that some instances have occurred, in which any infliction under death is too mild a punishment. It should be the maxim of every soldier never to be *surprised*, and of a general never to admit of such a declaration. Though not sanguinary, he views the effects of such cases in so criminal a light, that he could perform the office of executioner himself to an officer suffering such a circumstance.

Hayti

Hayti as being in a "savage state." It burns with all the fire of martial oratory, while breathing that bewitching eloquence which entwines and captivates the heart.* CHAP. V. 1804.

On the 8th of May he dispersed throughout the Spanish part of the island a cautionary proclamation, advising them to desist from countenancing the French soldiery, and the vain hopes of opposing him which they manifested; and on the 14th he set out from Cape François, proceeding by the Mole, to Port Paix and Gonaives, where he halted for a little time at his favorite town and head-quarters. From this time, and during the months of June and July, he employed himself in examining the western and southern provinces, repairing the injuries of war, and settling the distractions of their government. "The Aurora of peace" (to use their own expressions) "now began to afford the glimpse of a less stormy time," and the community to wear a natural appearance; notwithstanding the melancholy scenes of retributive devastation which occasionally unfolded themselves.

An event was brought about during his stay, which, while it savours of aggrandizement in the Chief, who had already been elevated to the highest place in the public confidence, served to combine the people more closely, and to present a more dignified character to their enemies. This was his elevation to the Imperial Dignity in a manner, and on terms not inferior

* See the Appendix.

CHAP. V. 1804.

to those which have raised other heroes, in times when heroism was the popular care.

Hayti erected into an empire under Jean Jaques Dessalines.

Whether the design originated from the similar event which had taken place in France, or had birth in the magnificent ideas which arise in a state bursting from the clouds of adversity into glory, is not determined; that it had an exalted basis is certain, and it was conducted in a manner comportable with the simplicity of the earliest institutions, and the refined elegance of modern courts.

General Dessalines having formally agreed to accept the dignity of Emperor, a meeting of the constituted authorities took place on the 8th of September at Port-au-Prince, to arrange the time and manner in which the will of the people should be executed; when that day month was fixed upon for the coronation, and a Programa* issued, of the different forms and ceremonies with which it should be attended.

A procession was formed representing the different functions of the state, depicted so as to shew how they affected its interest, thereby producing a grand and impressive picture, highly descriptive of the manners and principles of the people. In this procession, Education took the lead, as the first and most prominent local good; the Arts next, as little inferior; and Agri-

* See the Appendix.

culture

culture the third, as partaking of the first class, and at the head of the second; Foreign and National Commerce succeeded; then Justice and Legislation; followed by the Officers of Health; and last of all the Military. CHAP. V. 1804.

A superb amphitheatre was erected on a martial plain; when Jean Jaques Dessalines was declared Emperor of Hayti, amid the thunder of cannon, which was re-echoed as an acknowledgement by the Marine of other nations, in the harbour. The Church sanctified the event by a solemn *Te Deum*, and the day concluded by public rejoicings, apparently the most sincere that ever greeted a similar occasion.

CHAP.

CHAP. X. 1804.

culture the third, as partaking of the first class, and of the least of the second; Foreign and National Commerce succeeded; then Justice and Legislation, followed by the Officers of Health; and last of all [illegible]

A superb amphitheatre was erected on a martial plain; where Jean Jacques Dessalines was declared Emperor of Hayti, amid the discharge of cannon, which was re-echoed by an acknowledgement by the Marine of [illegible] in the harbour. The Church sanctified the event by a solemn Te Deum, and the day concluded by public rejoicings, apparently the most sincere that ever greeted a [illegible] occasion.

SUCH, then, was the [illegible] end of this eventful revolution; in which the Imperial dignity was the reward for the courage and experience of the Chief, who, profiting by the misfortunes of his brave and good predecessor, had more successfully combated his enemies,—those enemies who were weak enough to consider it possible, and easy to reduce to slavery a powerful body of men who had for some few years enjoyed a taste of the sweets of liberty. [illegible] it be asserted that [illegible] is little in any way inferior to that of the extraordinary man whose laurels have been sullied in the attempt to subdue him. [illegible]

The recurrence to the earliest state of [illegible] name and character of the government, with [illegible] more than three hundred years experience, is [illegible] could not originate in [illegible] or uninformed minds; nor is such the

CHAP.

CHAP. VI.

On the Establishment of a Black Empire, and the probable Effects of this Colonial Revolution.

CHAP. VI. 1804. Probable effects of the colonial revolution.

SUCH, then, with the close of the year 1804, was the end of this eventful revolution, in which the Imperial dignity was the reward for the courage and experience of the Chief, who, profiting by the misfortunes of his brave and good predecessor, had more successfully combated his enemies,—those enemies who were weak enough to consider it possible, nay, easy to reduce to slavery a powerful body of men who had for some few years enjoyed a state of the most perfect freedom; nor can it be asserted that his title is in any way inferior to that of the extraordinary man whose laurels have been sullied in the attempt to subdue him.

The recurrence to the earliest state of the new world for the name and character of the government, with the advantage of more than three hundred years experience, is an idea which could not originate in mean or untutored minds; nor is such the

CHAP. VI. 1804. Probable effects of the colonial revolution.

the character of any of the present rulers of Hayti. With respect to the future policy they may chuse to adopt, time alone can determine. Should they adhere to the basis on which they have founded their proceedings, and remain unmolested by European powers, they may arrive at the most enviable state of grandeur and felicity; but should any evil spirits obtain a footing amongst them, and interrupt the harmony which may otherwise be maintained, by occasioning factions to arise from old contentions, or new divisions, the frequent consequence of overgrown wealth or dominion, they will in all probability fulfil the prediction of Edwards, by becoming "savages in the midst of society, without peace, security, agriculture, or property."

But, in either case, their reduction to their former situation is impossible; and though Europe waste her armies, and exhaust her navies in the endeavour, the blacks of St. Domingo will be unsubdued; and if they cannot repel the invasion of a reiterated and extended force, they will cut them off, as hath been already observed, with a scythe more keen and rapid than that of time. Every year and every day has been, and will still continue, to be pregnant with experience to them, and no power on earth will be able to reduce them, while their population will continue to increase in a vast proportion. The writer has reiterated these sentiments for several years, and through a period in which their confirmation *appeared* more than doubtful; his opinions were disinterested, and unmingled with any prejudice, either local, political, or pecuniary, and every event has tended to strengthen them.

Probable effects of the colonial revolution.

Should it ever happen in the course of time, that any of the various means dispensed by providence to check the exuberance of population should fall on Hayti, either in the form of contagion, or by a multiplication of the various diseases, to which the African race are subject, in the degeneration of slavery; and that a white population should by that time be formed, capable of taking advantage of such a calamity; then, but not till then, should the neighbouring continent of America be in a state to colonize, or the policy of European governments desire the attainment of the most splendid colony of the Antilles, an opportunity might possibly be afforded.—Whether it would be rational on the score of justice, or humanity to do so, is a subject not to be argued at present. Those who undertake the project, if ever it should be undertaken, will be capable of defending it with plausibility.

But to this part of the subject the public attention is rarely directed; the danger of a community of manumitted slaves in the American Archipelago, is their chief objection to the new Empire of Hayti. With those who form their opinion on erroneous principles, fears of this kind may arise, as the unreflecting clown startles at his shadow on the moonlight sward. Whether Hayti exist or not, as an independent island, if the black population of the other colonies of the Antilles continue to increase as it has done during the last fifty years, and to overbalance that of the whites, no power but that of the exercise of humanity, can preserve them to their present possessors. The practise of this power, happily, is prevalent at present, and

CHAP. VI.
1804.
Probable effects of the colonial revolution.

it is hoped, and expected, that profiting by the past, it will be always co-equal with the increased wealth of the proprietors, and their capability of being liberal; but if it does not originate with themselves, that the smallest danger can arise to the colonies, from the Empire of Hayti, may be positively denied. The negroes, though sufficiently warlike and vindictive, when roused by revenge, court quiet, and are ardent in all the relations of life, when kindly treated by superiors. They would then with extreme difficulty, if at all, be persuaded to quit a situation of comparative ease, to join strangers in a bloody conflict. Besides, the inhabitants of Hayti could derive no advantage from such a union. They are not to be compared with the Maroons, or the Charaïbes, as they possess a territory with an organised government, and sufficient resources of their own, all which they must lose in proportion to the success of any project of ambition. Neither have they, nor do they want the maritime power so absolutely necessary for an attack on the other islands; and many other difficulties occur to prevent such a scheme.

Yet, as many events beyond the utmost stretch of foresight happen in the course of time, it is incumbent upon those in particular, whose local interest is concerned, to take due care to prevent the miseries which they appear prematurely to dread; for extra precaution is not so great an evil, as a deficiency of necessary care; to the Proprietors of the British colonies in particular it is recommended, to think an inducement to some degree of devotion among their slaves an object of importance, with a

1804.

Probable effects of the colonial revolution.

careful diffusion of morality. In the former, the more peculiar mysteries need not be included; nor in the latter that rigid system, which denies even the innocent gaieties of humble life. The personal care, too, of negroes, should be an object of more attention, than it is on certain occasions, with a view to preserve that health which is of so much value to their proprietors, as well as the comfort, necessary to render them satisfied with their condition. These attentions, including the care of pregnant females, added to those humane and salutary laws which already preclude excessive punishment, or labor, will always produce the most desirable effects, and be more certain than all the inflictions, that coercive measures can devise to prevent a spirit of deliberation (the first revolutionary system) among slaves.

And finally, if, it should appear from the concessions, which are already granted that the slaves in the colonies may be elevated from the consideration of being a species below, even to the lowest class of human society, the complaints which have formerly arisen, will soon have no grounds for existence; and those philanthropic minds which have been led, from the glorious principle of protecting "him that had none to help him," to countenance an enthusiasm, which has been of the most fatal tendency, will, no doubt, exert their beneficent offices in increasing the good effects, of what may have been already done. But this principle must always be preserved inviolable, (whether it militate or not against the policy of retaining distant colonies will not be argued,)—that no deliberative body should prescribe for the

 internal

CHAP. VI. 1804. *internal polity* of a country at a distance, such as precludes an intimate and constant knowledge of its concerns.

Probable effects of the colonial revolution.

The Enquiry into the Rise of the Black Empire of Hayti, thus concludes for the present. It is hoped a remarkable and correct picture will be found of a Revolution, which ranks among the most remarkable and important transactions of the day. It is, at least, untinctured with prejudice of any kind, unless that spirit can be so called, which inclines towards truth and humanity.

APPENDIX.

APPENDIX;

COMPRISING

DOCUMENTS

REFERRED TO IN DIFFERENT PARTS OF THE WORK:

TOGETHER WITH

AUXILIARY REMARKS.

APPENDIX.

No. I.

(Referred to in Page 131.—" The fascinating eloquence of the Abbé Gregoire," &c.)

Among the other Public Efforts of the Society of Amis de Noirs, was the following Letter of the Abbé Gregoire, Bishop of the Department of Loire and Cher, Deputy of the National Assembly, to the Citizens of Color in the French West Indies, concerning the Decree of the 15th May, 1791, which produced an immediate and striking Effect.

FRIENDS,

No. I. Enthusiastic address to the people of color, exciting them to deliberation, and consequently insurrection.

YOU *were* MEN;—you *are* now CITIZENS. Reinstated in the fulness of your rights, you will in future participate of the sovereignty of the people. The decree which the National Assembly has just published respecting you, is not a *favour;* for a favour is *a privilege*, and a privilege to one class of people is an injury to all the rest.—They are words which no longer disgrace the laws of the French.

In securing to you the exercise of your political rights, we have acquitted ourselves of *a debt:*—not to have paid it, would have been a crime on our part, and a disgrace to the constitution. The legislators of a free nation certainly could not do less for you than our ancient despots have done.

It

No. I.

Letter of the Abbé Gregoire.

It is now above a century that Louis XIVth solemnly acknowledged and proclaimed your rights; but of this sacred inheritance you have been defrauded by pride and avarice, which have gradually increased your burthens, and embittered your existence.

The regeneration of the French empire opened your hearts to hope, whose cheering influence has alleviated the weight of your miseries; miseries of which the people of Europe had no idea. While the white planters resident amongst us were loud in their complaints against *ministerial* tyranny, they took especial care to be silent *as to their own.* Not a hint was suggested concerning the complaints of the unhappy people of mixed blood; who, notwithstanding, are their own children. It is *we,* who, at the distance of two thousand leagues from you, have been constrained to protect these children against the neglect, the contempt, the unnatural cruelty of their fathers!

But it is in vain that they have endeavoured to suppress the justice of your claims. Your groans, notwithstanding the extent of the ocean which separates us, have reached the hearts of the European Frenchmen; for *they* have *hearts.*

God Almighty comprehends all men in the circle of his mercies. His love makes no distinction between them, but what arises from the different degrees of their virtues. Can laws then, which ought to be an emanation of eternal justice, encourage so culpable a partiality? Can that government, whose duty it is to protect alike all the members of the same great family, be the mother of one branch, and the step-mother only of the others?

No, Gentlemen:—you could not escape the solicitude of the National Assembly. In unfolding to the eyes of the universe the great charter of nature, your titles were traced. An attempt had indeed been made to expunge them; but, happily, they are written in characters as indelible as the sacred image of the Deity, which is graven on your countenances.

No. I. Letter of the Abbé Gregoire.

Already had the National Assembly, in the instructions which it prepared for the government of the colonies, on the 28th of March, 1790, comprized both the whites and people of color under one common denomination. Your enemies, in asserting the contrary, have published a forgery. It is incontestibly true, that when I demanded you should be expressly named, a great number of members, among whom were several planters, eagerly exclaimed, that you were already comprehended under general words contained in those instructions. M. Barnave himself, upon my repeated instances to him on that head, has at length acknowledged, before the whole Assembly, that this was the fact. It now appears how much reason I had to apprehend that a false construction would be put upon our decree!

New oppressions on the part of your masters, and new miseries on yours, until at length the cup of affliction is filled even to the brim, have but too well justified my apprehensions. The letters which I have received from you upon this head, have forced tears from my eyes. Posterity will learn, with astonishment and indignation, that a cause like yours, the justice of which is so evident, was made the subject of debate for no less than five days successively. Alas! when humanity is obliged to struggle

No. I.

Letter of the Abbé Gregoire.

so long against vanity and prejudice, its triumph is dearly obtained!

It is a long time that the society of *Ami des Noirs* have employed themselves in finding out the means to soften your lot, as well as that of the slaves. It is difficult, perhaps impossible, to do good with entire impunity. The meritorious zeal of this society has drawn upon them much obloquy. Despicable writers have lanced their poisonous shafts at them, and impudent libels have never ceased to repeat objections and calumnies, which have been an hundred times answered and refuted. How often have we been accused of being sold to the English, and of being paid by them for sending you inflammatory writings and arms? You know, my friends, the weakness and wickedness of these charges. We have incessantly recommended to you attachment to your country, resignation, and patience, while waiting the return of justice. Nothing has been able to cool our zeal, or that of your brethren of mixed blood who are at Paris. M. Raimond, in particular, has devoted himself most heroically to your defence. With what transport would you have seen this distinguished citizen, at the bar of the National Assembly, of which he ought to be a member, laying before it the affecting picture of your miseries, and strenuously claiming your rights! If that Assembly had sacrificed them, it would have tarnished its glory. It was its duty to decree with justice, to explain itself clearly, and cause its laws to be executed with firmness:—it has done so; and if, (which God forbid!) some event, hidden in the womb of futurity, should tear our colonies from us, would it not be better to have

have a loss to deplore, than an injustice to reproach ourselves with?

No. I. Letter of the Abbé Gregoire.

Citizens! raise once more your humiliated countenances, and to the dignity of men, associate the courage and nobleness of a free people. The 15th of May, the day in which you recovered your rights, ought to be ever memorable to you and to your children. This epoch will periodically awaken in you sentiments of gratitude towards the Supreme Being; and may your accents ascend to the vault of Heaven! At length you have a country. Hereafter you will see nothing above you but the law; while the opportunity of concurring in the framing of it, will assure to you that indefeasible right of all mankind,—the right of obeying yourselves only.

You have a country: and it will no longer be a land of exile, where you meet none but tyrants on the one hand, and companions in misfortune on the other; the former distributing, and the latter receiving, contempt and outrage. The groans of your afflictions were punished as the clamours of rebellion; and, situated between the uplifted poignard and certain death, those unhappy countries were often moistened with your tears, and sometimes stained with your blood.

You have a country: and happiness will shine on the seat of your nativity. You will now enjoy in peace the fruits of the fields which you have cultivated without compulsion. Then will be filled up that interval, which, placing at an immense distance from each other the children of the same father, has suppressed the voice of nature, and broke the bands of fraternity asunder.

 Then

No. I.
Letter of the Abbé Gregoire.

Then will the chaste enjoyments of conjugal union take place of of those vile sallies of debauchery, by which the majesty of moral sentiment has been insulted. By what strange perversion of reason can it be deemed disgraceful in a white man to marry a black or mulatto woman, when it is not thought dishonourable in him to be connected with her in the most licentious familiarity!

The less real worth a man possesses, the more he seeks to avail himself of the appearances of virtue. What can be more absurd than to make the merit of a person consist in different shades of the skin, or in a complexion more or less sallow? The man who thinks at all must sometimes blush at being a man, when he sees his fellow-creatures blinded by such ridiculous prejudices; but as, unfortunately, pride is one of those failings we most unwillingly part with, the empire of prejudice is the most difficult to subvert: man appears to be unable to arrive at truth, until he has exhausted his strength in travelling through the different paths of error.

This prejudice against the mulattoes and negroes has, however, no existence in our eastern colonies. Nothing can be more affecting than the eulogium made on the people of color by the inhabitants in that part of the world, in the instructions to those they have appointed their deputies to the National Assembly. The members of the Academy of Sciences pride themselves in reckoning a mulatto of the Isle of France in the number of their correspondents. Among ourselves, a worthy negro is a superior officer of the district of St. Hypolite, in the department of Gard. We do not conceive that a difference of color can be the founda-

tion

tion of different rights among members of the same political society: it is, therefore, we find no such despicable pride among our brave National Guards, who offer themselves to embark for the West Indies, to insure the execution of our decrees. Perfectly concurring in the laudable sentiments manifested by the inhabitants of Bourdeaux, they acknowledge with them, that the decree respecting the people of color, framed under the auspices of prudence and wisdom, is an homage rendered to reason and justice. While the deputies from the colonies have endeavoured to calumniate your intentions, and those of the mercantile part of the nation, the conduct of those deputies is perfectly contradictory. Ardently soliciting their own admission among us at Versailles; swearing with us in the Tennis Court not to separate from us until the constitution should be established, and then declaring when the decree of the 15th of May was passed, that they could no longer continue to sit with us! This desertion is a desertion of their principles, and a breach of their solemn oaths.

No. I. Letter of the Abbé Gregoire.

All those white inhabitants of the colonies who are worthy the name of Frenchmen, have hastened to abjure such ridiculous prejudices, and have promised to regard you in future as brothers and friends. With what delightful sensations do we cite the words of the citizens of Jacmel. "We swear to obey, without reserve, the decrees of the National Assembly respecting our present and future constitution, and even such of them as may substantially change it!" The citizens of Port-au-Prince tell the National Assembly the same thing, in different words:—"Condescend, gentlemen," say they, "to receive the oath which the municipality.

No. I. Letter of the Abbé Gregoire.

municipality has taken to you, in the name of the commons of Port-au-Prince, punctually to obey and execute all your decrees, and never to swerve from them in any respect whatever."

Thus has philosophy enlarged its horizon in the new world, and soon will absurd prejudices have no other supporters than a few inferior tyrants, who wish to perpetuate in America the reign of that despotism which has been abolished in France.

What would these men have said, if the people of color had endeavoured to deprive the whites of *their* political advantages? With what energy would they not have exclaimed at such an oppression! Inflamed into madness at finding that your rights have been pointed out to you, their irritated pride may perhaps lead them to make every effort to render our decrees ineffectual. They will probably endeavour to raise such disturbances, as, by wresting the colonies from the mother-country, will enable them to defraud their creditors of their just debts. They have incessantly alarmed us with the threat that St. Domingo will be lost, if justice be rendered to you. In this assertion we have found nothing but falsehood: we please ourselves in the belief, that our decree will draw the bands still closer which unite you to the mother country. Your patriotism, your interest, and your affections, will concur in inducing you to confine your commercial connections to France only; and the reciprocal tributes of industry will establish between her and her colonies a constant interchange of riches and good offices. If you act unfaithfully towards France, you will be the basest and most abandoned of the human race. But no, generous citizens, you will not become traitors to your country;

No. I. Letter of the Abbé Gregoire.

country; you shudder at the idea. Rallied, with all other good Frenchmen, around the standard of liberty, you will still defend our glorious constitution. The day shall arrive when the representatives of the people of color will cross the ocean to take their seats with us. The day shall arrive among you when the sun will shine on none but freemen; when the rays of light shall no longer fall on the fetters of slavery. It is true, the National Assembly has not yet raised the condition of the enslaved negroes to a level with your situation; because suddenly granting the rights to those who are ignorant of the duties of citizens, might, perhaps, have been a fatal present to them: but forget not, that they, like yourselves, are born to freedom and perfect equality. It is in the irresistible course of things that all nations, whose liberty has been invaded, shall recover that precious portion of their indefeasible inheritance!

You are accused of treating your slaves much worse than the whites: but, alas! so various have been the detractions with which you have been aspersed, that it would be weakness in us to credit the charge. If, however, there be any foundation for what has been advanced on this head, so conduct yourselves in future as to prove it will be a shameful calumny hereafter.

Your oppressors have heretofore endeavoured to hide from their slaves the lights of Christianity; because the religion of mildness, equality, and liberty, suits not with such blood-thirsty men. May *your* conduct be the reverse of *theirs*. Universal love is the language of the gospel; your pastors will make it heard among you. Open your hearts to receive this divine

 system

No. I. Letter of the Abbé Gregoire.

system of morality. We have mitigated *your* misfortunes; alleviate, on your part, those of the unhappy victims of avarice, who moisten your fields with their sweat, and often with their tears. Let the existence of your slaves be no longer their torment; but by your kind treatment of them expiate the crimes of Europe!

By leading them on progressively to liberty, you will fulfil a duty; you will prepare for yourselves the most comfortable reflections; you will do honor to humanity, and ensure the prosperity of the colonies. Such will be your conduct towards your brethren, the negroes; but what ought it to be towards your fathers, the whites? Doubtless you will be permitted to shed tears over the ashes of *Ferrand de Baudiere*, and the unfortunate Ogé, assassinated under the forms of law, and dying on the wheel for having wished to be free! But may he among you perish, who shall dare to entertain an idea of revenge against your persecutors! They are already delivered over to the stings of their own consciences, and covered with eternal infamy. The abhorrence in which they are held by the present race of mankind, only precedes the execration of posterity. Bury, then, in eternal oblivion every sentiment of hatred, and taste the delicious pleasure of conferring benefits on your oppressors. Repress even too marked expressions of your joy, which, in causing them to reflect on their own injustice towards you, will make their remorse still more poignant.

Strictly obedient to the laws, teach your children to respect them. By a careful education, instruct them in all the duties of morality; so shall you prepare for the succeeding generation virtuous citizens, honorable men, enlightened patriots, and defenders of their country!

No. I. Letter of the Abbé Gregoire.

How will their hearts be affected when, conducting them to your shores, you direct their looks towards France, telling them, "beyond those seas is your parent country; it is from thence we have received justice, protection, happiness, and liberty. There dwell our fellow citizens, our brethren, and our friends; to whom we have sworn an eternal friendship. Heirs of our sentiments and of our affections, may your hearts and your lips repeat our oaths! Live to love them; and, if necessary, die to defend them!"

(Signed) GREGOIRE.

Paris, 8th June, 1791.

No. II.

(Referred to, and its Substance explained, p. 113.)

Principes de la Première Assemblée Generale de St. Domingue.

No. II. Principles of the First General Assembly of St. Domingo, as published by one of its members in Paris.

Un principe d'oû sont émanés tous les travaux de l'Assemblée de la Colonie fut généralement adopté par tous ses membres, c'est que les colonies ne doivent intéresser la métropole, qu'en proportion des avantages qu'elles lui procurent. Cette considération dût acquérir, dans l'esprit de tous les colons, un caractère de

 légalité

No. II.

Principles of the First General Assembly.

légalitè à tous les moyens qui pouvoient assurer la prospérité de la colonie, et augmenter ses rapports avec la mère patrie.

Il auroit èté sans doute à souhaiter, et il seroit bein plus encore, qu'une même loi pût convenir à touts les climats, à toute espèce de mœurs, à toutes les populations; mais malheureusement les hommes ne sont pas les mêmes par tout; telle loi qui convient dans un endroit, seroit nuisible dans un autre.

L'Assemblée Générale envisagea donc la constitution de St. Domingue, sous trois rapports, toujours dirigés d'après son intérêt de rester unie a la métropole, et d'apres la révolution de l'empire.

1. Comme faisant partie intégrante de l'empire François.

2. Comme obligée de concourir par ses productions à la prospéritée de l'etat.

3. Comme assujettie par la dissemblance de son climat de ces mœurs et de sa population, à des besoins particuliers et differens de ceux de la metropole.

Division de la Constitution de St. Domingue.

Ces divers rapports diviser la constitution convenable à St. Domingue,

En lois générales;

En lois communes;

Et en loix particulières.

Loix Générales.

Le lois générales de l'empire, celles qui intéressent tous les

 François,

No. II. Principles of the First General Assembly.

François, dans quelque coin de la terre qu'ils soient placés, furent considérées comme obligatoires pour les colonies, sans aucun examen, sans aucune restriction.

Ces lois sont: la forme du gouvernment, le sort de la couronne, la reconnoisance du monarque, les déclarations de guerre, les traités de paix, l'organization générale de la police, et de la justice, &c. &c. L'intérêt des colonies se trouvant à cet égard confondu avec celui de toute la nation, l'Assemblée Nationale a seule le droit de décréter ces loix.

Loix Communes.

Les loix communes sont celles qui ont rapport aux rélàtiones de la métropole avec les colonies; c'est un contrat par lequel la France s'oblig ede protéger et defendre les colonies contre les puissances étrangères, de l'ambition desquelles elles devient droient l'objet. Cette protection ne devant ni ne pouvant être gratuite, les colonies doivent, en dedommager l'etat par les avantages du commerce. Délâ, le regime prohibitif dans les fers duquel la destinée les a condamnés à rester toujours; et quel que soit le degré de liberté dont jouisse la nation, les colonies seront toujours esclaves du commerce. C'est une position politique absolument inhèrent á leur position physiques, elles n'en laissent pas échapper le moindre murmure; elles savent bien que leur qualité de François ne leur donne pas de droit sur les déniers de l'etat; elles consentent donc à ne récévoir que de la France tous les objets de consommation que ses manufactures et son sol peuvent fournir; elles souservent encore à l'obligation de n'enivrer leurs desirs.

 qu'en

No. II. Principles of the First General Assembly.

qu'en France. Ce qu'elles demandent, ce qu'on ne peut leur réfuser, c'est qu'en consacrent ces conventions fondamentales, les abus que le regime prohibitif entraîne après lui soint détruits.

Loix Particulières ou Regime Interieur.

Les loix particulières sont celles qui n'intéressent que les colonies. De grands motifs ont porté la colonie de St. Domingue à s'en réserver la formation: 1. il est bien reconnu que les loix de St. Domingue ne peuvent être faites ailleurs que dans son sein: cette vérité fondamentale a échappé à son ennemi le plus cruel. M. la Luzerne, dans son mémoire presenté â l'Assemblée Nationale, le 27 Octobre 1789, (No. 2.) disoit que les colonies n'ont jamais pu être régies par les mêmes loix que le royaume, et qu'il a fallu toujours conférer le pouvoir â deux administrateurs de faire les loix locales, parce qu'il est une infinité d'infinités de convenances qu'on ne peut connoître que sur les lieux.

Ce que l'Assemblée Générale s'est réservée n'est donc que la portion du pouvoir législatif qui résidoit, contre le droit des hommes, dans les mains de deux satrapes, que la colonie n'intéresse que par les richesses qu'ils en retirent pendant leurs administration.

2. Il est contraire aux principes constitutionnels, que celui qui fait la loi n'y soit point assujetti.

Tous les hommes ont le droit de concourir à la formation de la loi à laquelle ils sont assujettis; mais nul ne peut concourir á la formation de celle qui ne l'assujettit pas.

Ce principe, seul éxige de la liberté individuelle, seul garant de la bienfaisance de la loi, qui n'a pas permis aux colons de St. Domingue

Domingue de douter que l'Assemblée Nationale, dispensatrice des bienfaits régénérateurs, n'approuvât cette disposition qui assure la propérité de St. Domingue.

No. II. Principles of the First General Assembly.

En effet, il ne peut pas en être des loix locales des sections éloignées de l'empire, comme des loix qui n'interessent que la France.

La loi décrétée pour le royaume est la même pour tous les cantons. L'universalité des députés de l'Assemblée Nationale sont intéressée à en examiner scrupuleusement tous les rapports, â en considérer tous les avantages et tous les inconvéniences. De sorte que l'intérêt que tous ont â ce que la loi, du vice de laquelle ils seroient eux mêmes les victimes, ne soit que le fruit d'une longue méditation, et de reflexions longuement et soigneusement diseutées, en assure la sagesse.

Le loix particulières de St. Domingue n'assujettissant que les habitans qui y resident ou qui y ont leur fortunes, n'interessent dans l'Assemblée Nationales que les douze députés des colonies.

3. Une des conditions essentielles, à la bonté de la loi, est que celui qui la fait, connoisse par faitements les rapports qu'elle doit avoir avec la constitution; nul ne peut connoître les particularités locales que celui qui est sur les lieux, parce que ces mêmes particularités changent et varient; et il faut que la loi soit faite, d'âprès ces variations.

4. Il est bien constant que les liens de la société sont les pouvoirs etablis pour en faire exécuter les conditions.

Le bonheur de toute constitution dépend absolument d'une action

No. II.

Principles of the First General Assembly.

action égale dans ces différans pouvoirs; c'est cette égalité seule qui en maintient l'équilibre.

Il faux necessairement qu'il existe à St. Domingue un pouvoir executif; car le malheur des sociétés veut que la raison n'aille jamais en politique quà côté de la force. Si ce pouvoir n'est balancé par aucun autre, il finira par tout envahir, et par substituer l'oppression aux bienfaits de la régénération à laquelle la révolution actuelle donne à tous les François le droit de pretendre. Il ne peuvent donc étre contenu dans ces bornes que par une masse proportionnée de pouvoir législatif, dont il ayent à redouter la surveillance.

5. Les principes de l'Assemblée Nationale s'opposent à ce qu'elle decrete la constitution particulière de St. Domingue. Celle de la France a pour base la liberté, l'égalité; celle de St. Domingue repose malheureusement sur la servitude, et une distinction de classes, d'où depend la conservation de cette superbe colonie. Tous les raisonnements possibles échouerent contre cette vérité.

Ces différentes observations, bien analysées dans l'Assemblée Générale, la rassurérent sur la crainte qu'elle avoit de ne point se trouver d'accord avec les principes de l'Assemblée Nationale, et de prêter à la calomnie le prétexte d'inculper ses intentions.

Les differens membres de l'Assemblée Générale etoint bien eloignés de prevoir que l'heureuse révolution qui à porté la joie et la enthousiasme dans le cœurs de tous les François, finiroit par porter à St. Domingue la deuil et la desolation. Qu'importe à la France, quelque soit notre régime domestique, pourvu qu'il tende tend a faire le bien de la colonie? Pourvu que nous soyons assujettis aux loix générales de l'empire? Pourvu que nous respections les rapports commerciaux? Pourvu que nous regardions la sujétion de ne traiter qu'avec la France, comme un juste dédommagement de la protection et des secours qu'elle nous accorde? Pourvu que nous éxécutions les décret de l'Assemblée Nationale, en tout ce qui n'est point contraires aux localités.

No. II. Principles of the First General Assembly.

Il importe à la France que nous soyons heureux, que nous consomions les denrées et les marchandises qu'elle peut nous fournir, et que nous lui envoyons en echange beaucoup de sucre, de caffé, d'indigo, de coton, de cacao, &c. &c. Enfin, il lui importe que la constitutione de St. Domingue soit telle, qu'elle unisse pour jamais cette colonie à la metropole, et qu'elle concoure, par ces richesses, a la prospérité de l'etat.

D'après ces reflexions, simples et vraies, l'Assemblée Générale de St. Domingue posa ses bases constitutionnelles dans son décret du 28 Maï (No. 3.)

No. III.

(Referred to in Page 157, where also the Substance is translated.)

No. III. Declaration of a dying conspirator, which if acted upon, might have checked the insurrection in its rise.

Testament de Mort d'Ogé.

Extrait des Minutes du Conseil Supérieur du Cap, l'an mil sept cent quatre-vingt-onze le neuf Mars, nous, Antoine Etienne Ruotte,

No. III.
Ogé's evidence against the conspirators.

Ruotte, Conseiller du Roi, doyen au Conseil Superieur du Cap, et Maria François Pourcheresse de Vertieres, aussi Conseiller du Roi au Conseil Supérieur du Cap, commissaires nommés, par la cour, à l'effet de faire exécuter l'arrêt de ladite cour, du 5 du présent mois, portant condamnation de mort contre le nommé Jacques Ogé, dit Jacquot, quarteron libre; lequel, étant en la chambre criminelle, et après lecture faite du dit arrêt, en ce qui le concerne; a dit et déclaré, pour la décharge de sa conscience, serment préalablement par lui prêté, la main levée devant nous, de dire vérité.

Que dans le commencement du mois de Fevrier dernier, si les rivières n'avoient pas été débordées, il devoit se faire un attroupement de gens de couleur, qui devoient entrainer avec eux les àtélier, et devoient venir fondre sur la ville du Cap en nombre tres considérable; qu'ils étoient même déjà réunis au nombre de onze mille hommes; que la debordement des rivières est le seul obstacle qui les a empêchés de se réunir; cette quantité d'hommes de couleur étant composée de ceux du Mirebalais, de l'Artibonité, du Limbé, d'Ouanaminthe, de la Grand Rivière, et généralement de toute la colonie. Qu' à cette époque, il etait sorti du Cap cent hommes de couleur pour se joindre à cette troupe. Que l'accusé est assuré que les auteurs de cette révolte sont les Declains, negrés libres de la Grand Riviere, accuses au procès; Dumas, n. l.; Yvon, n. l.; Bitozin, m. l. Espagnol; Pierre Gedard et Jean Baptiste, son frere, n. l. de la Grand Riviere; Legrand Mazeau et Toussaint Mazeau, n. l.; Pierre Mauzi, m. l.; Ginga Lapaire, Charles Lamadieu, les Sabourins, Jean Pierre

Goudy,

Goudy, Joseph Lucas, mulâtres libres; Maurice, n. l.; tous accusés au procés.

No. III. Ogé's evidence against the conspirators.

Que le grands moteurs, au bas de la côte, sont les nommés Daguin, accusé au procès; Rebel, demeurant au Mirabelais; Pinchinat, accusé au procès; et que l'accusé, ici présent croit devoir nous déclarer étre un des plus ardens partisans de la révolte, qui a mu en grande partie celle qui a éclaté dans les environs de St. Marc, et qui cherche à en excité une nouvelle; qu'il y a dans ce moment plusieurs gens de couleur, dans différens quartiers, bien résolus à tenir à leurs projets, malgré que ceux qui tremperont dans la révolte perdroient la vie; que l'accuse, ici présent, ne peut pas se ressouvenir du nom de tous; mais qu'il se rappelle que le fils de Laplace, q. l.; dont lui accusé a vu la sœur dans les prisons, a quitté le Limbé pour aller faire des récrues et ces soulvemens de gens de couleur sont soutenus ici par la presence des nommés Fleury et l'Hirondelle Viard, députés des gens de couleur auprés de l'Assemblée Nationale; que lui accusé, ici present, ignore si les députés se tiennent chez eux; qu'il croit que le nommé Fleury se tient au Mirabalis, et le nommé l'Hirondelle Viard, dans le quartier de la Grand Rivière.

Qui lui accusé, ici present, declare que l'insurrection des revoltés existe dans les souterrains qui se trouvant entre la Crête à Marcan et le canton du Giromon, paroisse de la Grande Rivière; qu'en conséquence, si lui accusé pouvoit etre conduit sur les lieux, il se feroit fort de prendre les chefs des révoltés; que l'agitation dans laquelle il se trouve, relativement à sa position actuelle, ne lui permet pas de nous donner des détails plus circonstanciés;

No. III.

Ogé's evidence against the conspirators.

qu'il nous le donnera par la suite, lorsqu'il sera un peu plus tranquil; qu'il lui vient en ce moment à l'esprit que le nommé Castaing, mulâtre libre de cette dépendance; ne se trove compris en aucune manière dans l'affaire actuelle; mais que lui accusé, nous assure que si son frère Ogé, eût suivi l'impulsion dudit Castaing, il se seroit porté à de bien plus grandes extrémités; qui est tout ce qu'il nous a dit pouvoir nous déclarer dans ce moment, dont lui nous avons donné acte, qu'il a signé avec nous et le gréffier.

Signé à la minute, J. OGE, RUOTTE, POURCHERESSE DE VERTIERES, et LANDAIS, gréffier.

Extrait des Minutes du Greffe du Conseil Supérieur du Cap, l'an mil sept cent quatre-vingt-onze, le dix Mars, trois heures de rélévée, en la chambre criminelle, nous, Antoine Etienne Ruotte, Conseiller du Roi, doyen du Conseil Supérieur du Cap, et Maria François Joseph de Vertieres, aussi Conseiller du Roi, audit Conseil Supérieur du Cap, commissaires nommés par la cour, suivant arrêt de ce jour, rendu sur les conclusions du procureur général du roi de ladite cour, à l'effet de procéder au recolement de la déclaration faite par le nommé Jacques Ogé, q. l.; lequel, aprés serment par lui fait, la main levée devant nous, de dire la vérité, et après lui avoir fait lecture, par la greffier, de la declaration du jour d'hier, l'avons interpellé de nous déclarer si ladite déclaration contient vérité, s'il veut n'y rien ajouter, n'y diminuer, et s'il y persiste.

A repondu que ladite déclaration du jour d'hier, contient vérité, qu'il persiste, et qu'ill y ajoute que les deux Didiers frères, dont

 l'un

No. III.

Ogé's evidence against the conspirators.

l'un plus grand que l'autre, mulâtres ou quarterons libres, ne les ayant vu que cette fois; Jean Pierre Gerard, m. l. du Cap, et Caton, aussi du Cap, sont employés à gagner les ateliers de la Grande Rivière, qu'ils sont ensemble de jour, et que de nuit ils sont dispersés.

Ajout encore que lors de sa confrontation avec Jacques Lucas, il a été dit par le dernier, que lui accusé, ici présent, l'avoit menacé de le faire pendre; à quoi lui accusé, a repondu audit Jacques Lucas, qu'il devoit savoir pourquoi que ledit Jacques Lucas n'ayant pas insisté, lui accusé n'a pas déclaré le motif de cette menace, pour ne pas perdre ledit Jacques Lucas; qu'il nous déclare les choses comme elles se sont passées; que ledit Lucas lui ayant dit qu'il avoit soulevè les ateliers de M. Bonancy, et de divers autres habitans de la Grand Rivière, pour aller egorger l'armée chez M. Cardineau; qu'au premier coup de corne, il étoit sûr que ces ateliers s'attrouperoient et se joindroient à la troupe des gens de couleurs; alors lui accusé, tenant aux blancs, fut révolté de cette barbarie, et dit au nommé Jacques Lucas, que l'auteur d'un pareil projet méritoit d'être pendu; qu'il eût à l'instant à faire rentrer les negres quil avoit posté dans differens coins avec des cornes; que lui accusé, ici present, nous déclare qu'il a donné audit Lucas trois pomponelles de tafia, trois bouteilles de vin et du pain; qu'il ignoroit l'usage que ledit Lucas en faisoit; que la troisième fois que ledit Lucas en vint chercher; lui accusé, ici présent, lui ayant demandé ce qu'il faisoit de ces boissons et vivres; ledit Lucas répondit que c'étoit pour les negres qu'il avoit dispersé de côté et d'autre; que ce qui prouve que

No. III.

Ogé's evidence against the conspirators.

ledit Lucas avoit le projèt de soulèver les nègres esclaves contre les blancs, et de faire égorger ces derniers par les prémiers; c'est la proposition qu'il fit à Vincent Ogé, frère de lui accusé, de venir sur l'habitation de lui Jacques Lucas, pour être plus a portée de se joindre aux nègres qu'il avoit debauché; que si lui accusé n'a pas révélé ces faits à sa confrontation avec ledit Jacques Lucas, c'est qu'il n'a pas voulu le perdre; qu'il a du moins la satisfaction d'avoir détourné ce crime horrible et cannibale; du'il s'étoit réservé de révéler en justice, lors de son élargissement; que ce même Lucas est celui qui a voulu couper la tête a deux prisonniers blancs, et notamment au sieur Belisle, pour lui avoir enlevé une femme; que Pierre Roubert ôta le sabre, des mains de Jacques Lucas, et appella Vincent Ogé, frère de lui accusé, ici present, qui fit des rémontrances audit Lucas; que cependant ces prisonniers ont déclarés en justice que c'étoit lui accusé qui avoit eu ce dessein; que même à la confrontation ils le lui ont soutenu; mais que le fait s'étant passé de nuit, lesdits prisonniers ont pris, lui accusé, pour ledit Lucas, tandis que lui accusé n'a cessé de les combler d'honnêtétês; qu' à la confrontation, lui accusé a cru qu'il étoit suffisant de dire que ce n'étoit pas lui, et d'affirmer qu'il n'avoit jamais connu cette femme; mais qu' adjourd'hui il se croyoit obligé, pour la décharge de sa conscience, de nous rendre les faits tels qu'ils sont, et d'insister à jurer qu'il ne l'a jamais connue.

Ajoute l'accusé que le nommé Fleury et Perisse? le premier, l'un des députés des gens de couleur près de l'Assemblée Nationale, sont arrivé en cette colonie par un bâtiment

Bordelais

No. III.

Ogé's evidence against the conspirators.

Bordelais avec le nomme l'Herondelle Viard; que le capitaine a mis les deux prémiers a Acquin, chez un nommé Dupont, hommé de couleur; et le nommé l'Hirondelle Viard, égalemen, député des gens de couleur, au Cap. Ajoute encore l'accuseé, qu'il nous avoit déclaré, le jour d'heir, que le nommé Laplace, dont le père est ici dans les prisons, faisant des récrues à Ovanaminthe, est du nombre de ceux qui ont marché du Limbé contre le Cap; que pour éloigner les soupçons, il est allé au Port-Margot, où il s'est tenu caché plusieurs jours, feignant d'avoir un fluxion; que ledit Laplace père a dit, à lui blanc, ne deposera pas contre lui malgré qu'il sache toutes ses démarches; qu'il etoit assuré que le nommé Girardieu, détenu en prison, ne declareroit rien, parce qu'il étoit trop son ami pour le découvrir; qu'en suite, si'l le denonçoit, il seroit forcé d'en dénoncer beaucoup d'autres, tant du Limbé que des autres quartiers.

Observe l'acusé que lorsqu'il nous a parlé de moyens employés par Jacques Lucas pour soulever les nègres esclaves, il a omis de nous dire que Pierre Maury avait envoyé une trentaine d'esclaves ches Lucas; que lui accusè, avec l'agrément d'Ogé le jeune, son frère, les renvoya, ce qui occasionna une plainte générale, le gens de couleur disant que c'étoit du renfort; que lui aecusé eut même à cette occasion un rixe avec le plus grand des didiers, avec lequœl il manqua de se battre au pistolet pour vouloir lui soutenir qu'étant libre et cherchant à être assimilé aux blancs, il n'étoit pas fait pour être assimilé aux nègres esclaves; que d'ailleurs soulevant les esclaves, c'étoit détruire les propriétés des blancs, et qu'en les detruissant, ils detruisoient les leurs propres; que depuis

que

No. II.

Oge's evidence against the conspirators.

que lui accusé étoit dans les prisons, il a vu un petit billet écrit écrit par ledit Pierre Maury à Jean-François Tessier, par lequel il lui marque qu'il continue à ramasser, et que le nègre nommé Coquin, à la dame veuve Castaing aînée armé d'une paire de de pistolet garni en argent et d'une manchette que ledit Maury lui à donné ueille à toute ce qui se passe, et rend compte tous les soirs audit Maury; qui est tout ce que l'accusé, ici present, nous declare, en nous coujurant d'être persuadés que, s'il lui étoit possible d'obtenir misérecorde, il s'exposeroit volontièrs à tous les dangers pour faire arrêter les chefs de ces revoltes; et que dans toutes les circonstances, il prouvera son zêle et son respect pour lès blancs.

Lecture à lui faite de sa déclaration dans laquelle il persiste pour contenir vérité, lui en donnons acte, quil a signé avec nous et le gréffier.

Signé à la minute J. Ogie, Ruotte, Pourcheresses de Vertieres, et Landais, gréffier.

Pour expedition collationée, signé Landais, gréffier.

No. IV.

No. IV.

(Referring to p. 169.)

Terms of Capitulation proposed by the Inhabitants of La Grande Anse (including the Quarter at Jeremie) represented by Mons. de Charmilly, possessed of full Powers by a Commission from the Council of Public Safety of the aforesaid Place, dated the 18th of August, 1793, and presented to His Excellency Major-General Williamson, His Majesty's Lieutenant-Governor of Jamaica, for his Acceptance.

First official paper of the British expedition to St. Domingo.

ART. I. That the proprietors of St. Domingo, deprived of all recourse to their lawful sovereign, to deliver them from the tyranny under which they now groan, implore the protection of his Britannic Majesty, and take the oath of fidelity and allegiance to him, and supplicate him to take their colony under his protection, and treat them as good and faithful subjects till a general peace, at which period they shall be finally subjected to the terms then agreed upon between his Britannic Majesty, the Government of France, and the Allied Powers, with respect to the sovereignty of St. Domingo.—Answer. Granted.

Art. II. That till order and tranquillity are restored at St. Domingo, the Governor appointed by his Britannic Majesty shall have

No. IV. 1804. have full power to regulate and direct whatever measures of safety and police he shall judge proper.—Answer. Granted.

Art. III. That no one shall be molested on account of any anterior disturbances, except those who are legally accused in some court of justice, of having committed murder, or of having destroyed property by fire, or of having instigated others to commit those crimes.—Answer. Granted.

Art. IV. That the Mulattoes shall have all the privileges enjoyed by that class of people in the British islands.—Answer. Granted.

Art. V. That if, at the conclusion of the war, the colony remains under the sovereignty of his Britannic Majesty, and order be established therein; in such case, the laws respecting property, and all civil rights, which were in force in the said colony before the revolution in France, shall be preserved; nevertheless, until a colonial assembly can be formed, his Britannic Majesty shall have the right of determining provisionally upon any measures which the general good and the tranquility of the colony may require; but that no assembly shall be called, until order is established in every part of the colony; and, till that period, his Britannic Majesty's governor shall be assisted in all the details of administration and police by a committee of six persons, which he shall have the power of choosing from among the proprietors of the three provinces of which the colony consists.—Answer. Granted.

Art. VI. That, in consequence of the devastations which have taken place in the colony by insurrections, fire, and pillage, the governor

No. IV.
Capitulation of the English at St. Domingo.

governor appointed by his majesty, on taking possession of the colony, to satisfy the demand of the inhabitants in these respects, shall be authorised to grant, for the payment of debts, a suspension of ten years, which shall be computed from the date of the surrender; and the suspension of all interest upon the same shall begin from the period of the 1st of August, 1791, and terminate at the expiration of the ten years granted for the payment of debts; but all sums due to minors by their guardians, or to absent planters by those who have the management of their property, or from one planter to another for the transfer of property, are not to be included in the above suspension.—Answer. Granted.

Art. VII. That the duties of importation and exportation upon all European commodities shall be the same as in the English colonies.—Answer. Granted. In consequence, the tariff shall be made public and affixed, that every one may be acquainted therewith.

Art. VIII. That the manufactures of white sugars shall preserve the right of exporting their clayed sugars, subject to such regulations as it may be necessary to make with respect to them.—Answer. Granted. In consequence, the duties upon white sugars shall be the same as were taken in the colony of St. Domingo, in 1789.

Art. IX. That the catholic religion shall be preserved and maintained, but that no other mode of evangelic worship shall be excluded.—Answer. Granted. On condition that such priests as have taken the oath prescribed by the persons exer-

No. IV.
Capitulation of the English at St. Domingo.

cising the powers of Government in France, shall be sent away, and replaced by others.

Art. X. The local taxes to acquit the expences of garrisons, and of the administration of the colony, shall be assessed in the same manner as in 1789, except the alleviations and remittances which shall be granted to the inhabitants whose property has suffered by fire, till their possessions are repaired. An account shall be kept by the colony of all the sums advanced on the part of Great Britain, for supplying the deficiency of the said taxes; which deficiency, as well as all the public expences of the colony (except those of his majesty's naval forces, destined for its protection) shall always be defrayed by the said colony.—Answer. Granted.

Art. XI. His Britannic Majesty's Governor of St. Domingo, shall apply to the Spanish government, to obtain restitution of the negroes and cattle sold by the Spanish territory by the revolted slaves.—Answer. Granted.

Art. XII. The importation in American bottoms, of provision, cattle, grain, and wood, of every kind, from the United States of America, shall be allowed at St. Domingo.—Answer. Granted. On condition that the American ships, which shall be employed in this trade, shall have only one deck; and this importation shall be allowed only as long as it shall appear necessary for the re-establishment or subsistence of the colony, or until measures have been taken for putting it in this respect upon the same footing as other English colonies; and an exact account shall be kept of the said vessels, with the descrip-

5 tion

tion of their cargoes, and shall be transmitted every three months to the Right Honourable the Lords Commissioners of his Majesty's treasury, as well as to one of the principal Secretaries of State; and on no account whatever shall any of the said vessels be allowed to take in return any production of the colony, except molasses or rum. No. IV. Capitulation of the English at St. Domingo.

Art. XIII. No part of the aforesaid conditions shall be considered as a restriction to the power of the parliament of Great Britain, to regulate and determine the political government of the colony.—Answer. Granted.

No. V.

(Referred to in Page 183.)

Copie de la Lettre de M. le Chevalier de Sevré, Commandant les Troupes Colonailes à Tiburon, au Colonel Whitlock, Commandant en Chef les Troupes de sa Majesté Britannique à St. Domingue.

"MONSIEUR LE GOUVERNEUR,

"Le Vaisseau, Le Capitaine Robert, qui est arrive ce matin dans notre port (et décidé à partir cette nuit,) me fournit une occasion sûre et prompte pour vous instruire des details de l'attaque qui a été faite par les brigands, sur nos postes lier, deux heures avant le jour. No. V. Dispatch of M. de Sevré, in the British service.

 "A trois

No. V.
Dispatch of M. de Sevré.

"A trois heures et demi, mon poste avancé placé à la Vigie, a été surpris par une armée au moins de 2,000 brigands, qui avoient avec eux deux pièces de campagne de 4 livres; ils ont entouré dans le même instant le fort et la ville. C'est avec peine que j'ai pu me retirer au fort avec ma garnison, où j'ai supporté une longue fusillade avant d'avoir été en état de riposter. Les brigands avoients tout en leur faveur, ils voyoient le fort, et le dominaient de toutes partes, et comme il ne faisoit pas jour nous ne pouvoins les appercevoir. Le combat duroit depuis deux heures, lorsque deux caissons de poudre, ont pris feu de la grande batterie, et l'ont entierement démontée en faisant sauter les canons dehors du fort. Ce malheureux événement m'a tué où blesse vingt hommes et découragé un instant la garnison, elle s'est remise de suite et a faite un feu violent sur l'ennemi: j'ai alors ordonné à quelques negres de Jean Kina, de sortir sur le chemin de la rivière; ils ont battu les brigands, et les ont forcé de se retirer dans le hauteurs.

"Je sui ensuite sorti avec environ 200 hommes negres ou blancs; et j'ai marché du côté de la ville en divisant ma troupe en deux collones, dont j'ai donné le commandement de l'une à M. Philibert, moi à la tête de l'autre; j'ai monté pour les cerner par derriere, et tacher de m'emparer de leurs pieces, mais la premiere collone n'ayant pu monter assez à tems, les brigands ont réussi a emmener leurs canons.

"Je n'ai pu faire poursuivre l'ennemi qui fugait, que jusques sur l'habitation *Gensac*, tant mes hommes étaient fatigués de s'être battu, pendant cinq heures, sans relâche.

"J'ai

No. V. Dispatch of M. de Sevré.

" J'ai eu en environ cent hommes victimes du combat, dont trente tués sur la place, et cent blessés, parmi lesquels il en mourut beaucoup; j'estime qu'ils ont au moins 500 hommes hors de combat: cent cinquante ont été trouvés morts sur le champ de battaile; et les chemins, par lesquels ils se sont retires, sont si couverts de sang, qu'ils doivent avoir un nombre tres considérable de blessés.

" La troupe Anglaise s'est conduite avec le courage qui la caractérise partout: le Capitaine Hardiman est dignè des plus grands éloges; je suis désespéré que vous me l'enleviez, il est dificile à remplacer par ces talens et ses vertus.

" Aussitôt apres le combat, j'ai ecrit à tous les commandans dans les quartiers de la dépendance pour qu'ils m'envoyent du secours; j'en attends à chaque moment, mais je suis bien renforcé par la presence de la frégate *l'Alligator* qui est arrivè ce matin.

" Je suis avec respect, &c.

(Signé) " LE CHEVALIER DE SEVRE

" *Tiburon*, 7 *April*, 1794."

No. VI.

No. VI.

Account of M. de Charmilly, Commissioner for the Capitulation with the British.

No. VI.

(Referring to p. 193, &c.)

———" *the indefatigable De Charmilly.*"

THE distinguished part this gentleman acted during the troubles in his adopted country, and the familiarity of his name to every description of persons concerned in the arrangement between Great Britain and St. Domingo, render some account of him, if not absolutely necessary, at least highly interesting to the reader. We have the power more readily to gratify this inclination, as M. de Charmilly has himself afforded the principal materials for the purpose, which we have translated from the work before quoted, entitled, "*Lettre à M. Edwards,*" &c.

"After," says he, "concluding my attendance at the University of Paris, and travelling through a considerable part of Europe, I arrived at St. Domingo in the beginning of the American war. A few months residence in the colony made me acquainted with its importance. Born with an activity hardly to be surpassed, and favoured with a strong constitution, I became desirous to make myself acquainted with the affairs of the island. During a residence at different times of fourteen years, in the full sense of the word I travelled over the whole colony, having been engaged in some important suits, administered to several large estates, and having business of great consequence in every part of the island, which made me acquainted with the principal planters in its various

No. VI.

Account of M. de Charmilly;

various districts. If you join to that the ambition of becoming one of the richest of its inhabitants, you may judge if I was not, more than any other person, in the possession of opportunities of information respecting the resources of its different provinces, and the advantages of its different manufactures; besides, my knowing personally almost all the officers of its administration, both military and civil; with the generous hospitality of the *Creoles,* and my independence of every tye. From all these reasons it may be concluded, that scarcely any inhabitant of the colony had a greater opportunity of knowing its affairs than myself.

"Returning to France at the end of the last war, I was grieved to see the baneful effects of those poisonous principles which the French had imbibed in America. I also saw, with deep concern, the establishment of that *philanthropic* sect, created first in Philadelphia, and afterwards transplanted to Europe. I then visited England, where I remained a few months; from thence I went to Jamaica, where I also resided some time.

"Since my return to St. Domingo, having re-established several plantations on my own account, I was under the necessity of acquainting myself with every thing that related to the commercial resources of the colony. I also had, in conjunction with Mr. de Marbois, the arrangement of the affairs of one of the most wealthy contractors of St. Domingo. A long residence at Port-au-Prince and the Cape, enabled me also to judge of every material occurrence that passed in the two principal cities.

"On

No. VI. Account of M. de Charmilly.

"On returning to my plantation, at the moment of the revolution, it will not appear surprising that I was nominated a member of the assembly of my parish, afterwards of that of the province where I resided, and, finally, deputy of the general colonial assembly.

"From the publication of the *Rights of Man*, I foresaw, with the most rational and well-informed inhabitants, the misfortunes that awaited the colony.

"Residing in the south part of the island, which was in a great measure indebted to the English, and particularly the merchants of Jamaica, for its establishment; and being, also, from frequent visits, perfectly acquainted with England, I happily turned my views towards its government, to ensure the safety of St. Domingo. This sentiment never abandoned me an instant from the first moment of the troubles; I constantly manifested it in my parish, in my province, and in the general assembly at St. Marc, where all my thoughts and actions were continually directed to the means of assuring its success.

"The torrent of revolutionary ideas had too much agitated every head, not to force the wisest people to conform to circumstances; and I freely own, that I was one of those who affected to believe in the possibility of an absurd independence; prefering it, for the interests of the island, *to the still more absurd idea*, of a sugar colony existing with the pretended *rights of man*. Unfortunately, persons of the greatest influence in St. Domingo, dazzled by the remembrance of the great commercial advantages derived, during the American war, from their increasing trade

 with

No. VI.

Account of M. de Charmilly.

with neutral nations, hoped, and pretended that it might exist independent, under the general protection of the European powers. My opinion was always, that such an independence could not take place, and that it was necessary for the colony to be under the protection of a mother country; and that it would be well if they were under that of a great nation like England. The diversity of opinions frustrated all my plans, and (mine being well known) obliged me to embark, with many of the resident proprietors, on board the Leopard. This was, with the view of flying from two parties; one of whom saw in us opponents to their ambition; and the other, the enemies of that anarchy which they thought of establishing in this delightful climate. Arrived in Europe, I soon discovered that France was lost; but still more, surely, was St. Domingo, if a power, interested to save her own colonies did not afford her relief.

"The melancholy intelligence of the disasters of St. Domingo, were first brought to Europe by the Daphne, an English frigate. I was the first, and only inhabitant, who came to England to confirm that news, of which I found a proof in two hundred letters, delivered to me by Captain Gardner, the commander of the vessel.

"In the year 1790, I had the honour of an interview with the ministers of his Britannic Majesty, and proposed to them the means of retaining their colonies, by saving St. Domingo. The facts which I communicated then, and have often since repeated, are recorded in the memorial which I submitted to government on the occasion. The revolutionary spirit, which had turned the

 heads

No. VI.

Account of M. de Charmilly.

heads of the French people, furnished the most just and wisest reasons for the British ministry to refuse an offer which had been expressed too late, was become by the effervescence of the colony, and the diminution of its revenues and produce, of too little importance to expose them to the event of a war with the French.

"I returned to Paris, but very soon (in 1792) the miseries of France and the king compelled me to seek an asylum in England. From that time I foresaw the certainty of a war; continually occupied for the welfare of my countrymen, and of the first colony in the world, I renewed my solicitations to the British government. In concert with other inhabitants, I never ceased labouring to prove to the ministers of Great Britain, that, if they saved not St. Domingo, the most considerable colony of the *Antilles*, they would not save any of *their* own.

"The French declared war against England in February, 1793. Then, the case of those who had exerted themselves to preserve the English and French colonies were heard; others had evinced as much zeal as myself, and I had no advantage over them but that of a better knowledge of the colony of St. Domingo, and being enabled to say—"*Behold what must be done: I will accomplish it, or perish!*"

"It is for the British ministers to judge, if I was so happy as to fulfil my promises; they were pleased to assure me so, and his Majesty himself deigned to testify to me, his approbation of the zeal and devotion, with which I had placed myself in his service."

The

The unfortunate end of this gentleman's services has been already sufficiently pourtrayed. After wasting that strength of which he formerly so much boasted, and covering himself with fruitless wounds, he had the mortification to see his great project fail, and to shelter himself under the position, that it had not failed in toto, since it had diverted the revolutionary principle from Jamaica. He had also the humiliation with a number of his cotemporaries, to see all his arguments in favor of subjugating the blacks, refuted, and to be obliged to pass the decline of an active life, in a species of dull and solitary exile, under the protection of the English government.

No. VI. Account of M. de Charmilly.

Notwithstanding his misconceptions M. de Charmilly has offered some sensible advice with regard to the island with which he was so well acquainted, and, it may be said, merited a more dignified fate. It was his ambition to be the legislator, and to become the saviour of his country; and it were to be wished that he had exerted himself in a cause in which, though unsuccessful, he might have enjoyed the merit of

———" Bravely falling with a falling state!"

But, alas! no such honors awaited him, he was doomed, even in obscurity, to be followed by the suspicious censures of his countrymen, for whom he was so proud to act, while he could expect no other sentiment than contempt from those against whom he vainly ventured his life.

 No. VII.

No. VII.

Letter of Toussaint to Admiral Smith.

No. VII.

(Referring to Page 264).

Documents illustrative of the Character and Manners of Toussaint L'Ouverture.

IT is always pleasing to trace the interchanges of civility in war between two great and benevolent minds; the following letter has been selected as a specimen of Toussaint's familiar intercourse from a variety of other papers of a similar description.

LIBERTY. EQUALITY.

At Cape François, the 5th January, 7th Year of the French Republic, one and indivisible.

Toussaint L'Ouverture, General in Chief of the Army of St. Domingo, to Edward Tyrrel Smith, Esq. Captain of his Britannic Majesty's Ship Hannibal.*

SIR,

LIEUTENANT STOVIN has performed the commission with which you charged him. As I was at the Cape when he arrived, he was conducted to me, and has brought me your letters of the 3d and 5th January, although addressed to the commandant of this place. I perceive that you have on board sixty-four French prisoners, which you propose to me to exchange, and which I would not have hesitated to do instantly if I had had the same number of prisoners here.

* Now Admiral Smith.

As

Liberté. *Egalité.*

Au Cap français le 16 nivose l'an septième de la Republique française, une et indivisible.

TOUSSAINT LOUVERTURE,

Général en chef de l'Armée de Saint-Domingue,

A Monsieur Edward Hyde Smith Commandant pour S. M. B. le Vaisseau St Annibal.

Monsieur le Commandant

Le Lieutenant Storin a rempli la mission dont vous l'avez chargé comme je me suis trouvé au Cap, il m'a été amené et m'a remis vos deux Lettres des 3 et 5 Janvier, quoique adressées au Commandant de cette Place. Je vois que vous avez à votre Bord 64 prisonniers français que vous me proposez d'échanger, ce que je n'eusse pas balancé de faire de suite si j'avais eu ici le même nombre de prisonniers

Mais mes principes d'humanité répondant parfaitement à ceux que vous me manifestez je vous ~~préviens~~ serai obligé de relaxer les prisonniers français ; je vous enverrai huit prisonniers anglais les seuls qui soient ici, à l'exception d'un qui ayant été la cuisse cassée se trouve à l'hopital. Pour le surplus je vous donnerai des lettres pour les ports de paix et le môle où je donnerai ordre de vous faire la remise des prisonniers qui vous reviendront. Et si par cas on ne pouvait completer ce nombre, je vous engage ma parole d'honneur de les remettre à votre disposition, lorsque le sort de la guerre en remettra à la mienne.

Dans le cas que vous ne feriez pas confiant dans les lettres que je vous

donnerai pour le mole & le Port de paix
alors vous pourrez transporter les prisonniers
français que vous avez fait dans ces endroits
où ils pourront être échangés. J'attendrai
votre réponse pour me servir de Gouverne.

Quoique le Porter, le Rhum et le
Jambon que vous avez eu la civilité d'adresser
au chef de cette ville ne me soit pas
particulièrem.t adressé je ne laisse pas que
de vous en faire mes remerciemens, je voudrois
avoir ici quelque chose qui put vous être
agréable, vous la recevriez. Je permetts à
votre Domestique de faire les provisions
dont vous pourrez avoir besoin

J'ai l'honneur d'être

Monsieur le Commandant,

Votre très humble &
obéiss.t serviteur

Toussaint Louverture

No. VII.
Letter of Toussaint.

As my principles of humanity correspond perfectly with those you manifest, I shall be obliged to you to release the French prisoners. I shall send you eight English prisoners, the whole that are here, with the exception of one, who, having had his thigh broken, remains at the hospital for it to be set. I will give you letters for Port Paix and the Mole, and I shall give the necessary orders that you may be furnished with the prisoners that will be coming to you; if it should happen that they do not complete the number, I promise you on my word of honor, that they shall be at your disposal whenever the fortune of war shall place them at my command.

In case that you should not be satisfied with the letters I give you for the Mole and Port Paix, you then can carry the French prisoners you have made to those places where they may be exchanged. I wait your answer to govern me.

Although the porter, the rum, and the ham which you have had the civility to address to the Chief of this City, were not particularly addressed to me, I cannot omit to return you my thanks. I wish there may be any thing here agreeable to you, and you shall receive it. I have given your servant permission to make any provision for which you may have occasion.

I have the honor to be, Sir,

Your most humble and

Obedient Servant,

TOUSSAINT L'OUVERTURE.

No. VII.

Extract from Mr. Reilly's Journal.

Brief Extract from the MS. Journal of Charles Reilly, Esq.

Port Royal, Jamaica.

ON the 16th of November, 1798, being ready for sea, Col. Harcourt and Capt. Reynolds came on board, and we set sail for Port-au-Prince, in St. Domingo.

On the 24th, being in the Bight of Leogane, saw a strange sail. In the evening came up with her: she proved to be an American bark from Port-au-Prince, bound to Philadelphia, with French passengers and property, which was sent into Port Royal.

On the 25th November came to anchor without gun-shot of the fort at Port-au-Prince, and sent in a flag of truce to prepare for a treaty with the Black General, Toussaint, then commanding the chief part of the island; but the boat returned with information that he was not there. We then got under weigh, and stood off towards Leogane. In the night we manned and armed the boats, and sent them along shore. In the morning they returned with a small copper-bottomed schooner, laden with coffee, and bound to St. Jago, in Cuba. They likewise took four open boats, one of which we sold for four hundred dollars back to a Frenchman, and in the others we sent the prisoners on shore.

On the 26th came to anchor off Leogane; sent a flag of truce, and was informed the general was at Aux Cayes. Got under weigh, and at noon came to an anchor there, out of gun-shot of the fort. Sent a boat on shore, and learned that Toussaint was at Gonaïves. An officer, however, came on board in a flag of truce, and told the captain we might send our boat ashore, and purchase what stock we wanted. Of this kindness we availed ourselves, from the extreme cheapness at which we were supplied. No. VII.

On the 27th we got under weigh, and on the 28th chased two strange sail. By noon we brought one of them to, which proved to be a government sloop from Cape François, bound to Port-au-Prince, laden with wines and provisions of all kinds. The schooner that had been previously taken, being manned and armed, she was sent one cruize, commanded by the purser, who soon returned with a schooner, laden with provisions, that had sailed with the same sloop. We took every body out of her except some ladies, who were passengers, and the same evening came to anchor in Gonaives Roads.

Sent a flag of truce on shore, and saw General Toussaint, who seemed very well pleased with the proposition of a treaty for trading, to and from Jamaica, and rendering every thing agreeable.

Next day we got under weigh, and stood off and on till evening, as the captain had promised to send all the prisoners on shore when they should send a small vessel for them. In the mean time the person who was sent prize-master, having intoxicated himself in the evening when the ship was running into her anchorage, he bore up for Port Royal, and behaved very unmanly to the poor distressed ladies. He would not allow them to open their trunks for clean clothes, nor would he allow them any of two cases of wine, which the captain had left entirely for them. The vessel came for the prisoners next morning, and they went on shore, but the Black General was exceedingly vexed at the treatment the ladies had received, as they were the wives of officers

No. VIII. cers in whom he had much confidence. This circumstance had nearly been the cause of much mischief, and the dissolution of the treaty, as he would hardly believe it was not intended by the captain, as all the male prisoners were returned with the exception only of one, who had preferred to remain with one of the ladies, who was his sister. In a short time, however, his temper warm, but not irascible, was appeased, and all was well.

On the 14th December a brig, the Mary, arrived from Jamaica, laden with provisions, and on the 6th we put the two gentlemen conducting the treaty on board her, when she hoisted the flag of truce, and we bore up for Port Royal, where we arrived on the 8th.

No. VIII.

(Referring to Page 264.)

Extract from the former Publication of the Author of this Work upon the then projected Expedition of St. Domingo, describing its Progress; and, from a Comparison with the subsequent Dispatches of the French General, demonstrative of the Verity of those Principles upon which he argued against its Adoption.

Anticipation of the fate of the French expedition by the author, published during its projection.

UPON what foundation the projectors of the French armament rested their hopes of success (supposing them not totally ignorant of what was to be attempted in the reduction of St. Domingo at present), other than the prowess of the First Consul, it is not easy to conceive—the astonishing difficulties that have been surmounted,

surmounted, and prodigies that have already been achieved by the invincible Bonaparte! But they should have recollected, that the improbable successes of that general were not unfrequently attributed to the CAUSE he supported!—certainly the best calculated to inspire young troops with a romantic idea of chivalry, and to carry them, unknowing, through dangers that would appal the most hardy veterans. How different is the object at present: detachments from armies, that held combined Europe at defiance, when resolved to be free, and gave peace to the conquered nations that no longer opposed their freedom, are embarked to expel their own spirit from another land; to suppress every generous emotion they had been accustomed to feel; and to again fill the furrows of a smiling country with blood—the blood of FREEMEN, WHOM THEY HAD THEMSELVES CREATED.

No. VII.

Anticipation of the fate of the French expedition.

"Unused to the sickening suspense of a maritime conveyance, they are painfully wafted to the seat of war in a noxious climate; they debark in a country rendered hostile by a series of inexplicable menaces, and prepared to meet with indignation those it considers as betrayers of the cause in which they had formerly bled!—Vanished is the enthusiastic spirit of bravery, that was wont to lead them to the fight, while other voices sound the Song of Liberty!

"Allons! enfans de la patrié
La jour de gloire est arrivé
Contre nous—de la tyrannée
L'etendart sanglant est elevée!
Entendez vous, dans la Campagné,

 Mugir

No. VIII.

Anticipation, &c.

Mugir ces ferocés soldâts,
Que viennent dans nos bras
Egorgés vhs fils et votre Campagné!
Aux armes!" ——*

"The hitherto victorious troops of the republic, land in various directions, beneath the heavy fire of forts well appointed; and mounted chiefly with brass ordnance: they press forward to—— what?—not to enter towns from which the enemy has fled precipitately, leaving behind them every comfort necessary for an army, requiring early rest to recruit; they enter cities, not merely evacuated, but no longer cities! to be mocked by the ruins of repose, and the destruction of necessaries they required.

"Recruited from their own magazines, or the trifling aid to be forced from a few Americans, they proceed into a country, every foot of which, when obtained, is deprived of all that can aid their enterprize. Troops, dispirited by novel tactics, and an enfeebling climate, are to pass their nights in the open air, and exposed to the nocturnal vapours, alone fatal to European habits, sustained only by provisions furnished from their own stores, with no more water than they have conveyed with them, and unable to proceed, or to return.

* "Ye patriot band!
The day of glory comes; against us see
The bloody standard rais'd of tyranny!
Hark! in your fields ferocious soldiers roar,
Your children and your country are no more!
Close to your breasts they come—
To arms!"—

"Occasional

No. VIII.

Anticipation, &c.

"Occasional aids, with peculiar good fortune, carried them farther into the interior, to experience all those difficulties in a more extensive degree; with a subtraction from their numbers and their comforts, in proportion to the victories they may obtain, and the difficulties they may surmount.

"On the other hand—

"A country is raised, to repel a horde of invaders, to whom are attributed the intentions of despoiling the land, and enslaving its inhabitants; a well-disciplined army in every part, intimately acquainted with every quarter of the island, inured to the climate, and habituated to the soil; trained to a long expectation of the attack, is prepared to meet them. Hardy, and unencumbered with stores, they sport with an harrassed enemy; and, when the day decides against them, leaving the enemy to burning towns, and mined plantations, they recede in safety within the next line of fortifications: were they even deprived of all adventitious aid,* the umbrageous plantain alone affords them repose and food, or they luxuriate in the varieties of the yam and the banana, refreshed by the streams, to which they readily find access; they rise unimpaired, to support the cause next their heart, and revel in proportion as their assailants are dismayed.

"Almost impenetrably fortified up to the very mountains of Cibao, whose inaccessible tops reach the heavens, Toussaint recedes with ease, faster than the wasting enemy can, with pain,

* Which is impossible, while every little coasting-bark from America brings a fresh supply; and an ample resource is found in every new situation.

No. VIII. Anticipation, &c.

pursue him; and in this way is he, in alliance with the very elements to be pursued through a route of this description 500 miles? I speak of the elements, for the period is fast approaching, when, in addition to the horrors already experienced, the rains will commence, whose overwhelming torrents will require portable towns to withstand them, where indifferent camp-equipage only can be conveyed; and, in this situation, if not before, I feel no hesitation in saying, that Le Clerc, lamenting his laurels, which have withered so untimely, will assimilate Macbeth, and exclaim, with heart-felt regret,—

> "There is no going hence, nor tarrying here!"

"All possible grounds of success, it is easily perceived, are done away—unless Toussaint, during his experience of his government, has acquired the knowledge of "expediency," and on that score is expected to sacrifice his adherents for a snug retirement!—a circumstance hardly to be looked for; or, that three or four millions of men, who have forgotten every other restraint than a voluntary sense of duty imposes, should easily be inclined to return to the dominion of the *cowskin!!!**

"The English government, in three years, employed above twenty thousand men, and expended thirty millions of money on St. Domingo; and its army, even then, was never able to penetrate five miles into the country; yet the French government

"* The instrument of punishment, no doubt, judiciously handled, by those young men, who perform their noviciate in the character of Overseers of the *Slaves*.

vernment proposes to exterminate the whole race of colour without the least delay. No. VIII. Anticipation, &c.

"*Veni vidi, vici!*—then—General Le Clerc has completed his career of extermination, and he sits down in the delightful vallies of St. Domingo without a single *rebel** to cultivate the soil; it must be supplied by a fresh, a continued importation of negroes, ignorant of labour, and without any to instruct them, at an excessive waste of time and of produce, and an expence of not less than one hundred millions at least!

"Whether France be adequate to colonize at this rate, I presume not to determine. Considering her at the acmé of her present power, I shall not wonder at the attempt, nor at her assuming all the concomitants of colonization,—corporate bodies, chartered companies, and the long train of monopolies, so fatal to the peace and the interest of nations.

"I have now only to add a few observations on those fears, and the promoters of them, which have obtained for the Dictator of France, in his scheme of retrieving to the mongrel government of that country the delightful island of St. Domingo, such an apparently universal patronage with even persons of discernment in this kingdom. To those intimately acquainted with the

"* To hear this term in France, at this present day, and the diminutive idea entertained of St. Domingo, as well as the contemptible opinion affected of Toussaint, excites risibility. The two former explain themselves; and it is sufficiently known that Toussaint is a more extraordinary character, and at this moment possessed of more *real* power than the Grand Consul! "Why may not I," says he, "hold absolute power here, as well as the First Consul in France?"—*(Original Note.)*

British

No. VIII. Anticipation, &c.

British colonies in the West Indies, these observations are not necessary; but there are many whose interests in the islands are by no means inconsiderable, who owe their principal information to those eternal babblers, who, without the most distant pretensions to knowledge, experience, or a common portion of common sense, fill every avenue with their alarms, and surprize every new week with a new hypothesis.

"These have affected to view in the establishment of a BLACK REPUBLIC in this extensive territory, the entire annihilation of all our possessions, the elevation of a revolutionary hydra, that breathes another Pandemonium of ills on the afflicted world! till the expedition of Bonaparte has been treated as a common cause, and much has been anticipated that could not be expected, if it could be wished.

"Nothing appears more evident to me, than that the system which, without the intervention of any of those accidents that some time change the face of things, is about to obtain in St. Domingo, is not one that will by any means lead to an extension of territory, or the diffusion of principles. In the possession of a vast island, such as it has been described, much would remain to be done at home, were they henceforward to remain in uninterrupted peace; the cultivation of vast tracts, the renovation of what has been destroyed, and the arrangements of their own interests, will indispensably preclude the interference of Toussaint with the government or opinion of the neighbouring islands.

2 "Added

No. VIII. Anticipation, &c.

" Added to this, what person acquainted with the respectable state of defence in which our islands are kept, can ever entertain the least fear respecting them?—Small as they comparatively are, possessed by planters of distinguished talents, defended by a militia prompt on all occasions; with an army well appointed on their shores, under the superintendance of ability and experience at home; and a navy round their coasts, the wonder of the world; what restless, romantic spirit could induce an attempt so certainly destructive in the effort, and fruitless in the event?"

" * Notwithstanding it has of late years been the fashion to consider the character of a planter as derogatory to humanity, and incapable of being blended with any of those qualities that ameliorate the condition of the species, every opportunity which I have had of judging has tended to convince me of the contrary. Nothing, indeed, can be more cruel than to single out any description of persons for public reprobation, as may suit the purpose of the fanatic or the partizan; and nothing is more fatal to the cause of truth than an implicit reliance on the vague reports of their enthusiasm, which must inevitably preclude the possibility of acquiring correct information, or adhering to facts if produced to their notice.—If the young and thoughtless squander the accumulations of their ancestors, it is certainly no evidence of general voluptuousness. If there are circumstances exceptionable in the conduct of the slave-trade, does it follow that the planter is a merciless executioner? Certainly not,—it would be hostile to his interest, and inexpedient in his situation. As merchants and as men, many are highly and extensively esteemed and regarded; and instances of affection and regret in the slaves, in whose torture they have been described to exult, are neither unfrequent or unrecorded.

No. IX.

No. IX.

First colonial regulation.

No. IX.

(Referred to in Page 321.—Documents respecting the colonial Administration of Le Clerc.)

First colonial Regulation of the Captain-General, extracted from the Official Gazette of St. Domingo.

ADMINISTRATION OF THE COLONY.

Head-Quarters, at the Cape, June 22, 1802.

IN the name of the French government,

The General in chief Captain-general, decrees as follows:—

In the French part of St. Domingo, the administration of the quarters and communes is confined to military commandants and councils of notables. The commandants to have the jurisdiction of police in their respective districts, and the chief command of the gens d'armerie. The councils of notables to be composed of proprietors or merchants, and to consist of five members, in the towns of Port Republicain, the Cape, and Des Cayes, and of three members in other communes. The members to be appointed by the colonial prefect; and every one so appointed to be compelled to accept the office. The military commandants are charged with the delivery (gratis) of passports for travelling in the colony, the suppression of vagrancy, the care of the police, the maintenance of cleanliness and health, the care of citizens newly arrived, the police of the prisons, and the regulation of weights and measures, in concurrence with the council of notables. Except in the case of flagrant crimes, the military commandants cannot arrest any citizen without an order from the Commandant of the quarter. The communes to provide for their own expences; the sums to be regulated by a decree of the general in chief, with the advice of the colonial prefect. No military commandant can put in requisition the labourers or the cattle of any plantation; the general in chief reserves that power to himself. The councils of notables to provide for the expences of the communes and for the imposts adopted by the commander in chief, with the advice of the colonial prefect. Those councils alone to deliberate upon the communal interests; all other assemblies of citizens are prohibited, and shall, if attempted, be considered as seditious, and dispersed by force. The councils to correspond immediately with the sub-prefects, by whom their members may be suspended, and finally dismissed by the colonial prefect. There shall be in each parish a commissary to register the public acts.

No. IX. Administration of Le Clerc.

(Signed) LE CLERC.

COMMERCE OF ST. DOMINGO.

By another decree of the general in chief,

French merchant vessels are to be admitted only in the ports of the Cape, Port Republicain, des Cayes and de Jacmel. Merchandize, or produce of the manufactures, or soil of France, not

No. IX. Administration of Le Clerc.

to be subject to any duty on importation. Colonial produce, exported by French vessels, to be subject to a duty on exportation.

Foreign vessels of the burden of 70 tons, and upwards, are permitted to enter the above four ports. French or foreign merchandize imported in them to be subject to a duty on importation, conformable to tariff. The produce of the colony exported by them to be subject to a duty on exportation.

Every captain of a French or foreign vessel must, on his arrival in port, before any other person on board lands, present himself before the captain general, and the colonial prefect, at the place of their residence, and in other ports to the general commandant, and the chief of administration, for the purpose of giving an account of his voyage. The captain shall transmit on the same day, to the commandant of the place, a declaration, written and signed, containing an account of the passengers he has on board: no passenger to disembark without the authority of the commandant.

The captain must, on the day of his arrival, remit the letters and packets in his charge to the director of the post at the port, and shall receive a discharge.

The captains of French and foreign vessels must, within a day after their arrival, transmit to the directors of the harbours, the bill of lading of their cargoes. All merchandize found on board which is not included in the bill of lading, will be confiscated.

Every captain of a foreign vessel must consign his cargo to a domiciliated merchant, who shall be personally responsible for the

No. IX. Administration of Le Clerc.

the payment of the duties on importation and exportation, and for the frauds which may be committed by the captains of the vessels consigned to him.

No French or foreign vessel shall be suffered to quit the ports, but on producing to the captain of the port the certificate of the director of the customs, stating that all the duties have been paid.

Every French or foreign vessel which shall be found in any of the ports, not designated in the decrees, or sailing within two leagues of the coast, shall be taken possesion of by the guard-vessels, and conducted into one of the designated ports, in order that the confiscation of the vessel and cargo may be adjudged by the captain general, on the report of the colonial prefect. The vessel making such capture, to be entitled to one-third of the value of the vessel and cargo confiscated.

TARIFF OF CUSTOMS IN THE FRENCH PART OF ST. DOMINGO.

IMPORTATION.

French merchandize and produce in foreign vessels, 10 per cent. on the value—Meal, biscuits, salt, provisions, wood for carpenters and buildings, cattle and sheep, horses, mules, poultry, &c. ditto 6 per cent. ditto.—Foreign merchandize, ditto, 20 per cent. ditto.

EXPORTATION.

The following are the most material articles:

Coffee in foreign vessels, 13 francs 33 cents. per quintal. —White sugar, ditto, ditto.—Brown ditto, 6 f. 67 c. ditto.

 —Cotton

No. IX. Administration of Le Clerc.

—Cotton, 30 f. ditto.—Indigo, 80 c. per lb.—Produce not enumerated, 20 per cent. on the value.—French manufactures in foreign vessels exempt from duty.

SUBSEQUENT COMMERCIAL REGULATION.

(In consequence of a remonstrance of the merchants and ship-owners of the city of Havre, &c. presented to the First Consul, Bonaparté, May 30, 1802, against the admission of British merchandize.*)

Head-Quarters at the Cape, Sept. 8, 1802.

In the Name of the French Government the Commander in Chief, Captain General, decrees as follows:—

Art. I. After the 1st of Vendemiaire, year 11, (Sept. 23, 1802), no other merchandize or articles of provision, except those specified in the annexed list, can be imported into the colony by foreign ships:—none can be exported by the same ships, but molasses, syrup, spirits, and rum; dye woods and wood for cabinet makers; guiacum, coffee, and provision, or merchandize of every kind imported by the French merchants.

II. After the same period, the duties on the merchandize and provisions specified in the annexed list, imported into the colony

* In this remonstrance is the following confession:—" Thanks be to our warriors, thanks be to your genius;—the English have come out of the long contest with much less glory than we have, but they have withdrawn from the struggle rich and astonishingly powerful. All is organised among them, and it will be long, very long, before we can vie with them in trade. We can only be saved from destruction by prohibitory regulations. A convalescent should not enter the lists with a mighty giant."

6. by

No. IX. Administration of Le Clerc.

by foreign ships, shall pay at the rate of ten per cent: duty *ad valorem* in the colony, according to a tariff, which the colonial prefect shall settle every three months, from the medium prices of the preceding three months, in the open ports of the colony.

The duties on colonial productions which, according to the permission granted by the first article, shall be exported in foreign vessels, shall pay, over and above, one half more than those exported in French ships, according to the tariff annexed to the decree of the 3d of Messidor last (June 22). These productions shall pay, besides the war tax, established by the decree of Messidor 25 (July 14).

Productions and merchandize arising from the French commerce, exported from the colony in foreign ships, shall pay no duties.

III. All merchandize and products not specified in the annexed list, imported by foreign vessels, are prohibited, reckoning from the 1st of Vendemiaire, year 11 (September 23, 1802). The captains of foreign vessels which arrive in the open ports of the colony before that period, shall be allowed to land their merchandize, on lodging a declaration at the custom-house.

Those which arrive in the open ports of the colony after Vendemiaire 1st (September 23,) until the 15th Brumaire next (November 6) inclusive, shall be allowed to land the unprohibited goods they have on board. In regard to those prohibited, they shall lodge a declaration of them, and shall be bound to produce them on their departure, under the pain of their vessels being confiscated.

After

No. IX.

Administration of Le Clerc.

After the 15th Brumaire (November 6) vessels, whose cargoes are not entirely composed of non-prohibited merchandize and productions, shall not be admitted into the ports of the colony. Those not coming within the case of being admitted, which shall procure admission by false declarations, or which, after baving been obliged to leave the said ports, shall be found effecting, or trying to effect a fraudulent landing, shall be confiscated, as well as the cargoes.

IV. Nothing in the present decree shall affect that of Messidor 5, which exempts from all duties, till the 30th of Frimaire, year 11 (December 21, 1802); oxen and mules imported into the ports of the Cape, Port Republicain, Des Cayes, and Jacmel.

All the dispositions of decrees relating to commerce and the customs, not contrary to the present decree, are also maintained.

V. The colonial prefect is charged with carrying the present decree into execution.

(Signed) LE CLERC.

List of the merchandize and productions, the importation of which by foreign ships is permitted, on paying a duty of ten per cent. *ad valorem*:—beer, bricks, coals, cables, and cordage; train oil, spermaceti oil, pitch, tar, resin, &c.; essence of turpentine, oats, barley, maize, flour, rice, biscuit, salt beef, salt pork, hams, sausages, &c. are not comprehended under this denomination; salt butter, mantagus, cod-fish, bacaga, &c.; salt mackarel, dried herrings, pickled herrings, shads, cod sounds, pickled mullets, stock-fish; live cattle, horses, mules, apes, hogs, sheep, ducks, fowls, turkies, geese; timber for building, spars, planks, oars, casks, &c. &c.

5

No. X.

M. Rainsford del. J. Barlow sculp.

The mode of training Blood Hounds in St. Domingo, and of

No. X.

(Referred to in p. [illegible])

[illegible] Account of the Nature and History of the [illegible] [illegible] used in the American Colonies.

ON the subject which it is [illegible] [illegible] [illegible] [illegible] the following particulars [illegible] [illegible] [illegible] [illegible] the numerous rude inventions [illegible] [illegible] ages to attain a superiority in war, was that of the use of beasts in a variety of ways, in conjunction with their regular armies. In Virgil [illegible] [illegible] [illegible] [illegible] against an opponent [illegible] and [illegible] [illegible] a ludicrous employment of *foxes*, driven with firebrands towards the enemy's camp. The war [illegible] and *elephant* are also represented as taking an active share in the battle at all times. The introduction of dogs, however, is not so generally [illegible] and one which [illegible] [illegible] [illegible] avail but in a very [illegible] degree. [illegible] first particulars [illegible] [illegible] acting with troops, is by Herrera, the [illegible] when describing the last conflict of Columbus with the Indians in 1492; [illegible] the Sleuth-hound of the Scots was in high repute as being early applied to discover the haunts of robbers; and Strabo is said to describe an attack upon the Gauls

[illegible] [illegible] Compton's Scriptural

7 [illegible]

† See the [illegible] part of this [illegible]

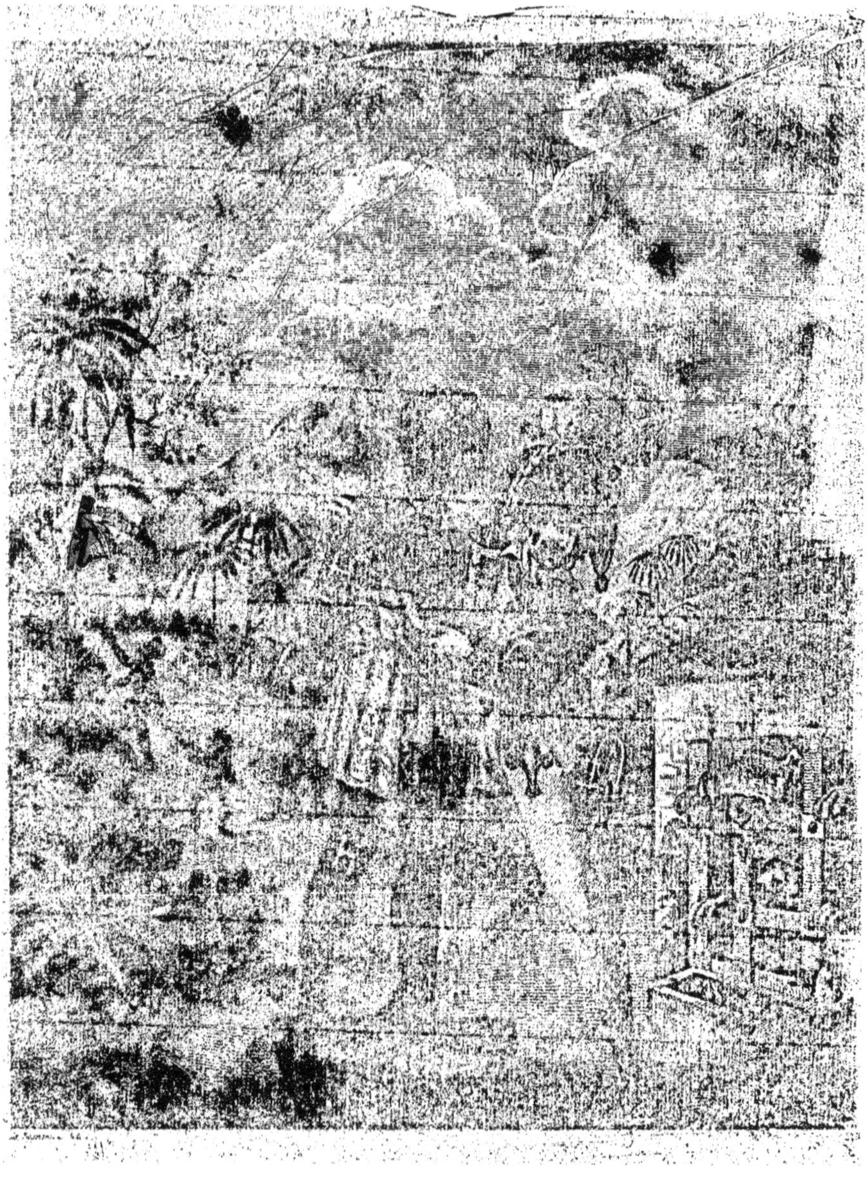

No. X. Account of the use and history of blood-hounds.

No. X.

(Referred to in p. 327, &c.)

Some Account of the Nature and History of the Blood-Hounds used in the American Colonies.

ON this subject which it is anxiously desired to impress upon the reader, the following particulars may not be unacceptable.—Among the numerous rude inventions of barbarous ages to attain a superiority in war, was that of the use of beasts in a variety of ways, in conjunction with their regular armies. In Virgil the effect of *bulls* sent in terrible array against an opponent is recorded, and Moses affords a ludicrous employment of *foxes*,* driven with firebrands towards the enemy's camp. The *war-horse* and *elephant* are also represented as taking an active share in the battle at all times. The introduction of *dogs*, however, is not so generally used, and one which is considered as likely to avail but in a very confined degree. The first particular mention of their use in acting with troops, is by Herrera, the Spanish historian, when describing the first conflict of Columbus with the Indians in 1492;† the Sleute-hound of the Scots was in much repute as being early applied to discover the haunts of robbers; and Strabo is said to describe an attack upon the Gauls

* Or Jackalls. See the curious observations on this subject in Tomlinson's Scriptural Translations, p. 273.

† See the former part of this work.

by

No. X.

History of the blood-hounds.

by dogs of the present description.* The character of decided enmity to man, however, seems to have been preserved only in Spanish America, and the writer is induced from many circumstances to think that the quadruped which is the subject of this account is, though of a similar species to the Irish wolf-dog breed, a native of the South Seas.

Whether or not the dog in a savage state would devour his master, as is asserted, shall not here be argued; it is certain that on the mode of rearing, and subsequent discipline for use, in war, much has always depended, and that (to the disgrace of human beings so employed) their education has been reduced to such a system, as to leave little of the natural character remaining.

With the persons who breed and have the care of these animals in Spanish America, the public are already sufficiently acquainted; but there are some facts which are not equally known, both as respect these people, and the mode of rearing the dogs, as particularly practised in St. Domingo, to which attention is at present confined. The first of these subjects will be explained by a comparison easily made; and of the latter the writer is indebted for an accurate knowledge to an intelligent friend, who had the care of those animals and their keepers in their troublesome passage from the Havannah to Jamaica, the same which

* This incident is on the authority of an obliging writer in the Monthly Magazine, in answer to a query on the subject on account of the present work, Strabo not being at hand for a reference.

forms

No. X.

The modern chasseur an exact counterpart of the ancient Buccanier.

forms a prominent subject of the history already given to the public on the occasion.*

Among the remains of the Buccaniers, (which are every where prevalent in St. Domingo and its vicinity, in the different *Trou's* which retain their names, and several local expressions,) are the costume and mode of life, in the Spanish chasseurs who

* Dallas's History of the Maroons. Mr. Quarrel (through the medium of a writer always intelligent, and sometimes eloquent) has excited the interest of the public to the whole of his services in relation to the expedition from Jamaica to Cuba, for the purpose of obtaining blood-hounds and their leaders; he has described a long round of difficulties, of

"Moving accidents by flood and field,"

all of which were overcome by the superior talents, the local, and even *maritime* skill of the commissioner! According to this account, the minutest object in the arduous business of the expedition was not only managed by him, during sickness or convalescence, but his bark was directed through peculiar courses, and battles fought successfully against a superior power, with a crew somewhat like Falstaff's regiment. But Mr. Quarrel forgot to name the Captain of the vessel which carried him to Cuba, and returned with the blood-hounds to Jamaica, or the wonder would have ceased; and this is the more singular, in a man of letters and enterprize, like Mr. Quarrel, from the exquisite delight and extensive information he must have received from the society of Captain Campbell; a gentleman, with enlarged ideas, high literary talents, the most consummate bravery, and unbounded nautical skill, who almost prefers (*under existing circumstances*,) the command of a little vessel like that which conveyed Mr. Quarrel and his charge! (and which is generally, or a considerable share, his own property,) *peculiarly* on account of its being *absolutely* under *his own* direction; and with a crew such as the commissioner very justly describes, he has performed more intrepid actions, and visited with success, more parts of the globe than any other officer of his age, which is happily not yet far advanced. The writer had reason to hope from the pen of him who has traced the steps of the injured Bruce in Abyssinia, a valuable paper on this, as well as other subjects relating to the Western Archipelago; but this, as well as other valuable communications intended for the public, in the possession of a mutual friend, was neglected, when

"*Old Ocean smil'd,*
"And, dancing on the tide of pleasure wild,
"Brisk Fame high-bounding, blew her echoing horn."

Pursuit of Fame, *a Poem.*

3 I conduct

No. X.

Mode of training blood-hounds.

conduct the blood-hounds. The hog-skin trowsers drawn on their limbs warm from the animal when shot wild in the woods, and the mode of preparing their food, (*boucaner*, a name at present synonimous with cooking in the island,) being common to both; and, in fact, every part of their dress, their migratory life, power of forbearance, and savage habits in the woods, all exhibit the ancient Buccanier in the modern Chasseur; and the portrait of the one when young, robust, and daring, is a very complete resemblance of the other.

The character of these people differed somewhat in the numbers which joined the French army, and were increased by tyros, when their operations became such a favorite relief in the actions between it and that of the blacks.

Mode of rearing the dogs.

With respect to the dogs, their general mode of rearing was latterly in the following manner. From the time of their being taken from the dam, they were confined in a sort of kennel, or cage, where they were but sparely fed upon small quantities of the blood of different animals. As they approached maturity, their keepers procured a figure roughly formed as a negro in wicker work, in the body of which was contained the blood and entrails of beasts. This was exhibited before an upper part of the cage, and the food occasionally exposed as a temptation, which attracted the attention of the dogs to it as a source of the food they wanted. This was repeated often, so that the animals with redoubled ferocity struggled against their confinement while in proportion to their impatience the figure was brought nearer, though yet out of their reach, and their food decreased, till, at the last extremity of desperation, the keeper resigned the figure, well charged with the nauseous food before described, to their wishes. While they gorged themselves with the dreadful meat, he and his colleagues caressed and encouraged them. By these means the whites ingratiated themselves so much with the animals, as to produce an effect directly opposite to that perceivable in them towards the black figure; and, when they were employed in the pursuit for which they were intended, afforded the protection so necessary to their employers. As soon as they were considered initiated into their business, the young dogs were taken out to be exercised in it, and trained with much exactness as possible. In some instances this extended to a great length, but in general their discipline could not permanently retain them under the command of their leaders, the consequence is obvious.

No. X. Mode of training blood-hounds.

The common use of them in the Spanish islands was in chace of runaway negroes in the mountains. When once they got scent of the object, they immediately hunted him down, unless he could evade the pursuit by climbing up a tree, and instantly devoured him: if he was so fortunate as to get from their reach into a tree, the dogs remained about it yelping in the most dreadful manner, till their keepers arrived. If the victim was to be preserved for a public exhibition of cruelty, the dogs were then muzzled, and the prisoner loaded with chains. On his neck was placed a hoop with inverted spikes; and hooks outward, for the purpose of entangling him in the bushes, or elsewhere. Should the unhappy wretch proceed faster than his wearied pursuers, or attempt to run from them, he was given up to

No. X.

Accidents arising from blood-hounds.

the dogs, who instantly devoured him. With horrid delight the chasseurs sometimes preserved the head to expose at their homes, as monuments of their barbarous prowess.—Frequently on a journey of any length these causes were, it is much feared, feigned for the purpose of relieving the keepers of their prisoners, and the inhuman wretch who perpetrated the act, on his oath of having destroyed his fellow creature, received the reward of ten dollars from the colony!

If the most dreadful accidents among the blacks were ascribed, and it is apprehended justly, to the troops of blood-hounds in the very spots on which they were reared, what was not to be expected on the seat of war, amidst innumerable prejudices, and the powerful motive of self-preservation? when every one conceived himself justified in contributing an act of barbarity to the common cause, while it arose, perhaps, out of his own cruel disposition. The writer shrinks from the task of description in this place, yet the concealment will not excite the detestation he urges against the very idea of ever again introducing these animals under any pretext to the assistance of an army.* But indifferently kept, the

* The defence of his friend (certainly a most laudable motive in these degenerate times, notwithstanding the old proverb *Amicus Plato, amicus Socrates, sed magis amica veritas*) has led the ingenious writer before alluded to (Mr. Dallas) to some arguments in favor of blood-hounds, however cautiously introduced, not less glaringly false. Such is that, of the use of *house-dogs*. The writer need not call the attention of this gentleman (with whose sensibility of character he is not unacquainted) to the following obvious facts in behalf of their mutual country. The house-dog commonly used in the united kingdom, is the barking cur, who is not capable of a dangerous attack, and his use is only to create alarm; and even when a more powerful species are used, as the Newfoundland breed, they never kill or wound,

the dogs frequently broke loose in the vicinity of the Cape, and infants were devoured in an instant from the public way! At other times they proceeded to the neighbouring woods, and surprizing an harmless family of laborers at their simple meal, tore the babe from the breast of its mother, or involved the whole party, and returned with their horrid jaws drenched in the gore of those who were acknowledged, even in the eyes of the French army, as innocent, and therefore permitted to furnish them with the produce of their labor. Huts were broken into by them, and

No. X. Ferocity of blood-hounds.

* * * * * * * * * * *

the picture becomes too dreadful for description even for the best of purposes.

---

wound, except they are aggravated, of which several curious instances have recently occured; two are in the immediate recollection of the writer; one, he believes, at an inn near Hounslow, where a servant being detected by the faithful guard in the act of robbing the house at night, he threw him down on the spot, and placing himself upon him, held him there uninjured till the morning, when he delivered him into other custody. Another was, when an housekeeper remaining in a house alone, where a quantity of plate was deposited, borrowed for one night the dog of a neighbouring butcher to protect her, who, in the following morning presented her with a culprit before the side-board, in the person of a relation of her master:—the rest of the story is too invidious. If at any time an accident occurs, (which is not frequent,) of a dog injuring any one in the smallest degree, the writer never yet knew a master who would not immediately destroy him, and surely none desire to see even the nightly thief lacerated and devoured, instead of his injury prevented; but if even the position of Mr. Dallas were just, the case would by no means apply.

No. XI.

No. XI.

Commercial regulation of Rochambeau.

No. XI.

(Referred to in Page 335.)

The first colonial Regulation issued during the Government of Rochambeau.

ARRETE OF THE GENERAL IN CHIEF.

I. THE arrêté of the Captain-general of the 15th Fructidor, 10th year, which permits the importation of different articles of produce in this colony in foreign bottoms, paying 10 per cent. duty is received.

II. Foreigners may import into this colony all wares and merchandize not enumerated in the abovementioned arrêté, subject to a duty of 20 per cent. *ad valorem.*

III. The colonial-prefect shall make out every six months a tariff of the value of all the wares and merchandize imported under the second article. The duty of 20 per cent. shall be fixed by this tariff.

IV. The importation of goods permitted by the fifth and second article of this arrêté shall only take place at the Cape, Port Republican, and the Port of St. Domingo.

V. The present arrêté shall be in force immediately after its publication.

VI. The

No. XII. Capitulation of the French army.

VI. The colonial-prefect is charged with the execution of the present arrêté, which shall be printed, published, and posted up, and inserted in the Official Gazette.

(Signed) D. F. N. ROCHAMBEAU, Capt. Gen.

December 19, 1802.

No. XII.

(Referred to in Page 345.)

Documents respecting the Evacuation of St. Domingo, by the French Army under Rochambeau; from the London Gazette, and other authentic Sources.

ARTICLES OF CAPITULATION BETWEEN THE FRENCH GENERAL ROCHAMBEAU, AND THE BLACK GENERAL-IN-CHIEF OF SAINT DOMINGO.

French and Native Army.

THIS day, the 27th Brumaire, of the 12th year, according to the French æra, and the 19th of November, 1802, according to the common æra, the adjutant-commandant, Duveysier, having received full power from General Rochambeau, Commander-in-chief of the French army, to treat for the surrender of the Town of the Cape, and Jean Jacques Dessalines, general of the native Army

No. XII. Capitulation of the French army.

army, being also authorised to treat on the occasion, have agreed on the following articles, viz.

I. The Town of the Cape, and the forts dependent thereon, shall be given up in ten days, reckoning from to-morrow, the 28th of Brumaire (Nov. 18), to the general-in-chief, Dessalines.

II. The military stores which are now in the arsenals, the arms, and the artillery of the town and forts, shall be left in their present condition.

III. All the ships of war, and other vessels which shall be judged necessary by Gen. Rochambeau, for the removal of the troops and inhabitants, and for the evacuation of the place, shall be free to depart on the day appointed.

IV. All the officers, military or civil, and the troops composing the garrison of the Cape, shall leave the place with all the honours of war, carrying with them their arms, and all the private property belonging to their demi-brigades.

V. The sick and wounded who shall not be in a condition to embark, shall be taken care of in the hospitals till their recovery; they are specially recommended to the humanity of Gen. Dessalines, who will cause them to be embarked for France in neutral vessels.

VI. General Dessalines, in giving the assurance of his protection to the inhabitants who shall remain in the country, calls at the same time upon the justice of General Rochambeau to set at liberty all the natives of the country (whatever may be their colour,) as they cannot be constrained, under any pretext of right, to embark with the French army.

No. XII. Capitulation of the French army.

VII. The troops of both armies shall remain in their respective positions, until the tenth day after the signature hereof, which is the day fixed on for the evacuation of the Cape.

VIII. The General in Chief Rochambeau will send, as a hostage for the observance of the present stipulation, the Adjutant-General Commandant, Urbain de Vaux, in exchange for whom the General in Chief Dessalines will send an officer of the same rank.

Two copies of this convention are hereby executed in strict faith, at the head-quarters on the Heights of the Cape, on the day, month, and year aforesaid.

(Signed) DUVEYSIER.
DESSALINES.

Correspondence between the Commander-in-Chief of the French Army of St. Domingo, and Capt. Loring, of his Majesty's Ship the Bellerophon, commanding a blockading force off Cape François.

ARMY OF ST. DOMINGO.

Head-Quarters at the Cape, 27th Brumaire, An. 12, of the French Republic.

The General-in-Chief to Commodore Loring, commanding the Naval Force of his Britannic Majesty before the Cape.

SIR,

TO prevent the effusion of blood, and to save the remains of the army of St. Domingo, I have the honour to send you two offi-

No. XII. Capitulation of the French army.

cers charged with instructions to enter into an arrangement with you. The General of Brigade Boyé, &c. and the Commodore Barré, are ordered to transmit this letter to you. I have chosen them to have the honour of treating with you.

I have the honour, &ç. &c.

D. ROCHAMBEAU.

Copy of the Propositions made by the General Rochambeau, to evacuate Cape François.

I. THE General Rochambeau proposes to evacuate the Cape; himself and his guards, consisting of about 4 or 500 men, to be conveyed to France without being considered prisoners of war. Not granted.

II. The Surveillant and Cerf to be allowed to carry him and suite to France. Not granted.

(Signed) JOHN LORING.

Bellerophon, off Cape François, Nov. 19, 1803.

SIR,

I HAVE to acquaint you, on the subject communicated to me by General Boyé and Commodore Barré, of your desire to negotiate for the surrender of Cape François to his Britannic Majesty, that I send for the purpose, and to know your final determination, Captain Moss, of his Majesty's ship La Desirée, in order to agree with your wishes in so much as is consistent with the just rights of his Britannic Majesty on that point.

I have

I have also to inform you my instructions confine me to the French officers and troops in health being sent to Jamaica, and the sick to go to France or America. The transports to convey them being first valued, and security given by the commander in chief, for the due payment of the valuation by the French republic. The white inhabitants of the Cape will not be permitted to go to Jamaica.

No. XII. Capitulation of the French army.

Such are the parts of my instructions, with which I am bound to comply in any agreement for the surrender of Cape François.

I have the honour to be, &c.

(Signed) J. LORING.

GENERAL ROCHAMBEAU, Commander-in-Chief, &c. &c. &c.

[B.] COLONY OF ST. DOMINGO.

Head-Quarters at the Cape, 27th Brumaire, in the Year 12.

THE GENERAL IN CHIEF OF THE ARMY OF ST. DOMINGO, &c. &c. &c. TO COMMODORE LORING, &c.

SIR,

I HAVE received the letter which you have done me the honour to write to me. As your propositions are inadmissible, I must beg of you to consider the preceding letter as not having been received.

I have the honour to be, &c.

D. ROCHAMBEAU.

British

No. XII.

Capitulation of the French army.

British Account of the Capitulation of the French Army of St. Domingo, in the Letter of Sir John Thomas Duckworth to Sir Evan Nepean.

Port Royal, Dec. 18, 1803.

SIR,

HAVING, in my letter No. 3, by this conveyance, stated to you, for the information of my Lords Commissioners of the Admiralty, that General Rochambeau had made proposals for capitulating, which, though inadmissible, I thought soon must lead to others more reasonable; the event has justified my opinion; but I am sorry to say that officer, whose actions are too extraordinary to account for, had, on the 19th ultimo, (previous to his proposal to Captain Loring, through the General of Brigade Boyé, and Commodore Barré) actually entered into a capitulation with the black General Dessalines, to deliver up the Cape to him, with all the ordnance, ammunition, and stores, on the 30th; I conclude, flattering himself that the tremendous weather, which our squadron was then, and had been, experiencing for three weeks, would offer an opening for escape, but the perseverance and watchfulness thereof precluded him from even attempting it. On the 30th, the colours of the Blacks were displayed at the forts, which induced Captain Loring to dispatch Captain Bligh, to know General Dessalines' sentiments respecting General Rochambeau and his troops; when, on his entering the harbour he met Commodore Barré, who pressed him in strong terms to go on board the Surveillante, and enter into some capitulation, which would put them

No. XII. Capitulation of the French army.

them under our protection, and prevent the Blacks from sinking them with red-hot shot, as they had threatened, and were preparing to do, which Captain Bligh complied with, when, they hastily brought him a few articles they had drawn up; which he (after objecting to some particular parts, that they agreed should be altered, to carry his interpretation to Jamaica) signed, and hastened to acquaint General Dessalines, that all the ships and vessels in port had surrendered to his Majesty's arms, and with great difficulty he obtained the promise to desist from firing, till a wind offered for carrying them out (it then blowing hard directly into the harbour; this promise he at length obtained, and the first instant the land-breeze enabled them to sail out under French colours, which, upon a shot being fired athwart them, the vessels of war fired their broadsides, and hauled down their colours, except the Clorinde, a large frigate of thirty-eight guns, who unluckily took the ground abaft, and was forced to throw most of her guns overboard, and knocked her rudder off, when there was great apprehensions for her safety; and I am informed by the captains of the squadron, that we must attribute the saving her (apparently without further damage) to the uncommon exertions and professional abilities of acting Lieutenant Willoughby, with the boats of the Hercule, who, I trust, will be honoured with their lordships' protection.

Captain Loring, after seeing the generality of the prizes taken possession of, left the Theseus and Hercule to fix a temporary rudder to the frigate, and bring the remainder with them, bearing away for the Mole, and on the 2d summoned the General of

 Brigade

No. XII. Capitulation of the French army.

Brigade Noailles, who commanded there, to capitulate; this he declined doing, asserting that he had provisions for five months; and herewith I transmit a copy of his letter. The numerous and crowded state of the prisoners on board all the prizes, and their being without provisions, making it necessary for Captain Loring to proceed to Jamaica, he arrived here the 5th with the Elephant and Blanche, also the Surveillante and Vertu thirty-eight gun frigates, and various other prizes, leaving the La Pique to blockade the Mole, who anchored in this port the 8th, and acquainted me that General Noailles had evacuated the night he refused to capitulate, bringing in with her five out of the six vessels in which the garrison had embarked, a brig with the general on board only escaping. I send a vessel of war to England, with General Rochambeau and those officers who are said to have participated in his cruelties at the Cape, I am, &c.

J. T. Duckworth.

No. XIII.

No. XIII. Declaration of the Independence of St. Domingo.

No. XIII.

(Referred to in Page 345.)

Declaration of the Independence of the Blacks of St. Domingo.

PROCLAMATION OF DESSALINES, CHRISTOPHE, AND CLERVAUX, CHIEFS OF ST. DOMINGO.

In the Name of the Black People, and Men of Color of St. Domingo:

THE Independence of St. Domingo is proclaimed. Restored to our primitive dignity, we have asserted our rights; we swear never to yield them to any power on earth; the frightful veil of prejudice is torn to pieces, be it so for ever. Woe be to them who would dare, to put together its bloody tatters.

Oh! Landholders of St. Domingo, wandering in foreign countries, by proclaiming our independence, we do not forbid you, indiscriminately, from returning to your property; far be from us this unjust idea. We are not ignorant that there are some among you that have renounced their former errors, abjured the injustice of their exhorbitant pretensions, and acknowledged the lawfulness of the cause for which we have been spilling our blood these twelve years. Toward those men who do us justice, we will act as brothers; let them rely for ever on our esteem and friendship; let them return among us. The God who protects us, the God of Freemen, bids us to stretch out towards them our conquering

 arms.

No. XIII. Declaration of the Independence of St. Domingo.

arms. But as for those, who, intoxicated with foolish pride, interested slaves of a guilty pretension, are blinded so much as to believe themselves the essence of human nature, and assert that they are destined by heaven to be our masters and our tyrants, let them never come near the land of St. Domingo: if they come hither, they will only meet with chains or deportation; then let them stay where they are; tormented by their well-deserved misery, and the frowns of the just men whom they have too long mocked, let them still continue to move, unpitied and unnoticed by all.

We have sworn not to listen with clemency towards all those who would dare to speak to us of slavery; we will be inexorable, perhaps even cruel, towards all troops who, themselves forgetting the object for which they have not ceased fighting since 1780, should come from Europe to bring among us death and servitude. Nothing is too dear, and all means are lawful, to men from whom it is wished to tear the first of all blessings. Were they to cause rivers and torrents of blood to run; were they, in order to maintain their liberty, to conflagrate seven eighths of the globe, they are innocent before the tribunal of Providence, that never created men, to see them groaning under so harsh and shameful a servitude.

In the various commotions that took place, some inhabitants against whom we had not to complain, have been victims by the cruelty of a few soldiers or cultivators, too much blinded by the remembrance of their past sufferings to be able to distinguish the good and humane land-owners from those that were unfeeling and

No. XIII. Declaration of the Independence of St. Domingo.

and cruel, we lament with all feeling souls so deplorable an end, and declare to the world, whatever may be said to the contrary by wicked people, that the murders were committed contrary to the wishes of our hearts. It was impossible, especially in the crisis in which the colony was, to be able to prevent or stop those horrors. They who are in the least acquainted with history, know that a people, when assailed by civil dissentions, though they may be the most polished on earth, give themselves up to every species of excess, and the authority of the chiefs, at that time not firmly supported, in a time of revolution cannot punish all that are guilty, without meeting with new difficulties. But now-a-days the Aurora of peace hails us, with the glimpse of a less stormy time; now that the calm of victory has succeeded to the trouble of a dreadful war, every thing in St. Domingo ought to assume a new face, and its government henceforward be that of justice.

Done at the Head-Quarters, Fort Dauphin, November 29, 1803.

(Signed) DESSALINES.
CHRISTOPHE.
CLERVEAUX.

True Copy, B. AIME, Secretary.

No. XIV.

Proclamation for the abjuration of the French nation.

No. XIV.

(Referred to in p. 348.)

Proclamation for a solemn Abjuration of the French Nation.

LIBERTY OR DEATH!—NATIVE ARMY.

THE GENERAL IN CHIEF TO THE PEOPLE OF HAYTI.

CITIZENS,

IT is not enough to have expelled from your country the barbarians who have for ages stained it with blood—it is not enough to have curbed the factions which, succeeding each other by turns, sported with a phantom of liberty which France exposed to their eyes. It is become necessary, by a last act of national authority, to ensure for ever the empire of liberty in the country which has given us birth. It is necessary to deprive an inhuman government, which has hitherto held our minds in a state of the most humiliating torpitude, of every hope of being enabled again to enslave us. Finally, it is necessary to live independent, or die. Independence or Death! Let these sacred words serve to rally us—let them be signals of battle, and of our re-union.

Citizens—Countrymen—I have assembled on this solemn day, those courageous chiefs, who, on the eve of receiving the last

last breath of expiring liberty, have lavished their blood to preserve it. These generals, who have conducted your struggles against tyranny, have not yet done. The French name still darkens our plains: every thing recals the remembrance of the cruelties of that barbarous people. Our laws, our customs, our cities, every thing bears the characteristic of the French.—Hearken to what I say!—the French still have a footing in our island! and you believe yourselves free and independent of that republic, which has fought all nations, it is true, but never conquered those who would be free! What! victims for fourteen years by credulity and forbearance! conquered not by French armies, but by the canting eloquence of the proclamations of their agents! When shall we be wearied with breathing the same air with them? What have we in common with that bloody-minded people? Their cruelties compared to our moderation—their colour to ours—the extension of seas which separate us—our avenging climate—all plainly tell us they are not our brethren; that they never will become such; and, if they find an asylum among us, they will still be the instigators of our troubles and of our divisions. Citizens, men, women, young and old, cast round your eyes on every part of this island; seek there your wives, your husbands, your brothers, your sisters—what did I say? seek your children—your children at the breast, what is become of them? I shudder to tell it—the *prey of vultures*. Instead of these interesting victims, the affrighted eye sees only their assassins—tigers still covered with their blood, and whose terrifying presence reproaches you for your insensibility,

No. XIV.

Proclamation for the abjuration of the French nation.

No. XIV. Proclamation for the abjuration of the French nation.

bility, and your guilty tardiness to avenge them—what do you wait for, to appease their manes? Remember that you have wished your remains to be laid by the side of your fathers—When you have driven out tyranny—will you descend into their tombs, without having avenged them? No: their bones would repulse yours. And ye, invaluable men, intrepid Generals, who, insensible to private sufferings, have given new life to liberty, by lavishing your blood; know, that you have done nothing if you do not give to the nations a terrible, though just example, of the vengeance that ought to be exercised by a people proud of having recovered its liberty, and zealous of maintaining it. Let us intimidate those, who might dare to attempt depriving us of it again: let us begin with the French; let them shudder at approaching our shores, if not on account of the cruelties they have committed, at least at the terrible resolution we are going to make—To devote to death whatsoever native of France should soil with his sacrilegious footstep, this territory of liberty.

We have dared to be free—let us continue free by ourselves, and for ourselves; let us imitate the growing child; his own strength breaks his leading-strings, which become useless and troublesome to him in his walk. What are the people who have fought us? what people would reap the fruits of our labours? and what a dishonourable absurdity, to conquer to be slaves!

Slaves—leave to the French nation this odious epithet; they have conquered to be no longer free—let us walk in other footsteps; let us imitate other nations, who, carrying their solicitude into futurity, and dreading to leave posterity an example of cowardice,

No. XVI.

Proclamation for the abjuration of the French nation.

cowardice, have preferred to be exterminated, rather than be erased from the list of free people. Let us, at the same time, take care, lest a spirit of proselytism should destroy the work—let our neighbours breathe in peace—let them live peaceably under the shield of those laws which they have framed for themselves; let us beware of becoming revolutionary fire-brands—of creating ourselves the legislators of the Antilles—of considering as a glory the disturbing the tranquility of the neighbouring islands; they have not been, like the one we inhabit, drenched with the innocent blood of the inhabitants—they have no vengeance to exercise against the authority that protects them; happy, never to have experienced the pestilence that has destroyed us, they must wish well to our posterity.

Peace with our neighbours, but accursed be the French name—eternal hatred to France: such are our principles.

Natives of Hayti—my happy destiny reserves me to be one day the centinel who is to guard the idol we now sacrifice to. I have grown old fighting for you, sometimes almost alone; and if I have been happy enough to deliver to you the sacred charge confided to me, recollect it is for you, at present, to preserve it. In fighting for your liberty, I have laboured for my own happiness: before it shall be consolidated by laws which shall ensure individual liberty, your chiefs whom I have assembled here, and myself, owe you this last proof of our devotedness.

Generals, and other chiefs, unite with me for the happiness of our country: the day is arrived—the day which will ever perpetuate our glory and our independence.

No. XIV.

Proclamation for the abjuration of the French nation.

If there exist among you a lukewarm heart, let him retire, and shudder to pronounce the oath which is to unite us. Let us swear to the whole world, to posterity, to ourselves, to renounce France for ever, and to die, rather than live under its dominion—to fight till the last breath for the independence of our country.

And ye, people, too long unfortunate, witness the oath we now pronounce: recollect that it is upon your constancy and courage I depended when I first entered the career of liberty to fight despotism and tyranny, against which you have been struggling these last fourteen years; remember that I have sacrificed every thing to fly to your defence—parents, children, fortune, and am now only rich, in your liberty—that my name has become a horror to all friends of slavery, or despots; and tyrants only pronounce it, cursing the day that gave me birth; if ever you refuse or receive with murmuring the laws, which the protecting angel that watches over your destinies, shall dictate to me for your happiness, you will merit the fate of an ungrateful people. But away from me this frightful idea: You will be the guardians of the liberty you cherish, the support of the Chief who commands you.

Swear then to live free and independent, and to prefer death to every thing that would lead to replace you under the yoke; swear then to pursue for everlasting, the traitors, and enemies of your independence.

J. J. Dessalines.

Head-quarters, Gonaives, 1st Jan. 1804,
1st Year of Independence.

No. XV.

No. XV.
Communication on the appointment of a governor-general for life.

No. XV.

(Referred to in Page 354.)

Communication of the Intentions of the Black Government on the Appointment of a Governor-General for Life.

LIBERTY OR DEATH!

A PROCLAMATION.

Jean Jacques Dessalines, Governor-General, to the Inhabitants of Hayti:

CRIMES, the most atrocious, such as were hitherto unheard of, and would cause nature to shudder, have been perpetrated. The measure of their cruelty overflowed. At length the hour of vengeance has arrived, and the implacable enemies of the rights of man have suffered the punishment due to their crimes.

My arm, raised above their heads, has too long delayed to strike. At that signal, which the justice of God has urged, your hands, righteously armed, has brought the axe to bear upon the decrepit tree of slavery and prejudice. In vain had time, and more especially the infernal politics of Europeans, defended it with triple brass; you have stripped it of its armour; and have placed it upon your heart, that you may become (like your natural enemies,) cruel and merciless. Like an overflowing and mighty torrent, that bears down all opposition, your vengeful fury has

No. XV.

Communication on the appointment of a governor-general for life.

swept away every obstacle to its impetuous course. Perish thus! all tyrants over innocence, all oppressors of mankind!

What then? Bent for many ages under an iron yoke, the sport of the passions, or the injustice of men, and of the caprices of fortune; mutilated victims of the cupidity of white Frenchmen; after having fattened by our toils, these insatiate blood-suckers, with a patience and resignation unexampled, we should again have seen that sacrilegious horde attempt our destruction, without any distinction of sex or age; and we, whom they call, men without energy, of no virtue, of no delicate sensibility, should not we have plunged in their breast the dagger of desperation? Where is that Haytian so vile, Haytian so unworthy of his regeneration, who thinks he has not fulfilled the decrees of the Eternal, by exterminating these blood-thirsty tygers? If there be one, let him fly; indignant nature discards him from our bosom; let him hide his infamy far from hence; the air we breathe, is not suited to his gross organs; it is the air of liberty, pure, august, and triumphant.

Yes, we have rendered to these true cannibals, war for war, crime for crime, outrage for outrage; yes, I have saved my country; I have avenged America. The avowal I make in the face of earth and heaven, constitutes my pride and my glory. Of what consequence to me is the opinion which contemporary and future generations will pronounce upon my conduct? I have performed my duty; I enjoy my own approbation; for me, that is sufficient. But, what am I saying? The preservation of my unfortunate brothers, and the testimony of my own conscience, are

not

No. XV.

Communication on the appointment of a governor-general for life.

not my only recompence: I have seen two classes of men, born to cherish, assist, and succour one another—mixed in a world, and blended together—crying for vengeance, and disputing the honor of the first blow.

Blacks and Yellows, whom the refined duplicity of Europe for a long time endeavoured to divide; you, who are now consolidated, and make but one family; without doubt it was necessary that our perfect reconciliation should be sealed with the blood of your butchers. Similar calamities have hung over your proscribed heads; a similar ardor to strike your enemies has signalized you: the like fate is reserved for you, and the like interests must therefore render you for ever one, indivisible, and inseparable. Maintain that precious concord, that happy harmony, amongst yourselves; it is the pledge of your happiness, your salvation, and your success; it is the secret of being invincible.

It is necessary, in order to strengthen these ties, to recal to your remembrance the catalogue of atrocities committed against our species; the intended massacre of the entire population of this island, meditated in the silence and *sang-froid* of the cabinet; the execution of that abominable project to me was unblushingly proposed, when already begun by the French, with the calmness and serenity of a countenance accustomed to similar crimes. Guadaloupe pillaged and destroyed; its ruins still reeking with the blood of the children, women, and old men put to the sword; Pelage (himself the victim of their craftiness), after having basely betrayed his country and his brothers; the brave and immortal Delgresse, blown into the air with the fort he defended, rather

No. XV. Communication on the appointment of a governor-general for life.

than accept their offered chains. Magnanimous warrior! that noble death, far from enfeebling our courage, serves only to rouse within us the determination of avenging or of following thee. Shall I again recal to your memory the plots lately framed at Jeremie? the terrible explosion that was to be the result, notwithstanding the generous pardon granted to these incorrigible beings at the expulsion of the French army? The deplorable fate of our departed brothers in Europe? and (dread harbinger of death) the frightful despotism exercised at Martinique? Unfortunate people of Martinique, could I but fly to your assistance, and break your fetters! Alas! an insurmountable barrier separates us; yet, perhaps a spark from the same fire which enflames us, will alight on your bosoms: perhaps, at the sound of this emotion, suddenly awakened from your lethargy, with arms in your hands, you will reclaim your sacred and indelible rights.

After the terrible example I have just given, sooner or later Divine Justice will unchain on earth some mighty minds, above the weakness of the vulgar, for the destruction and terror of the wicked. Tremble! tyrants, usurpers, scourges of the new world! Our daggers are sharpened, your punishment is ready! Sixty thousand men, equipped, inured to war, obedient to my orders, burn to offer a new sacrifice to the manes of their assassinated brothers. Let that nation come who may be mad or daring enough to attack me. Already at its approach, the irritated Genius of Hayti, arising from the bosom of the ocean, appears; his menacing aspect throws the waves into commotion, excites tempests, and with his mighty hand disperses, or dashes fleets in

5 pieces;

pieces; to his formidable voice the laws of nature pay obedience; disease, plague, famine, conflagration, poison, are his constant attendants. But why calculate on the assistance of the climate and of the elements? Have I forgot that I command a people of no common cast, brought up in adversity, whose haughty daring, frowns at obstacles, and increases by dangers? Let them come, these homicidal cohorts? I wait for them with a firm, and steady eye. I abandon to them freely the shore, and the places where cities have existed, but woe to those who may approach too near the mountains! It were better for them that the sea received them into its profound abyss, than to be devoured by the anger of the children of Hayti.

No. XV. Communication on the appointment of a governor-general for life.

"War, even to Death, to Tyrants!" this is my motto; "Liberty! Independence!" this is our rallying cry.

Generals, Officers, Soldiers, somewhat unlike him who has preceded me, the Ex-General TOUSSAINT L'OUVERTURE, I have been faithful to the promise I made to you, when I took up arms against tyranny, and whilst the last spark of life remains in me I will keep my oath. "Never again shall a colonist, or an European, set his foot upon this territory with the title of master or proprietor." This resolution shall henceforward form the fundamental basis of our constitution.

Should other chiefs, after me, by pursuing a conduct diametrically opposite to mine, dig their own graves, and those of their own species, you will have to accuse only the law of destiny, which shall have taken me away from the happiness and welfare of my fellow-citizens. May my successors follow the path I shall

No. XV. Communication on the appointment of a governor-general for life.

have traced for them! It is the system best adapted for consolidating their power; it is the highest homage they can render to my memory.

As it is derogatory to my character, and my dignity, to punish the innocent for the crimes of the guilty, a handful of whites, commendable by the religion they have always professed, and who have besides taken the oath to live with us in the woods, have experienced my clemency. I order that the sword respect them, and that they be unmolested.

I recommend anew, and order all the Generals of Departments, &c. to grant succours, encouragement, and protection, to all neutral and friendly nations, who may wish to establish commercial relations in this island.

Head-Quarters at the Cape, 28th April, 1804, first year of independence.

The Governor-General, (Signed) DESSALINES.

A true Copy,

The Secretary-General, JUSTE CHANLATTE."

No. XVI.

No. XVI.

Cautionary proclamation to the Spaniards against treachery to the Blacks.

No. XVI.

(Referred to in Page 355.)

Caution to the Spaniards.

LIBERTY OR DEATH!

A PROCLAMATION.

Jean Jacques Dessalines, Governor-General, to the Inhabitants of the Spanish Part of the Island:

SCARCE had the French army been expelled, when you hastened to acknowledge my authority; by a free and spontaneous movement of your heart, you ranged yourselves under my subjection. More careful of the prosperity than desirous of the ruin of that part which you inhabit, I gave to this homage a favourable reception. From that moment I have considered you as my children, and my fidelity to you remains undiminished. As a proof of my paternal solicitude, within the places which have submitted to my power, I have proposed for Chiefs, none but men chosen from amongst yourselves. Jealous of counting you in the rank of my friends, that I might give you all the time necessary for recollection, and that I might assure myself of your fidelity, I have hitherto restrained the burning ardor of my soldiers. Already I congratulate myself on the success of my solicitude, which had for its object, to prevent the effusion of blood; but at this time a

fanatic

No. XVI.

Cautionary proclamation to the Spaniards against treachery to the Blacks.

fanatic priest had not kindled in your breasts the rage which predominates therein; the incensed Frerand had not yet instilled into you the poison of falsehood and calumny.—Writings, originating in despair and weakness, have been circulated; and immediately some amongst you, seduced by perfidious insinuations, solicited the friendship and protection of the French; they dared to outrage my kindness, by coalescing with my cruel enemies. Spaniards, reflect! On the brink of the precipice which is dug under your feet, will that diabolical minister save you, when with fire and sword I shall have pursued you to your last entrenchments?

Ah! without doubt, his prayers, his grimaces, his relics, would be no impediment to my career. Vain as defenceless, can he preserve you from my just anger, after I shall have buried him, and the collection of brigands he commands, under the ruins of your capital! Let them both recollect that it is before my intrepid phalanx that all the resources and the skill of Europeans have proved ineffectual; and that into my victorious bonds the destiny of the Captain-General, Rochambeau, has been surrendered. To lure the Spaniards to their party, they propagate the report, that vessels laden with troops have arrived at St. Domingo. Why is it not the truth? They little imagine that, in delaying to attack them until this time, my principal object has been to suffer them to increase the mass of our resources, and the number of our victims. To spread distrust and terror, they incessantly dwell upon the fate which the French have just experienced; but have I *not* had reason to treat them so? The

wrongs

No. XVI.

Cautionary Proclamation to the Spaniards against treachery to the Blacks.

wrongs of the French, do they appertain to Spaniards; and must I visit on the latter the crimes which the former have conceived, ordered, and executed on our species! They have the effrontery to say, that, reduced to seek safety in flight, I am gone to conceal my defeat in the southern part of the island. Well, then! now let them learn that I am ready; that the thunderbolt is about to fall on their heads. Let them know, that my soldiers are impatiently waiting for the signal to go and reconquer the boundaries which nature and the elements have assigned to us. A few moments more, and I shall crush the remnant of the French under the weight of my mighty power.

Spaniards! you, to whom I address myself, solely because I wish to save you; you who, for having been guilty of evasion; shall soon preserve your existence only so far as my clemency may deign to spare you; it is yet time; abjure an error which may be fatal to you, and break off all connection with my enemy, if you wish your blood may not be confounded with his. Name to me, without delay, that part of your territory on which my first blow is to be struck, or inform me whether I must strike on all points without discrimination. I give you fifteen days, from the date of this notification, to forward your last intentions, and to rally under my banners. You are not ignorant, that all the roads of St. Domingo in every direction, are familiar to us; that more than once we have seen your dispersed bands fly before us. In a word, you know what I can do, and what I dare; think of your preservation.

Receive here the sacred promise which I make—not to do any

No. XVI. Cautionary proclamation to the Spaniards against treachery to the Blacks.

any thing against your personal safety or your interest, if you seize upon this occasion to shew yourselves worthy of being admitted amongst the children of Hayti.

Head-Quarters at the Cape, May 8th, 1804, first year of independence,

The Governor-General, (Signed) DESSALINES.

A true Copy,

The Secretary-General, JUSTE CHANLATTE.

No. XVII.

(Referred to in Page 356.)

Programa issued to direct the Order of the Ceremonies on the Coronation of Jean Jacques, the First Emperor of Hayti.

Port-au-Prince, Sept. 8.

Ceremony of the Coronation of Emperor.

ON the 8th of October all the troops of the garrison, in the best order possible, will march under arms to the Champ de Mars at two o'clock, A. M. precisely, and form in square battalions.

A detachment of grenadiers immediately to form a line to the house of the Commandant-General of Division.

At three o'clock the Members of all the Civil and Military Authorities, having assembled at the Government House, will proceed from thence to the Champ de Mars in the following procession: No. XVII.

A Platoon of Grenadiers.
The Public Teachers,
Conducting a great Number of their Pupils.
The Deputation of the Body of Artisans,
Preceded by a Chief Artisan.
A Deputation of Agriculturists,
Preceded by one of their principal Members.
A Deputation of Foreign Commerce,
Preceded by one of its Members.
A Deputation of National Commerce,
Preceded by one of its Members.
The Members of Justice, and the Ministerial Officers.
The Health Officers of the Army, attached to the Division.
The Officers of the Military Marine.
The Etat-Major of the place, connected with that of the Circuit.
The Administrators, and those in their employ.
The General commanding the Divisions,
Accompanied by his Etat-Major.
A Platoon of Grenadiers.

Arrived at the Champ de Mars, all the drums shall beat a march, and the procession shall advance to an Amphitheatre which shall be prepared for its use.

No. XVII. The Act announcing the nomination of the "Emperor," (DESSALINES) shall be read in a loud and intelligible voice!

A discharge of musketry and of cannon, which shall be repeated by all the forts of the city, and vessels in the harbour, shall follow the reading of the act.

The ceremony of the Coronation shall next take place on a throne, elevated in the midst of the Amphitheatre, and surrounded by all the great Officers of the Empire.

The ceremony shall be announced by a triple discharge of cannon and musketry.

After the ceremony, the troops shall file off to the church, and form in order of battle.

The Procession, in the order abovementioned, shall also advance to the Church, where a *Te Deum*, in thanksgiving for this memorable day, shall be sung.

During the *Te Deum*, a third discharge of cannon and musketry shall take place.

After the *Te Deum*, the Procession shall return, in the same order, to the house of the General of Division.

The Fete shall terminate by a grand illumination in all parts of the city.

Done at Port-au-Prince, the 6th September, 1804, the first year of independence,

The General of Division,

(Signed) A. PETION.

No. XVIII.

(Referred to in Page 91, &c.)

A View of the Distribution of the Black Force in the French Colonies at the Revolution of St. Domingo, from the Official Returns.

	Chief Places, or Jurisdictions.	Quarters, or Parishes.	No. of negroes.
Northern Part	THE CAPE	The Cape and its dependencies	21,613
		The *Petite Anse* and Plain of the Cape	11,122
		L'Acul, Limonade, and St. Susan	19,876
		Morin and the Great River	18,554
		Dondon and *Marmelade*	17,376
		Limbé and Port Margot	15,978
		Plaisance and *Le Borgne*	15,018
	FORT DAUPHIN	Fort Dauphin	10,004
		Ouanaminthe and *Valliere*	9,987
		The *Ferrier, Rouge,* and the *Trou*	15,476
	PORT DE PAIX	*Port de Paix*, Little St. Louis, Jean Rabel, &c.	29,540
	MOLE ST. NICHOLAS	The Mole and Bombarde	3,183
Western Part	PORT AU PRINCE	Port-au-Prince, &c.	42,848
		Arcahaye	18,553
		Mirebalais	10,902
	LEOGANE	Leogane	14,896
	ST. MARK	St. Mark, the Little River, Verettes, and Gonaïves	57,216
	LITTLE GOAVE	Little Goäve, Great Goäve, and *Le Fond des Nigres,*	18,829
		L'Anse à Vaux, and Le Petit Erou	13,229
	JEREMIE	Jeremie and Cape Dame Maria	20,774
Southern Part	THE CAYES	The Cayes and Torbuk	30,937
	TIBURON	Cape Tiburon and *Les Coteaux*	8,153
	ST. LOUIS	St. Louis, Cavaillon, and Aquin	18,785
	JACMEL	Jacmel, Les Cayes, and Baynet	21,151
		51 Parishes.	464,000

Eastern Part, not yet ceded to the French.

The difference between the above total and that furnished in page 91, is to be accounted for by the erroneous statements of the planters to lessen the amount of the taxes, and other causes.

No. XIX.

ADDITIONAL REMARKS, &c.

IT was intended to insert in this place a number of papers with which the author has been furnished, as collateral evidence of the sentiments which occur in his work in favor of the people of color; but, on re-considering the accumulation of matter on this subject produced by the discussion of the slave trade, and the accessibility of the works of Barbot,* Bosman,† Smith,‡ &c. which all tend to shew the capacity of the African, and the eligibility of his native state, he has been led to think it less necessary; and shall, therefore, merely add the communication of an ingenious friend on the subject of *substituting European laborers for African cultivators;* and a quotation from an intelligent and respectable writer,§ which as perfectly accords with his own sentiments, as it surpasses his powers of describing them.

" It is significantly enquired by Postlethwaite,|| ' Whether Africa will not admit of a far more extensive and profitable trade with Great Britain than it ever yet has done? and whether the

* Account of Africa. † Description of Guinea. ‡ Voyage to Guinea.

§ The Reverend Joshua Larwood, R. N. || Dictionary of Trade and Commerce.

latter

latter might not supply their colonies and plantations with whites instead of blacks?' No. XIX.

"The first of these enquiries may be readily answered in the affirmative; and the latter demonstrated without difficulty. The condition of Africa is now, only what Britain was once; and the slavery of its inhabitants, that which has existed in every age. The one can be remedied by the means which have constituted the rise of all states; and the existence of the latter is inconsistent with the present refinement of the other three quarters of the world.*

---

* The author desires not to be considered as *adopting* this writer's sentiments. He is, however, of opinion with M. de Charmilly, (so often quoted in this work, and never unprofitably,) who has the following judicious ideas of negro amelioration, which have been, he is happy to be informed, partly acted on. "If I require (says he) the continuation of the trade, I also require that it should be conducted under more vigilant laws than exist at present, for the advantage of the negroes, the planter, and the merchant, in short, that well digested laws be established for regulating the tonnage of the trading ships. They should not exceed three hundred tons, nor be less than two hundred; for if the ship be large, it continues trading too long, and the scurvy and other diseases breed among the negroes first acquired; and if too small, they are too ill at ease. It ought to be settled how many negroes should be carried in each ship, according to the size, without a possibility of evading the law. It should be prohibited to export from Africa any negro more than twenty years old. Man at this age is yet capable of attaching himself to a new country, climate has but little influence upon him, and he leaves in his native land few objects of attachment, compared with the older negro, who leaves a wife and children.

"No negro should be embarked without first being inoculated; several surgeons should be attached to a ship, who should all make oath, before the sale of negroes commences in the colony to which they may be brought, that they have not by any means driven in, or repelled the maladies of negroes, which kill so great a number. These measures I admit would be more expensive, and the fitting out a trading ship would at first cost the person equipping it a still greater sum, which would finally be borne by the planter, who would be well indemnified; for, instead of purchasing two or three negroes, he would only purchase one, whom he would more easily preserve, and who would work more readily, &c."

Without,

No. XIX.

"Without, however, referring to humane, or even refined considerations, the proposition about to be made takes its stand solely on the ground of expedience. Among the numerous reasons assigned for a rigorous treatment of negroes, are, besides their constant inclination to revolt, a decided inefficiency, and incredible expence. The high price of their first purchase, the risk of desertion, or of death, by a variety of peculiar maladies; and if neither occur, that their labor is not, by many degrees, equal to that of an European. That many Europeans support the climate with great ease, and particularly those who are abstemious, is certain; it becomes then an obvious fact, that if a sufficient number of laborers could be obtained from Europe for the cultivation of the colonies, no objection could arise to their adoption. The purchase of the negro would be saved, and the colonies relieved from his maladies, while the acquisition of property, and the evitation of the invidious distinction of complexion, would suppress that inclination to rebellion which the very character of slavery inspires; while the steady toil of the European laborer, even under every disadvantage, could not fail to equal the lax exertion ascribed to the negro.

"With regard to obtaining cultivators for her colonies from the population of Britain, little doubt can exist when the advanced state of this country is considered, and the various means, which, under the appearance of inflictions, are ordered for checking the exuberance of that population that would otherwise tend to its own destruction;* and surely moderate toil, even under a vertical

* See Malthus on Population.

sun,

sun, with sufficient provision of every kind, would not be a greater evil than that of vagrancy, or an heart-rending despondency, under the pressure of numerous evils; nor, even where the climate overcame the constitution, would the infliction be more terrible than that of war, contagion, or suicide. No. XIX.

"It is not intended here to recommend the introduction of felons, a resource always insufficient, but to project the prevention rather than the punishment of crimes. It is well known, and has been *partially* confirmed by a writer, whose declaration, as an intelligent magistrate* has had much weight, that in the metropolis alone there constantly exists an incredible number of persons, who, at a period of life when they may be considered capable of any exertion, and many of them are prepared for that of an important nature, are without the possibility of obtaining any employment of their talents, and often without the means of procuring sustenance; accessible, therefore, to the insidious approaches of vice, and the contemplated victims of a refined police, for they are soon necessarily within the knowledge of its accurate officers, and are at liberty only to exert their claim to its notice. Would it not be a happy salvation from guilt to induce by some liberal system these starving beings from the threshold of sin, to an honest exertion of their faculties, and a suitable provision? and surely if the obnoxious trade be asserted to exist principally "to save the lives of such negroes as are taken captives in African warfare, and who would otherwise have been sacrificed;" the

* Colquhoun, Police of the Metropolis.

humane

No. XIX. humane sentiment may at least be expected to extend to the unhappy subjects of Britain, whose lives, yet equally innocent, are becoming less secure, and who, without some interposition of Providence will be sacrificed to offended justice.

"The number of those who come under this description throughout Britain is amply sufficient to supply the colonies. Even in London they are estimated by the writer just quoted at, it is believed, 50,000, and may be easily conceived to extend every where to a considerable number. A timely encouragement on a liberal and rational plan, would select from every quarter the objects calculated for the end, and no fear could be entertained in regard to qualifications for the business,—a subjection to the whip only excepted; and those who had felt the scourge of fate with severity, might if necessary sufficiently submit to a servile obedience by gentle gradations.

"Such a class of cultivators would increase the prosperity of a colony by a variety of means, and insure its affection to the mother country; while by obtaining establishments, each fresh importation, instead of rebellious views, would be inspired with the most pleasing prospects, and most cheering energies for labor.

"It may be safely determined, that by a liberal communication with its extensive coast, the continent of Africa would furnish an advantageous intercourse to Britain, and that a white population of laborers in the colonies is not only possible, but would produce the most desirable benefits to the colonies, and also to the mother country."

In

In a miscellaneous work intituled *Erratics*, by the gentleman before alluded to, forming a *mélange* of the most exquisite composition, illustrative of human nature, and general history, are the following traits of negro excellence; communicated with perfect freedom from bias to either side, which leaves us in doubt, whether most to admire the subjects or the relator. No. XVIII.

In the church-yard of Walton, the *Erratic* is attracted by an elegant Latin memorial over the grave of two Africans, husband and wife, whose faithful services obtained for them this honorable distinction from Sir Patrick Blake, Bart. their master; this we will not injure by quotation, but proceed to its consequent reflections.

"Martha," (says the sensible writer,) "plucked a few sprigs of clover from the grave, placed one in her own bosom, distributed the others to her companions, and with an eye ready to gush, took me by the arm, &c. * * * * On our way, however, we could not refrain from pouring forth our ardent and merited eulogium upon the dignified virtue and grateful affection of the worthy *Baronet* who thus generously recorded the exalted qualities of his exemplary adherents. Indeed, I could even now dwell with delight upon the great credit reciprocally reflected by these parties, so fortuitously and so fortunately cast within the sphere of each other's benevolence; a mutual connexion, cemented by such exalted humanity on one side, and on the other by such cordial and consummate fidelity, that nothing less decisive and fatal than the *febris vitæ filum abrupens* could have caused to decrease or decay.

No. XVIII. —"So captivating a memorial of candid, gentlemanly, family, and liberal attachment, ought to reckon against a few West India delinquencies, and to discourage indiscriminate crimination and prejudice.

"Well, alas! too well do you and I know (for often, too often, have we seen) that there have been (I will not say are) the most flagrant violations of all human feelings, and the most atrocious wantonness of an accursed barbarity; but, amongst the noxious weeds which have disgraced the soil of the different colonies, and contaminated the atmosphere of the Antilles, let us contemplate this attractive and fragrant flower, which sheds around its balmy perfume, and counteracts the poisonous influence of such deleterious productions.

"The *quem in deliciis labuit* of our epitaph is a very just expression of the domestic and affectionate *Cotto.* Nor are the Cottos of sable hue more rare, or less estimable, than their fairer sisters of European celebrity. The most animated and attractive examples of pure and ardent love to the husbands of their hearts, and the fathers of their offspring, are as strikingly exhibited under the roofs of various negro huts, as are any where displayed in the families of the old world. In the laudable duties of wedded life, and the maternal offices to the precious pledges of connubial intercourse, the transported and enslaved matrons of Africa are not to be surpassed by the enlightened and free females of the freest land.

"That they possess the finer feelings of the soul in a very eminent degree, and are delicately prompt to the most fascinating propensities

propensities of humanity, is not only apparent in their domestic and laborious stations on shore; but what incontrovertible proofs have we not seen of their steady and useful courage on board our ships of war! No. XVIII.

"Well then might the classical and Sallustian conciseness of the Shepperton Epitaph address the candor of its readers with the generous admonition of—

"Disce ab Æthiope virtutem, et ne crede colori."

* * * * * * *

"To virtuous Afric, lib'ral reader turn
There, from her sable sons, this maxim learn:
To no complexion is the charm confin'd,
In every climate grows the virtuous mind."

Epitaph on Benjamin and Cotto Blake; Erratics, vol. ii. p. 209.

THE END.

INDEX.

A

INDEX.

B

C

Declaration

INDEX.

E

F

G

H

INDEX.

Directions to the Binder for placing the Plates.

NEW

NEW AND POPULAR WORKS

NOW PUBLISHING BY

JAMES CUNDEE, AT THE ALBION PRESS, IN IVY-LANE,

PATERNOSTER-ROW, LONDON.

THE SPORTSMAN'S CABINET:

OR,

A CORRECT DELINEATION

OF THE VARIOUS

DOGS USED IN THE SPORTS OF THE FIELD;

Including the Canine Race in general; consisting of a series of rich and masterly Engravings of every distinct Breed, from original Paintings, taken from Life, purposely for the Work, by P. Reinagle, Esq. R. A.; engraved in the Line Manner by Mr. John Scott, interspersed with beautiful Vignettes, engraved on Wood, by Messrs. Bewick and Nesbitt, the whole forming a Collection of superb Sporting Subjects, worthy the Attention of Amateurs of Field Sports, and Admirers of the Arts in general; a comprehensive, historical, and systematic Description of the different Species; their Qualifications, peculiar Properties, and predominant Propensities; the various Pursuits and agreeable Sports to which they individually become appropriate, and the Means by which they are respectively trained; occasionally interspersed with authenticated Anecdotes of the Sagacity, Memory, Fidelity, Affection, Courage, Perseverance, and every other distinguished Feature appertaining to each particular Kind; including such Remarks upon Greyhounds, Hounds, Pointers, Spaniels, and all Dogs engaged in the Sports of the Field, as will necessarily comprehend a collateral View of Hunting, Coursing, Shooting, &c. &c. with a complete Review of the different Diseases to which they are subject, and the most approved and efficacious Modes of Treatment and Cure; concluding with a scientific Disquisition upon the Distemper, Canine Madness, and the Hydrophobia.

This Work is printed in an elegant Style, in two Volumes super-royal Quarto, price 6l. 10s. in Boards, or in twenty-five Numbers, at 5s. each, one or more of which may be had at a time.

There are twenty-eight Copper Plates, and nearly an equal number of Engravings on Wood.

SELECT

MODERN CLASSICS;

Comprehending faithful Translations of the most esteemed Productions of German, French, and Italian Authors, with a Critical Account of their Lives, accompanied by Notes, Historical and Biographical, including Zimmermann, Marmontel, La Fontaine, Montaigne, Fontenelle, Barthelemy, Klopstock, Gellert, Haller, Rollin, Florian, Fenelon, St. Pierre, Gessner, Genlis, Goethe, Lavater, Buffon, Sturm, Schiller, Garve, Wieland, Lessing, &c. &c. &c.

Plan of Publication.—I. The Select Modern Classics is printed with a new type, cast for the purpose, in an elegant style.—II. The work is regularly published once a fortnight.—III. There are two editions; each Number of the fine will contain the proof impression of a portrait, or highly-finished historical engraving, and five sheets of foolscap 8vo. hot-pressed, price 1s. 6d. The common edition generally consisting of 96 pages of small 12mo. with similar embellishments, will be sold for 1s. each Number.—IV. The first Number, commencing with Zimmermann on Solitude, was published on the 1st of December, 1804, and the succeeding Numbers regularly at the periods before stated. Directions will be given with the last Number of each work for placing the Cuts; complete Indexes, &c. &c. For Amateurs of the Graphic and Typographic arts, about 50 copies are printed in large Post Octavo, and hot-pressed, with Proof Impressions of the Plates, price 2s. each Number.

The first Ten Numbers will comprise the celebrated Production of Zimmermann on Solitude, Forming two elegant Volumes, enriched with Eleven superb Engravings from original Designs, by the most eminent Artists.—Each distinct Production will be arranged so as to comprise a certain quantity of Numbers, leaving it at the option of the Purchaser, either to continue the Publication, or decline it, at the conclusion of any particular Work.

*** The Work is in a state of great forwardness, in which the same uniformity of elegance is preserved, and will be continued in a style superior to any other publication of the same size and price. The admired production of the Death of Abel, by *Gessner*, succeeds the present work.

To

BOOKS published by JAMES CUNDEE.

To Noblemen, Gentlemen, and Divines, who have received their Education at the University of Oxford, as well as to Amateurs of the Fine Arts, the following splendid Work is recommended, elegantly printed in Imperial Folio, and enriched with correct and beautifully engraved Views of Oxford, illustrated by elegant Letter-press, and published Monthly, in Numbers, Price 8s. each,

A GRAPHIC AND DESCRIPTIVE TOUR

OF THE

UNIVERSITY OF OXFORD;

Comprehending general PICTURESQUE VIEWS; correct Representations of all the PRINCIPAL PUBLIC BUILDINGS, with their History and present State, and the Academic Costume.—To be completed in Twenty-five Numbers.—These Views will constitute elegant and appropriate Ornaments, as Furniture Prints.

Elegantly printed in Two Volumes, small Octavo, containing near Two Thousand Pages of Letter-press, and Sixty-six correct picturesque Delineations of the various Beauties of England and Wales, and a Whole-Sheet coloured Map, price 1l. 5s. extra boards;

THE

TRAVELLER'S GUIDE;

OR,

ENGLISH ITINERARY;

Containing accurate and original Descriptions of all the Counties, Cities, Towns, Villages, Hamlets, &c. and their exact Distances from London; together with the Cathedrals, Churches, Hospitals, Gentlemens' Seats, (with the Names of their present Possessors) Manufactures, Harbours, Bays, Rivers, Canals, Bridges, Lakes, Salt and medicinal Springs, Vales, Hills, Mountains, Mines, Castles, Curiosities, Market Days, Fairs, Inns for Post Horses, &c.; the whole comprising a complete Topography of ENGLAND and WALES. To which are prefixed, GENERAL OBSERVATIONS ON GREAT-BRITAIN; including a correct Itinerary from London to the several Watering and Sea-Bathing places, Lists of Inns in London; Mail Coaches; Wharfs; Packet-Boats; Rates of Porterage; Postage of Letters; and every other useful Information, equally calculated for the Man of Business and the inquisitive Traveller.

BY W. C. OULTON, Esq.

Elegantly printed in Small Octavo, enriched with Twenty-Two Engravings, Price 9s. in Boards,

THE

THESPIAN DICTIONARY;

OR,

DRAMATIC BIOGRAPHY OF THE PRESENT AGE;

Containing Sketches of the Lives, Lists of Productions, various Merits, &c. &c. of all the principal Managers, Dramatists, Composers, Commentators, Actors, and Actresses, of the united Kingdom; interspersed with numerous original Anecdotes. Forming a complete Modern

HISTORY OF THE ENGLISH STAGE.

*** From the very favourable Reception which the first Edition of this Work met with, the Proprietors have been enabled to embellish the present Edition with *Fifteen additional* Engravings. It is also on a larger Type, and considerably reduced in Price.

J. CUNDEE, PRINTER,
Ivy-Lane.